W9-CFB-588

Keats, Shelley,
and
Romantic
Spenserianism

Greg Kucich

Keats, Shelley, and Romantic Spenserianism

The Pennsylvania State University Press
University Park, Pennsylvania

Library of Congress Cataloging-in-Publication Data

Kucich, Greg.
  Keats, Shelley, and romantic Spenserianism / Greg Kucich.
      p.   cm.
  Includes bibliographical references.
  ISBN 0-271-00706-0 (alk. paper)
  1. English poetry—19th century—History and criticism. 2. Keats,
John, 1795–1821—Knowledge—Literature. 3. Shelley, Percy Bysshe,
1792–1822—Knowledge—Literature. 4. Spenser, Edmund, 1552?–
1599—Influence—Keats. 5. Spenser, Edmund, 1552?–1599—Influence—
Shelley. 6. Romanticism—England—History—19th century.
  I. Title.
  PR590.K83   1991
  821'.709—dc20   90–30966

Copyright © 1991 The Pennsylvania State University
All rights reserved
Printed in the United States of America

It is the policy of The Pennsylvania State University Press to use acid-free
paper for the first printing of all clothbound books. Publications on un-
coated stock satisfy the minimum requirements of American National Standard for Information Sciences—Permanence of Paper for Printed Library
Materials, ANSI Z39.48–1984.

For Dennis Lamb

Contents

List of Illustrations

Abbreviations and Citations

The following abbreviations are used parenthetically in the text:

LJK   *The Letters of John Keats.* Ed. Hyder Edward Rollins. Cambridge, Mass.: Harvard University Press, 1958. 2 vols.

KC   *The Keats Circle.* Ed. Hyder Edward Rollins. Cambridge, Mass.: Harvard University Press, 1965. 2 vols.

LPBS   *Letters of Percy Bysshe Shelley.* Ed. Frederick L. Jones. Oxford: Clarendon Press, 1964. 2 vols.

PW   *Shelley: Poetical Works.* Ed. Thomas Hutchinson; revised by G. M. Matthews. London: Oxford University Press, 1970.

SP   *Shelley's Prose.* Ed. David Lee Clark. Albuquerque: University of New Mexico Press, 1954.

FQ   *The Faerie Queene.* Ed. Thomas P. Roche. Princeton: Princeton University Press, 1978.

C   *The Critical Heritage: Spenser.* Ed. R. M. Cummings. New York: Barnes & Noble, 1971.

R   *The Romantics Reviewed, 1793–1830: Contemporary Reviews of British Romantic Writers.* Ed. Donald Reiman. New York: Garland, 1972. 9 vols.

Quotations of Keats's and Shelley's poetry, unless otherwise noted, refer to Jack Stillinger's *The Poems of John Keats* and G. M. Matthews's *Shelley: Poetical Works.*

Quotations of *The Faerie Queene* are taken from Thomas P. Roche's edition and cited by book, canto, and stanza number. All references to Spenser's shorter poems follow *The Yale Edition of the Shorter Poems of Edmund Spenser* (Ed. William Oram et al.).

Quotations of passages from *The Faerie Queene* that Keats marked follow the text of the editions that he used.

Acknowledgments

My intellectual and emotional debts to those who have supported
this project are legion, and my gratitude is only exceeded by my
regret that I have not space enough to single them all out here. I
shall ever remain deeply indebted to all those scholars who have
built up the great traditions of Spenser studies and Romantic scholarship. Several recent influences, however, deserve special mention.
For the pleasure of their advice, their encouragement, and their ongoing conversation, I would like to thank Jack Stillinger, S. K.
Heninger, A. C. Hamilton, Robert Gleckner, Stuart Peterfreund,
Daniel Watkins, and Stephen Fredman. My thoughts on Spenser
have been guided at Notre Dame by Theresa Krier, who has just
published a book on Spenserian perception, *Gazing on Secret Sights:
Spenser, Classical Imitation, and the Decorums of Vision.* My research as-
sistant, the Reverend Ninan Tharakan, provided essential service in
the early stages of this project. Christopher Fox, who labors with
gusto down the hallway from my office, has shown me the excitement of scholarship and the supreme value of friendship. George
Bornstein first taught me about Romanticism, and his support of my
work has never slackened. My debt to him only increases with time.
To Stuart Curran and Joseph Wittreich, I am especially grateful for
the intellectual friendship and the generosity of spirit they have extended to me as a continual source of enrichment.

For institutional support, I would like to acknowledge the funding
and leave time provided by the National Endowment for the Hu-
manities and Notre Dame's Institute for Scholarship in the Liberal
Arts. I have been fortunate to receive ongoing and essential research assistance from the staffs of the Huntington Library, the
Newberry Library, the Houghton Library, the New York Public Library, the British Library, the Victoria & Albert Museum Library,
and the Keats House Library. Philip Winsor and Cherene Holland
of The Pennsylvania State University Press have provided invaluable
editorial support in guiding this work to its final stage. Portions of
Chapter 2 were originally published as "The Duality of Romantic

Spenserianism" (*Spenser Studies* 8 [1990]: 287–307) and "Leigh Hunt and Romantic Spenserianism" (*Keats-Shelley Journal* 37 [1988]: 110–35). The section on Keats and Charles Brown's Spenser volumes in Chapter 4 first appeared as "'A Lamentable Lay': Keats and the Marking of Charles Brown's Spenser Volumes" (*The Keats-Shelley Review* 3 [1988]: 1–22). An earlier version of the *Prometheus Unbound* section was printed as "The Spenserian Psychodrama of *Prometheus Unbound* (*Nineteenth-Century Contexts* 12 [1988]: 61–84). I am grateful to the editors of these journals for allowing me to reproduce or elaborate on these earlier publications.

A special note of gratitude should be addressed to my friends at Keats House: Christina Gee, Roberta Davis, and Judith Knight. Coming to know them has been one of the nicest rewards of all. And thanking Ruth Yarger, who has sustained me through it all, is one of my greatest pleasures yet. Peter Atkins continues as a true brother in spirit and deed. Rachel G. McLean remains, as ever, "the root of all that ioyous is."

Introduction

Spenser has ever been a favorite among the poets, but the Romantics loved him in an exceptional way and to an extreme that is unique in literary history. Southey liked to think of himself as the reincarnated "Spirit of Spenser," and he claimed to have read *The Faerie Queene* thirty times (quoted in Hard 128). Scott, as he put it, "devoured . . . whole cantos" of *The Faerie Queene* in boyhood and poured out Spenserian stanzas of his own throughout his long poetic career (*Letters* 1:320). Hazlitt called Spenser "the most poetical . . . of poets" (*Lectures* 68). Lamb labeled him "the Poet's Poet" (quoted in Hunt, *Imagination and Fancy* 51). And it was Keats's legendary "ramping" through *The Faerie Queene* as an adolescent that made him become a poet (*KC* 2:148), an experience that characterizes much of the flowering of Romanticism. The collective appearance between 1790 and 1830 of the first variorum Spenser edition, multiple reprintings of eighteenth-century Spenserian commentary, countless periodical discussions of Spenserian topics, and some 150 recorded poetic adaptions, some of them ranking among the period's finest poems, suggests how thoroughly Spenser informed and inspired Romantic literary culture.[1] Leigh Hunt, who proudly branded himself a "Spensero-philist" (*Correspondence* 2:264), summarized: "The most poetical poets of the last and present generation have all passionately admired him; and no stanza has been so popular as the magnificent one of his invention" (*Literary Criticism* 447).

Spenser's tremendous impact on Romanticism is virtually a commonplace of literary history. It is also well known that he became a remarkably fertile muse for Keats and Shelley in particular, giving them a song and a vision to sing about in a series of richly creative encounters that are now the stuff of literary legend. Harold Bloom calls him Shelley's ever-present "ancestor" (*Map of Misreading* 149), and Angus Fletcher finds him responsible for the outpouring of Shelley's "deeper skills" (341). According to Keats's first biographers, *The Faerie Queene* "awakened" the young poet's "genius," whose "soul

1. My count of Romantic Spenserian poems is based upon Davies's compilation.

arose into poetry" imbued with the enchantment of Spenser's "fairy world" (*KC* 2:55–56). It may come as a surprise, then, to learn how little has been written about these profound gifts. Despite all the recent work on Renaissance/Romantic dynamics, there is no book on the general subject of Romantic Spenserianism.[2] Indeed, most of the prodigious amount of the Romantics' commentary on Spenser has never even been reprinted, which has left us dependent on a few inadequate collections of Spenser criticism to frame any judgments about what he meant to his nineteenth-century descendants. Anthologies of his historical reception usually limit the Romantic section to a few abridged and often-repeated commentaries (Alpers, *Edmund Spenser;* Cory, *Critics;* Elliott; Mueller). The Critical Heritage Spenser volume (Cummings) and the three major studies of Spenser's developing reputation (Wurtsbaugh; Wasserman, *Elizabethan Poetry;* De Maar) all stop chronologically before the full advent of Romanticism. *The Spenser Encyclopedia,* apparently, will not contain a separate entry surveying and assessing the Romantics' overall reaction. There have been very few specialized studies of Spenser's relation to Keats or Shelley. None of them is of substantial length (with the exception of Carlos Baker's dissertation on Spenser and Shelley), and most of them were written long before the advent of influence theory helped us better understand the complexity of poetic relations.[3]

Robert Gleckner (*Blake's Prelude, Blake and Spenser*) and Joseph Wittreich (*Visionary Poetics*) have recently reminded us of the richness and importance of this long-overlooked Spenserian context in Romantic poetry. But their studies are specialized by nature and not designed to consider Spenserian influences outside of Blake's context. What they do tell us, besides a great deal about the Blake/Spenser relationship, is how much more we could learn about Romantic poetics from a sustained effort to characterize the general nature of the period's conversation with Spenser and the special role that Keats and Shelley played in it as two of his greatest admirers

2. There have been several dissertations written on Spenser and the Romantics, to which I am indebted (Pitts, Richards, Zimmerman). Traugott Bohme's 1911 reference work on Spenser's evolving reputation goes up to Shelley and can still be useful.

3. Curran provides a summary of the limited body of criticism related to Spenser's impact on Shelley ("Spenser and Shelley"). The Keats/Spenser dynamic is frequently mentioned throughout Keats scholarship, especially by Gittings (*John Keats, The Mask of Keats*), Bate (*John Keats*), and Vendler. But the only substantial study exclusively devoted to it since the dated and relatively unhelpful works of Read and Bhattachereje is Karel Stepanik's article on "The Problem of Spenserian Inspiration in Keats's Poetry."

and subtlest readers during the period. Yet as Stuart Curran has recently noted, Shelley scholars—and the same could be said of Keats circles—remain "loath" to investigate this Cave of Mammon ("Spenser and Shelley").

The cause of this reluctance is a long-standing scholarly distaste for the Romantics' seemingly perverse habit of trivializing Spenser's thought in fatuous worship of his beauty. Hazlitt's notorious advice to relish Spenser's "sensuality" instead of "meddling" with his allegory has been taken to epitomize this unfortunate bias (*Lectures*, 35, 38). Hunt's florid hymns to Spenser's luxury suggest even more strikingly why the Romantics' role in Spenserian history has been so widely slighted: "Divine Poet!" Hunt characteristically exclaims of Spenser, "sitting in the midst of thy endless treasures, thy luxurious landscapes, and thy descending gods! . . . We have found consolation in thee at times when almost everything pained us, and when we could find it in no other poet of thy nation, because the world into which they took us was not equally remote. . . . [I]n coming to thee, we have travelled in one instant thousands of miles, and to a quarter in which no sin of reality is heard" (*Literary Criticism* 456). Such outbursts became a regular feature of Romantic Spenserianism, and a sampling of them has been collected and reprinted as the basis for the twentieth century's dismissal of what Paul Alpers has called the Romantics' "tired and hackneyed view of . . . [Spenser's poetry], one that is justly outmoded. . . . [Its] characterization of Spenser's passivity, sensuousness and love of beauty . . . makes *The Faerie Queene* seem a monument to 'poeticalness' in a bad sense" (*Edmund Spenser* 68–69). This is the standard way that Spenser scholars look at the Romantics, with A. C. Hamilton disparaging "romantic indulgence in the poem's sensuous surface" (4), Maureen Quilligan lamenting that to "the eye of much nineteenth . . . century criticism, Spenser's most typical procedures have been well nigh invisible" (20), and Benjamin Lockerd echoing her by wondering why the aspects of Spenser's art that we now appreciate were "invisible" to nineteenth-century readers (17). With Hunt and Hazlitt taking such Phaedria-like excursions toward unreal Spenserian quarters, it is not hard to understand why Alpers's camp has silenced the Romantics—"rescued" Spenser from them, as he puts it (*Edmund Spenser* 3)—and why so few voices have arisen to defend them.

Yet our perception of their error has been distorted all along by our exclusionist focus on a small, spectacular body of writings that constitutes only a fraction of Romantic Spenserianism. And even that fraction has been removed from its immediate context and read in a reductive manner. Gleckner (*Blake and Spenser*) and Wittreich (*Visionary Poetics*) have shown in their readings of Blake's visionary Spenser how the intellectual dimension of his art could profoundly inspire the Romantics. If we consider the full sweep of their conversation with him, we will find that they were in fact deeply divided about his thought and his beauty. Moreover, in their contrary responses to him they came to recognize a dialectical cast of mind in his own poetry that became strikingly apposite to their own modern experience of self-debate and skeptical interiority.

Recent scholarship on Romanticism has come increasingly to understand the mentality governing the era's poetics in terms of what Susan Wolfson calls a "fundamentally interrogative character" (*The Questioning Presence* 18). Citing Hartman and de Man on the "indeterminacy" of Romantic mental acts, she finds the poetry "critically implicated in perceptions that provoke inquiry, experiences that elude or thwart stable organizations, events that challenge previous certainties and require new terms of interpretation" (18). Earl Schulze calls this process "self-critical irony" (31), a habit of mind that has become the center of a series of recent books on Romantic irony, dislocation, and mental doubling (Simpson, Mellor, Rajan). Peter Thorslev summarizes these processes of self-debate as the "Romantic dialectic," which is "basic to much, even to most Romantic poetry in England" (67). For Leon Waldoff, the "Romantic dialectic" entails a fundamental competition between the claims of imagination and reality (*Keats and the Silent Work* 80, 36). Stuart Curran also finds one of the principal controlling tensions of Romantic poetry the drama between imaginative idealism and relentless realism (*Poetic Form* 128–57). Whatever terms or points of reference one might choose to emphasize amid this debate, the fundamental concern shared by all these critics is with the act of the mind doubling in on itself—an act that increasingly became, as the second generation of Romantic poets developed, the central dynamic of the era's poetic discourse. It was the Romantics' widespread and ever-deepening recognition of Spenser's habitual inclination toward just such a frame of mind, one that particularly embodies the contraries of idealism and actuality, that ultimately made him such an essential figure in the psychodrama of their poetry.

As the Romantics became increasingly sympathetic to what they saw as Spenser's own experiences of self-division, moreover, they began to receive him as an unusually flexible, even vulnerable mentor. And here, within the context of their particularly acute sensitivity to the problems of an overbearing poetic tradition, they found something in him that was even more personally compelling: his unique way of appearing as what Keats called a "great bard" who was also accessible and reassuring. Spenser, the arch-poet of dreams and fairy fantasies, had always charmed young readers. The point was often repeated throughout the eighteenth and nineteenth centuries that his enchantments had made him unequaled in giving birth to young poets and that the experience of being "fathered" by him was unconditionally joyful. Abraham Cowley's poetic "birth" in the mid-seventeenth century was representative: "this [a copy of Spenser's poems] I happened to fall upon, and was infinitely delighted with the Stories of the Knights, and Giants, and Monsters . . . and by degrees with the tinkling of the Rhyme and Dance of the Numbers, so that I think I had read him all over before I was twelve years old, and was thus made a Poet as irremediably as a Child is made an Eunuch" (C 86). The echoing recollections of generations of poets following Cowley—including Dryden, Pope, Scott, Southey, and Keats, among many others—testify to Spenser's natural ascendancy as the chief poet who makes other poets. Yet as innocent or spontaneous as this kind of inspiration may have been, the idea of his genial influence grew more and more strategically valuable as England's poets began to feel the increasing burden of the past in the eighteenth and nineteenth centuries. It became a source of reassurance to cultivate under pressure, whether or not one actually felt a Cowley-like spontaneity of joy in Spenser's rhyme. And when it was reinforced and complemented by the developing sense of his self-divided vulnerability, it turned him into an invaluable icon of generous poetic transmission illuminating an otherwise forbidding palace of poetic fame.

In this unique and interrelated combination of a mentality that addressed the Romantics' deepest acts of self-debate, and did so with seeming benevolence, Spenser became one of their great empowering muses. Their strategies for incorporating him into their own poetics reached a peak of sophistication just as Keats and Shelley were being born into poetry in the second decade of the nineteenth century. And it is because those two poets emerged precisely within the ripest conditions ever for Spenserian revisionism, and acted on the situation with a brilliance that left all their peers behind, that I have chosen to make them the focal points of my study of Romantic Spenserianism.

Such an inquiry must be grounded, at first, in the earlier eighteenth century, for most of the principal concerns and strategies of Romantic Spenserianism originated there and cannot be fully appre-

ciated apart from it. I do not intend my study of the evolutionary
process through which the eighteenth century transmitted Spenser
to the Romantics to be merely a chronicle of Spenserian echoes or
allusions. Neither do I seek to discuss every facet of Spenserianism
that emerged in the eighteenth and nineteenth centuries. Rather, I
am concerned with what I see as the enabling line of Spenserianism
that flowed through Dryden, Thomson, Beattie, and eventually culminated in the interrogative "dialectic" of Romanticism, that part of
the Spenserian tradition that ultimately helped give the Romantics,
Keats and Shelley in particular, articulate voice.

In tracing the progress of what Shelley would call Spenser's "kindling" influence on the generations, I intend to show that, contrary
to common assumptions, there was neither a sharp division between
the eighteenth century's idea of him and the Romantics' nor even
such a single entity as a Romantic Spenser, or an eighteenth-century
Spenser. Instead, multiple visions of him competed and overlapped
throughout both periods.[4] And from that complicated, often divisive
conversation about how to understand him arose the steadily deepening impression of his interrelated accessibility and contemporaneity that set the conditions for his vital role in the poetry of
Keats and Shelley.

Learning how eighteenth-century Spenserianism flowed into their
endeavor may broaden our emerging revaluation of the complicated
processes by which the Romantics did not so much revolt against
their immediate literary background as absorb, extend, and transform it for their own purposes. To see how that experience of cultural transmission shaped their overall response to the more distant
and formidable tradition of England's Renaissance is also to expand
our current ways of thinking about poetic influence and its impact
on their achievement. For in their conversations with an earlier past,
the Romantics felt neither the paralytic anxiety that a Bloomian
reading might locate nor a secure confidence about their stance in
relation to their ancestors. Instead, they consciously sought out a
variety of psychological and aesthetic mechanisms to help them overcome, or at least withstand, the pressures of a literary tradition they
often felt bearing down on them. How Spenser helped diminish
some of that strain is a key to part of his appeal for them and a

---

4. Richard Frushell, in one of the few recent studies of Spenserian imitation, notes
that the numerous Spenserian formats in eighteenth-century poetry grew out of and
equaled in variety the wide number of different aesthetic tastes and fashions in the
period's literary culture (Frushell, "Spenser and the Eighteenth-Century Schools"
176).

dramatic illustration of their passionate struggle to work out their own creative salvation by redeeming the past. Our recognition of the different yet comparably enabling ways that Keats and Shelley received him can thus ultimately strengthen our continuing effort to distinguish their respective places within Romanticism's overall poetic project.

As we follow the complicated pathways through which the Romantics' rejuvenation of Spenser helped facilitate their emerging poetics, we may also find that they have something worthwhile to teach us about his own artistry. The renaissance in Spenser studies of the last two decades has largely come about from a series of breakthrough readings elucidating his infinitely complicated methods for rendering "psychic reality" (MacCaffrey 6, 33), which we now find grounded in his constitutional "play of double senses," his deep experience of the endless oppositions of ideality and "the pressures of the world." This "dialectic," A. Bartlett Giamatti summarizes, "what we call the dual impulse—goes on forever at the heart" of *The Faerie Queene* (69). It also goes on forever, albeit in radically transmuted form, at the heart of Romanticism. Among Spenser scholars, Isobel MacCaffrey and Michael Murrin have been sensitive to that transformation, noting how the Romantics increasingly interiorized Spenser's allegory and displaced its "cosmological" truths with "psychological" ones (Murrin 202). I take that astute suggestion as the starting point for my investigation of the sustained process by which such a revisionary dynamics ultimately issued in some of the Romantics' most "perfect" poems (Curran, "*Adonais* in Context" 181). Instead of assuming that the "intervening centuries [between us and Spenser] could not define or even appreciate" the aspects of his art we are now "rediscovering" (Lockerd 11, 18)—or worse, that neither Keats nor Shelley "had a clue to what *The Faerie Queene* is all about" (Sale 130)—we might take a lesson from the Romantics, especially Keats and Shelley. In their voyages to what Fletcher characterizes as Spenser's "core of profound ambivalence" (273), they carried out in their poetry one of the most engaging criticisms ever of the strengths and limitations of his "double vision" (Cheney 3).[5]

5. Bloom should be taken seriously when he urges Spenser scholars to deepen their understanding of *The Faerie Queene* by reading it through the Romantics' revisionary criticism: "The use made of Spenser by Shelley and Blake (and less substantially, though as extensively, by Keats) is an important part of the critical history of *The Faerie Queene* which Spenser scholars are not wise to neglect, however curiously backwards a technique it may seem to approach a prototype, the Garden of Adonis, by means of its imaginative derivatives, Blake's Beulah or Shelley's various earthly paradises" (*Shelley's Mythmaking* 178).

THE SPENSERIAN CONTEXT: INCENTIVES TO CONVERSATION

PART 1

Spenser in the   1
Eighteenth Century

To survey the full range of Spenser's impact on the period from the Restoration to Johnson's age would require a book-length inquiry along the lines of Dustin Griffin's recent work on Milton in the eighteenth century. I wish to focus this chapter, instead, on the one center of eighteenth-century Spenserianism from which most of the rich complexity of the Romantics' response flowed: the period's ever-deepening impression of Spenser's unique adaptability within England's formidable poetic tradition. Matthew Prior's exclamation at the start of the century could be taken as the motto of this Spenserian strain: "Who reads that bard desires like him to write . . . still tempted by delight" (*Colin's Mistakes*, lines 9–10). Decades later near the close of the century James Beattie felt even more strongly about this phenomenon, explaining how much Spenser "pleased" and inspired him while all the other "great masters" of the past seemed beyond "reach" ("Preface" to *The Minstrel; Dissertations* 152). A majority of England's leading literary figures from Prior's generation to Beattie's shared that experience, sensing a congeniality in Spenser that made him distinctly attractive in contrast to his more foreboding peers. How this response developed throughout the century to establish the grounds for the Romantics' fascination with his duality and his accessibility is the concern of this chapter.

I

Spenser had inspired criticism and imitation before Dryden,[1] but his admirers in the later seventeenth century were the first to make the

1. Although Spenser enjoyed a great popularity among his immediate followers in the early seventeenth century—such as Drayton, Browne, Wither, and the Fletchers—he fell out of favor as the century developed, his reputation sinking so deeply that by 1658 William London excluded him from a *Catalogue of the most vendible books in Eng-*

issue of poetic influence a central part of his legacy. This development grew out of England's new concern with poetic tradition and its threatening power, the subject of W. J. Bate's pioneering work on the burden of the literary past. Milton's death, as Bate writes of Dryden's response, seemed to conclude what Dryden called the "Gyant Race" of England's great Renaissance poets (*The Burden of the Past* 1– 29). Its achievement seemed fixed as a towering monument forever to remind succeeding poets—the "puny generations" that Shelley would lament—of their belatedness.[2] Discussion particularly focused on the narrow possibilities of epic accomplishment, considered the supreme measure of poetic vitality, in the aftermath of Milton's gigantic labor. Griffin may be right to qualify Bloom's image of Milton as the great inhibitor, arguing instead for the eighteenth century's rich extension of Milton's pastoral, his odes, and his myth of a recovered paradisiacal garden. But to most Neoclassical and Romantic poets, epic remained the ultimate standard for judging one's stature next to what Keats called the towering "Cliff of Poesy." And beginning with Dryden's era, widespread apprehensions arose that in this fundamental context Milton overshadowed everyone. John Dennis and Issac Watts noted how a consensus about Milton's preeminence was gradually building, as was reflected in a 1691 article for the *Athenian Mercury* titled "Which is the best Poem that ever was made and who . . . deserves the Title of the best Poet that ever was." The indisputable conclusion was that "Milton's *Paradise Lost* . . . will never be equal'd" (*C* 223). Attempts to "improve" that inimitable poem, which usually meant paraphrasing it in heroic couplets, struck many as the "abus[e]" of a "sacred tradition" (quoted in Wurtsbaugh 13). It was therefore difficult to resist Dryden's succinct and penetrating conclusion: "This man cuts us all out" (quoted in Havens, *The Influence of Milton* 21). With Milton threatening to close off the highest

---

land. For a sustained discussion of Spenser's impact on Elizabethan and Jacobean poetry, see Grundy (*The Spenserian Poets*). Wells and Cummings have collected extensive commentary on Spenser from 1579 to 1715.

2. As Bate has pointed out (*Burden* 24–25), there was no lack of literary critics in the eighteenth century to celebrate complacently the progress of modern poetry. But the period's most perceptive minds acknowledged uneasily what seemed to be their own age's undeniable inferiority to the Renaissance past. Addison, for instance, cautioned that those contemporary poets who blithely criticized their Renaissance predecessors "too slightly passed over . . . the Beauties in our antient English Poets . . ." (quoted by Wasserman, *Elizabethan Poetry* 40). Steele made a similar point about "Each Pygmy genius" who "dares" prescribe or rival "Great Shakespear's . . . boundless Wit" (quoted by De Maar 29).

kind of poetic election, Spenser's admittedly great but incomplete and problematical epic began to seem an alternative, more flexible line of tradition to extend. The appeal of this contrast helped catalyze in Dryden's age the first large-scale burst of Spenserian activity, and it would become an increasingly important stimulant for the escalating Spenserianism of the eighteenth century.

Although Spenser has always had a kind of magically inspiring effect on the poets, it was actually the emerging strategies of Neoclassical literary theory that made him now appear so opportunely flexible. Bate has taught us to understand the era's preoccupation with correctness as a defense against the threatening power of Renaissance poetry—a way of being different from a superlative tradition while criticizing or controlling its raw energy, "reducing" those "Gyants" of the past "to size or manageability" (*The Burden of the Past* 23).[3] This strategy helps explain the pervasive duality of Restoration writing on the Renaissance, with critics like Dryden both reverencing great predecessors and chastizing their egregious faults. It has been customary to associate this duality, as it persisted into the eighteenth century, with a critical tendency to distinguish between poetic form and content. Milton, as Wasserman tells us, was praised for his sublime theme and deprecated for his convoluted style (*Elizabethan Poetry* 17). Yet many faithful proponents of stylistic correctness loved the very "rude" poetics of the Renaissance that they officially condemned. Dryden, writing in his own well-sculpted couplets, yearned nostalgically for the "boist'rous" wit of the previous age. Other readers liked Wyatt's "Excellent Verses" and Drayton's "Harmony of Numbers." And Renaissance love songs, which were usually characterized in terms of their barbarously rough lyricism, found a sympathetic readership throughout the Restoration and the eighteenth century.[4] This contradictory enthusiasm for a discountenanced style has puzzled more than one critic of the Renaissance presence in that epoch. But if we relate the contradiction to Bate's idea of Neoclassi-

---

3. A group of more recent critics has extended and elaborated Bate's notion of Neoclassical theory as a defense mechanism. Maureen Quilligan explains that "it was convenient for Dryden to locate his grand rival's paternal seat in . . . the gothic, unneoclassical excesses of *The Faerie Queene*, reserving for himself a continental correctness" (19). Jean-Pierre Mileur characterizes Neoclassical theory as "a highly rationalized defense against the greatness of the native tradition" (167). Dryden's Neoclassicism, Griffin argues, helped him resist "the pressure of Miltonolatry" and preserve a space "still left open for a modern poet to write an epic" (141).

4. Wasserman catalogues these enthusiastic responses to Renaissance lyricism (*Elizabethan Poetry* 26–48, 153–91).

cal theory as a defense mechanism, we can see the period's writers using the aesthetics of correctness to limit or, as Dryden put it, to "tame" Renaissance poetic qualities they profoundly admired. Undoubtedly, there were many naive readers who worshiped unconditionally at the temple of Bossu. But for those who fully understood the growing threat of belatedness, there was a more subtle strategic value in Neoclassical aesthetics and the control it could exert over the Renaissance past. No Renaissance poet of high caliber proved so susceptible to such "taming" as Spenser.

This was especially true of *The Faerie Queene*, whose unusual vulnerability as an incomplete, highly eccentric work presented a welcome contrast to the seeming intransigence of Milton's more Classical epic model. Readings of Spenser consequently grew more frequent during the Restoration, and they regularly focused on *The Faerie Queene* as a divided work—superlative in many of its poetic qualities and richly deserving of emulation, yet seriously flawed in terms of Neoclassical theory and therefore quite open to refinement. Nearly everyone agreed that on the merit of *The Faerie Queene* Spenser belonged with England's greatest poets. To Rhymer, he was "great Spenser," to Dryden "Master" Spenser (*C* 207, 204). "He was, in a word," summarized the editor of the 1679 edition of his collected works, *The Works of that Famous English Poet, Mr. Edmond Spenser*, "completely happy in everything that might render him Glorious, and Inimitable to future Ages" (i). But for all his acknowledged greatness, he was quite imitable or, as Gleckner has shown, at least correctable, when approached through the mechanism of Neoclassical theory (*Blake and Spenser* 18). His diction was uncouth, his narrative lacked unity, his stanza was irregular, his imagination chaotic, his allegory inappropriate for epic action. These flaws were consistently mentioned, often in the same breath with soaring praise.[5] And everyone seemed to regret his indebtedness to Ariosto, whose model had debauched, in Rhymer's phrase, "great Spenser's judgement" (*C* 207). These objections had grown so commonplace by the end of the seventeenth century that Addison could write the following critique of *The Faerie Queene* without, as he later confessed, having even read it: "But now the mystic tale, that pleas'd of yore, / Can charm an

---

5. Rhymer, Davenant, Bysshe, and Dryden all lamented his "unhappy choice of so long a stanza." Davenant, Fuller, and Dryden condemned his obsolete diction. Blackmore and Temple felt his allegory was excrescent. These judgments have been assembled and discussed by De Maar (32–37), Wurtsbaugh (10–13), and Wasserman (*Elizabethan Poetry* 17–32).

understanding age no more; / The long-spun allegories fulsome grow, / While the dull moral lies too plain below" (*Epistle to Sacheverell*, lines 23–26).

Addison's slighting of Spenser's ineffective moralism suggests a great deal about the special influence strategies at work in this dichotomous criticism, for his comment arose from a heated debate about the center of Spenser's genius and the possibilities of emulating it. It is common for us to think of Neoclassicism's obsession with the moral part of Spenser. And, indeed, many who praised him in Dryden's generation seemed most impressed with his teaching skills. Edward Phillips, Milton's nephew, honored him as the "immortal" poet who sang "the sum of Christian and moral virtues." In Spenser's epic, argued Sir William Temple, "Morality" and "Instruction" replace "Story" as "the Subject of an *Epick Poem*" (*C* 199, 222). Such praises, echoed by the next two generations of critics, made up one of the dominant themes of eighteenth-century Spenserianism. Yet as pious as Spenser's Restoration readers may have been, their bias toward his moralism was neither so exclusive nor so straightforward as it appears. Many of them felt most strongly attracted to his sheer poetical abundance, that teeming profusion of musicality, pictorialism, and imaginative inventiveness that twentieth-century readers have characterized as his "protean resources" (MacCaffrey vi). In fact, those like Dryden and Pope who looked upon him as a master located his genius fundamentally in this poetic wealth. Measuring up to it oneself, however, was an intimidating challenge. But, as Addison revealed, setting out to correct the way he beat that gold into moral lectures seemed quite manageable. As much as one might feel astonished by the "force of . . . [his] Genius," explained Temple, "his Moral lay so bare, that it lost the 'Effect'" (*C* 222). Hence the emphasis on his moralism, which could not overlook the inadequacies in his manner of articulation, proved to be a strategic way of "taming" the "Gyant." Moreover, a duality of response, mixing reverence for his poetry with ambivalence about his moral efficiency, could place his followers in the unique position of aligning themselves with a surpassing talent who still needed major refinement.

We can trace that strategy working its way out in the period's specific divisions about his poetic and moral gifts. To many readers, like a reviewer of Beaumont's *Psyche*, he was the "Master of Poetry," not morality, "a Model fit to be imitated by all the succeeding Pretenders to that Art" precisely because of his "protean resources" (*C* 231, 233). The author of *Spencer Redivivus*, a 1687 adaptation of *The Faerie Queene*, celebrated above everything else his "*Poetical Genius*," the "wonderful Variety, Beauty, and Strength" of his "extraordinary" inventions (iv). And a very young Pope was becoming captivated, as he recalled years later, with the "gallery of pictures" in *The Faerie Queene*, which gave him "a vast deal of delight" throughout his life (quoted in Spence, *Observations* 182). Others, like Samuel Woodford, who composed a new version of Spenser's lost *Canticles* in 1679, found the "melting Strains" of his "Song" the mark of his "Genius." "[N]ever any other," Samuel Wesley concluded, "must expect to enjoy . . . such a prodigious Poetical Copia" (*C* 208, 210, 231). We shall find that last pronouncement one of the basic axioms of Spenserian history. No matter what one said about his excellent learning, it was his "prodigious Poetical Copia" that fundamentally made up his "Genius," that astonished his followers while also cutting them out. There was plenty of room, however, to make him a clearer, more effective moralist. His "Good *Christian* Thoughts," declared Henry Hall, must be liberated from his "Rhime." To purify him, many concluded, one needed only to impose on his "Design" the "rules of Bossu" (*C* 227, 222, 233, 228). Hence to recognize what Dennis perceptively called his overall "strange inequalities," honoring his "Poetical Genius" while stressing his inadequate moralism, proved an effective means of cutting oneself back into a great poetic tradition. How unique that opportunity was to Spenser's situation is suggested by Dennis's conclusion that where Spenser needed the "Rules" grafted onto him Milton was utterly complete unto himself (*C* 229).

Dryden was particularly sensitive to these special possibilities of controlling Spenser with Neoclassical theory. On the surface, his dichotomous reaction to Spenser appears consistent with the era's conventional distinction between the laudable content and the flawed style of Renaissance poetry. He reverenced Spenser's intellect, proclaiming that "no man was ever born with a greater genius, or had more knowledge to support it." Yet he also delivered "many Censures" on Spenser's stylistic eccentricities, concluding that the discipline of Bossu's "Rules" was necessary to correct such lapses (*C* 203, 205). He was far from unequivocal on this point, however, for his "Censures" revealed more of his wish to circumscribe Spenser's genius than any aesthetic displeasure he may have felt about that unusual style. In fact, he often expressed a profound love of its graces. Spenser was a great master in our language, he argued in apparent disregard of Bossu's rules, "who saw much farther into the Beauties of our Numbers than those who immediately followed [him]" (*C* 205). Those "Beauties," Dryden noted in a personal annotation of the *Mutabilite Cantos*, inspired the musical harmonies of his own

"Ode on St. Cecilia's Day."[6] "I must acknowledge," he could thus conclude, "that Virgil in Latin, and Spenser in English, have been my Masters" in versification (*C* 302). This last revelation, with its confessional tone of acknowledgment, suggests Dryden's awareness of the way his official displeasure with Spenser's numbers belied his more private relishing of them.[7] The contradiction seems less a sign of deception or confusion than a testament to Dryden's sharp understanding of how Spenser's poetic mastery was unusually susceptible to the limiting strategies of Neoclassical theory.

Spenser's appeal as a flexible giant was not confined to Dryden. It also registered in the special emphasis now given to his pliant disposition. It was perhaps a stroke of good luck, for poets with an eye to the past and to Milton's particularly foreboding austerity, that Spenser had always been renowned for his gentle temperament. His admirers in the early seventeenth century liked to celebrate his sweet tenderness as a love poet. But Dryden's contemporaries were unusually keen to promote his overall mildness, perhaps even to exaggerate it, as if they sensed how naturally such an image grew out of their discussion of his vulnerabilities and how much it could augment the growing attractiveness of his pliancy. The editor of the 1679 collection of Spenser's works claimed tenderness of sentiment as the most distinguishing feature of his entire corpus: "He was . . . of a temper strongly tender, and amorous; as appears everywhere in his Writings, but particularly in his Laments on the Death of *Sir Philip Sidney,* and in his incomparable *Daphnaida* (i). In building up this image of a tender-minded poet, Spenser's admirers began to stress the patiently endured misfortunes of exile, poverty, and public neglect recorded in his *Complaints.* The 1679 editor representatively introduced him as "ill-treated" Spenser. Thus Oldham's lamentable 1683 portrait of a gentle, much-suffering bard prescribed what was fast becoming the standard way of looking at Spenser: "Famish'd his Looks appeared his eyes sunk in, / Like Morning-Gown about him

6. Dryden's annotated copy of the 1679 edition of Spenser's works is now located in the Wren Library of Trinity College, Cambridge. His annotation on the "St. Cecilia's Day" source is reprinted in Wells (275).

7. It was a strategic evasion that at least one nineteenth-century critic of Spenser recognized. John Wilson, who wrote a series of articles on Spenser for *Blackwood's Edinburgh Magazine* in the 1830s, thought that Dryden had "lied" in preferring the correctness of Waller to the richness of Spenser (quoted in Zimmerman 19). Wasserman notes the pervasiveness of such evasions in eighteenth-century responses to the Renaissance, cautioning that "Augustanism . . . does not often treat publicly of its unfashionable interests" (*Elizabethan Poetry* 35).

hung his Skin: / A Wreath of Laurel on his Head he wore, / A book inscrib'd the Fairy Queen he bore" (quoted in Cory, *The Critics of Edmund Spenser* 51). The juxtaposition here of the sorrowing persona of the *Complaints* with the epic writer of *The Faerie Queene* suggests the precise nature of Spenser's new appeal. He appeared as a great, laurel-wreathed epic bard who was also soft and pliable. That image gradually became established as a literary stereotype that would grow more and more attractive as the problem of poetic influence progressively intensified throughout the eighteenth century.

The writers of Dryden's generation openly voiced the special relief they felt under Spenser's mild sway. Many of them felt inspired to become poets specifically because of his benevolent characteristics. Cowley remembered how the "tinkling" of Spenser's rhyme first moved him to write poetry (*C* 86). For Oldham, it was the "rich copiousness" of "Spencer's Muse" that gave him the courage to overcome his "modesty" and assume the "liberty" to make verses (*C* 300). The impression here of Spenser's beneficial parentage was particularly important to Dryden, who spoke of Spenser's legacy in terms of fluid "lineal descents" and happy "families" of successor poets. Dryden was particularly intrigued by the precedent of congenial poetic transmission, the "infusion sweete," that Spenser had himself established in his claim that "the Soul of *Chaucer* was transfus'd into his Body; and that he was begotten by him Two hundred years after his Decease" (*C* 205). "Ne dare I like," Spenser had begun his continuation of Chaucer's Squire of Dames Tale, "but through infusion sweete / Of thine owne spirit, which doth in me surviue, / I follow here the footing of thy feete, / That with thy meaning so I may the rather meete" (*FQ* 4.2.34). If Dryden's interest in this happy version of the family romance was at all representative, and we shall see that the passage continued to fascinate poets throughout the eighteenth century, we may conclude that just as England's poets were first starting to experience Oedipal conflicts with their forebears they began approaching Spenser as a generous, noncombative father. It was not long before the image of a kindly "Father Spenser," as Prior put it in *Colin's Mistakes* (1721), became another significant literary stereotype.

Such an encouraging "Father" immediately gave his poetic sons an unusual confidence about revision, which registers dramatically in the late seventeenth century's most notable Spenserian work, *Spencer Redivivus* (1687). An attempt to regenerate or enhance Spenser, as the title declares, the poem reveals how confidently Neoclassical strategy was used to reduce his size and improve his achievement. Its anonymous author, like Dryden, maintains a dualistic response, with his theoretical criticism qualifying his deep regard for Spenser's "Poetical Copia." He acknowledges the beauty of the "Essential Design" of *The Faerie Queene* while arguing, on the basis of Neoclassical rules, for the need to "abbreviate" the narrative (iv). In fact, he finds Spenser's poetic manner so eccentric as to warrant a complete stylistic overhaul of *The Faerie Queene*. He rewrites all of Book 1, replacing its "antiquated Verse . . . obsolete language . . . and tedious stanza" with modern "Heroic Numbers" (iii). Thus he confidently plunges into the redemption of Redcrosse's tale:

> A Worthy Knight was riding on the Plain,
> In Armor Clad, which richly did Contain
> The Gallant Marks of many Battels fought,
> Tho' he before no Mortal Habit fraught.
>   (lines 1–4)

We may cringe at the outcome of thus "regularizing" Spenser's style. But we should recognize the importance of such a revisionary strategy, whatever its aesthetic limitations, in helping to answer Neoclassicism's worries about its own belatedness. Efforts to "correct" the rough style of Renaissance poets were, of course, quite common throughout the Neoclassical period. But they did not often project the aura of self-assurance that regularly characterized the work of Spenserian writers like the *Spencer Redivivus* poet, who proudly claimed in his subtitle to have "totally laid aside" Spenser's "obsolete" style. Another anonymous rehabilitator of Spenser, who produced in 1716 a prose version of the story of Timias and Belphoebe titled *Memoirs of Fairyland,* proclaimed that he was quite ready to "say after" Spenser in a new way (vii). Such confidence seemed quite justified to many readers, like the poet who commended the author of *Spencer Redivivus* for giving Spenser's "Lines" considerable "advantage" (*Spencer Redivivus* 8). Milton revisionists, on the other hand, were much more diffident about their tampering with a great tradition. Hopkins, who put Books 1 and 2 of *Paradise Lost* into rhymed couplets in 1699, worried about his "abuse" of Milton's "sacred verse." Marvell apologized for all those who might "presume" to impose rhyme on *Paradise Lost*. And Pope, several decades later, denounced Milton's refiners as "caricatures" of the original.[8] There were parodists like John Philips, of course, who seemed to relish

---

8. Wurtsbaugh discusses Hopkins's comment (13). Thorpe records the responses of Pope and Marvell (335, 349). Frushell says no imitators "presumed . . . to overgo the model" ("Spenser and the Eighteenth-Century Schools" 175), but it would appear that such a "presumption" both occurred and created deep ambivalence about its merits.

toying with Milton's style. But for the most part, his adapters regarded their own enterprise with a wary uncertainty from which the
Spenserians were free. This contrast became increasingly important
for the history of poetic revisionism in the eighteenth century.

Several new developments in the Spenserian criticism of the early
eighteenth century made Spenser's adaptability seem even more
pronounced. John Hughes, who in 1715 produced the first scholarly
edition of Spenser's works, was very much concerned with the new
pressures of literary influence, regretting that the "great mass of invention has been opened long ago, and little new ore seems to have
been discovered or brought to light by later ages" (xliii). Spenser,
whose eccentric talents had always puzzled critics, seemed to give
Hughes a wide, unexplored cavern of raw material from which new
ore could be refined. In preparing an elaborate critical apparatus,
he thus displayed a strong interest in Spenser's openness to interpretation and his flexibility for adaptation. Most significantly,
Hughes developed the first theoretical defense of Spenser's allegory
and did so in such a way as to enhance greatly his unique reputation
as a malleable giant. Spenser's Restoration critics had almost univer-
sally deplored the allegorical mode of *The Faerie Queene,* viewing that
enterprise as incompatible with the genre of Classical epic. But
Hughes set out to define *The Faerie Queene* as an allegorical poem
governed by principles distinct from the strategies of Classical epic.
In this important new argument, which came to be known as the
"Gothic" view of *The Faerie Queene,* Hughes described Spenser's epic
as a compendium of allegorical portraits whose loose arrangement
resembles the eccentricities of Gothic architecture. His thesis is most
significant for my reading of Spenserian history in providing a theoretical basis for regarding Spenser as a great but flawed poet, a master artist worthy of emulation yet uncommonly open to refinement.[9]

Such a "Gothic" epic, Hughes argues, features imaginative portraiture and moral instruction in discrete allegorical scenes instead of
fostering, in Classical epic fashion, the narrative unity of a complete
poem: "[T]he whole Frame of it [*The Faerie Queene*] would appear

---

9. Gleckner finds Hughes locked into Neoclassical systems, which make his elu-
cidations of Spenser's genius both highly conventional and "notably unhelpful" (*Blake
and Spenser* 20). I wish to suggest, though, how Hughes's Neoclassical systematizing
was not so automatic or naive. Its strategies for defining Spenser's unusual contradictions helped reduce him "to size" (Bate, *Burden* 23) and initiated an evolving theory of
his unique accessibility that eventually culminated in Romanticism's conviction of his
elect status as a fluid transmitter of Renaissance "Poetical Copia."

monstrous, if it were to be examin'd by the Rules of Epick Poetry.
. . . But as it is plain the Author never design'd it by those Rules, I
think it ought rather to be consider'd as a Poem of a particular kind,
describing in a Series of Allegorical Adventures or Episodes the
most noted Virtues and Vices" (xliii). According to this standard, *The
Faerie Queene* must be judged by the inventive quality of detached
allegorical episodes, which Hughes measures according to four crite-
ria: the liveliness, elegance, consistency, and moral clarity of the fable. Such an unclassical test makes Spenser's narrative disunity seem
less significant than the fabulous portraiture and the moral lessons
scattered so prodigally throughout his allegory. It is precisely the
abundance of these qualities that Hughes cites as the principal
strengths of his "Gothic" poem: "The chief Merit of this Poem con-
sists in that surprizing Vein of fabulous Invention, which runs thro
it, and enriches it every where with Imagery and Descriptions more
than we meet with in any other modern Poem" (lviii–lix). Besides
simply delighting us, Hughes adds, these inexhaustible bursts of
"Poetical Magic" deliver a vigorous moral at those moments when
their fantastic creations are rising upon us most thickly. Hence the
"minute Beauties" of Spenser's "Figures" are everywhere accompanied by such "truly sublime . . . Thoughts" as "we may imagine
our excellent *Milton* to have study'd" (liv–lv). It is the multiplicity of
such brilliant flashes in "this beautiful and moral Poem," Hughes
concludes, that should move readers to praise Spenser as a superlative "Gothicist" instead of condeming him as a failed Classicist (cxiv).

Hughes was thus the first of many eighteenth-century critics to
recommend taking Spenser on the terms of his own unique genius.
Yet Hughes takes away as much as he gives, for in differentiating
between Classical and Gothic style he clearly subordinates the merit
of the latter. Spenser may have deliberately chosen an eccentric design for *The Faerie Queene*, and he may have succeeded quite well in
carrying out the strategies of that plan, but Hughes still regards any
such "Gothick" program as inherently inferior to the aesthetics of
classical epic. He therefore insists on judging Spenser by Gothic instead of Classical standards while simultaneously implying Spenser's
limitations in his abandonment of the Classical mode: "[T]o compare
it [*The Faerie Queene*] therefore with the Models of Antiquity, would
be like drawing a Parallel between the *Roman* and the *Gothick* Architecture. In the first there is doubtless a more natural Grandeur and
Simplicity. . . . tho the former is more majestick in the whole, the
latter may be very surprising and agreeable in its Parts" (xliii–
xliv).This hierarchy of "Roman" and "Gothick" art makes it possible

for Hughes to find "Exception" with the very Spenserian "Model" he is defending. He can thus speak in the same breath of Spenser's "Excellencies" and his "Faults," his great "Abundance" in the Gothic style and his "most obvious Defects" in departing from Classical aesthetics (xlii–xliii). While explicating the legitimate strategies of Spenser's eccentric style, for instance, Hughes regrets the unevenness of his stanza, tries to regularize his unusual orthography, and wishes that more of *The Faerie Queene* approximated the narrative unity of Book 1. In this mixed reaction Hughes was following earlier critics who had used Neoclassical theory to diminish Spenser's idiosyncratic genius. But his Gothic argument built up a new theoretical conclusiveness about Spenser's "strange inequalities." Pope certainly understood the attractiveness of that point when, writing to Hughes, he declared that "Spenser has been ever a favourite poet to me: he is like a mistress, whose faults we see, but love her with them all" (quoted in Elliot 13). Love her, we might add, *because* of them all.

It seems hardly coincidental that just as Spenser's vulnerability was growing more provocative, his readers increasingly came to think of him as a gentle friend, or even a soft mistress. Dryden's generation had felt this, too, but not with quite the enthusiasm that suggests how intriguing the idea of his pliancy was now becoming. Hughes, not surprisingly, was one of its leading proponents. The unifying focus of his life of Spenser, the most extensive one yet published, centers on the tender, melancholy spirit with which Spenser greeted a series of misfortunes—that spirit of gentle endurance that Cheney has described as his "characteristic mode of personal reference" (3). Beginning with the "pathetical Complaints" about Rosalind's cruelty in *The Shepheardes Calender,* Hughes enumerates the long train of political and domestic sufferings expressed with poignant grief throughout Spenser's poetry. Though showing little critical interest in the *Complaints,* Hughes emphasizes their personal quality as "the Sighs of a miserable Man" and gives them large scope in his biography in order to stress the pathos of Spenser's hard life and the still deeper poignance of his sorrowful yet ever gentle endurance (ix).

This special attention to his mildness was the principal means by which most of his admirers now characterized him. Prior, one of the early eighteenth century's most prolific Spenserian poets, called him "gentle Edmund" and celebrated his "friendly love" (*Colin's Mistakes,* lines 90, 92). Samuel Croxall, Spenser's first major eighteenth-century imitator, thought of him as a tender poet of sorrow: "See gentle Colin, Silver Mulla weeps / And wets the dewy shore when you lament" (*An Original Canto of Spencer,* 4). In *Memoirs of Fairyland*

and Samuel Wesley's *The Battle of the Sexes* (1723), Spenser appears as a kindhearted, melancholy tutor. Here, in this image of a beneficent guide lies the greatest significance of all the new discussion about Spenser's gentleness, for the emphasis on his mildness was broadly taken as a license to assume his congenial encouragement toward poetic disciples. Hence Wesley's *The Battle of the Sexes* begins with a dedicatory poem featuring Spenser's benevolent, fatherly approval of the imitation:

> Spencer, a glorious Shade . . .
> With Joy looks down to see a Son arise,
> That thus on Earth the Father's Place supplies;
> With Joy, he sees you modestly excel.
> And pleas'd beholds you imitate so well.
>   (lines 26–31)

Prior, in the self-portrait from *Colin's Mistakes* that opened this chapter, similarly declared how "much he lov'd" a kind, encouraging "Father Spencer." That such a Spenser was more of a fabricated product of the early eighteenth-century literary imagination than a historical personage emerging from biographical research suggests how powerfully the image of his benevolence replied to the age's concern about its own cultural past. And the institutionalization of "Father Spencer" as a literary stereotype that persisted well into the nineteenth century, even when more accurate biographies diminished its historical validity, implies the significant degree to which that image could relax those beset with the shadowy giants of tradition.

The early eighteenth-century Spenserians discovered how this effect could be enhanced by stressing the playfulness of Spenser's imagination. They were the first to notice in any substantial way what Leigh Hunt would call his "child-like" love of hyperbolic fantasy (*Literary Criticism* 453), that penchant for excess that Leigh DeNeef (102) and James Nohrnberg (196–97) have characterized as his "joco-serious . . . light-heartedness." Hughes's colleagues might not have gone so far as to agree with Alpers that parts of *The Faerie Queene* may be ranked among "the great comic poems in English" (*Poetry of The Faerie Queene* 405). But they did specifically praise his comic extravagance for the way it pleasantly cajoled and tempted young poets toward emulation, which is the subject of Frushell's recent article, "Spenser and the Eighteenth-Century Schools." Hughes thought that Spenser's relish for the kind of Gothic excess that delights young imaginations made him an irresistible coaxer of nascent poets, "the Father of more Poets among us, than any other of our Writers; Poetry being first kindled in the Imagination, which Spencer writes to, more than any one, and the Season of Youth being the most susceptible of the Impression" (xx). With this emphasis, the friendly father also took on the attributes of a playmate who nurtured and shared the wild, supernatural fantasies of his poetic children. Simply writing in his archaic style, what Prior called wearing a "farthingale," induced a prankish spirit of play. Others noted how his exuberance inspired comic exaggeration in his followers, who were like the "raskall many" dancing around the dead dragon's "monstrous large extent" (*FQ* 1.12.9) in their delight with the grotesqueness of such scenes as the description of Errour's vomit:

> Therewith she spewed out of her filthy maw
> A floud of poyson horrible and blacke,
> Full of great lumpes of flesh and gobbets raw,
> Which stunck so vildly, that it forst him slacke
> His grasping hold, and from her turne him backe:
> Her vomit full of bookes and papers was,
> With loathly frogs and toades, which eyes did lacke.
>
> (*FQ* 1.1.20)

Scenes like this may seem "remarkable" in their "horror" to some contemporary Spenser scholars (DeNeef 102). But to Hughes's generation, they mainly seemed to encourage frolicsome forms of imitation.

Croxall, for instance, cites the precedent of Spenser's "Raillery" and begins his own *Original Canto of Spencer* (1714) with the transparent hoax of a bumbling editor, Nestor Ironside, discovering a lost Spenser manuscript. That "recovered" document abounds with the high-spirited grossness of the following portrait of Archimago, like a modern Errour, feeding his hellish brood:

> For this their Office good, the Sorcerer
> Forth from a Wallett which beside him hung,
> Threw many gobbet Offals, of good Cheer,
> Which they devour'd with Cries that loudly rung,
> And wagg'd their Tails, and lilled out their Tung.
> . . . from their inly Maw their Loads they did upspew.
>
> (lines 181–89)

Whatever allegorical function may have resided in Spenser's portrait of scurrilous theological pamphleteering is subordinated here to "child-like" indulgence in sublime vulgarity. Pope's better-known portrait of "Obloquy" in his Spenserian imitation, "The Alley" (1727), takes this tendency of "toying" with Spenser's excess, as Shenstone later called it, to the furthest extreme:

> Her Dugs were mark'd by ev'ry Collier's Hand,
> Her Mouth was black as Bull-Dogs at the Stall:
> She scratched, bit, and spar'd ne Lace ne Band,
> And Bitch and Rogue her Answer was to all;
> Nay, e'en the Parts of Shame by Name would call:
> Yea when she passed by or Lane or Nook,
> Would greet the Man who turn'd him to the Wall,
> And by his Hand obscene the Porter took,
> Nor even did askance like modest Virgin look.
>   (lines 37–45)

Burlesque, of course, pervaded the eighteenth-century poetic scene.[10] But in the special case of Spenserian imitation, the "Raillery" seemed at least partly warranted by the master. Moreover, its execution forged a spirit of conspiratorial glee among Spenser and his fellow "Raillers." As a counterbalance to our standard reading of the moralistic bias of eighteenth-century Spenserianism, we should remember how much these early followers "toyed" with their jocular "Father." A measure of how significant that experience could prove in reducing the pressures of literary competition may be gauged by the way Spenserian play became a popular literary tradition, appealing to a long stream of eighteenth-century and Romantic writers from Pope to Keats and continuing even to this day in the imitations and "discovered" Ironside-like manuscripts that are featured in the Porlock Society meetings of the annual Spenser at Kalamazoo conference.

As much as Spenser may have seemed a welcoming figure, however, to follow him into poetry required finding some important contemporary relevance in his mode of thinking or seeing. That concern would dominate the history of Spenserian revisionism. The lack of any such affinity beyond a generally shared commitment to moralism is probably why Dryden's generation produced so few Spenserian poems. The early eighteenth-century writers found a more specific bond, however, in rescuing his imaginative form of

10. For a sustained study of eighteenth-century burlesque poetry, see Bond.

allegorical didacticism—"wondrous truths in pleasing dreams" (Prior, *Ode Humbly Inscribed to the Queen*, line 19)—from the disrepute into which it had fallen during the late seventeenth century. Their revaluation of the principles of his moral allegory helped popularize that creative form of instruction. Addison, for instance, became a great proponent of moral "Fable[s]" (*C* 225). This general recovery of allegory, in turn, sparked the sudden appearance of numerous Spenserian fables and set the grounds for the spate of Spenserian didactic allegories that eventually flooded the eighteenth century. But much as these early eighteenth-century poets approved of Spenser's allegorical mode and wished to integrate it with their own intellectual and aesthetic concerns, there was method to their bias. They perpetuated, even refined, the Restoration strategy of emphasizing Spenser's moralism in order to correct its blemishes.

The early eighteenth-century poets found fault with the same kind of irregularity of expression that their immediate predecessors had stressed. Prior, for instance, felt that Spenser's "numbers" needed to be made "more harmonious" (*An Ode Humbly Inscribed to the Queen* 173). Croxall found his "Stile" obsolete and his allegorical intentions often "hard to tell" (*An Original Canto of Spenser* 5). But besides extending what was by then a fairly conventional method of refining Spenser's style, the early eighteenth-century writers developed a whole new revisionary strategy for modernizing his allegory. They were particularly drawn to the political and historical dimensions of his allegory, and in such a way as to reinforce their confidence about improving his achievement. Hughes characterized large segments of *The Faerie Queene* as "a kind of figurative Representation of Queen Elizabeth's Reign" (lxiii). Prior thought Spenser especially commendable for celebrating "Eliza's" rule (*An Ode Humbly Inscribed to the Queen*, line 11), just as Croxall praised him for singing the "Glories of Eliza's Reign" (*An Ode Humbly Inscribed to the King*, line 6). This interest in Spenser's nationalism encouraged the adaptation of his political themes to contemporary subjects, which did more than punctuate the relevance of his allegory. With Britain on the rise militarily and economically in the early eighteenth century, it was tempting in such adaptations to boast cultural equality with, if not superiority to, the politicians and poets of Elizabethan England. Hence in *An Ode Humbly Inscribed to the Queen* (1706), Prior could sincerely make what may now seem an egregiously rash comparison between himself and Spenser, in which he envisions himself buoyed up by the winds of English progress to soar past his illustrious model:

When bright Eliza rul'd Britannia's state,
. . . .
An equal genius was in Spenser found.
But, greatest Anna! while thy arms pursue
Paths of renown, and climb ascents of fame,
Which nor Augustus, nor Eliza knew;
What poet shall be found to sing thy name?
. . . if the sovereign lady deigns to smile,
I'll follow Horace with impetuous heat,
And clothe the verse in Spenser's native style.
And by these examples rightly taught to sing,
And smit with pleasure of my country's
   praise,
Stretching the plumes of an uncommon wing,
High as Olympus I my flight will raise.
                                    (lines 21–38)

Few would claim now that Prior or any of his colleagues flew so
high. But the confidence they were fashioning for Spenserian revision would be so modified and strengthened through succeeding
generations as to help make Keats and Shelley, eventually, true
eagles on the wing.

As Prior's generation tried to build on that foundation themselves,
they located the one major tension point from which the history of
Spenserian revisionism would branch out during the eighteenth century: how to affiliate oneself with a "Poetical Genius" lavishly skilled
in the crafts of beauty while also regularizing that talent along the
corrective lines of Neoclassical revisionism. It would have been a
much easier task, if, like the *Spencer Redivivus* poet, one simply felt
obliged to smooth out Spenser's style and clarify his moralism. That
is the way many historians of eighteenth-century Spenserianism understand its revisionary program. But most eighteenth-century
writers felt that to place oneself in his tradition fundamentally meant
going to school, as Dryden put it, in his harmonies of versification,
or, according to Pope, in his "gallery of pictures." Prior's example
shows how difficult it was to do that and patch up his blemishes at
the same time.

Prior loved Spenser's "Beauties" as much as anyone, and trying to
reproduce them became one of the primary aims of his adaptations.
He found that the dominant traits of Spenser's style were not all that
difficult to imitate precisely because they were so eccentric, which
made any approximation of them, howsoever remote, at least remi-

niscent of no one but Spenser himself. Simply scattering a few archaisms and writing in something like *The Faerie Queene* stanza, Prior felt,
entitled one to claim a certain affinity with what he called "Spenser's
native style" (*An Ode Humbly Inscribed to the Queen,* line 34). However
superficial that form of imitation might have appeared to the likes of
Samuel Johnson ("Life of Prior" 117), it demonstrated both the relative easiness of linking oneself with Spenser and the importance,
notwithstanding the general push to regularize him, of approaching
his "native style." I will return to the first point in chapter 2 because
it developed into an increasingly important aspect of Romantic Spenserianism. But for now, I wish to concentrate on the extent to which
Prior appreciated and worked on that "native style." In his preface
to *An Ode Humbly Inscribed to the Queen,* he praised the "height of
imagination," the "lovely" descriptive richness, the felicity of language, and the harmony of "numbers" in Spenser's poetry (178). His
annotations of *The Faerie Queene,* as W. L. Godshalk has shown, reveal a special interest in the pictorial and musical prodigality of
Spenser's pageant scenes. Prior's conscious effort to approximate
these qualities may be traced in the following stanzas on Marlborough's return to combat against the French:

> As the strong eagle in the silent wood,
> Mindless of warlike rage and hostile care,
> Plays round the rocky cliff or crystal flood,
> Till by Jove's high behests call'd out to war,
> And charg'd with thunder of his angry kind,
> His bosom with the vengeful message glows;
> Upward the noble bird directs his wing,
> And, towering round his master's earth-born foes,
> Swift he collects his fatal stock of ire,
> Lifts his fierce talon high, and darts the forked fire.
>
> Sedate and calm thus victor Marlborough sate,
> Shaded with laurels, in his native land,
> Till Anna calls him from his soft retreat,
> And gives her second thunder to his hand.
> Then, leaving sweet repose and gentle ease,
> With ardent speed he seeks the distant foe;
> Marching o'er hills and vales, o'er rocks and seas,
> He meditates, and strikes the wondrous blow.
> Our thought flies slower than our general's fame:
> Grasps he the bolt? we ask—when he has hurl'd the flame.
> (lines 41–60)

Many of the rudimentary features of Spenser's Gothic "manner," as Prior understood it, are latent here—most obviously the occasional archaism ("behests") and the approximation of Spenser's epic stanza, but also the use of extended imaginative similes, the exotic descriptive painting, and the cultivation of assonance and alliteration for musical effect ("Plays round the rocky cliff or crystal flood"). More than a simple dabbler in Spenserian words, Prior clearly wished to incorporate something, in however limited a fashion, of Spenser's "Poetical Copia."

No one, however, would mistake the stanzas I have quoted for Spenser's. Indeed, Prior probably would have been unhappy with such an error, for he was also determined to regularize Spenser's genius and clarify his moralism. Prior's pursuit of those aims demonstrates the revisionary strategies of eighteenth-century Spenserianism in full operation. Though sensitive to Spenser's "Beauties," Prior also realized how vulnerable they were to a Neoclassical criticism and how much room for innovation could be cleared by applying such a standard of judgment. Hence the contradictions, recalling Hughes's divided remarks on Gothic and Classical art, in his preface. He could proclaim that Spenser was tremendously "knowing" in the mysteries of style while arguing, from his Neoclassical rostrum, that Spenser suffered from an obsolete diction, indulged too deeply in descriptive flourishes, and needed to be made "more harmonious" (178). This is precisely what Prior attempted to do in his imitation, turning Spenser's stanza into the symmetrical ten-line unit, rhyming *ababcdcdee*, that came to be known as the "Prior stanza." Within this more evenly regulated unit, he divided the syntax of individual lines into coupletlike structures, with each line usually end-stopped and frequently balanced by a medial caesura. He severely limited Spenser's archaisms, cultivating in their place a characteristically Augustan linguistic decorum. He curtailed Spenser's descriptive and musical luxury in favor of a more insistently didactic and politicized allegory about the progress of England's continental campaigns. And he abandoned the digressive, overlapping progress of Spenserian narrative for a briskly paced, sequential account of Marlborough's recent victory over the French.

Similar ways of modernizing Spenser were attempted by Prior's contemporaries. Wesley, for instance, used the ten-line stanza in his satire on contemporary social relations, *The Battle of the Sexes*, and Croxall, in *An Original Canto of Spenser*, attempted to finish the story of Britomart and Artegall in a new allegory that would also figure the rise of Britain's international power in the eighteenth cen-

tury.[11] This last example is particularly significant, as it shows how
the diffuseness of Spenser's narratives encouraged continuations or
completions in the interests of refinement. An anonymous "Gentle-
man of Trinity" tried to complete the *Mutabilitie Cantos* in 1729. And
Croxall, himself, wrote *Another Original Canto of Spencer's Fairy Queen*
(1714). With a model as open-ended as Spenser's, such attempted
completions could be ventured endlessly, and they were throughout
the eighteenth century. These new, more conventionally unified
poems departed so radically from Spenser that one is tempted to
agree with Johnson that writers like Prior, Wesley, and Croxall, in
their pursuit of originality, "no longer imitate . . . Spenser" ("Life of
Prior" 117). But this was exactly the point, not so much to "imitate"
him as to "improve" him by carrying his native genius, which Prior
and others certainly appreciated, into a modern, more refined context.[12]

As much as this particular marriage of tradition and innovation
served a crucial eighteenth-century need to build a second temple of
poetry over the grounds of the first, there was one fundamental
drawback in the early revisions of Spenser that would also persist
throughout the century. In refining Spenser's achievement, the
moderns had sacrificed many of those qualities on which they found
his greatness depending: his love of beauty, his gift for music, and
his teeming imagination. The basic strategies of Neoclassical Spenserianism were designed precisely to remove competition with these
strengths by pointing out their putative liabilities. But in suppressing
the monumental part of Spenser to clear space for originality, the
early eighteenth-century poets more or less consigned themselves to
inferiority. Prior understood this problem quite clearly. On one occasion, he abandoned his Neoclassical stance in pursuit of those
"Beauties" that he always relished and knew he was losing by regularizing Spenser. In *Colin's Mistakes*, a short paean to feminine
beauty, he retained the ten-line stanza. But in all other respects he
honored those Gothic irregularities that the new Spenserians were

11. Croxall also celebrated England's rising national power in his 1714 Spenserian
imitation, *An Ode Humbly Inscribed to the King.*

12. Griffin, in characterizing eighteenth-century theories of imitation, finds this
dialectic of the past and the present a crucial outgrowth of the eighteenth century's
self-conscious mission to match, integrate, and perhaps excel its great Renaissance
inheritance. "[A]daptation represents both cultural continuity (tradition preserved
and maintained) and cultural vigor (tradition renewed in contemporary terms)" (71).
The "final motive" of eighteenth-century poets who imitated Renaissance models,
Griffin argues, is "the wish to realize some possibilities latent in the original, suggested
but left undeveloped . . ." (68).

bent on correcting. He abandoned didactic allegory completely in favor of sensuous description. He broke down the symmetrical couplet structure of Neoclassical Spenserian poems for a more varied run of the line. And he used frequent archaisms, combined with a profuse deployment of assonance and alliteration, to create a musical euphony approximating something like the ringing gold bars that Yeats heard in the march of Spenser's stanzas (*Essays* 379). The following luxurious lines show how much Prior admired a "native" Spenser relatively untouched by Neoclassical innovation:

> . . . that bright form that pleaseth so mine eye,
> Is Jove's fair Daughter Pallas, gracious queen,
> Of liberal arts; with wonder and delight
> In Homer's verse we read her, well I ween,
> That in love of his Grecian master's flight,
> Dan Spencer makes the fav'rite goddess known,
> When in her graceful looks fair Britomart is shown.
>   . . . .
> As Colin mus'd at evening near the wood,
> A nymph undress'd, beseemeth, by him past,
> Down to her feet her silken garment flow'd,
> A ribbon bound and shaped her slender waist,
> A veil, dependent from her comely head,
> And beauteous plenty of ambrosial hair,
> O'er her fair breast and lovely shoulders spread,
> Behind fell loose, and wanton'd with the air.
> The smiling Zephyrs call'd their am'rous brothers:
> They kissed the waving lawn, and wafted it to others.
>   (lines 34–80)

This sensuous type of imitation may seem closer to Spenser's "native style" than the characteristic Neoclassical adaptation. But it is also more derivative and, in the direct rivalry it thus invites with Spenser's own "Poetical Copia," more conclusively inferior to its model, which is probably why Prior could at times forget about the "delight" of Spenserian imitation and "drop my pen" at the daunting task (quoted in Frushell, "Spenser and the Eighteenth-Century Schools" 196). That uneasiness may very well explain why the major poets of the era, Pope and Dryden, never essayed a sustained Spenserian poem, and why the entire period never produced any Spenserian poetry among its leading achievements. It did lay the foundations, though, for a confident attitude toward Spenserian revision.

And it established a working precedent for such adaptations, which in spite of changing literary tastes and shifting attitudes toward the Renaissance would help guide the next generation of poetic revisionists. But it only raised without solving the problem of how to wed Spenser's richest talents with modern innovation. That unsettled conflict provoked a hostile critical reaction to the early Spenserian poems and caused a pronounced decline in Spenserian activity during the second and third decades of the eighteenth century. With the "Affectation" of Croxall's Spenserianism under the attack of reviewers (*The Examiner Examined* 4), few Spenserian poems appeared in the next twenty years. The same dilemma would continue to limit the significance of Spenserian poetry throughout the first half of the eighteenth century. Yet ironically and in the typical wavelike pattern of Spenserian activity throughout the eighteenth century, that drawback also heightened the growing impression of Spenser's "strange inequalities" and his consequent openness to revision. The early eighteenth-century writers had thus opened the door, but just barely, into a Spenserian mansion of many beckoning apartments.

II

When most critics refer to the Spenserian revival of the eighteenth century, they are usually thinking only of the Spenserian literature that appeared between the mid-1730s and the early 1760s. This span of roughly twenty-five years witnessed one of the greatest outpourings ever of Spenserian activity. Hughes's complete works, long out of print, was republished. Four separate editions of *The Faerie Queene* appeared, some with elaborate critical apparatuses. Numerous scholars began calling for a variorum Spenser. Two books devoted to Spenser were issued, John Jortin's *Remarks on Spencer's Poems* (1734) and Thomas Warton's two-volume *Observations on The Fairy Queen of Spencer* (1754, expanded and reprinted in 1762). Paintings of subjects from *The Faerie Queene* began to proliferate in public exhibitions (Bradley). William Kent, the famous gardener and illustrator, designed a series of illustrations for *The Faerie Queene*. Sculptures modeled on figures from Spenser's epic began to appear in the fashionable gardens of country estates. And upwards of fifty Spenserian poems were published during these years.[13] So pervasive was

13. My count is based on the catalogues of Spenserian poems compiled by Wasserman (*Elizabethan Poetry*) and Davies.

this Spenserian vogue that by the 1750s Johnson had wearied of it all and wished to put an end to what seemed like a craze gone out of control.

Historians of Spenser's reputation like Wasserman have called attention to this mid-century Spensermania, reminding us that the Romantics were not the first modern writers to embrace Spenser on a large scale. But the exact causes of it have remained elusive. Most discussions of eighteenth-century Spenserianism tend to assess it as one continuous unit and thus fail to observe the distinct historical situation of the mid-eighteenth-century revitalization of Spenser. Hence questions about how and why it arose and lapsed at specific times, and how it both extended and modified earlier forms of Spenserianism, have never been sufficiently addressed.[14] These are questions that bear significantly on the central issue of how the mainline Spenser tradition of the eighteenth century developed into Romantic Spenserianism. The mid-eighteenth-century writers, themselves, can supply the best answers in their special concern with elaborating those earlier claims for Spenser's unique flexibility amid an intransigent literary tradition.

In *The Burden of the Past,* Bate has amply shown how the eighteenth century's early concern about the domineering stature of England's Renaissance tradition grew into a major crisis around the middle of the century. It was then becoming apparent that the Neoclassical experiment to refine the literary past was only circumscribing modern poetry, ensuring its subordination to the spontaneous largesse of the Renaissance. Numerous tracts like William Duff's *Essay on Original Genius* (1767), John Brown's *Dissertation on the Rise . . . and Corruptions of Poetry and Music* (1763), and Edward Young's influential *Conjectures on Original Composition* (1759) began to appear, many of which categorically announced the moderns' inferiority to

---

14. The standard way of accounting for the mid-century Spenserian onrush has been to invoke generally the period's growing interests in antiquarianism (Wurtsbaugh 60), landscape portraiture (Wasserman, *Elizabethan Poetry* 117–18), and Gothicism (De Maar 11). There can be no doubt that Spenser's congeniality to these tastes played an important role in his rising popularity among mid-eighteenth-century poets and critics. Yet most of these trends had started decades before Warton wrote his *Observations* in 1754. And as quite general aesthetic vogues embodying a diffuse range of interests, they can only partially explain such a precise, explosive, and highly focused phenomenon as the burst of Spenserianism that engaged virtually every major literary figure in England for a short period during the middle of the eighteenth century. How that phenomenon relates to or differs from the century's earlier, less volatile rush toward Spenser has never even been raised as a consideration in the standard works on eighteenth-century Spenserianism.

their gigantic ancestors, Classical and English.[15] Discussion predictably focused on the epic, still considered the fundamental measure of literary greatness. And, here, it was Milton who seemed to cut everyone out more thoroughly than ever before. Negative reactions to *Paradise Lost* certainly existed. Johnson's ambivalent, sometimes flagrantly hostile Milton criticism has always troubled his admirers. Bentley's attempt to "correct" Milton's irregularities is notorious, as is Lauder's even more sensational effort to discredit Milton. But the hyperbolic, erratic nature of this resistance implies, in itself, a troubled defensiveness about Milton's overwhelming impact, which was not at all confined to those who tried so openly to diminish him. For there was indeed good reason to feel defensive. The period's general response to Milton, as an epic bard, was rapidly turning into something like worship for a godlike Power who dwelt apart. Witness the following claims: "[Milton] excelled all other English poets. . . . In [*Paradise Lost*] there is a nobleness and sublimity . . . which transcends, perhaps, that of any other poem." "[He exhibited] the highest possible range of mind in the English language." "[He] is in a supreme rank . . . with which all other poets compare but as second class." "[He is] an Oracle . . . a noble Genius, perhaps the greatest that ever appeared among men" (quoted in Havens, *The Influence of Milton* 8, 27). Still more telling of the profound reverence now accorded Milton was the hesitation with which many critics ventured any negative comments. Jortin, who riddled Spenser with criticism, guardedly began his limited notice of problems in *Paradise Lost:* "I think it will not be cavilling to say. . ." (174). Noting how pervasive this wariness had become, a critic for the *Monthly Review* complained in 1760: "Whoever at this time ventures to carp at *Paradise Lost,* must whisper his criticism with caution" (quoted in Havens 24). Miltonolatry may have irritated some critics—Johnson grumbled about the "contest" in praising *Paradise Lost* (quoted in Havens 8)—but it posed an unprecedented dilemma for any poet seeking to improve upon

---

15. Bate writes: "By the middle of the eighteenth century there was an almost universal suspicion that something had gone wrong in the neoclassic adventure. And nothing could be more parochial than to associate this, as has so often been done, with merely a budding Romanticism restive against 'neoclassic tradition.' The uneasiness went far deeper, and afflicted those who strongly sympathized with the stylistic mode (or modes) of neoclassic poetry and art. This is especially true by the second half of the century. . . . Whatever else can be said of the spate of critical writing that suddenly begins in the middle of the eighteenth century in England, we can describe it as an attempt, however confused at first, to reground the entire thinking about poetry in the light of one overwhelming fact: the obviously superior originality, and the at least apparently greater immediacy and universality of subject and appeal, of the poetry of earlier periods" (*Burden* 45, 48).

England's epic tradition. As Thomson bluntly put it, "we live in times too late" (*The Castle of Indolence*, II, 199).[16]

Given this problematical situation, it does not seem coincidental, or simply an outgrowth of new fashions, that a less intimidating maker of English epic like Spenser should have suddenly become so popular. Although his strong presence in England's epic line was by now undisputed, the contrast of his recent drop in popularity with Milton's great upsurge must have reinforced the unusual aura of flexibility already considered basic to his role in the epic tradition. How Spenser's milder impact might affect the question of modern epic achievement did indeed become a central issue in his revival. Attention focused on his own epic precedent, to the general exclusion of his shorter poems. Unlike Milton's shorter works, which were edited and imitated throughout the eighteenth century, Spenser's waited nearly a century after Hughes's work to be reprinted. It was not that the mid-eighteenth century was unsympathetic to lyrical poetry. More to the point, there was something about Spenser's epic that was so compelling as to minimize interest in his lyrics. It is significant that such an exclusive curiosity about *The Faerie Queene* was also confined to professional literary circles. Spenser never enjoyed Milton's currency among common readers, as witnessed by the many eighteenth-century critics who lamented the reading public's ignorance of him.[17] This distinctly literary interest in *The Faerie Queene* may be understood in terms of the way Griffin explains the fascina-

---

16. It seems necessary here to qualify Griffin's contention that "Acknowledging Milton's greatness . . . seems not to have induced in eighteenth-century writers any distance or anxiety. . . . [Pope and his contemporaries seem] to have been quite free of any taint of anxiety of influence or untroubled by the burden of the past" (3, 156). Milton's impact may have provided an untroubling inspiration, as Griffin argues, for eighteenth-century experiments with the ode, the sonnet, the masque, and the novel. But when it came to facing up to the "supreme rank" of his epic achievement, the ultimate test to which most eighteenth-century and Romantic poets subjected themselves, acknowledging the "second class" status of the moderns and experiencing the pain of inferiority that such a recognition enforced seemed inescapable. Pope, as even Griffin observes, called himself "a worse writer, far, than Milton" (157). And rather than expressing what Griffin characterizes as "appropriate modesty" (157), Pope's self-deprecation seems more a product of the troubled sense of his own belatedness that forced him, on another occasion, to speak of himself as a "degenerate offspring" of his poetic forebears (quoted in De Maar 104).

17. One of Wasserman's general conclusions in *Elizabethan Poetry* is that Milton and Shakespeare were much more popular than Spenser with the general reading audience. Over one hundred editions of *Paradise Lost* appeared during the eighteenth century, and over fifty editions of Shakespeare's plays. The century only produced nine editions of *The Faerie Queene*, though Ralph Church's 1758 edition was specifically designed for a common reading public.

tion with Milton's shorter works among eighteenth-century men of letters. For a literary generation feeling increasingly closed in by the Renaissance's mountainous achievement, Milton's odes and Spenser's epic offered spaces to build upon that tradition. Spenser's legacy, by opening up the great epic line, must have seemed especially intriguing. Collins made a point of noting that where Milton had closed the curtain on epic vision "from every future view," Spenser could still transmit "amplest power" to at least a select few (*Ode on the Poetical Character*, lines 17–22, 72–76). His particular attractiveness in this respect can be traced in the way Collins's generation extended those earlier theories for demonstrating his rare flexibility.

One of the most hitherto puzzling features of mid-eighteenth-century Spenserianism is the same contradictory attitude that informed the Spenserian criticism of Dryden and Hughes. The new writers continued to mix lavish praise with extensive faultfinding, both responses often directed to the same aspect of Spenser's art. Thus John Upton, arguably the most insightful of the new generation of critics, both praised "the pause of . . . [Spenser's] verse" and condemned its "hitching" rhythm (*Spenser's Faerie Queene* 2: 369, 365). Jewel Wurtsbaugh, noticing a similar duality in Thomas Warton's reading of *The Faerie Queene*, finds him endlessly wavering "between his fondness for a poet who 'makes such perpetual and powerful appeals to the fancy' and his regard for 'that decorum which nature dictated, and which the example and the precept of antiquity had authorized'" (120). At a loss to account for this recurrent paradox, Herbert F. Tucker resorts to such phrases as "critical equivocation" and "doubleness of response" (327). Equivocation there certainly was, but it was less a product of critical confusion than an outgrowth of the strategy used by Hughes's generation to honor Spenser as the Mammon of poetry while checking his bounty with complaints about the mistaken way he turned it to instruction.

A moralistic bias drove much of the Spenserianism of the mid-eighteenth century, producing numerous critical disquisitions on the more overtly didactic allegories of *The Faerie Queene*, such as the procession of the seven deadly sins at the House of Pride or the description of Proserpina's garden in Mammon's cave. It was also responsible for scores of imitative allegories about the dangers of ignorance, lewdness, intemperance, and a host of other vices. The didactic extremism of these poems is enough to make us shake our heads with Frushell ("Spenser Imitations") and wonder what Spenser had to do with any of it. But, as before, the moralism here was not so naive. For while there were those who cared only about Spenser's severe truth, many saw a great deal more. At bottom, and with a growing appreciation of romance traditions making them even less reserved than Hughes's generation about poetical opulence, the mid-eighteenth-century writers were astonished by Spenser's "Poetical Copia." "What an invention," Richardson exclaimed, "What painting! What colouring displayed throughout the works of that admirable author!" (quoted in Wasserman, *Elizabethan Poetry* 95). To Goldsmith, Spenser was a "great magician" who "charmed" his readers to "tread the regions of fancy" (467). Collins greeted him in that same fantastic landscape, invoking his "visions wild" as the ideal manifestation of the "poetical character" (*Ode on the Poetical Character,* line 22). Thomas Warton tried to incorporate his rustic beauty into his own imitation, "A Pastoral in the Manner of Spenser," and he declared that he loved the "magic" of a "wildly-warbled song" more than anything else in Spenser (*Ode to Pleasure,* line 157). It was clearly this magical "well-head of Poesie," as Richard Hurd put it, that placed Spenser "highest among the poets" (112, 120). Yet because of their homage to this poetical fertility, many admirers also agreed with Richardson that "no man will ever come up to Spenser" (quoted in Wasserman, *Elizabethan Poetry* 95). It seemed just as clear, however, that many could come up to and surpass him in the clarity with which they expressed their moralism.

This is precisely how those intrigued by Spenser articulated their criticism, in terms of the considerable incentive for improvement he had dangled forth in all his erratic prodigality. "You know very well," wrote Upton to Gilbert West, one of the mid-eighteenth century's most prolific Spenserian imitators, "that but half the poem of the *Fairy Queen* is now extant: the stories therefore, as well as allegories, being incomplete, must in many instances appear very intricate and confused" (*Letter* 2). West certainly understood the implications of that point, which are just becoming apparent now to twentieth-century Spenser scholars,[18] for he produced two popular imitations

---

18. DeNeef argues for the endless, liberating play that readers experience in extending Spenser's meaning, but the point could just as easily be applied to the way eighteenth- and nineteenth-century poets have responded to *The Faerie Queene.* Spenser's poems, DeNeef claims, "are essentially unfinished because they are offered only as groundpaths for a reader's subsequent invention, as incentives to conversation, rather than completed orations. The critical urge to sum up, to draw the activity of interpretation to a literal close, runs directly counter to Spenser's own refusal to allow such an enterprise" (175). Harry Berger makes a similar point in arguing for the irresolution at the heart of what he calls "the Spenserian dynamics" ("The Spenserian Dynamics"). Jonathan Goldberg has presented the most radical reading of the "endlesse worke" that readers, and poets I would add, engage in while extending

of Spenser that extended cantos of *The Faerie Queene* and contributed whole new episodes. The poem is "unfinisht," added Ralph Church, editing *The Faerie Queene* in 1758. There were many "omissions" to be filled out and "many little oversights" in need of correction (1:xxiii; 3:445). Joseph Spence, in *Polymetis* (1747), may have been the most unsparing in listing these "Defects" and pointing out where Spenser needed correction in his moral allegory. But nearly every critic or imitator of Spenser in the mid-eighteenth century made some trenchant point about those "Defects" and their need for refinement. What lay at the bottom of all these remarks was put most succinctly by Upton in a studied understatement whose carefulness of phrasing suggests just how much it meant next to that "one overwhelming fact" of the past's "obviously superior originality": "I do not suppose . . . [Spenser] infallible" (*Letter* 32). This was no small conclusion to make about any of those giants from before the flood, let alone one to whom "no man could ever come up."

To elaborate this idea of Spenser as a lofty yet approachable eminence, the mid-eighteenth-century writers expanded all the previous "doubling" methods for asserting his "strange inequalities" and unusual flexibility. Hughes's Gothic theory reappeared in the 1750 reprinting of his edition and in Tonson's 1758 edition of *The Faerie Queene*. It became one of the most common ways of assessing *The Faerie Queene*, but its special maneuver for limiting while acknowledging Spenser's genius was executed with much more sophistication.

Warton, for instance, made a more complex version of that strategy the central thesis of his *Observations*, the era's most substantial critical study of Spenser. With a new antiquarian zeal, Warton shows how Spenser adapted the French, Italian, and English romances of earlier poets to create an unprecedented work of imaginative allegory written in a distinct Gothic tradition. Insisting even more strenuously than Hughes on the need to judge Spenser according to this background, Warton ventures the most powerful argument to date for reading Spenser on his own terms. At the same time, however, and again like Hughes, he implicitly rates the Gothic style inferior to the Classical. And, counter to his own principle, he goes on to criticize the various "monstrous and unnatural" excesses by which Spenser violated Classical propriety. He even cites the Abbé du Bos, as Dryden had done in a related context, to demonstrate the basic

---

Spenser's "endlessly indecipherable" meanings and his deliberately inconclusive quests (6–7).

incoherence of allegorical narrative (2:109, 322). In this negative response, Warton also exceeds Hughes, providing a list of Spenser's faults so lengthy as to provoke a self-admonishing apology for treating his subject so harshly.[19] Such "critical equivocation" enables him, like Hughes, to qualify everything he gives to Spenser. But he far exceeds Hughes in the degree of both his support and his criticism, which makes Spenser seem all the greater and lesser at the same time—or put another way, all the more provocative as a blemished mistress.

The usefulness of Neoclassical theory in thus equivocating about Spenser is most apparent in Warton's particular reactions to the "Poetical Copia" of *The Faerie Queene*. The Gothic theory entitled him to commend it, and his exuberant praise reveals a profound admiration for Spenser's poetical "magic." He characterizes one of Spenser's greatest strengths, for instance, as a sheer delight in luxurious description. Such descriptive opulence, Warton argues, depends moreover on Spenser's manifold beauties of versification: "[T]he fullness and significancy of Spenser's descriptions is often owing to the prolixity of his stanza, and the multitude of his rhymes" (1:160). Spenser's metrical delights warrant further praise for their strictly musical pleasure: "It is also remarkable that his lines are seldom broken by transpositions, antitheses, or parentheses. . . . His sense and sound are equally flowing and uninterrupted." His archaic diction, Warton continues, had "much improved upon [Chaucer's]" in fostering such harmonies (1:170, 190). But above all, Warton revels in the fecundity of Spenser's enchanting imagination. Writing of the tradition of sorcerous creators that Spenser heads, Warton finds such imaginative enchantment the deepest measure of "true poetry": "[S]uch are their tuneable Graces of magic and enchantment . . . that they contribute, in a wonderful degree, to rouse and invigorate all the powers of imagination: to store the fancy with those sublime and alarming images, which true poetry best delights to display" (2:323). Put together, these remarks make Spenser appear the undisputed master of "true poetry."

Yet Warton cuts back on each claim by reprimanding Spenser for failing, in the ecstasies of his imagination, to practice decorum and clarity of instruction. Thus Spenser's imaginative "exuberance" often makes him carelessly fabricate "monstrous and unnatural" vulgarities. His descriptions are frequently "offensive." His stanza im-

19. Warton was taken to task by William Huggins in *The Observer Observ'd* (1756) for his "too usual virulence" in setting himself up as Spenser's judge and "accuser" (4).

poses a "bondage of riming" productive of redundant and super-
fluous expression. His allegory is often confusing in its "imperti-
nent" mixture of pagan and Christian sources. And amid the "ex-
travagancies" of his imaginative portraiture, the "meaning" of his
allegory is frequently "occult," often indiscernible. Few writers, Warton would seem to conclude in this second verdict, stumbled so fa-
tally as Spenser in the "capital fault[s]" of his allegory (2:87–101).
Warton's energetic scrupulousness in ferreting out those "faults"—
he even commends the "ingenious discernment" of Spence's search
for "Defects" (2:95)—suggests how important it could be to find that
room where one could "come up to" Spenser.

   This is not to imply that Warton was disingenuous in his readings
of The Faerie Queene, or that he tried to contain Spenser with a superficial criticism whose tenets he did not personally uphold. His Observations carry out a sustained Neoclassical analysis of Spenser's weaknesses, and his private annotations of The Faerie Queene fully
substantiate his commitment to this critical position.[20] But he also
had to acknowledge a passionate enthusiasm for Spenser's erratic
genius that partook of his era's more spontaneous devotion to the
enormous strength of the Renaissance. And in this special context,
he recognized how effectively Neoclassical theory could restrain a
natural power like Spenser's. In fact, he saw how vulnerable Spenser
was, unique among all the mighty dead, to such a strategy. Thus he
opens his Observations by noting the peculiar division of personal and
theoretical reactions that Spenser alone arouses, a split that makes it
possible if not irresistible to extol and censure him at once: "In reading Spenser, if the critic is not satisfied, yet the reader is transported" (1:24). Although Warton sides here with the transported
reader, it is the unsatisfied critic guided by what Warton calls a "deliberate judgment" who controls much of the Observations. Such an
equation, in which judgment limits desire and towering genius receives a frame, came to dominate a fast-growing critical establish-
ment of Spenser commentary in the mid-eighteenth century.

   The writings of Richard Hurd and John Upton, the period's two
other leading Spenser critics, show how deeply rooted this mode of
equivocation had become in Spenser scholarship. Looking to both
Hughes and Warton, Hurd repeats their injunctions to read The

   20. At the end of his heavily annotated edition of the 1596 edition of The Faerie
Queene, now in the British Library, Warton wrote two full pages of detailed notes on
Spenser's "absurd" imaginative and stylistic excesses. He also made numerous run-
ning comments about such breaches of Neoclassical standards as the apparent lack of
unity in Book 4 of The Faerie Queene and the indecorum of the rustic language of The
Shepheardes Calender.

Faerie Queene as a Gothic allegory governed by a set of principles different from those of Classical epic. Thus he begins his influential Spenser chapter in *Letters on Chivalry and Romance* (1762): "[Spenser] could have planned, no doubt, an heroic design on the exact classic model. . . . But the charms of fairy prevailed. . . . Under this idea then of a Gothic, not a classical poem, the *Fairy Queen* is to be read and criticized" (56). Hurd even shares with Warton a natural preference for the poetic enchantments of Spenser's Gothic style: "I principally insist upon . . . [the] preeminence of the Gothic manners and fictions, as adapted to the ends of poetry, above the classic" (76). "[P]hilosophical or historical truth," Hurd goes on, anticipating what Hazlitt would say fifty years later, is less important in Spenser than "*poetical truth;* a very slender thing indeed, and which the poet's eye, when rolling in it's finest frenzy, can but just lay hold of" (92). "True poetry," he might have said with Warton, resides in Spenser's eccentric beauty.

Yet also like Warton, Hurd contradicts his basic claims, qualifying each with appeals to "judgment" and complaints that Spenser had not exercised more of it. Thus while privileging the Gothic style, Hurd admits that the Classical model may still be "the truest . . . because the simplest." In fact, he continues, the principles of Classical unity are bound "to discover and expose the nakedness of the Gothic" (67, 71). Hence the whole moralizing enterprise of *The Faerie Queene* seems quite "defensible," but Spenser had carried it out in an "untimely" fashion (74, 116). To prove that point, Hurd brings Neoclassical standards to bear on *The Faerie Queene* against his own insistence on a Gothic reading. He is determined, for instance, to find "unity" in the epic and dubiously locates it in Spenser's "design" of Gloriana's court as a radius from which the poem's action extends. Where he cannot impose such unity, Hurd faults Spenser's "considerable" lack of clarity, such as his frequent distortion of narrative continuity in the interests of Gothic extravagance.[21] These direct reversals of the case for a Gothic Spenser make it seem as if there are two different Hurds in the essay. And in a way that is not uncommon for mid-eighteenth-century Spenserian writings, there are: Warton's transported reader and his judgmental critic. Echoing Warton, Hurd acknowledges just such a division at the end of his essay:

21. Rosemond Tuve commends Hurd for protecting Spenser from "the error of forcing the different logic of epic design upon materials and purposes unsuited to it" (343). But that allegiance to Spenser's "native style" (Prior, *An Ode Humbly Inscribed to the Queen*, line 34) for which Hurd has rightly been commended by generations of Spenser scholars, makes up only one-half of his "doubleness of response"(Tucker 327).

What we have lost [through Neoclassical criticism], is a
world of fine fabling; the illusion of which is so grateful
to the charmed Spirit; that in spite of philosophy
and fashion, Faery Spenser still ranks highest among the
Poets. . . . Earth born critics . . . may blaspheme,
But all the Gods are ravish'd with delight
Of his celestial Song, and music's wondrous might.
                                                    (120)

Hurd was genuinely ravished with "Faery Spenser," but he also
knew as an earthborn critic of the mid-eighteenth century that blasphemy could be useful. Its attention to what he called the "mis-
alliance" of Gothic strength and Classical weakness in *The Faerie
Queene* could reveal just how seductive Spenser was as a beautiful yet
flawed mistress in need of purification.

John Upton practiced the most severe form of blasphemy in his
Spenser criticism. Upton is now considered most notable for his
scrupulous correction of textual errors, his careful elucidation of
Spenser's sources, and his intelligent annotations of numerous passages in *The Faerie Queene*.[22] But his criticism is more significant in
the history of Spenserianism for its ingenious balance of Gothic and
Neoclassical approaches to *The Faerie Queene*. In his *Letter Concerning
a New Edition of Spencer's Faerie Queene to Gilbert West* (1751), Upton
constructs a more elaborate version of Hughes's Gothic reading. He
argues for the beautiful variety of allegorical episodes in *The Faerie
Queene*, which like Hurd he compares to the divergent pathways of a
Gothic garden. Yet he also notes the inferiority of this plan to Classical epic, and he conducts so extensive a survey of Spenser's impro-
prieties that he pauses to wonder aloud, "But 'tis surprizing I should
dwell so long upon faults, when I have so many beauties all around
me" (32). Although he proceeds to tell a cautionary tale of a gentle-
man who overlooked the beauties of a garden in his fixation on the
weeds, Upton wants to find Spenser's weeds, admitting at one point
to be "looking for something to blame in Spenser" (30). His combination of Gothic transport and Neoclassical judgment, of course,
makes Spenser's flowers look simultaneously like weeds, and such is
the basic reading put forth in his 1758 edition of *The Faerie Queene*.

---

22. Upton is frequently cited in the Johns Hopkins variorum edition of Spenser's
works (Greenlaw) as an editor of considerable critical insight and scholarly familiarity
with Spenser's historical and literary sources. His readings figure centrally in Tucker's
article about the contribution of eighteenth-century Spenser scholarship to our own
understanding of *The Faerie Queene*.

For that work, Upton takes the revolutionary step of viewing *The Faerie Queene* as a Classical epic that fulfills all the major principles of the tradition built up by Homer, Virgil, and Milton. In opposition to the growing consensus about *The Faerie Queene* as a Gothic fragment, Upton begins his argument: "[I]n the epic poem the unity of the action should never be violated by introducing any ill-joined or heterogeneous parts. This essential rule Spenser seems to me strictly to have followed" (1:xx). Instead of simply refuting the Gothic theory, however, Upton shapes a more complicated form of the Gothic/Neoclassical split. In trying to make his subject a Classicist, he ultimately reinforces the divided view of Spenser's shakiness on Neoclassical grounds and his natural strength in the land of fairy.

The narrative of *The Faerie Queene*, Upton premises his argument, forms a unified Classical paradigm—beginning in medias res with one hero, Arthur, connecting various subplots as Achilles does in the *Iliad*—that the six concluding books were meant to complete. (Upton skirts the question of whether those books were lost, according to one tradition, or left unfinished at Spenser's untimely death.) This claim never won many followers in Spenserian circles. But it did highlight, considering that huge absence of the second, so-called unifying half of *The Faerie Queene*, Spenser's obvious inferiority to those great makers of completed epics with whom he was being compared. Any attempt to place him among the eternals, then, would have to drop such comparisons and judge his eccentric achievement on its own terms. The appeal here of the Gothic theory is obvious, and Upton, notwithstanding his wish to find the Classicist in Spenser, comes to celebrate the same "Poetical Copia" that constitutes for Warton and Hurd the "true poetry" of *The Faerie Queene*. Thus he praises Spenser's "luxuriant fancy," commends the "beauties" of his music, and marvels at the way his rhymes and meters "accord so well" with his patterns of thought. These combined qualities, Upton concludes, invite all readers to become "spectator[s]" ("transported" ones, we might add) of Spenser's brilliant, "imaginary" world (2:339, 349, 341, 346).

In focusing on this poetical abundance, however, Upton ultimately reinforces the era's prevailing sense of its vulnerability to the strictures of Neoclassical "judgment," for his basic impulse to read *The Faerie Queene* as a Classical epic compels him to reproach the lack of clarity in Spenser's Gothicism, however appealing its beauty may be. Upton cuts back on his encomia more radically than any of his contemporaries. He feels repelled by the "odious" vulgarity of descriptions like the portrait of Errour. He blames Spenser's archaisms for torturing the language into subservience to rhyme. Most emphatically—and this from the man who wonders how Spenser's "rhyme could so well accord with reason"—he complains again and again of the "wicked rhymes" that obfuscate Spenser's meaning and make his stanzas "jingle" and "hitch" (1:xl, xxxv; 2:366). As the period's single most influential commentary on Spenser, this divided reading thus helped consolidate the emerging idea of Spenser as a poet of "strange inequalities" possessing a rare mixture of unparalleled poetic beauties qualified by enormous lapses in judgment.

That scholarly idea took root in the collective imagination of mid-eighteenth-century critics, poets, and general readers. The lesser critics of Spenser all presented a similarly divided analysis, often directed to a more popular reading audience. Thus in his 1751 edition of *The Faerie Queene* Thomas Birch condensed his overall estimate of Spenser into this dualistic claim: "The Fairy Queen, notwithstanding all the Defects either of the Plan or Execution, may be justly considered as one of the noblest Efforts of Genius in any Age or Language" (xxxi). The editor of Tonson's 1758 *Faerie Queene* also concluded, "Yet with all its imperfection, it must be said, that his [Spenser's] diction is . . . much more sublime and beautiful than that of any English poet, who had written before him" (x). Ralph Church, editing *The Faerie Queene* in 1758, praised Spenser's great "variety" while apologizing for his many "oversights" (445). "[With] all his faults," Goldsmith summarized, "no poet enlarges the imagination more than Spenser" (468). Thus with all its enormous defects, *The Faerie Queene* could still be considered one of the grandest poems ever written. No single work, in the estimation of the mid-eighteenth century, hovered so dramatically between weakness and sublimity. No other great writer seemed quite so accessible to change and refinement. The excitement of following in the footsteps of such an incomplete giant may be measured by William Wilkie's confident prognostications about his own Spenserian adaptation, *A Dream: In the Manner of Spenser* (1769):

> Nor are your tales [Wilkie's own] I wot so loosely yok'd,
> As those which Colin Clout did tell before;
> Nor with descriptions crowded so, and chok'd,
> Which, thinly spread, will always please the more.
> Colin, I wot, was rich in Nature's store;
> More rich than you, had more than he could use:
> But mad Orlando taught him bad his lore:
> Whose flights, at random, oft misled his Muse:
> To follow such a guide, few prudent men would chuse.
> (lines 109–17)

No single passage better encapsulates the heart of the mid-eighteenth century's dichotomous reading of Spenser, or points out so succinctly how that reading made him such a promising model for revision. Poetically, he was overflowing, one of the greatest ever, "More rich than you." But in putting his wealth to practical purposes, he was "misled" and in need of improvement. That is precisely why Wilkie was expressing his creative ambitions in Spenserian stanzas instead of, say, Miltonic blank verse.

Questions must emerge at some point about how consciously Spenser's readers intended to cast him in this provocative role. Their dualistic responses may stem in part from their recognition that his eccentricity would not fit within any one traditional form of classification. But the fact that their impression of his vulnerability to criticism reinforced their curiosity about his reputation for mildness suggests a deeper, more complicated interest in those riches of his that needed polishing. Though biographers were beginning to question the veracity of his toils under court oppression, most of his mid-eighteenth-century readers liked to stress the gentle manner in which he bore a host of worldly disappointments. Theophilus Cibber thus remarked in 1753: "It is agreed on all hands, that the distress of our author helped to shorten his days, and indeed, when his extraordinary merit is considered, he had the hardest measure of any of our poets. It appears from different accounts, that he was of an amiable sweet disposition; humane and generous in his nature" (100). Even the sobersided Upton thought Spenser's "amiable disposition" one of his most noteworthy features (*Spenser's Faerie Queene* 1: 306). Joseph Warton best summarized the wide consensus on this last point, characterizing Spenser as a "sweet and amiable allegorical poet" predominantly given to "tender and pathetic feeling." "To imitate Spenser on a subject that does not partake of the pathos," he went on, "is not to give a true representation of him, for he seems to be more awake and alive to all the softness of nature, than almost any writer I can recollect" (31).

Spenser's perceived generosity was particularly significant in relation to his impact on poetic disciples. Like their immediate predecessors, but with still greater enthusiasm, mid-eighteenth-century writers acclaimed his rare habit of nurturing young poets. William Thompson regarded "gentle Edmund" as a kind "Father" whose "sweetness" enriched his own song (*Sickness*, II, 24–29). Spenser's playfulness, Shenstone happily declared, made one love to "trifle" with him (*Letters* 55). Others noted how "no writers have such power as he to awaken the Spirit of Poetry in others. . . . [M]ore Poets have sprung from Spenser than all other English writers" (quoted in Wasserman, *Elizabethan Poetry* 92; Cibber 99). Kindly, even impish, in his disposition and particularly encouraging to his followers, "gentle Edmund" thus appeared more like an avuncular friend than a stern patriarch. Cibber could note the resulting tendency to admire his unparalleled talent not only without intimidation but with the warmth of a welcomed intimacy: "No writer ever found a nearer way to the heart than he, and his verses have a peculiar happiness of recommending the author to our friendship, as well as our admiration" (99). Amiable friend, soft mistress, benevolent father: the pattern of these recurring personae, so different from the predominant idea of a forbidding Milton, should indicate how much the mid-eighteenth century's response to Spenser's divided achievement was answering its deepest qualms about Dryden's somber evaluation of a modern era forever "cut out" from England's poetic heritage.

Perhaps the most telling sign of this special interest in him as a unique facilitator of poetic transmission lies in the way his mid-eighteenth-century critics focused on his own art as a model of generous and immensely successful poetic revisionism. We all know, Upton declared, "what an imitator of the poets *Spenser* is" (*Letter* 38). It was also common knowledge, as Thomas Warton summarized, how much he had "improved upon" Chaucer, Ariosto, and a host of other models (*Observations* 1:190, 273). No one knew better, Upton explained, "when to add, or diminish, or vary [his sources], as his subject requires" (*Letter* 38, 12). The "superbly inventive and original" quality of that revisionism is a given in Spenser scholarship today (Tuve 345). But even more important to mid-eighteenth-century critics was the spirit of generous and enabling transmission with which Spenser brought the past into himself. That famous claim to have absorbed Chaucer's spirit through "infusion sweete"—itself adapted from Lucretius, as Jortin noted (98)—captivated nearly everyone's attention. We need only remind ourselves of all those echoes about being cut out to realize how encouraging it must have been to find Spenser setting himself up as a model for "sweete" poetic infusions. The implication here of how his own legacy might "surviue" in the present, how one might "follow" the "footing" of his own "feete," was so inspiring for Warton that he thought of it in terms of spiritual rehabilitation. As he annotated Redcrosse's miraculous renewal in the "well of life," he compared it to Spenser's rejuvenation of his own sources and expressed "rapture" at "contemplating the chymerical energy of true genius, which can produce so noble a transmutation, and whose virtues are not less efficacious and vivifying in their nature than those of the miraculous water here displayed" (*Observations* 1:75). This stunning gloss makes Spenser a great champion of the "vivifying" energy of poetic transmission, hence a kind of savior for the belated eighteenth century and the authorizing agent, in his own allegory, for all those readings of his redemptive inspiration. It was a role to be counterpointed with Upton's sense of Milton as a "conqueror [who] . . . deck[ed] himself in the spoils" of his vanquished sources (*Letter* 23). Such a lesson was eagerly consumed by mid-eighteenth-century poets, and it supplied the critical basis from which Shelley would eventually build up his own theory of "vivifying" poetic influence.

We can trace the great appeal of this model of invigoration in the way the poets, those to whom the ultimate task of opening up the past fundamentally devolved, actually responded to Spenser. They all acknowledged his greatness, but they focused most particularly on the flexibility and generosity that critics were so warmly ascribing to him. Though Thomson honored him as "my Master" (*The Castle of Indolence,* II, 468), he fondly thought of this "Master" as "gentle Spenser, fancy's pleasing son" (*The Seasons,* "Summer," lines 1572–75). Shenstone felt the same way, emphasizing "a peculiar tenderness of sentiment remarkable throughout his works" ("Preface" to *The Schoolmistress*). Robert Potter called him "Lov'd Spenser . . . the tenderest bard that ere empassion'd song" (*A Farewell Hymne to the Country,* lines 238–44). And William Mickle similarly appealed to "the gentle breast / Of haplesse Spenser . . . Fancy's sweetest impe" (*Syr Martyn,* lines 13–14). Shakespeare may have been considered a kindhearted spirit, and Jonson a hale fellow, but this attention to Spenser's tenderness was unique in its warmth and its concentration. For the poets, it meant that Spenser came to them with open arms, welcoming them, as Keats envisioned it in *Calidore,* into the Renaissance palace of poetry. If Milton brought on the Oedipal anxieties that Bloom emphasizes, a very different "Father Spencer" made them feel, as Robert Lloyd put it at the start of his Spenserian imitation, shielded as a "Son under the Protection of the Father" (*The Progress of Envy* x). It should therefore come as no surprise to find Gray declaring that he "never sat down to compose poetry without reading Spenser for a considerable time previously" (xvii).

The flexibility that made Spenser appear so accessible also began to suggest his most profound intellectual relation to a modern age, for the dualistic readings of *The Faerie Queene* inevitably raised suspicions of his own internal conflict between poetic luxury and intellectual responsibility. Perhaps there were not simply two readers of Spenser in every response. It might be that there were actually two

Spensers at odds in the poetry itself, a teacher of truth and a poet of beauty: "the sacred and seductive" Spenser that Leigh Hunt would recognize a century later ("English Poetry" 749), or the "dramatic" and "didactic" Spenser that Berger has honored in our own time (*The Allegorical Temper* 122). Thomas Warton, Hurd, Upton, and many others acknowledged that his "fine fabling" had actually diverted him from his intellectual purpose, either to the detriment of his art (the opinion of most), or to the benefit of his genius for poetic luxury. Ariosto could be blamed for seducing him away from his moral obligations. Or conversely, as Goldsmith argued in an important anticipation of Romantic claims, he was to be commended for leaving "reason" and "the ways of the present world" behind so as to charm us "without instruction" (467–68). Either way, his innate duality of mind began to emerge in the mid-eighteenth century as one of the most notable features of his art. Upton, as Tucker has recently argued (334), even concluded that such a dynamic of opposites makes up the central interest of *The Faerie Queene*. Thomas Warton was particularly intrigued by Spenser's hermaphroditical figures, like Venus in her temple, and he sensed that many such characters could be viewed as "visible and external symbols" of mind, their duality embodying Spenser's own divided psyche (*Observations* 1:96–97; 2:77). These penetrating insights, transmitted to the Romantics and elaborated by them, suggested how trenchantly Spenser could speak to a poetic age in fundamental conflict between imaginative idealism and intellectual realism. Ultimately then, the Neoclassical strategy of revealing Spenser's accessibility also became one of the keys to unlock his profound relevance for modern poetics. That intersection, as it developed through the latter half of the eighteenth century, made him one of the great enabling muses of Romanticism.

III

One of the strongest lines of transmission through which this idea of Spenser reached the Romantics came out of the Spenserian poetry of the mid-eighteenth century. The Gothic theory gave poets an efficient strategy for improving Spenser, by making him a better Classicist and a more effective moralist, but it also suggested the need to integrate his native stylistic opulence with Neoclassical innovation. A number of mid-eighteenth-century Spenserian poems, it is true, simply followed Prior's method for correcting his erratic genius by intensifying his didacticism and regularizing his style. The growing appeal of didactic allegory made this form of adaptation all the more attractive. Hence the earlier methods for "improving" Spenser were all used extensively. Works like Gloucester Ridley's *Psyche* (1747), Samuel Boyse's *Albion's Triumph* (1743), Robert Bedingfield's *The Education of Achilles* (1747), Upton's *A New Canto of Spencer's Fairy Queen* (1747), and Robert Lowthe's *The Choice of Hercules* (1747) even outdid the early eighteenth-century poems in their stylistic regularity (often framed in Prior's stanza), their contemporary nationalism, their insistent didacticism, and their effort to "complete" *The Faerie Queene* with "new cantos." This type of determinedly moral poem, flagging its virtue in its title, is what we often think of as eighteenth-century Spenserian art. But many of Spenser's imitators, the ones who became most important for the Romantics, applied the Gothic theory to their poems and tried to bring Spenser's "Poetical Copia" into their corrective innovations. Tensions thus arose, reduplicating the age's divided critical opinion of Spenser, between truth and beauty. That dualistic condition of Spenserian poetry eventually inspired a form of adaptation that explored Spenser's own perceived divisions of mind as a model for the psychodrama of modern poetic experience.

The writings of West show how deeply engrained this character of duality was becoming in mid-eighteenth-century Spenserianism. West also wrote "new" cantos of *The Faerie Queene*, featuring familiar characters like Archimago and Redcrosse, in which the style is regularized and the allegory is both modernized and made tediously plain. *Education, a Poem: in Two Cantos, Written in Imitation of the Style and Manner of Spenser's Fairy Queen* (1751), a drama about England's mission to refine the morals of her youth, recalls Prior's works with its mechanically regular stanzas and its concluding allegorical figure of England surveying rich fields of a "future fame" that surpasses the accomplishments of any preceding era, specifically Elizabeth's:

> Fired with th' idea of her future fame,
> She rose majestic from her lowly stead,
> While from her vivid eyes a sparkling flame,
> Out-beaming, with unwonted light o'erspread
> That monumental pile; and as her head
> To every front she turn'd, discover'd round

> The venerable forms of heroes dead;
> Who for their various merit erst renown'd
> In this bright fane of glory shrines of honour found.
>
> On these that royal dame her ravish'd eyes
> Would often feast; and ever as she spied
> Forth from the ground the lengthening structure rise
> With new-placed statues deck'd on every side,
> Her parent breast would swell with generous pride.
>
> (lines 811–24)

West was also sensitive, however, to the increasing talk about a Gothic Spenser. Thus he tried more extensively than anyone in Prior's generation to approximate Spenser's musical, descriptive, and imaginative beauties. The following description of Archimago's fabricated visions in *Abuse of Travelling, a New Canto of Spenser's Fairy Queene* (1739), for instance, shows how substantially West cultivated poetic qualities that we would associate more with Spenserian opulence than with Neoclassical regularity—the musical play of assonance and alliteration, the rhythmical sway of lines interwoven across couplet structures, the melodic tone of polysyllabic archaisms like "withouten," and the pictorial richness of lush, exotic landscape poetry:

> A spacious plain the false enchaunter show'd,
> With goodly castles deck'd on every side,
> And silver streams, that down the champain flow'd,
> And wash'd the vineyards that beside them stood,
> And groves of myrtle; als the lamp of day
> His orient beams display'd withouten cloud,
> Which lightly on the glistering waters play,
> And tinge the castles, woods, and hills with purple ray.
>
> (lines 101–8)[23]

Such indulgences are always limited in West's poems, however, controlled invariably by the regularizing habits of his Neoclassical Spenserianism. That refining impulse bespeaks his confidence about improving a gentle, flexible Spenser. Yet his experiments with both

23. As much as the description here aspires to a Spenserian lushness, however, we should be aware of Pitts's helpful reminder that much of the pictorialism in these mid-eighteenth-century imitations owes as much to emerging theories of landscape art as to Spenser's own examples (104–22).

these Gothic and Neoclassical formats reveal the extent to which Spenser's flexibility was encouraging dualities of style and outlook in mid-eighteenth-century adaptations.

Those contraries, indeed, were rapidly becoming a central feature of Spenserian poetry. We have been conditioned by the regularizing strategies of mid-eighteenth-century Spenserian poets to dismiss their works as dull moral allegories that have little to do with Spenser (Pitts 49; Wasserman, *Elizabethan Poetry* 131–32; Frushell, "Spenser Imitations"). But the fact is, many of them loved to indulge in his stylistic opulence. Mickle wished to reproduce his "wantonness of description" (541). Moses Mendez emulated his "numbers sweeter than the crystal rill / The which o'er breaking pebbles pleasing reigns" (*The Blatant Beast*, II, 55–56). William Thompson, calling him "the most descriptive and florid of all our English poets," shows in "An Hymn to May" (1758) what extremes of luxury these Spenserian poets could reach:

> By the warm sighs, in dewy even-tide,
> Of melting maidens, in the wood-bind groves,
> . . . .
> With dew bespangled by the hawthorn buds
> With freshness breathing, by the daisy'd plains,
> By the mix'd music of the warbling woods,
> And jovial roundelays of nymphs and swains;
> In the full energy, and rich array,
> Delight of Earth and Heaven! O blessed May!
> From Heav'n descend to Earth: on Earth vouchsafe to stay.
> (lines 43–56)

The poets who thus indulged, however, still felt in almost every case a conflicting urge to correct Spenser. Mickle insisted that his own narrative and moral "should be one" (541). Mendez made English patriotism the center of his imitations. And Thompson in *Sickness* (1745) wrote one of the most laborious, stylistically mechanical pieces of didactic allegory in the history of Spenserianism. The mood of mid-eighteenth-century Spenserian poets was thus one of confidence about transforming their model, but the actual character of their poetry assumed a duality of style and focus that would eventually sensitize them to Spenser's own fundamental contraries.

Several ingenious new forms of adaptation were actually designed to sustain this growing dynamic of truth and beauty in Spenserian art. One such innovation, which we shall see to be of great impor-

tance to Shelley, balanced those Spenserian contraries through a
particular extension of the "dream-vision" motif that Cheney (19),
Nohrnberg (79), and many others find to be a central component of
The Faerie Queene. This kind of adaptation features a human protagonist who dreams of, or is magically transported to, some celestial
land usually ruled over by a fairy goddess. Such a format—to be
found in works like Samuel Boyse's *The Vision of Patience* (1741),
Thomas Denton's *The House of Superstition* (1762), William Jones's
The Palace of Fortune (1769), Wilkie's *A Dream*, and even in West's
Education—encouraged the voluptuous language and description
that was growing so popular in Spenserian art. Hence Jones lavishly
displays the Acrasian riches of his visionary kingdom:

> Fresh lawns, and sunny banks, and roseate bow'rs,
> Hills white with flocks, and meadows gemm'd with flow'rs;
> Cool shades, a sure defence from summer's ray,
> And silver brooks, (where wanton damsels play)
> Which with soft notes their dimples crystal roll'd
> O'er colour'd shells and sand of native gold;
> A rising fountain play'd from every stream,
> Smil'd as it rose, and cast a transient gleam,
> Then, gently falling in a vocal show'r,
> Bath'd every shrub, and sprinkled every flowr,
> That on the banks, like many a lovely bride,
> View'd in the liquid glass their blushing pride;
> Whilst on each branch, with purple blossoms hung,
> The sportful birds their joyous descant sung.
> (lines 77–90)

From the vantage point of such beautiful scenes, however, the mortal dreamers of these poems look out upon the trials of human experience and learn an important moral lesson. Here the corrective impulse toward regularity and overt instruction, often of a particularly
contemporaneous nature, becomes manifest. Jones's protagonist
learns a "sage example," delivered in crisp heroic couplets, about the
asps "hidden beneath the bowers of bliss!" The young disciple of
West's *Education* receives a more historically specific lecture about
the intellectual decline of England's youth in the eighteenth century.
And Wilkie's dreamer, in a conclusion that strikingly demonstrates
the ultimate purpose of refining Spenser in these moralistic sections,
learns to tighten up the "loosely yok'd" tales of *The Faerie Queene*.
    An even more popular strategy for mixing Spenser's old graces

with modern lessons was to bring his pastoralism into a contemporary context. As the mid-eighteenth-century vogue for rural poetry like Gray's *Elegy* and Goldsmith's *Deserted Village* increased, Spenser's naive manner naturally became more attractive. *The Shepheardes Calender* is the only Spenser text other than *The Faerie Queene* that drew much attention during the eighteenth century. It was not only Spenser's generic pastoralism that attracted readers, however, but also what they called the "simplicity" of *Faerie Queene* episodes like Una's straying on an ass—"sweet images of humility," C. S. Lewis calls them (352). What seemed to make this simple pastoral style so appealing was the likelihood of being able to reproduce its beauties. It was clearly easier to approximate the naive diction, the rural descriptions, and what Shenstone called the "pretty metre" (*Letters* 42) of Spenser's pastoral manner than the densely packed opulence of highly wrought scenes like the Bower of Bliss. Going so far as to improve on his "simplicity" was also more of a manageable goal than trying to outdo him in stylistic luxury. One could always write even more naively than he did, dropping his occasional conceits and artificial-sounding archaisms (Murrin would call it "cleansing the Temple" [203]). The archaic quality of that temple presented yet another incentive to refine Spenser's pastoralism, for the spirit of antiquity that was predominant in his rustic world offered a particularly strong contrast with the contemporary scenes of instruction in the poetry of his modern followers. To highlight that incongruity could only emphasize his obsolescence and reinforce the feeling of progressiveness so important to those who revised him.

In *The Schoolmistress* (1737–48), the most successful of these adaptations, Shenstone both "cleanses" his rustic beauty and grafts onto it a contemporary style of didacticism. Shenstone's description of an unpretentious rural garden, for instance, characterizes the new idea of simplified Spenserian graces that was emerging in the mid-eighteenth century:

> Herbs too she knew, and well of each could speak
> That in the garden sipp'd the silvery dew;
> Where no vain flower disclos'd a gawdy streak;
> But herbs for use, and physic, not a few,
> Of grey renown, within those borders grew:
> The tufted basil, pun-provoking thyme,
> Fresh baum, and marygold of cheerful hue;
> The lowly gill, that never dares to climb;
> And more I fain would sing, disdaining here to rhyme.
>
> (lines 91–99)

Shenstone also uses this kind of rustic coloring as the decoration for his scenarios of modern instruction. Shunning the literary land-scapes of Spenserian pastoral, he describes a common scene from eighteenth-century rural life, the country schoolhouse, in order to deliver the kind of lessons about contemporary experience that earned *The Schoolmistress* a place among the "Moral Pieces" of John-son's *English Poets*. Hence it concludes with this warning to the schoolchildren about the wastefulness of eighteenth-century court life:

> Enjoy, poor imps! enjoy your sportive trade,
> And chase gay flies, and cull the fairest flowers;
> For when my bones in grass green sods are laid:
> For never may ye taste more careless hours
> In knightly castles, or in ladies' bowers.
> O vain to seek delight in earthly thing!
> But most in courts where proud Ambition
>   towers;
> Deluded wight! who weens fair Peace can spring
> Beneath the pompous dome of kesar or of king.
>   (lines 270–78)

Besides the sense of improvement here in purifying Spenser's beauty and wedding it to such overt moralism, this kind of modern pastoral also deepened the eighteenth century's impression of his geniality. Shenstone could not overlook the ludicrous contrast of his homely Spenserian mode with the lofty epic style that informs much of *The Faerie Queene*. In fact, he began *The Schoolmistress* as an off-handed parody of that style, in the manner of Pope's "The Alley." Ringing Spenserian phrases describing the plight of the school-mistress's wards, "They grieven sore, in piteous durance pent" (line 15), were meant to contrast comically with the bathetic context of a country schoolhouse. As Shenstone proceeded with his mock-heroism, however, he began to sense and appreciate the same tendency in Spenser for playfulness, simplicity, even vulgarity that Pope and others were noting. "[I] take great delight," he explained after work-ing on *The Schoolmistress*, "in his [Spenser's] simplicity, his good na-ture, &c. . . . I am now . . . from trifling and laughing at him really in love with him" (*Letters* 42). This sympathy with Spenser's inherent naivete inspired Shenstone's more ambitious idea of a modern pas-toral correcting and extending Spenser's own example. It also vali-dated the whole concept of simplifying Spenser, which after all seemed only an extension of his own natural tendencies, a claim that certainly could not be made about Milton. As Pope realized, efforts to write Miltonic poems on domestic themes, like Philips's imitations, only produced bombast or absurd incongruities with the elevated quality of Milton's character. Shenstone's alternative thus revealed an important way to strike intimacies with Spenser that would both extend his native cast of mind and facilitate the duality that was becoming central to the works of his followers.

A stream of Spenserian poems influenced by *The Schoolmistress* followed, like Henry Mackenzie's *The Old Bachelor* (1776), Burns's "The Cotter's Saturday Night" (1786), Potter's *A Farewell Hymne to the Country* (1749), Gavin Turnbulls's *The Cottage* (1788), and Beattie's *The Minstrel* (1771–74), all of which essay, in some substantial way, Shenstone's balance of moralism and beauty. That duality made such a profound impact on the Romantics because it eventually became a psychological as well as a stylistic consideration. Instead of simply blending didacticism with stylistic graces, the Shenstonian poems began to dramatize the poet's actual division between his intellectual duty and his aesthetic pleasure. The action of Spenserian poems began to take place, as Coleridge would later say, in "mental space" (*Literary Remains* 94), that region in which the poet's own deepest contraries of mind contend. With the landscape of Spenserian adaptation thus shifting inward, the self-reflexive "inscape," as Berger calls it ("Two Spenserian Retrospects" 5), of Spenser's own mental universe became more and more apparent to his readers. It was the Romantics' eventual recognition of the contrary acts of mind going on throughout his internal universe that ultimately moved them to find so much of themselves in his art. The beginnings of this breakthrough are apparent in Robert Potter's little-known but highly significant adaptation of the *Epithalamion, A Farewell Hymne to the Country.*

Though obviously seeking a Shenstonian balance of rural beauty and didactic instruction, Potter gives a new character of mental division to this dynamic. He tries to reproduce both the luxurious nature imagery and the dexterous meters of Spenser's marriage song. But experiencing the great difficulty of tracing Spenser's opulent "trewe verse"—"The footing of whose feet / I, painefull follower, assay to trace" (lines 244–46)—Potter follows Shenstone's plans for a more manageable adaptation. Thus he simplifies Spenser's pastoral style and focuses his own narrative, like Shenstone's, on the differences between healthy experience in the country and the corruptions of modern court life:

>   Ye lordlings great, that in proude citties wonne,
>   Which gently-cooling breezes never bless;
>   In gorgeous palaces with heat foredonne,
>   Come here and envy at my littlenesse.
>   All on a hanging hill, a simple home,
>   For its small tenant roome,
>   Safe-nested in the bosom of a grove,
>   Where pride, and strife, and envie never come,
>   Nor any cares, save the sweet cares of love.
>   (lines 147–55)[24]

This Shenstonian distinction between rural pleasure and courtly decadence receives an important new twist in Potter's closing stanzas. There he debates the conflicting pulls of indolence in the country and duty in the metropolis. He finally acquiesces to his obligations, as the title of his poem implies, but only with deep regret for the loss of rural innocence: "Break then thy rural pipe. . . . These woodnotes wild, this flowre-perfumed aire, / And thy sweet-streaming yare, / Must charm no more" (lines 310–13). This is not so straightforward a matter as trying to combine stylistic beauty with regimented instruction. Rather, Potter's own division between intellectual responsibility and the pleasures of poetry becomes the climactic concern of his poem.

That conflict gradually emerged as a central component of late-eighteenth-century Spenserianism, with works like Hugh Downman's *The Land of the Muses* (1768) opposing fancy to judgment and Beattie's *The Minstrel* contrasting rural dreaminess with worldly action. It is not hard to see how pointedly this tension addressed those emerging Romantic divisions between realism and imagination. Shenstone's Spenserian pastoral, with Potter's specific mental focus, thus became a highly favored poetic model for the Romantics, expanded in Wordsworth's *The Female Vagrant* (1798), Thomas Campbell's *Gertrude of Wyoming* (1809), John Reynolds's *The Romance of Youth* (1817), John Clare's *The Village Minstrel* (1821), and a host of minor Romantic pastoral poems in Spenserian stanzas. But it was finally Thomson's *The Castle of Indolence* (1733–34) that showed the Romantics how Spenser's "inscape" could best fit their own situation. *The Castle of Indolence* was the most popular mid-eighteenth-

---

24. Wasserman, recognizing Potter's genuine lyrical talent, notes that he "shook off the whole neoclassic system of versification and, with considerable success, entered into what Coleridge called 'the swan-like movement of Spenser'" (*Elizabethan Poetry* 150).

century Spenserian poem among the Romantics, for many of the same reasons that *The Schoolmistress* attracted so much attention. Like Shenstone, Thomson balances didacticism with pastoral beauty, but he conducts his oppositions along Potter's specific lines and with much greater sophistication than any of his contemporaries. He simplifies Spenser's pastoral style in Shenstone's manner, enjoying what he calls the "ludicrous" effect of Spenserian archaisms and settings dressed out in homely garb (*The Castle of Indolence*, 455). But while he welcomes this "trifling" and the relief from severe poetic competition that it brings, he also seeks to produce a richer semblance of Spenser's stylistic luxury. And, unlike most Spenserian poets of the eighteenth century, he has the talent to do so. His landscape descriptions are thus more stylized than Shenstone's and closer to Spenser's blissful bowers, despite their deliberate "simplicity," than anything else written in the eighteenth century:

> Join'd to the prattle of the purling rills,
> Were heard the lowing heards along the vale,
> And flocks loud-bleating from the distant hills,
> And vacant shepherds piping in the dale:
> And now and then sweet Philomel would wail,
> Or stock-doves plain amid the forest deep,
> That drowsy rustled to the sighing gale;
> And still a coil the grasshopper did keep,
> Yet all these sounds yblent inclined all to sleep.
> (I, lines 28–36)

In the second canto of *The Castle of Indolence* Thomson rejects this indolent world as morally irresponsible, and he turns to Shenstone's practice of modernizing Spenser's archaic pastoral scene with didactic sermons on contemporary forms of immorality. Yet the soporific charm of his pastoral descriptions, as many commentators have noted, reveals his own deep inclination toward poetic luxury. Hence a conflict like Potter's emerges at the center of *The Castle of Indolence*. The complexity with which Thomson articulates that tension constitutes his great contribution to Romantic Spenserianism.[25]

Instead of simply narrating his conflicting desires, like Potter, Thomson plays them out within an elaborate allegorical frame-

25. See Newlyn for a particularly useful discussion of the relation of Thomson's Spenserian dualities to Romantic poetics. That relation has also been explored by Parker and Schulman.

work. He even subtitles *The Castle of Indolence* "An Allegorical Poem" and characterizes Spenserian art in his preface as fundamentally allegorical. Even more significant for the Romantics, however, is his manner of deepening the interiority of Spenser's own allegory to make it a more effective vehicle for a modern drama about the poet's divided commitments to imagination and realism. The allegory of *The Faerie Queene*, as Thomson understood it, actually contains the basic design for this psychodrama. One of the central tensions in *The Faerie Queene* that eighteenth-century commentators often noted is the conflict between enchantment, fomented by evil wizards like Archimago, and moral responsibility, practiced most representatively by Una and Arthur. Thomas Warton, for instance, was fascinated by Archimago's magical enticements and Una's stalwart virtue (*Observations* 2:124–25). Struggling between these two extremes, central characters like Redcrosse and Guyon labor toward spiritual maturation. Although many eighteenth-century readers saw this drama operating within moral categories of temptation and virtue, we have seen how some important critics were reinforcing Thomson's sense of the allegory's relation to Spenser's own aesthetic divisions. That Spenser scholars are still debating the exact relationship between Archimago and Spenser, both makers of gorgeous illusions, suggests that Thomson was far from misguided to see the "inner condition" of self-division in Spenser's allegories of enchantment. Indeed, Thomas Warton, annotating *The Faerie Queene*, thought Thomson was absolutely right to find so much in Spenser.[26] The problem in Spenser for Thomson, though, was not that he had fallen short as a moralist, but rather that he had buried this mental debate, lost track of it, in his compulsion to teach a lesson. *The Castle of Indolence* became Thomson's attempt to release that buried psychological dynamic through what Gleckner has called "significant allusion": a direct response to a precursor meant to redeem "the eternal verities" shrouded in his errors (*Blake and Spenser* 1–2).

This kind of revisionary allusiveness is most apparent in Thomson's presentation of Indolence, the wizard in command of the castle. Indolence is a poet, a maker of illusions who shares much in common with Archimago. His castle habitation, for instance, abounds with the same kind of deceptive beauty that characterizes Archimago's hermitage:

---

26. Warton's annotations of scenes of enchantment in *The Faerie Queene* frequently refer to Thomson's celebrations of idleness in *The Castle of Indolence*.

In lowly dale, fast by a river's side,
With woody hill o'er hill encompass'd round,
A most enchanting wizard did abide,
Than whom a fiend more fell is no where found.
. . . .
The landscip such, inspiring perfect ease,
Where Indolence (for so the wizard hight)
Close-hid his castle mid embowering trees,
That half shut out the beams of Phoebus bright,
And made a kind of checker'd day and night.
(I, 10–13, 55–59)

Thomson calls Indolence a "wicked wight" and condemns him, just
as Spenser judges Archimago, on moral grounds. Yet the poetic
graces of Indolence prove harder to reject. His magnificent illusions
encourage his followers to become dreamers. And the visionary
splendor of their reveries, described with a seductively opulent
Spenserian style, suggests Thomson's tentative approval of their indulgence as the legitimate activity of imaginative poets. They gaze in
delighted wonder at their dreams,

As when a shepherd of the Hebrid isles,
Plac'd far amid the melancholy main,
(Whether it be a lone fancy him beguiles;
Or that aerial beings sometimes deign
To stand embodied, to our senses plain)
Sees on the naked hill, or valley low,
The whilst in ocean Phoebus dips his wain,
A vast assembly moving to and fro:
Then all at once in air dissolves the wondrous show.
(I, 262–70)

The Keatsian question in this passage focuses the debate at the heart
of Thomson's psychodrama: is poetic imagination to be cultivated as
a form of insight, a visionary apprehension of "aeriel beings," or
shunned as a "lone fancy," a lie against intellectual responsibility?
Divided by these competing claims, Thomson alternately thinks of
devoting himself to realistic writing—"actions fair"—and poetic enchantment—"love's enchanting woes" (I, 282, 286). Where Spenser
ultimately presents Archimago's story in a moral context and then
unmasks its evil intrigues, Thomson thus preserves or redeems the

inner dynamic of poetic division in this allegory and leaves it unresolved.

He further unveils this form of Spenserian interiority by heightening its role in one of Spenser's favorite scenes of mental conflict: the sumptuous banquet hall, a standard feature, for example, in the Castle Joyeous, the House of Pride, and Busyrane's castle. The "costly arras . . . pretious stone . . . endlesse richesse . . . [and] gorgeous array" of the House of Pride's hall signify the moral temptations and dangers of excess (1.4.6–8). Thomson's chamber, as its association with "rural poets" and dreaming bards implies, does not so much embody moral conflict as it elaborates his poem's ongoing duality of artistic temptation and prudence:

> The rooms with costly tapestry were hung,
> Where was inwoven many a gentle tale;
> Such as of old the rural poets sung,
> Or of Arcadian or Sicilian vale:
> Reclining lovers, in the lonely dale,
> Pour'd forth at large the sweetly-tortured heart;
> Or, sighing tender passion, swell'ed the gale,
> And taught charm'd echo to resound their smart;
> While flocks, woods, streams, around repose and peace impart.
> . . . . the bard in waiting there
> Cheer'd the lone midnight with the Muse's love:
> Composing music bade his dreams be fair,
> And music lent new gladness to the morning air.
> (I, 317–70)

The ambiguity of this passage makes its complex aesthetic focus all the more evident. Soft luxury and reclining lovers in Spenser's festal halls betray moral degeneracy. Thomson's portrait both summons all those negative associations and qualifies them with a much more fruitful description of imaginative indolence. The spacious rooms "swell" with pleasure, just as the lovers' songs "swell" the gale. The tapestry tells a "gentle tale" sung by "rural poets." The bard's song "cheers" the night and "gladdens" the morning. If the poetic activity of this scene reminds us of Spenser's treacherous luxury, it must also surprise us with its many implications of fecundity. For Thomson, the choice between artistic luxury and responsibility is not so straightforward as Spenser's moral equations. And in this recovery of the hidden drama of Spenser's castle allegory, it is left open-ended.

Thomson did make that choice in the end, however, siding rather tediously with intellectual duty in canto 2 of *The Castle of Indolence*. But that decision ultimately tells us more about the dynamics of eighteenth-century Spenserianism than the limitations of Thomson's art. While it may register some insecurity about his aesthetic irresolution, it more directly reveals his dependence on the eighteenth-century's basic strategy for refining Spenser—that is, regularizing his style and clarifying his didacticism. As much as Thomson may have seen himself enriching the complexity of Spenserian allegory, he was finally unwilling to disagree with Spenser on the need for moral conclusiveness. Thus finding himself, at last, in Spenser's own position of unmasking evil, there was only one effective form of maintaining his originality: the standard Neoclassical strategy of refining Spenser's instruction. Thus for canto 2, in a scenario reminiscent of many eighteenth-century Spenserian poems, he modernizes the narrative of Guyon and the Palmer destroying Acrasia's bower. He replaces those characters with allegorical figures representative of eighteenth-century progress, the "knight of arts and industry" attended by a moralistic bard, both of whom set out to destroy the fanciful world of Indolence. The luxurious descriptions of Spenser's model episode are replaced by extended lectures on modern duty, patriotism, and industry, which are framed in the austere, modern style of Neoclassical Spenserianism:

> They talk'd of virtue, and of human bliss.
> What else so fit for man to settle well?
> And still their long researches met in this,
> This *truth of truths,* which nothing can refel:
> "From virtue's fount the purest joys out-well
>   (II, 316–19)

The independence from Spenser that Thomson seeks is evident here, but clearly to the aesthetic detriment of *The Castle of Indolence*. More obviously than any other eighteenth-century poem, Thomson's work demonstrates the limitations of the eighteenth century's plan to mix beauty and didacticism in its Spenserian art. Yet *The Castle of Indolence,* in the mental drama of its first canto, also suggests the kind of "significant allusion" required to make a more successful Spenserian art. That example helped establish the idea of redeeming Spenser's psychological duality from his moral absolutism, which, if extended, could bring him into the "doubling" center of Romantic poetics.

Thomson's poem clearly had the most to teach the Romantics about Spenser's relevance to their own situation. Wordsworth annotated his copy of *The Castle of Indolence* with a Spenserian poem about his own conflicting attractions to imaginative luxury and intellectual responsibility. Coleridge spoke warmly of "that most lovely poem, The Castle of Indolence" (*Unpublished Letters* 33) and incorporated its dichotomies into his most powerful lyric on his own deep divisions between moral duty and the imaginative "shapings of the unregenerate mind," "The Eolian Harp."[27] Keats extended the divisions of mind in Thomson's castle motif, as we shall see, to shape his own personal allegory about modern poetic experience. But *The Castle of Indolence* did not make up the only eighteenth-century line transmitting Spenser's dualism to the Romantics. The major Spenser critics of the eighteenth century were frequently reprinted and studied throughout the Romantic period.[28] Although there was much dissatisfaction with their source hunting and their moral glosses, their interest in Spenser's divided aims drew considerable attention. Hunt, for instance, quoted Hurd and Warton on the two Spensers when making his own most forceful claims about Spenser's divided psyche (*Imagination and Fancy* 52). This kind of reaction also characterizes the Romantics' general reading of eighteenth-century Spenserian poetry. They thoroughly explored its diverse forms—Wordsworth, for example, could quote Moses Mendez—and while many of them were ambivalent about moral didacticism like West's, they prized the kind of duality that pervades eighteenth-century Spenserian poems. It was the one feature of Beattie's *The Minstrel*, for instance, that Byron emphasized in the preface (4–5) to his own

27. See Newlyn (113).
28. Warton's *Observations* went through new editions in 1807 and 1820. Hurd's *Letters on Chivalry and Romance* was reprinted in 1811. Todd's variorum edition of Spenser's complete works (1805) includes sustained essays on Spenser by Hughes, Upton, Spence, Warton, and Hurd. Its eight volumes also feature voluminous eighteenth-century comments on specific Spenserian passages, which—if Hunt's annotated copy of Todd is at all representative—were thoroughly poured over by the Romantics. Eighteenth-century commentary frequently appeared, moreover, in the Spenser volumes of the many collected editions of the British poets, compiled by editors like Bell, Aikin, and Chalmers, which went through multiple reprintings throughout the Romantic period. Chalmers even made a special point of commending "the many criticisms" of Spenser written during the eighteenth century ("Life of Spenser" 10–11). Eighteenth-century Spenserian poetry was available to the Romantics in a wide body of reprintings. In his eighteen-volume anthology of eighteenth-century verse, *Bell's Classical Arrangements of Fugitive Poetry* (1789–1810), John Bell includes two volumes of Spenserian poems, a decision that in itself suggests how popular those works remained around the turn of the nineteenth century.

Spenserian epic, *Childe Harold's Pilgrimage* (1812–18). Overall, then, the Romantics created a specialized idea of eighteenth-century Spenserianism, redeeming its fine duality from the dross of its moral extremism. And that redemption inspired them to see how recovering Spenser's own dichotomous vision could empower the doubling energies at the center of their unfolding poetics.

The duality of eighteenth-century Spenserianism, we recall, had emerged from theories about Spenser's openness to revision. That duality was also transmitted to the Romantics, we shall see, in a way that similarly reinforced impressions of his flexibility. It was only such a combined sensitivity to his psychological relevance and his accessibility that inspired them to carry out such an elaborate creative dialogue with him. The idea of a "gentle Spenser" came to them as a much-needed, in some cases indispensable, source of reassurance about travelling with those mighty poets who inspired their vision. One of the final twists of eighteenth-century Spenserianism was particularly significant in bolstering that important sense of confidence. The plethora of mid-eighteenth-century imitations, many of them relentlessly dull, provoked a strong anti-Spenser backlash in the last third of the century, much of which was indirectly focused on the regularizing innovations. Complaints were raised, for instance, about the "tedious langour" of Spenser's stanza and the "kind of task-reading" required to get through his laborious allegories (Hume 376). Johnson called Spenserian imitation "the plaything of fashion," and he declared that Spenser's model was "of no value . . . what our ancestors have wisely thrown away" ("Life of West" 137; *Samuel Johnson* 218). The number of imitations plummeted between 1760 and 1790, and no one tried to bring out a substantial edition of Spenser until early in the nineteenth century. Even Shenstone and Thomson, despite their success with *The Schoolmistress* and *The Castle of Indolence,* remained skeptical about the lasting merit of their Spenserian works, for the eighteenth century's long history of discovering Spenser's faults, much as it may have encouraged revision, always cast some doubts on the validity of imitating him. Spenserian poetry continued to be read suspiciously, as more of a "plaything" than a serious artistic enterprise, and both Thomson and Shenstone chose to stake their reputations on other works. By 1770, resistance to Spenser and his imitators had so calcified that one *Monthly Review* critic could fulminate: "The Fairy Queen is frequently laid down almost as soon as it is taken up! because it abounds with loathsome passages!" ("Critical Observations" 306–7). In 1779 the situation seemed so desperate that an anonymous defender of Spenser, hoping to repair his "exploded . . . Authority," tried to rescue his thought from what seemed the hopeless muddle of his poetry by putting *The Faerie Queene* into a two-volume prose work titled *Una and Arthur* (v). "Poor Spenser," lamented Hurd, "must for ought I can see, be left to the admiration of a few lettered and curious men: While the many are sworn together to give no quarter . . . [to] his song" (111–12).[29]

It would take yet another generation, and a still more innovative way of incorporating Spenser into mainstream aesthetics, before adaptations of his poetry would gain a central place in England's literary culture. However, the burden that weighed him down throughout the eighteenth century, and the specific resistance he met late in the period, actually made him all the more attractive to the Romantics. From their position, that critical history seemed a record of increasing abuse and misunderstanding from which he badly needed to be rescued. Hence their enthusiasm for him only intensified, as did their sense of his unusual openness and vulnerability. It was difficult, then, to find anyone among the mighty dead who spoke to their hearts both so meaningfully and with so much encouragement about the new directions their conversation with the Renaissance might take.

29. Recognizing this plunge in Spenser's popularity among poets and critics—and there were many other devastating claims, like Hume's, that Spenser may retain "his place on the shelves . . . but he is seldom seen on the table" (376)—offers an important qualification to our general assumptions about the great rise of Spenserianism toward the end of the eighteenth century. Gleckner can take it for granted, for instance, that "the latter quarter of the eighteenth century" witnessed a tremendous "spate of Spenserianism" (*Blake and Spenser* 6). In fact, the outburst of Romantic Spenserianism did not fully get under way until the last decade of the century, and it was preceded by a marked decline in Spenser's reputation that actually created the desire for a rejuvenation of interest in the book that had so seldom been seen out on the table.

The Duality of
Romantic Spenserianism

The great eruption of "Spensero-philism," as Hunt would say, around the turn of the nineteenth century has usually been viewed as a dramatic revolution in Spenserian history, a new revival movement quite distinct from the eighteenth-century tradition and spectacularly myopic in its obsession with what Yeats called "Spenser's power of describing bodily happiness and bodily beauty at its greatest" (*Essays* 383). Some dispute remains whether or not this development was salutary, with scholars like Patrides commending the Romantics' celebration of Spenser's beautiful craftsmanship and others like Alpers regretting how their superficial biases misdirected generations of readers away from his intellectual depth. But nearly everyone agrees on the revolutionary character of Romantic Spenserianism. Wasserman reminds us that Spenser's beauty was deeply appreciated throughout the eighteenth century and that the Romantics "built upon a framework that had been laboriously constructed throughout the eighteenth century" (*Elizabethan Poetry* 252). Yet even he feels their borrowing was narrow in their primary concern with what we have until now considered a minor branch of the eighteenth-century background, the purely aesthetic strain of its Spenserianism (139). I wish to suggest, however, that the Romantics took much more from the eighteenth century, and that it was what they learned about Spenser's special relevance to their own situation that inspired the phenomenal surge of their Spenserian writing. Romantic Spenserianism neither struck out a whole new path for itself nor simply followed a Phaedria-like course toward unreal beauty. Instead it gathered up the most complex traditions of Spenserian history and carried them forward into a more fruitful range of poetic revisionism.

I

The wide scope and particular emphases of the Romantics' reading in eighteenth-century Spenserianism suggests how thoroughly they absorbed this background and its special focus on Spenser's adaptability. Eighteenth-century Spenserian poetry and criticism became their major guide for learning how to read Spenser, and we have seen how the frequency of its reprinting suggests the serious attention they gave to it. They were so deeply steeped in eighteenth-century Spenser criticism, in fact, that complaints about the burden of absorbing it all were not uncommon. Hunt, Wordsworth, and Scott all agreed that Todd's critical apparatus was marred by the way it overwhelmed readers with eighteenth-century commentary. Although this deluge of material could provoke some irritation, especially with the elaborate source-hunting of critics like Warton and Upton, it served an important purpose in focusing the Romantics' interest on Spenser's accessibility and his doubleness of vision. It is no coincidence that the two mid-eighteenth-century poems most deeply engaged with those attributes, *The Schoolmistress* and *The Castle of Indolence,* became the most popular Spenserian imitations among the Romantics.

The eighteenth-century's delight with Spenser's benevolent and "vivifying" inspiration became even more compelling for the Romantics. Although they were not the first to struggle with poetic influence, they encountered what Thomas McFarland has called "the originality paradox" on an entirely new scale of intensity (*Originality* 2). Hence, the kind of fascination that the eighteenth century had felt for a malleable Spenser increased proportionately with the Romantics' stronger experience of the burden of the past. We are in need of a detailed study examining the precise degrees of their influence anxiety and the related enthusiasm they would have felt about the image of a pliable Renaissance giant. Such a study is beyond the scope of this book. Yet it is essential to outline the parameters of the Romantics' debate about tradition, especially as it focused on the encroachment of Milton's legacy, in order to appreciate their profound attraction to the eighteenth century's notion of Spenser's flexibility.

✓   Stuart Curran has shown us how the Romantics conceived of their poetic enterprise as a "second Renaissance," a deliberate turning away from the Neoclassical experiment in order to reproduce, perhaps even to surpass, what had come to seem England's true poetic tradition: its first Renaissance (*Poetic Form* 14–28). We should make no mistake about their euphoria in setting out to generate a monumental poetic rebirth. It was a heady time for poetry, "a second spring in our poetry" proclaimed Francis Jeffrey ("Keats's Poems" 203). But raising what everyone considered to be "a second spring" also provoked comparisons with the original spring on a level of directness that the eighteenth century had warily avoided. The second Renaissance, in fact, had to define itself in terms of its relation to the first, and that compulsion gave rise to unprecedented apprehensions about the overbearing power of the past.

As early as 1787, Henry Headley was speaking with calm resignation about his own age's sense of doomed inferiority to the past: "If we seriously and impartially examine the clusters of poetical names that shone, and were concentrated in the space of ninety-one years from the accession of Elizabeth . . . to the restoration of Charles the second, and compare them with those who have respectively flourished from that time to this, a period of an hundred and thirty-eight years, we shall find the phalanx of older classics but little affected by a comparison with the more modern musteroll" (xv).[1] Headley's martial imagery was not coincidental. Along with images of giantism —Hazlitt, speaking of the Renaissance, often invoked those "giant-sons of genius" who "tower above" their successors (*Lectures* 45)— such imagery appears time and again in the Romantics' debate about the past, revealing their impression of being cast into an embattled relationship with domineering forebears. That experience, Hazlitt explained, often left them intimidated, near despair about the prospect of ever trying to build a second Renaissance: "What *niche* remains unoccupied? What path untried? What is the use of doing anything, unless we could do better than all those who have gone before us? What hope is there of this?" (*Lectures* 195). Those who struggled against hopelessness and tried to do better were sometimes commended. Coleridge, wrote one reviewer, impressively took on the Renaissance "giants in intellect" (*R* part A, 1:34). It was more common, however, for such attempts to meet with regret about the puny appearance of the moderns expending their limited strength like so many "Lillipution counterfeits," as one reviewer put it, in the shadow of Brobdingnagian ancients (*R* part B, 1:163). Hence Coleridge was cautioned against "dwelling with ardent love on the gigantic prodigies of Elizabeth, and James" (*R* part A, 2:746). Sir Walter

---

1. Echoes of Headley's assessment recurred throughout the Romantic period. Thus a reviewer of Ford's plays declared in 1811 that the Renaissance "has always appeared to us by far the brightest [era] in the history of English literature,—or indeed of human intellect and capacity. There never was, any where, any thing like the sixty or seventy years that elapsed from the middle of Elizabeth's reign to the period of the Restoration" ("The Dramatic Works of John Ford" 275). Hazlitt, surveying the evolution of English literary history, looked upon the present age as the anticlimactic last act of a drama whose "catastrophe" had come "in the first or second act" (*Lectures* 168).

Scott concluded that "in those days were giants in the land and we are but dwarfs beside them" (*Letters* 1:353). And Hazlitt summarized the entire situation when his trenchant understatement about Byron's plays expressed what many were thinking generally about the second Renaissance: "That was not the way of our first . . . writers" (*R* part B, 3:1592).

This was an unavoidable hard "fact . . . star[ing] us plainly in the face," Hazlitt said in response to those "sanguine theories" about a "second spring" (*Lectures* 45). Even Jeffrey had to admit: "[I]t is impossible not to be struck with the fact" of the priority of England's "rude times" (*R* part B, 2:918).[2] Milton, more than anyone else, drove that fact home. Like their eighteenth-century predecessors, the Romantics, at least at first, ranked epic as the highest poetic genre. "Every major poet," Curran writes, "planned an epic (though all were not executed) and minor bards issued them in profusion" (*Poetic Form* 159). Certainly there were quarrels, as there had been in the eighteenth century, with some parts of *Paradise Lost*. Blake, of course, imagined Milton wandering in eternity waiting for someone to redeem the errors of his epic. But for the most part, the Romantics echoed the eighteenth century in judging *Paradise Lost* as the greatest English example of the form. Their singular love of the Renaissance, moreover, and their disengagement from the eighteenth century's formulaic faultfinding, left them adulating Milton with an enthusiasm that surpassed all previous heights of praise. *Paradise Lost*, they concluded with a new kind of absoluteness, stood above all poems of all times, and the following encomia became commonplace: "the noblest composition on the most awful subject that ever employed an earthly pen. . . . Milton is the first because the sublimest poet that ever adorned the world. . . . Before the greatness displayed in Milton's poem, all other greatness shrivels away" (Duff 244; quoted in Shawcross 2; Stockdale 102, 117). Such breathless assessments made writing a Miltonic epic the supreme test of inven-

2. In his distrust of the second Renaissance, Hazlitt went so far as to theorize about the ineluctable diminishment that besets all cultural traditions: "The greatest poets, the ablest orators, the best painters, and the finest sculptors that the world ever saw, appeared soon after the birth of these arts, and lived in a state of society which was, in other respects, comparatively barbarous. Those arts, which depend on individual genius and incommunicable power, have always leaped at once from infancy to manhood, from the first rude dawn of invention to their meridian height and dazzling lustre, and have in general declined ever after. . . . [I]n the earlier stages of the arts, as soon as the first mechanical difficulties had been gotten over, and the language was sufficiently acquired . . . [the] giant-sons of genius . . . rose by clusters, and in constellations, never so to rise again!" (*Lectures* 45–46).

tion, which is why so many Romantic poets conceived of their creative projects, as Wordsworth did in the *Prospectus* to *The Recluse*, in terms of a challenge to Milton. It is true that for many of the period's minor poets, there was "no anxiety of influence" stopping them from making an assault on the "high slopes" of this "Parnassus" (Curran, *Poetic Form* 160). But the era's more gifted writers, like their counterparts in the eighteenth century, were more sensitive to the severity of that ascent. With the notable exception of Blake, who walked through eternity purified and strengthened by wrestling with Milton,[3] they predominantly felt their own greatness being shriveled away, "melted down" as Hazlitt put it or "gormandized" in Keats's anxious phrase, by such encounters with "the sublimest poet that ever adorned the world" (quoted in Wittreich, *The Romantics on Milton* 381; *LJK* 1:255).

Again and again, the Romantics were reminded of their impotence next to this "conqueror," as Upton had put it, who "deck[s] himself in the spoils of the conquered." Wordsworth was rebuked for aspiring "to sit in Milton's chair." Byron was laughed at for "wrestling with Milton upon his own ground." All such competitors, wrote one periodical critic, appeared sadly "dwarfish" (*R* part A, 1:378; part B, 1:275).[4] Coleridge had to admit that trying to adapt or improve on Milton was like struggling "to push a stone out from the pyramids with the bare hand" (*Conversations* 550). The deepening sense of being totally overcome in such a contest may best be represented by Percival Stockdale's recollection of Dryden's verdict. "This man," Stockdale said of Milton, "cuts us all out" (164). It was a cutting out that had never appeared, we may suspect, quite so absolute. While numerous bardlings continued to take on Milton with a faith of success that Curran finds both "comic and moving" (*Poetic Form* 160), the feeling of inferiority among more sophisticated writers was so strong that it became an open topic of discussion, one of the most serious problems that the Romantics recognized in their own literary culture. "There is, in all [our] . . . attempts," Jeffrey explained, "an air of anxiety . . . [that arises] from the fact of [our] . . . being, too

---

3. Amid the proliferation of recent work on the Blake/Milton dynamic, Joseph Wittreich's two major studies, *Angel of Apocalypse* and *Visionary Poetics*, have centered our understanding of that titanic struggle by which Milton's prophetic spirit is redeemed in Blake's poetry.

4. Another critic rebuked the entire Lake School for trying to copy "the manner of our older poets" while failing to write "as those great poets would have written" ("The Dramatic Works of John Ford" 283). And Hunt was advised to give up Shakespeare and Milton "as he would fly from giants" (*R* part C, 2:714).

obviously and consciously, imitators" (*R* part B, 2:920). I do not
mean simply to suggest the Romantics' paralysis under the weight of
Milton's tradition. As Wittreich, Sperry, Curran, and others have
shown, Milton's pressure did inspire the major Romantics to shape a
number of ingenious creative strategies for lifting themselves up to
his stature. I wish to emphasize, however, their sense of the extreme
difficulty of that task—like pushing a stone out from under the pyramids with one's bare hand—and the urgency they felt to locate or
create methods for carrying it out. Solutions were not easy to come
by. But there was at least one compelling mechanism of response
available to them, transmitted intact from the eighteenth century:
the reading of Spenser's epic tradition as a flexible alternative to
Milton's that even more directly addressed, in its dualities, their own
most entrenched aesthetic divisions.

II

The Romantics may have learned from Thomas Warton's generation how to see two sides of Spenser, but their own experience of
his doubleness was much keener. For one thing, they found the
eighteenth-century method of limiting the past on the grounds of
indecorum no longer tenable, which meant that most restraint about
celebrating Spenser's beauty could be dropped. Their conscious emulation of the overall "Poetical Copia" of the Renaissance inclined
them all the more to Spenser's bowers of bliss. Although their luxu-
riating in those bowers was neither so extreme nor so exclusive as we
have believed, it was undertaken with a more enthusiastic spirit than
any previous literary generation had known. What comes as more of
a challenge to our traditional reading of Romantic Spenserianism,
however, is a countering interest in Spenser's thought, which proved
to be equally strong. Most of the Romantics, notwithstanding their
adoration of his beauty, considered his "mental space" one of the
most significant parts of his poetic universe. Many of them went so
far as to praise his moralism above everything else in his art. To call
him both a dreamer and a thinker was not simply to note the variety
of his achievement. For the Romantics, it meant locating fundamental conflicts between his didactic and imaginative characters. Their
focus on those conflicts was essential to their deepening impression
of his unique adaptability. The mid-eighteenth-century writers may
have helped shape that perception of Spenser for them. But its distinctive features were significantly altered by new developments in

Spenserian history, which gave it a different, more profound relevance for the Romantics' own poetics.

The most important of these new shaping forces was James Beattie's influential Spenserian imitation, *The Minstrel*, a two-canto narrative in Spenserian stanzas about the wanderings and maturation of a young poet named Edwin. Though it first appeared in the early 1770s and followed a number of Thomson's strategies, it made so many major innovations on the eighteenth-century background that it should be considered the cornerstone of the new tradition of Romantic Spenserianism.[5] It became the Romantics' favorite model of Spenserian poetry, going through some two dozen reprintings between 1770 and 1821 and inspiring numerous imitations of its narrative. Wordsworth copied sections of it into his manuscripts of *The Prelude*, and identified with its story so deeply that Dorothy once described him in Beattie's own phrase about Edwin: "He was a strange and wayward wight." In the preface to *Childe Harold's Pilgrimage*, Byron cited it as the primary model for his own Spenserian epic. Keats associated it with his earliest poetic inspiration and, like his friend John Hamilton Reynolds and many of the other Romantics, tried to continue its narrative.[6] What made *The Minstrel* so attractive was its elaborate drama about a maturing poet's division between imaginative beauty and intellectual truth. Thomson had grappled with that conflict in his allegory, but no one before Beattie had treated the subject so extensively and with such directness. This development opened up an entirely new area for Spenserian poetry, one that became a major source and inspiration for the great outpouring of Romantic Spenserianism.[7]

Beattie's single greatest innovation on the Spenserian background is to bring this personal drama into prominent relief, making what he calls "The Progress of Genius" the dominant concern of *The Min-*

5. Wasserman does not believe that Beattie adapted "Spenserian elements" to any "new purposes" in *The Minstrel* (*Elizabethan Poetry* 131). It is true that he built his poem on Thomson's foundation, but he extended that precedent in ways that eventually developed into the Romantics' most innovative breakthroughs in Spenserian art.

6. For an extended account of the Romantics' references to *The Minstrel*, see King (*James Beattie* 105–32). Mary Moorman provides a detailed account of Wordsworth's ongoing fascination with *The Minstrel* (60–61).

7. King, writing of the poem's impact on the Romantics, argues that *The Minstrel* "is the first deliberate attempt in English to trace the development of the poet's own mind and imagination." Signs of its deep influence on Romantic poetry are abundant in the many "minor and major poets who repeated its phrases and cadences, who often derived their ideas about nature from it, who used it as a model for their poems, and who even to an extent developed their attitudes and lived their lives according to its theories" (*James Beattie* 91, 108).

strel.[8] Where Thomson had hinted at the personal applications of his allegory, Beattie clearly identifies Edwin as a projection of his own psyche, "a picture of myself" (quoted in King, *James Beattie* 91). He just as clearly grounds that self-portrait in the growing conflicts of a young poet torn between the luxuries of the imagination and the duties of the intellect. To extend such a drama out of Spenser's own example and consistently sustain it meant going much further than Thomson in making "significant allusions" to the psychological truth hidden beneath the moral veil of Spenser's allegory. Edwin appears as a kind of medieval pilgrim who, like Spenser's questing knights, experiences danger and division in his journey. But he is a minstrel not a Christian warrior, his quest is aesthetic not spiritual, and his trials are those of the troubled artist not the wandering soul. Most Spenser scholars today would agree that such a personal context is part of the multivalent "inscape" of *The Faerie Queene.* But Spenser never gives it such priority, nor does he pursue its conflicts to the extent that Beattie does. As Beattie sees it, the drama of Guyon halting his progress to gaze at the bathing nymphs should be recovered as an allegory of the poet's open-ended division between truth and beauty.

That revisionary move constitutes the central action of *The Minstrel.* Early in his travels, during what Beattie describes as his "fond romantic youth" (II, 263), Edwin frolics in imagination as a "visionary boy" delightfully filling the skies with fanciful constructs:

> And first, a wildly murmuring wind 'gan creep
> Shrill to his ringing ear; then tapers bright,
> With instantaneous gleam, illumed the vault of night.
>
> Anon in view a portal's blazon'd arch
> Arose; the trumpets bid the valves unfold;
> And forth a host of little warriors march,
> Grasping the diamond lance, and targe of gold.
>   (I, 303–9)

Edwin's cherished visions dissolve in the second canto of *The Minstrel,* however, when he meets a "hoary Sage" who lectures him on

---

8. Beattie explained that he chose to write in the nine-line Spenserian stanza precisely because its large room encourages a vigorous play of his own shifting emotions: "Not long ago I began a poem in the style and stanza of Spenser, in which I purpose to give full scope to my inclination, and be either droll or pathetic, descriptive or sentimental, tender or satirical, as the humour strikes me; for, if I mistake not, the manner which I have adopted admits equally of all these kinds of composition . . ." (*Life* 249).

the painful realities of experience. This instruction leaves him torn between his pleasant realms of fancy and the grim truths of temporal existence. Forcing himself to confront "dreadful truth," he yearns at the same time to relive "those tranquil days . . . When Fancy roam'd through Nature's works at will, / Uncheck'd by cold distrust, and uninform'd by ill" (II, 258–61). He finally heeds the "words of Truth" (II, 477), abandons fancy, and devotes himself to the sober realities of "Philosophy" and "Science." But his history ends inconclusively, with Beattie himself, like the narrator of Keats's "Ode to a Nightingale," forsaking a world of fancy to which he still relentlessly clings. "Adieu, ye lays that Fancy's flowers adorn," he declares, "Ye flowery lays, adieu!" (II, 550, 558). The Keatsian ambivalence of that farewell becomes apparent when the "unavailing woe" that Beattie experiences in confronting the death of a friend leaves him reaching to the very end toward Fancy's "soothing voice" and "placid eyes" (II, 550–67). The "progress of genius" thus extrapolates what for Beattie is the true drama of Spenserian pilgrimage: the poet's irreconcilable division between "dreadful Truth" and the "soothing voice" of imagination.

To redeem that drama successfully from Spenser's allegory, Beattie also introduces several key narrative, structural, and stylistic innovations. Perhaps the most influential of them is his new way of handling the narrative incompletion of Spenserian poetry. Throughout the eighteenth century, writing a fragmentary Spenserian canto ostensibly in the spirit of Spenser's unfinished epic had been largely a transparent ploy to evade the severe demands of long narrative poetry. But the open indeterminacy of Edwin's conflict justifies a fragmented narrative structure that reinforces the new kind of divisive psychological experience controlling *The Minstrel*. In deliberately fracturing his narrative to advance his poem's psychology, Beattie could even claim to be extending that characteristic lack of closure in *The Faerie Queene*, a "structure of undoing," that Goldberg finds an essential element of Spenser's vision of the "disequilibrium" in human experience (xi, 6). Where Spenser's "broken text" (1) implies the necessity of endless pilgrimaging in a fallen world, Beattie's even more radically inconclusive ending suggests the modern poet's perpetual conflict about his own aesthetic mission. Structural incompleteness, so often an awkward feature of eighteenth-century Spenserianism, now becomes a sophisticated component of the emerging theme of "disequilibrium" in a totally different order of Spenserian poetry.

To reinforce this new "play of double senses," Beattie capitalizes on another potential awkwardness of eighteenth-century Spenseri-

anism, that of incorporating Spenser's medieval motifs into a contemporary social or political context, presenting chivalric warriors as
knights of "industry." Beattie extends Shenstone's rudimentary effort to make an asset of that contrast by turning the distinction between past and present into a central part of his overall conflict
between imagination and reality. He accomplishes this by connecting
the Gothic "days of yore" (I, 21) with "Fairyland . . . Sicilian groves,
or vales of Arcady" (I, 93–94) and the contemporary world of "Science . . . Art and Industry" with "Truth" (II, 427–29). When Edwin,
a medieval minstrel, encounters the truths of eighteenth-century cultural progress, Beattie's narrative does not lurch anachronistically
between two historical periods so much as it highlights the poem's
ongoing conflict between the ideal and the real. Edwin's dilemma,
choosing between the careers of a Gothic minstrel or a modern philosopher, thus encapsulates Beattie's ongoing struggle between
imaginative and intellectual art.

   This strategy helps Beattie solve another major problem of
eighteenth-century Spenserian poetry: how to integrate Spenser's archaic diction with a contemporary language. For Beattie, the inappropriateness of Spenserian diction in an eighteenth-century poem
is not a hurdle to overcome but an incongruity to cultivate, as a way
to elaborate his divisions between old and new, ideal and real. "Antique expressions" are thus avoided on a general basis in *The Minstrel*, he explains, but admitted "where they seemed to suit the subject" (*Life* 1). They most suit the subject in those sections that dwell
fondly on the Gothic "days of yore." Words like "ween," "besprent,"
and "wight" inform Edwin's visionary moments, but they disappear
during the sage's lecture on modern truth. Hence the poem's linguistic incongruity punctuates its divided mental action.

   Beattie cultivates prosodic dichotomies for similar thematic purposes. He often describes the flexibility of Spenser's stanza in terms
of its capacity to encompass archaic and contemporary poetic
rhythms. Thinking of the opulent style of Spenser's Renaissance poetics, for instance, Beattie praises the stanza's "harmonious . . . variety of pause," its "complex modulation" like that of "blank verse,"
and its "wonderfully delightful pomp and majesty of sound." Yet he
also notes how it allows "the sententiousness of the couplet," a quality one would much more readily associate with eighteenth-century
poetics (*Life* 114, 1). By juxtaposing both of these styles and their
different historical associations, Beattie reinforces the fundamental
conflict between old beauty and modern truth in *The Minstrel*. Hence
the early sections of the poem are informed with a "harmonious,"

"complexly modulated" style that evokes Spenser's own Gothic opulence and the imaginative sensibility that Beattie associates with it:

> But who the melodies of morn can tell?
> The wild brook babbling down the mountain side;
> The lowing herd; the sheepfold's simple bell;
> The pipe of early shepherd dim descried
> In the lone valley; echoing far and wide
> The clamorous horn along the cliffs above;
> The hollow murmur of the ocean-tide;
> The hum of bees, the linnet's lay of love,
> And the full choir that wakes the universal grove.
>   (I, 334–42)

In the later sections of *The Minstrel,* however, Beattie resorts to a regular coupletlike style to promote the modern world of European experience:

> "Hail, sacred Polity, by Freedom rear'd!
> Hail, sacred Freedom, when by law restrained!
> Without you, what were man? A grov'lling herd,
> In darkness, wretchedness, and want enchained.
> Sublimed by you, the Greek and Roman reign'd
> In arts unrivall'd! O, to latest days,
> In Albion may your influence unprofaned
> To godlike worth the generous bosom raise,
> And prompt the sage's lore, and fire the poet's lays!
>   (II, 388–96)

Through this prosodic incongruity, and its expression of two different world views, Beattie transforms the single greatest stylistic problem in eighteenth-century Spenserian poetry into an operative vehicle for his new mental drama.

What ultimately turned that drama into a leading model for Romantic Spenserianism was Beattie's extension of the vogue for Spenserian simplicity and pathos that Shenstone had started in the mid-eighteenth century. The psychodrama of *The Minstrel,* notwithstanding its complexity, encourages this kind of tender emotionality in two ways. Because the poem features mental divisions that cause Edwin great sorrow, the pathos of suffering becomes one of its major concerns; that pathos is also associated with a domestic context, as the poem's mental action focuses on Edwin's imaginative re-

sponses to nature and rustic life. The first stage of his mental evolution, in a scenario of profound importance for Wordsworth, develops according to the beneficial influence of Nature's "boundless
store / Of charms" (I, 73–74). In the preface to *The Minstrel* Beattie
celebrates the "simplicity" of this rural context (*Life* 1), and he makes
its genial influence on the human psyche a focal point of Edwin's
early history:

> Fret not thyself, thou glittering child of pride,
> That a poor villager inspires my strain;
> With thee let Pageantry and Power abide:
> The gentle Muses haunt the sylvan reign;
> Where through wild groves at eve the lonely swain
> Enraptured roams, to gaze on Nature's charms:
> . . . .
> These charms shall work thy soul's eternal health,
> And love, and gentleness, and joy impart.
>   (I, 28–33, 82–83)

To maintain this aura of simplicity, Beattie often resorts to the
rather plain diction and uncomplicated metrics of the lines just
quoted. He also naturalizes the allegory of *The Faerie Queene*, heightening what Hamilton calls its "literal" level, the "sense of reality" it
yields in its straightforward presentations of "wretched" experience
(39, 222), such as the description of Scudamour's look of silent "dis-
may" and "anguish" that follows his learning of Amoret's purported
infidelity (4.1.50). In extending this dimension of *The Faerie Queene*,
Beattie creates an entirely new model of Spenserian adaptation for
the Romantics to follow.

   To "cleanse" Spenser's Temple, or increase his naturalism, Beattie replaces his allegorical landscapes of the mind—like Busyrane's
Castle or the House of Care—with a series of realistic nature descriptions followed by reflections about their influence on Edwin's
psyche. A lengthy description of ocean cliffs, for instance, focusing
on "th'enormous waste of vapour, toss'd / In billows, lengthening to
the horizon round" (I, 185–86), prompts a sustained reflection on
the way such striking landscapes expand Edwin's imaginative
powers: "In darkness, and in storm he found delight" and stimula-
tion to behold "truth sublime" (I, 192, 244). This descriptive/reflec-
tive style, as I will call it, became a dominant mode in Romantic
Spenserianism for several reasons. In simplifying Spenser's allegory,
it deepened common impressions of his mildness while enabling the

kind of "improvement" that Shenstone had practiced in a much more limited way. It also provided a format for exploring mental division that was, quite frankly, much looser and less demanding than traditional Spenserian allegory. Overall, then, it gave Spenser's growing reputation for adaptability a new kind of resonance for the Romantics.

Yet despite all these promising transformations of eighteenth-century Spenserianism in *The Minstrel,* many of the Romantics still found it locked into an outworn homiletic tradition. As much as Beattie may have wanted to hold the real and the ideal in dramatic tension, the latter half of his poem drops into the kind of tedious moral didacticism that characterizes canto 2 of *The Castle of Indolence.* Banal passages like the following one on the "philosophic sage" become the norm:

> 'Tis he alone, whose comprehensive mind,
> From situation, temper, soil, and clime
> Explored, a nation's various powers can bind,
> And various orders in one Form sublime
> Of policy, that 'midst the wrecks of time,
> Secure shall lift its head on high.
> (II, 486–91)

The monotony of Beattie's lecturing may be explained by what Gloucester Ridley called, after struggling through his own long Spenserian poem, the "punishment" of trying to maintain stylistic and mental energy throughout an extended Spenserian narrative (v). This problem would become increasingly apparent as the Romantics experimented with longer and longer adaptations. But another difficulty that beset so many eighteenth-century poets, the problem of how to improve Spenser, seems as significant here. All of Beattie's innovations are designed to reinforce a tension that he regards as fundamental to Spenser's poetry. But despite his sympathy with that tension as a poet, Beattie is also a philosopher who at last endorses the certain "truths" that his own "philosophic sage" declares. The best way, then, for him to improve on Spenser's dualities, and here Thomson supplied a lesson, is finally to resolve them more clearly than Spenser does, to become an eighteenth-century moralist instead of a perplexed poet. This conventional resolution left Coleridge subtitling *The Minstrel* "The Decay of Genius" (quoted by King, *James Beattie* 132). A new way of transforming Spenserian dualities had to be devised for Romanticism to redeem the "Genius" it found in *The Minstrel.* How that transformation occurred makes up the central history of Romantic Spenserianism.

III

It has been customary to explain the great boom of Spenserianism around the turn of the nineteenth century as an outgrowth of the Romantics' natural affinity with Spenser's "Poetical Copia" and its power to kindle imaginative vision (Wasserman, "Keats" 132; Grundy, *Elizabethan Poetry* 92–93; Petit 97). Most of them agreed that one of the remarkable experiences in reading Spenser is the effect of enchantment induced, as Hunt put it, by the "luxurious palette" of his descriptions (*Literary Criticism* 421). Coleridge felt that one of his greatest strengths is "a passion for the beautiful . . . [and] the voluptuous," which gives his art a "dream-like" beauty (*Literary Remains* 80). Lamb, who urged Coleridge on one occasion to imitate Spenser's "soothing fantasies," loved the "bewildering dreaminess of imagery" in his "faery grounds" (*Letters* 85; *Lamb as Critic* 156–57). Southey thought nothing more delightful in reading Spenser than the pleasure of "lingering out the day" in the shade of his enchanting imagery (quoted in Haller 31). Hazlitt, characterizing Spenser's manner as "picturesque from his intense love of beauty," summarized: "The poet takes us and lays us in the lap of a lovelier nature, by the sound of softer streams, among greener hills and fairer valleys. . . . He waves his wand of enchantment—and at once embodies airy beings, and throws a delicious veil over all actual objects" (*Lectures* 35).

That "enchantment," celebrated by Hunt as "never perhaps to be met with elsewhere" (*Literary Criticism* 421), seemed equally dependent on Spenser's musicality. Coleridge often spoke ecstatically of Spenser's stanza, "that wonderwork of metrical Skill," passionately admiring "the indescribable sweetness" and the "fluent projection" of its modulated rhythms (*Collected Works* 12: part 1, 116; *Literary Remains* 91). Southey honored Spenser as "the great master of English versification, incomparably the greatest master in our language" (quoted in Haller 264). Hunt loved the enchanting effects of the "perpetual honey" of his versification (*Imagination and Fancy* 51). This intoxication with his "honeyed" rhythms extended to his archaic diction, whose antique character seemed an ideal complement to the overall enchantment of his sounds. For Campbell, it is "beauti-

ful in its antiquity, and like the moss and ivy on some majestic building, [it] covers the fabric of his language with romantic and venerable associations" (*Specimens* 125). Such a "Gothic" language, Hunt
argued, creates the effect of a "fine, lazy, luxurious, far-off, majestic
dream" (*Literary Criticism* 447). Hazlitt, as was often his custom in
critical matters, put it most eloquently: "His versification is at once,
the most smooth and the most sounding in the language. It is a labyrinth of sweet sounds . . . that would cloy by their very sweetness, but
that the ear is constantly relieved and enchanted by their continual
variety of modulation. . . . The undulations are infinite, like those of
the waves of the sea: but the effect is still the same, lulling the senses
into a deep oblivion of the jarring noises of the world, from which
we have no wish to be ever recalled" (*Lectures* 44).

This rapture with a gorgeous Spenser who transports us beyond
the "jarring" world to Hunt's "quarter in which no sin of reality is
heard" became one of the great moving energies of Romantic Spenserianism. It was also responsible for what has been considered the
one damning feature of the Romantics' response to Spenser: their
complete disregard for his thought in their extreme worship of his
beauty. To be sure, they were ambivalent at times about the intellectual dimension of his allegory, feeling that his sense of moral responsibility had blemished his true genius as "the Poet's Poet." His
allegory, Hazlitt claimed, is "a drawback on the poetry" (*Complete
Works* 11:490); it detracts from "the brilliance of his fancy" according
to Hunt (*Imagination and Fancy* 49).[9] This bias for his luxury over his
thought led many of the Romantics to read and represent him in
fragmentary episodes of beauty instead of tracing out his sustained
narrative and allegorical patterns. *The Faerie Queene* thus became, in
Hunt's phrase, "an enchanted stream to dip into" for droughts of
pleasure (*Imagination and Fancy* 49). The Romantics' passion for such
"dipping" took them beyond *The Faerie Queene* and made them the
first post-Renaissance writers to honor in any substantial way
Spenser's shorter poetry, where they found numerous enchanting
streams in the *Epithalamion, The Shepheardes Calender, Muiopotmos,* the
sonnets, and the *Complaints.* Gathering these scenes together in a catalogue of gorgeous pictures seemed one of the best ways to present
Spenser. Hence anthologies like Hunt's "A Gallery of Pictures from
Spenser" (1833). Campbell's Spenser section in his *Specimens of the*

9. Coleridge found "the dullest and most defective parts of Spenser [to be] . . .
those in which we are compelled to think of his agents as allegories . . . " (*Coleridge's
Miscellaneous Criticism* 30).

British Poets (1819), and Hazlitt's Spenser chapter in his *Lectures on the English Poets* (1818) tend to represent the Romantics' Spenser as a poet of beautiful fragments.[10]

That poet of luxury inspired some of the Romantics' richest poetic moments, giving Keats his "La Belle Dame Sans Merci," as Yeats claimed, "and his 'perilous seas in faery lands forlorn.'" It was such a "poet of the delighted senses" that one important strain of Romantic Spenserianism bequeathed to nineteenth- and twentieth-century writers (Yeats, *Essays* 370). The sensationalism of this teaching, however, has blinded us to the wider context of debate in which it first emerged. If we consider the full range of the Romantics' reaction to Spenser, we will discover that their worship of his "Poetical Copia" occurred within a much broader discussion of his conflict between ideal beauty and intellectual responsibility. The more they considered that division, the more applicable it seemed to their own fundamental split over the claims of imagination and realism, and the more they found his experience of duality intertwined with his character of flexibility. It was their debate over those related points, as it developed and grew more sophisticated in the early nineteenth century, that ultimately made Spenser such a profound influence on their art.

We can trace the intersection of these concerns in the Romantics' curiosity about Spenser's unusual flexibility as a great but divided talent whose critical reception still remained unfixed. Part of his strong appeal, as we have already seen, rose out of his declining reputation in the late eighteenth century. *The Minstrel* was a rare success among a drastically reduced body of Spenserian poems from this period. Because it modified Spenser in so many ways, moreover, it often gave the impression of leaving him behind and thus did not reverse the flagging interest in him. This lack of attention became a topic of major literary interest, something to deplore and to be

10. Hunt made an outline of Spenser's enchanting passages in his own edition of Todd's Spenser, marking the flyleaf of each volume with a list of "Beautiful sequestered scenes" including such passages as Una among the satyrs, Proserpina's garden, the Masque of Cupid, Pastorella in the woods, and of course the Bower of Bliss. (Hunt's annotated copy of Todd's Spenser is located in the Victoria & Albert Museum Library. His annotated copy of Craik's Spenser collection is at the University of Iowa Library. The Victoria & Albert Museum Library and the University of Iowa Library have granted permission to quote from these texts.) As a sign of how much Spenser's shorter poems engaged the Romantics, we should note Lamb's dissatisfaction, when buying an edition of Spenser for Wordsworth, with a volume that only contained *The Faerie Queene*. He returned it for a complete edition of Spenser's poetry, which he promptly passed on to Wordsworth (Hard 132).

aroused by at the same time because it highlighted his unfixed status within an otherwise intractable literary tradition. Headley wrote in 1787 that "it is to be lamented [that Spenser's works] . . . are so rarely explored for present use" (xviii). It was quite significant to Headley's generation that such a lapse extended beyond the popular readership into the center of England's professional literary circles. John Aikin found "the students of English verse . . . unacquainted" with Spenser (4). Todd's variorum Spenser and the new inclusion of Spenser's life in an 1810 reprinting of Johnson's *English Poets* were therefore less the products of burgeoning interest in Spenser than parts of a movement to redress his neglect in the world of letters. That such a movement grew so rapidly is a measure not only of the Romantics' natural affinity for Spenser but also of their fascination with a great Renaissance poet whose "admirable" qualities, as Philip Neve put it, seemed intertwined with his current "neglect" (17), or, we might add, with what emphasized his limitations.

The real attractiveness of this new situation surfaces in the Romantics' eagerness to find it strengthening the old notion of what had always made Spenser appear so accessible, his "strange inequalities." It was Beattie's recent experiment, however, that gave this point a special new significance. His autobiographical focus on the conflicts of a poet renewed interest in the eighteenth century's idea of Spenser's divided achievement. *The Minstrel* made Wordsworth and Byron, for instance, associate the Spenserian heritage with self-division,[11] and it focused attention on that same dynamic in the Spenserian poem that it most obviously follows, *The Castle of Indolence*. Some of the Romantics simply repeated the eighteenth-century's dichotomous evaluation of Spenser's "Poetical Genius" and fallen "judgment."[12] Others, as we have seen, gave priority to Spenser's beauty; they reversed the equation, honoring his luxurious style while regretting, as Sir Walter Scott representatively said, "the tedium of [his] . . . long continued allegory" (*Letters* 2:227). Wherever one's aesthetic biases rested, however, the basic notion of Spenser's uneven accomplishment became the focal point of Romantic reactions. His works were to be regarded as "delightful" but "full of . . . inconsistencies and faults" ("Todd's Edition of Spenser's

11. The line from *The Minstrel* that had the most resonance for Wordsworth, as we have seen, was the one characterizing Edmund's perplexed and "wayward" personality. Byron opened his Spenserian epic, *Childe Harold's Pilgrimage*, with a preface about the waywardness of his own protagonist.
12. Stockdale, for instance, invoked Dryden's mixture of praise and blame, calling such criticism "equally just in its censure, and in its praise" (19).

Works" 412), at once "course" and "mellifluous" (Headley xviii, xxii), inexhaustibly "rich" and painfully "tedious" (Scott, "Todd's Edition of Spenser" 203, 209). In short, as one reviewer concluded, it was "difficult to say whether the excellencies or the defects are the greatest" (R part B, 2:566). If anything, as this sample of commentary suggests, Spenser's appearance as a flawed mistress received even more attention than it had in the eighteenth century, for there were now more ways to think about how he had compromised his craft. Even his most passionate worshippers among the Romantics noted self-division as his principal characteristic. The "knowing reader" of Spenser, Hunt acknowledged, becomes accustomed to "flats" between "delicious places," to "spots in a sun" (Literary Criticism 451, 455). Hazlitt concluded that one must regard Spenser, ultimately, as possessing "rich and varied and magnificent" gifts mixed inextricably with glaring "faults." The Faerie Queene, he added, encompassses this division so fundamentally that one could even read it as two books, one "very superior" to the other (Lectures 43).[13]

Beattie's recent innovations gave this image of self-division a new character of flexibility that made Spenser seem more gentle and amenable to revision than ever before. The great popularity of Edwin's sorrowful conflicts made Spenserian poetry synonomous with tender suffering and simple emotions. In fact, so many pathetic narratives in Spenserian stanzas followed The Minstrel that Lamb characterized "Spenser-like verse" as consisting of "all manner of pitiable stories . . . love—friendship—relationship, etc." Hence one reviewer of "Spenser-like verse" claimed that writers of "modernized imitation[s] of Spenser's manner . . . have a sort of hereditary right to be as . . . pathetic as . . . [they] please" (quoted in Hard 129; "Psyche, with Other Poems" 152). Given this "hereditary right," it was only natural to associate such demonstrative pathos with Spenser's own troubles and conflicts, whose poignant articulation seemed to make up the essence of what the early Romantics came to think of as his distinctive "manner." Stockdale found him "peculiarly happy in the plaintive, and pathetic strain" (27), and Headley stressed his unique talent for unlocking "the sacred source of sympathetic tears" (xxviii). Duff located the one controlling feature of his art in his "talent" for "the invention of . . . pathetic sentiment," represented by such examples as the "lamentations of Una" and "the melting tenderness of pas-

---

13. Hunt explained: "In short, he has a variety of faults, real or supposed, that would be intolerable in writers in general. This is true. The answer is that his genius not only makes amends for all, but overlaps them and makes them beautiful" (Imagination and Fancy 49).

sion" in Guyon's address to the orphan Ruddymane (230). Wordsworth found the part of Spenser closest to his heart in those stories
and took them as the model for his own tales of "life's ordinary
woes" (*The White Doe of Rylstone*, line 54), which is why Coleridge
declared of Wordsworthian simplicity: "I remember no poet whose
writings would safelier stand the test of Mr. Wordsworth's theory,
than SPENSER" (*Coleridge's Literary Criticism* 62).

If the idea of self-division was at the heart of the Romantics' critical assessment of Spenser, this attendant notion of what Coleridge
called his "constitutionally tender" personality (*Coleridge's Literary
Criticism* 143) inspired their deepest sympathies with him. Here, they
could draw upon and elaborate a line of eighteenth-century Spenserianism with which they were intimately familiar. Blake's portrait
of Spenser reveals how thoroughly they absorbed and enriched the
eighteenth century's idea of a Spenser made tender by all his conflicts (Fig. 1). Its image of Spenser surrounded by dancing fairies
and adorned with a heavy medallion containing a portrait of Queen
Elizabeth figures Blake's view of a poet deeply divided between ideological commitments and imaginative delights. That conflict appears
to weigh Spenser down, his ambivalent expression seeming "hardly a
happy one."[14] It is the poignant character of his sad ambivalence,
which appears to project a mixture of sorrow and tenderness, that
would have seemed most appropriate to the Romantics. Just such a
character, amply borne out by the legendary accounts of his patient
suffering, is featured in the two portraits of Spenser the Romantics
were most accustomed to seeing: Thomas Cook's engraving for the
frontispiece of John Bell's edition of *The Poetical Works of Edmund
Spenser* (1778), which Keats probably used in his final months, and J.
Collyer's engraving for the frontispiece of Todd's variorum edition
(Figs. 2 and 3). The tender and somewhat melancholy countenance
in these portraits seems to preside over the Romantics' standard
characterizations of Spenser. Hazlitt, usually hard-nosed in his literary judgments, always thought affectionately of Spenser's "romantic"
and "pensive tenderness" (*Complete Works* 5:379). Todd stressed the
"amicable temper" and "gentle disposition" of "the tender-minded
Spenser" (lvi, clxvi, cxxvi). Lamb described him as "Our elder Bard,
Spenser, a gentle Name" (*Letters* 1:41). And Wordsworth summa-

14. Gleckner, *Blake and Spenser* 11. Irene Taylor has characterized Spenser's countenance as bearing a look of "supercilious elegance" (104). Gleckner is probably right,
however, to place more emphasis, as Blake seems to have done himself, on the iconography of burdensome weights and constricting forces that seem to oppress
Spenser in the portrait.

Fig. 1. Blake's *Edmund Spenser*, from *Heads of the Poets*. (By permission of Manchester City Art Galleries)

EDMUND SPENCER.

From an Original in Lord Chesterfields Collection   Cook fec

Printed for John Bell near Exeter Exchange Strand London Dec! 15.th 17[

Fig. 2. Cook's engraving of Spenser for the frontispiece of Bell's edition of *The Poetical Works of Edmund Spenser* (1778). (By permission of the Newberry Library)

Fig. 3.   Collyer's engraving of Spenser for the frontispiece of Todd's variorum edition of *The Works of Edmund Spenser* (1805). (By permission of the
Hesburgh Memorial Library, University of Notre Dame)

rized: "In all that Spenser writes, you can trace the gentle affectionate spirit of the man" (*Critical Opinions* 265).

Our recognition of this deep sympathy for Spenser's "soft and
feeling heart" ("Todd's Edition of Spenser's Works" 413) should
readjust our conventional notions of the airy character of Romantic
Spenserianism, for it eventually led to a new, deeper appreciation of
Spenser's emotional poignance from which we can still profit today.[15]
But its most immediate value lay in the contribution it made to the
Romantics' sense of Spenser as a profoundly benevolent poet amid a
threatening literary tradition. How much that impression mattered
to them is suggested by their deliberate manipulation of historical
facts in order to preserve it, which is particularly notable in their
creative misreading of Spenser's political situation. It would be natural to assume that his aristocratic politics alienated most of them, and
adverse judgments by Blake, Shelley, and others certainly appeared.
But the dimension of Spenser's political life that seemed most inter-
esting was his purported hardship under the sway of a hostile Elizabethan court. With intriguing consistency, the Romantics down-
played his obsequiousness to Elizabeth in order to highlight his
complaints of ill treatment at the hands of an unsympathetic bureau-
cracy. This bias was all the more significant in its tendency to stress
his patient, gentle endurance under such hostile conditions. Coleridge thus wrote representatively of the "unjust persecution of Burleigh, and the severe calamaties, which overwhelmed [Spenser's] . . .
later days. These causes have diffused over all of his compositions 'a
melancholy grace,' and have drawn forth occasional strains, the
more pathetic from the gentleness. But nowhere do we find the least
trace of irritability, and still less of quarrelsome or affected contempt
of his censurers" (*Coleridge's Literary Criticism* 75). Thomas Dermody
was thus only stating a commonplace when he characterized
Spenser's political experience in this way: "Here Mulla's minstrel,
sweetest Spencer roves, / And warbles heav'nly his dejected lay . . .

15. Spenser scholars have been sensitive, for some time now, to what Alpers had
called the "humanity" of *The Faerie Queene* (*Poetry* 314): the pathos of human suffering
that testifies, as Hamilton puts it, to Spenser's profound awareness of "the wretched-
ness of life" (222). Benjamin Lockerd puts considerable emphasis on the recurrent
theme of "suffering and separation" in *The Faerie Queene* (77). And Cheney discusses
the "oasis of 'natural' or spontaneous emotion[s] . . . of suffering" in Calidore's book
(2, 17). But only Georgia Crompton has studied what she calls the "sufferer's syndrome" of Spenser's characters in a sustained way (119). The Romantics' considerable
understanding of Spenser's pathos suggests one of the most significant contributions
they can make (especially, as we shall see, in Keats's case) to an area of modern
Spenser scholarship in need of elaboration.

Burleigh crushed blithe fancy's son" ("The Cave of Patronage," lines 41–42, 71).

The most provocative aspect of this bias is the way it was even maintained in the face of overwhelming evidence to the contrary. Todd took great pains, carefully citing a wide array of historical documents, to prove once and for all that Spenser had not been slighted by Elizabeth's court, that in fact he had always benefited, up to the very end, from the patronage of his superiors. The evidence was compelling; land grants, pensions, and offices were given to him throughout his life. But on this one point, many of the Romantics emphatically dissented, notwithstanding their lack of any countering evidence. Hunt, for instance, annotated this part of Todd's biography with a series of petulant rebuttals: "An office which did not last . . . Value *seventeen pound odd,* land and subject to the drawbacks and necessity of cultivation, rebellion, fire & sword . . . Did he always get it[?]" ("Annotations of Todd's Spenser" I:clxx). Thomas Campbell credited Todd's account, but he still honored Spenser's tender, brokenhearted complaints about the ill will of politicians (*Specimens* 175). Clearly, there was something of great value in the idea, even if it were only a fiction, of Spenser's pathetic suffering.

How much that idea helped the Romantics relax with Spenser may be seen in their recurrent experience of playing with him. The gentle child in him had appealed to Cowley, Pope, Thomson, and many others before, who had felt inspired to "trifle" like Shenstone with such a gamesome poet. But Shenstone's impression of his boyish insouciance was now experienced much more pervasively and with greater jubilance than ever before. Coleridge called Spenser the "darling Poet" of Southey's childhood (*Collected Works* 3: part 2, 459–60). Lamb depicted him as "The Lady muses' dearest darling child" (*Letters* 1:41). Hazlitt found his playful imagination fulfilling "the delightful promise of our youth" (*Lectures* 35). And Hunt, honoring him as an "immortal child," thought that in reading him "our boyhood is again existing, full of belief, though its hair be turning grey" (*Literary Criticism* 456). The true wealth that such a "darling Poet" opened up for the Romantics lay in their eagerness to sport with this poetical "child."

The cluster of first-generation writers grouped around Wordsworth, for instance, liked to confirm their nascent artistic sensibilities by playing Spenserian games. Southey nicknamed a dour, self-righteous Oxford colleague "Talus" and Coleridge became known to his close friends as "Satyrane," the iconoclast. Coleridge also finished a comic preface to his early Spenserian poem "The Raven" (1798) by signing himself "Cuddie," and he referred to his "Lines in the Manner of Spenser" (1795) as "Little Potatoes in the Manner of the Pine Apple" (Mounts, "Wordsworth's Transparent Sobriquet" 203–5). Such Spenserian play also helped solidify his nascent friendship with Wordsworth. Several months after their first meeting, he sent Wordsworth this punning lyric on "Spencers," a fashionable short-coat: "Said William to Edmund I can't guess the reason / Why Spencers abound in this bleak wintry season, / Quoth Edmund to William, I perceive you're no Solon— / Men may purchase a half-coat, when they cannot a whole one" (quoted in Mounts, "Wordsworth's Transparent Sobriquet" 201). Lamb also strengthened his ties to both Wordsworth and Coleridge through such Spenserian play, often commending Coleridge's Spenserian trifles and laughing with Wordsworth over the story of a clerk's confusion of Edmund Spenser and Robert Spencer (1769–1834), a minor poet and translator.[16] This kind of "Spenserianizing," as Hunt would later call it (*Correspondence* 1:310), left Lamb feeling intimate enough with a friendly Spenser to speak of him quite disarmingly as "Ned Spenser" (*Works* 429). In the same spirit, Wordsworth could invoke him as "that gentle Bard . . . Sweet Spenser . . . I call him Brother, Englishman, and Friend!" (*The Prelude*, III, 281–85). Considering how Bloom has sensitized us to the Oedipal pressures at work whenever the Romantics looked back upon their poetic "fathers," we should not lightly pass over this rare appeal to a "Friend." Could one ever dream of calling Milton "Jack"?

We may register the great appeal of this idea of a gentle, friendly Spenser by noting how Beattie's simple pathos, itself developed out of Shenstone's example, became one of the dominant features of first-generation Romantic Spenserian poetry. Of course, there was nothing unusual any more about pathos in Spenserian art. But the degree to which it pervaded the Romantics' early Spenserianism was quite new, the sign of a growing tendency to associate Spenser and anything Spenserian with tenderness of feeling. Burns's "The Cotter's Saturday Night," a short poem in Spenserian stanzas about the domestic simplicity of rustic life, emerged as one of the more popular poems of the late eighteenth century.[17] Numerous adaptations followed, all extending the strain of pathetic sentiment in *The Minstrel*. Their titles, alone, indicate the new preeminence of tender emotion in the first great wave of Romantic Spenserian poetry:

16. Mounts recounts these events in his two informative articles on the Spenserian activities of the Wordsworth circle.

17. The fact that Burns probably never even read Spenser reveals how pervasive his reputation for pathos had grown.

The Scholar's Funeral (1825), *The Children's Dance* (1825), *The Solitary Tutor* (1813), *The Village Minstrel* (1821), *The Country Parson* (1797), *The Poor Man's Sabbath* (1804). Wordsworth's *The Female Vagrant*, a domestic tragedy in Spenserian stanzas about guilt and betrayal, falls squarely within this new vogue. But it may be Campbell's *Gertrude of Wyoming*, another tale of broken relationships, that best suggests the benefits to be gained from walking hand in hand with a warm-hearted Spenser.

Although these sentimental imitations were written in Spenserian stanzas and meant generally to expand Spenser's pastoralism, none of them follows Spenser very closely, least of all *Gertrude of Wyoming*, which recounts a British-fomented Indian massacre of an idyllic co-lonial settlement in prerevolutionary America—not the sort of event anyone would be accustomed to expect from reading *The Faerie Queene*. Yet to be "un-Spenser-like" in some demonstrative way, as Lamb put it (*Letters* 1:102), was precisely the point. Like Shenstone and Beattie before him, only in a more obvious mannner, Campbell sought to outdo Spenser on the score of pathos. *Gertrude of Wyoming*, explained one reviewer, is so "abundantly simple" and pathetic in its narration of Gertrude's death that neither Beattie nor Spenser nor anyone else could have "presented so perfect and powerful an image of sympathetic sorrow" as the following scene ("Gertrude of Wyo-ming" 252):

> Hushed were his Gertrude's lips! but still their bland
> And beautiful expression seemed to melt
> With love that could not die! and still his hand
> She presses to the heart no more that felt.
> Ah, heart! where once each fond affection dwelt,
> And features yet that spoke a soul more fair.
> Mute, gazing, agonising as he knelt,—
> Of them that stood encircling his despair,
> He heard some friendly words;—but knew not what they were.
> (III, 280–88)

Tearjerkers like this, written in the rather facile metrics of Camp-bell's style, may seem eminently forgettable to us. But for the early Romantics, they helped solidify that important image of "Ned Spenser" and demonstrated how his friendship might help engender an original revisionary art. In a "modernized imitation of Spenser's manner," we recall one periodical critic annnouncing in 1811, "the writer seems to have a hereditary right to be as . . . pathetic as he pleases." He also seemed to have the inspiration, we might add, to be more pathetic, more simple, and hence more innovative than the original master of pathos, Wordsworth's "Brother, Englishman, and Friend."

One of the best measures of how accessible the Romantics found this brotherly Spenser lies in their experience with his stanza. Eighteenth-century writers like Prior, as we have seen, had discovered how one might claim a tentative affiliation with Spenser simply by composing in his stanza, or in an approximation of it. But the Romantics made that point one of the theoretical cornerstones of their Spenserian aesthetics. The mere act of writing in so individualistic a stanza as Spenser's, many of them argued, instantly forged a connection with Spenser. As Coleridge put it, the stanza "always, more or less, recalls to the reader's mind Spenser's own style" (*Coleridge's Literary Criticism* 21). Moreover, the possibilities for success in thus recalling "Spenser's own style" seemed immense, despite the obvious complications of his stanza and the distinct problem of preserving one's own identity within a form so thoroughly owned by someone else. Chalmers, for instance, quoted Beattie to argue for the ease with which so many imitators had deployed the stanza ("Life of Spenser" 3). His claim was echoed by one of the reviewers of his edition of the British poets, who argued: "There is no form of verse in our language, in which so many successful poems have been written" ("Chalmers's English Poets" 72). The invocation of Beattie, here, suggests why the stanza seemed so manageable. Beattie, we recall, had linked the facility of writing in Spenserian stanzas with the simplified, free-flowing style he came to associate with Spenserian art. That idea of a roomy, uncomplicated metrical unit, especially amenable to the expression of a variety of emotional sentiments, is precisely how the early Romantics tended to characterize Spenser's stanza. Its "loose" harmony, wrote one periodical critic, "has afforded room enough for . . . [the] expansion of thought . . . and sentiment" (*R* part B, 1:450). Its modern imitators, explained another, have exploited its "absolute freedom from the necessity of compressing language or concentrating thought" (*R* part B, 4:1731). Freed from such restraints, Byron felt that he could "scribble" more easily in Spenser's stanza, the "measure most after my own heart," than in any other meter (*Letters* 2:210; 4:13).

It was the Romantics' negative criticism of the stanza, however, that most fully reveals why such "scribbling" seemed to bring them so much apparent success. The simple and unrestrained facility with which many poets were using the stanza, some reviewers complained, manifested a diffusion of prosodic intensity and a misguided departure from Spenser's own condensed metrical complexity—a failure, as Keats would later say, to hoard stylistic beauty as Mammon did his gold. The "prejudices [now] connected with it," one reviewer argued, tend to "dilute its strength" and sacrifice its "compression of thought" (*R* part B, 1:400–401). Another, criticizing the "feebleness" and "lengthened garrulity" of the modern Spenserian style, thought that its reductive simplicity undermines the overall merit of the poetry (*R* part B, 4:1731). In raising such complaints, these reviewers were indeed pinpointing the major thrust of contemporary Spenserian stylistics—that is, a simplification of Spenser's own opulence. But, at least in the eyes of the poets, they were reading the situation backward. Instead of seeing that simplification as a diffusion of Spenser's richness, one could view it as a deepening of his own intrinsic simplicity. A "languorous," sometimes even "nerveless" flow of the line, everyone acknowledged, made up one basic dimension of Spenser's own prosody (*R* part B, 4:1731), whether one counted it as a drawback to the poetry or a stylistic grace. To extend what Hunt called Spenser's own "child-like propensity" of style (*Literary Criticism* 453) could thus mean improving on the simplistic character that his art had come to embody for so many of the Romantics. The strong degree to which they felt themselves inspired by that conviction may be estimated by the staggering number of Spenserian stanzas that they facilely produced: there are 290 stanzas in James Willyams's *The Influence of Genius* (1816); 325 in Henry Boyd's *The Woodman's Tale* (1805); 372 in Mary Tighe's *Psyche* (1795); 1,849 in James Bland Burges's *Richard the First* (1801); and 1,936 in J. H. Wiffen's translation of Tasso's *Jerusalem Delivered* (1824). For the first time ever, if we consider the sheer volume of these stanzas, Spenserian poetry could truly be said to have broken out of its esoteric circles to acquire an immense popularity among a wide readership. Such enormous productivity could and did invite aesthetic disaster. But more important for us to recognize is the unprecedented accessibility that a warmhearted Spenser was projecting, an openness that would eventually lead to poetry that would live in the surer hands of Byron, Keats, and Shelley.

As much as Spenser's accessibility meant to the Romantics, however, it could not in itself spark their tremendous burst of adaptations or sustain the complicated mental dynamics of the long Spenserian poems they began producing. It was their increasing association of his tender vulnerability with his divided psyche that finally made him such a compelling model. Their ability to form that association and see into his doubleness of vision actually developed from a much broader appreciation of the intellectual dimension of his allegory than we have hitherto been willing to grant them.

Notwithstanding their rapture over his gorgeous style, they tended to find his allegory more intriguing than anything else in his art; and it was not the allegory's beautiful excess, however much that may have appealed to Hunt and others, that ultimately seemed most important to them. What mattered the most—and this goes most radically against our stereotypical assumptions—was what Coleridge called its "mental space" (*Literary Remains* 94), much of which the Romantics were the first to uncover. Blake thought Spenser's greatest relevance for the present age lay in the visionary character of his allegory, which transcended what Yeats called his "official morality" to embrace the eternal truths of prophetic vision (*Essays* 369). Wordsworth and Coleridge agreed, with Coleridge likening Spenser's allegorical vision to the profound range of insight in Classical mythology (*Literary Remains* 90–91) and Wordsworth finding it revelatory of the "highest" spiritual truths to a degree comparable with the writings of Milton and the Hebrew prophets (*Prose Works* 35). Here was a depth of vision in Spenser that even the eighteenth century, for all of its emphasis on his thought, had not begun to explore. The politics of his allegory could seem just as important to the Romantics. Sir Walter Scott was particularly interested in the "political allegory couched under . . . [Spenser's] tissue of Romantic fiction" (*Letters* 2:227), and he shaped his own longest Spenserian imitation, *The Vision of Don Roderick* (1811), as an extended political allegory. Coleridge, fascinated by the chronicle of the British kings that Arthur reads, felt that the national politics of Spenser's allegory made up one of the most engaging aspects of his art: "In Spenser we see the brightest and purest form of that nationality which was so common a characteristic of our elder poets. . . . To glorify their country—to elevate England into a queen, an empress of the heart—this was their passion and object" (*Literary Remains* 96). This attraction to the political Spenser increased as the Irish problem began to flare up anew around the turn of the nineteenth century. Once again, as Coleridge, Wordsworth, Scott, and many others attested, Spenser's *View of the State of Ireland* acquired a significant political relevance. It was reprinted in Todd's 1805 variorum and separately in an 1809 Dublin edition. Despite some objections to its harshness, it received wide praise as an "excellent and profound" political treatise ("Todd's

Edition of Spenser's Works" 416), and one that could still provide "useful" instruction for England's management of Ireland. These explorations of Spenser's intellectual world tended to center in what many of the Romantics considered its most important area, its "inscape," or as Lamb penetratingly wrote, its "copy" of "mental processes" (*Lamb as Critic* 157). Blake's illustration of "The Characters in Spenser's Faerie Queene," for instance, performs a sustained critique of the interiority of *The Faerie Queene*.[18] Coleridge, who was mainly thinking of that psychic landscape when he recorded his astonishment at Spenser's "mental space," found the allegory of *The Faerie Queene* expressing a range of psychological movements as complicated as the human "nervous system" (*Notebooks* part 1, 4358).[19] Calling *The Faerie Queene* "altogether allegorical," William Duff singled out what appeared to him the most striking examples of the "passions" of "life and action" in the stories of Despair, Malbecco, Mammon, and Care—episodes that would, as testaments of Spenser's deep thinking into the human heart, continue to fascinate many of the Romantics (205, 215, 221).[20] The drama of passions in the Despair episode seemed especially notable, inspiring paintings by Fuseli, Severn, and Benjamin West among others (Bradley 37–38). Southey found this sequence best illustrating Spenser's "often amazingly subtle perceptions of the workings of the mind" (Haller 241). Aikin emphasized its "strength" of mental characterization and placed it "almost at the head of all such fiction" (13). And Hazlitt considered it "one of the finest things in Spenser" (*Lectures* 38). Hazlitt actually became one of the most eloquent spokesmen ever for the presence of complex mental evocations throughout Spenserian allegory, claiming that the interweaving allegorical narratives of *The Faerie Queene* delineate "the truth of human passion" (*Lectures* 43). Looking into that "truth," where MacCaffrey finds "the interior human world . . . of Spenser's allegory" (6), has become one of the

18. See Gleckner's *Blake and Spenser* for an exhaustive study of Blake's reaction to Spenser's mental world in this portrait.

19. Coleridge was particularly fascinated by the evocation of Scudamour's "mental suffering" in the House of Care episode (*Literary Remains* 94; *Seven Lectures* xlvi–xlvii), a passage whose interiority always brought Hunt back to the burdens of his own heart (*Correspondence* 2:212–13).

20. Philip Neve, for instance, thought Spenser wielded a "masterly pen" in depicting the emotions of fear, confusion, and astonishment in such passages (21). George Crabbe similarly praised his evocations of "love, hatred, scorn, or anger," and he invoked this form of genius as the "Muse of my Spenser, who so well could sing / The passions in all" (*The Birth of Flattery*, lines 1–2).

major preoccupations of recent Spenser scholarship.[21] Clearly, the Romantics would have understood why our own attention to what MacCaffrey calls Spenser's "psychic reality" (86) has inspired a profound new respect for the range of his allegory.

It was this sensitivity to his "inscape" that enabled the Romantics to recognize how his experience of conflict and pathos entailed a special understanding of the "psychic reality" of divided consciousness. Hazlitt may have been deeply moved by strong displays of pathos, like Florimel's outpouring of sorrow in the witch's hut (*Complete Works* 10:81). But he always thought Spenser was at his best when depicting the mind in conflict, as in the story of Malbecco torn by jealousy and love or the plight of Guyon among the temptations of Mammon's cave. The poetics of this mental theater so intrigued the Romantics, in fact, that they began to formulate theories of how its stylistic and allegorical processes worked. Godwin, for instance, anticipating modern theories of Spenserian psychodynamics, argued that mental tension in *The Faerie Queene* arises from the allegorical strife of combatants representing polarities of thought. He cited Spenser's handling of the divisiveness of love during confrontations between such antagonists as Britomart and Busyrane, Belphoebe and Braggadocchio, Britomart and Malecasta, all of whom figure warring attitudes toward love and sexuality (*Uncollected Writings* 488). Most of those who painted the Despair episode were inspired by a similar understanding of the psychic conflict in the struggle between Una and Despair over the fate of Redcrosse's soul. Hazlitt added that Spenser also uses imagery of place, as many scholars are now arguing, to visualize states of mental division. Hence the "portentious massiness of the forms, the splendid chiaro-scuro, and shadowy horror" of Mammon's cavern all make visible the "terror" and "distress" of Guyon (*Lectures* 42).

21. Fletcher finds the "iconography" of Spenser's art particularly meaningful as a "basis" of "psychology," and he characterizes the allegory of *The Faerie Queene* as "a symbolism that conveys the action of the mind" (244, 278). Nohrnberg describes the action of Spenser's epic as "the metaphor of interiority" (740). DeNeef focuses on the poem's "internal dialogues" (13). Alpers might not find all Spenser scholars agreeing with his conclusions about the absolute primacy of "psychological realities" in *The Faerie Queene* (*Poetry* 108). But no one could deny that the great rejuvenation of Spenser scholarship in the last two decades largely proceeds from, elaborates on, and qualifies the following conviction. "Spenser's poetry," Alpers summarizes, "has its characteristic excellences when it is rendering the realities of human psychology. . . . Spenser's concern is preponderatingly with psychological truths . . . " (311–12). For a useful summary of the ongoing debate about how to interpret the psychological dynamics of Spenser's allegory, see Lockerd (12–25).

Finally, and here anticipating a point central to Hamilton's reading of mental action in *The Faerie Queene*, both Hunt and Hazlitt
argued that Spenser's prosodic modulations make an ideal stylistic
complement for his various forms of allegorizing the mind's shifting
impulses. Hazlitt thought that his poetry not only delights the ear
but also keeps pace with the "action" of his story and dramatizes "the
movement of the sentiment" (*Lectures* 44). Hunt, despite his adoration of the voluptuous laziness in Spenser's "variety of pauses" (*Imagination and Fancy* 57), agreed with Hazlitt on its other capacity to
advance the tide of mind. He frequently adjured readers to hear the
rhythm of passion in Spenser's modulations. The turbulent rhythms,
for example, of Una's outcry against Redcrosse's desertion—"How
does he find in cruel heart to hate / Her, that him lov'd, and ever
most ador'd / As the god of my life? Why hath he me abhorr'd"
(1.3.7)—provoked this comment on the passions they delineate: "It
is a striking instance of the beauty of that 'acceleration and retarda-
tion of true verse' which Coleridge speaks of. There is to be a hurry
on the words *as the*, and a passionate emphasis and passing stop on
the word *god;* and so of the next three words" (*Imagination and Fancy*
82). One of Hunt's young disciples, John Hamilton Reynolds, attributed his choice of Spenser's stanza in *The Romance of Youth* to precisely this effect. The stanza is the "most capable of variety in the
language," Reynolds said in his preface, and its modulations seem
unusually effective for the rendering of "feelings" and "thoughts"
(34). Hunt's two more famous protégés, Keats and Shelley, would
learn a similar lesson.

As much as the Romantics may have "dipped into" isolated
pockets of beauty in Spenser, then, they also worked through his
allegories in a sustained fashion to trace the intricate pathways of
their mental labyrinths. Hunt drew up a personal *Faerie Queene*
of "Beautiful sequestered scenes," but he also crossed the entirety of
Spenser's mental landscape, as he put it, in three "regular readings"
of the complete epic ("Annotations of Todd's Spenser" 7:250). And
Hazlitt rebuked those who "cannot get through Spenser's *Faerie
Queen*, and pronounce . . . all allegorical poetry tedious" (*Complete
Works* 1:138). When it came to voyaging through similar ground in
their own poetry, the Romantics felt especially inspired by what appeared to be the dramatic center of Spenser's allegorical world: the
mind's particular division between real and ideal experience. Our
own explorations of that specific dichotomy, Spenser scholars now
generally agree, is most responsible for the astonishing fecundity of
critical writings on Spenser in the last two decades. Giamatti, discuss-

ing "the vulnerability of [Spenser's] ideal revelations to the pressures of the world," argues that the "dialectic—or what we call the dual impulse—goes on forever" at the center of *The Faerie Queene* (49, 69). Cheney finds the "double vision" behind that "impulse" making up the "subject matter" of the poem (5, 20). MacCaffrey, who is the most "Romantic" of Spenser's recent critics, concludes that his poetry "has its life . . . [i]n the intersection between visible actuality and invisible transcendence" (358). As we look back now to that endlessly provocative Spenserian "intersection," we may find that the Romantics, especially in their Spenserian poems, have already been there and can do much to enlighten our own understanding of the terrain.

Wordsworth's early poem in Spenserian stanzas, *The Female Vagrant*, focuses on a madwoman's difficulty in separating reality from nightmarish delusions. His more elaborate revision of the tale, titled *Guilt and Sorrow*, probes more deeply into the psychological dynamics of guilt-ridden hallucinations and the mind's struggle to recover a hold on reality. His shorter Spenserian poem, "Stanzas Written in My Pocket Copy of *The Castle of Indolence*" (1802), specifically adapts Thomson's division between fancy and realism to his own vacillation between a poetry of imaginative indolence and one of responsible action. Blake's short imitation of Spenser balances "truth's beams" against "fairy dreams," and his portrait of Spenser's characters reveals in endless variety his fascination with the "studied contrariousness" of their mental states (Gleckner, *Blake and Spenser* 229). Coleridge's playful imitation, "Lines in the Manner of Spenser," examines a similar conflict by juxtaposing real and ideal visions of the poet's wife, a division treated with greater elaboration in the more well known though less obviously Spenserian lyric "The Eolian Harp." Campbell's *Gertrude of Wyoming* shifts continually between reveling in the pastoral beauty of an idyllic, Pennsylvanian bower of bliss and lamenting bitterly over the political disasters of England's Indian war against America. And Tighe's *Psyche*, one of the more extensive Spenserian treatments of this conflict between real and ideal experience, presents a sustained allegory about the progress of a mind seeking to balance its ideals of romance with the untidy realities of human love.[22]

---

22. Similar dualities can be traced throughout the less significant Spenserian poems of the period. Charles Lloyd, a sometime poetic collaborator with Coleridge, took up the theme of romance versus realism in his Spenserian imitations "A Poetical Effusion" (1795) and "Stanzas: Let the Reader Determine Their Title" (1819). Scott's *The Vision of Don Roderick* swerves throughout its ninety-three Spenserian stanzas between

It would not be an exaggeration to claim that such a deep immersion in Spenserian dualism helped condition the overall play of double senses at the heart of Romantic interiority, prompting Wordsworth, for instance, to think of himself as a Spenserian "pilgrim" at the outset of his own greatest mental quest, *The Prelude*. But the strategies for understanding Spenser's own experience of a divided mind and how that experience might be integrated with a modern poetics remained rudimentary during the first decade of Romanticism. No sustained theoretical discussions of the topic emerged; a number of critics, however, looking primarily to Beattie's example, were beginning to entertain thoughts about how a modern form of Spenserian allegory should appear. The poets, following Beattie as well, were also beginning to experiment with ways of making Spenser's duality fit their own.

For the early Romantics that process of integration did not mean jettisoning Spenser's philosophy, as we might assume. Very few were yet ready to drop what one reviewer commended as the "instructive allegory" ("Psyche, with Other Poems" 140). The object, instead, was to curb the "instructive" impulse of Spenser's allegory in order to create more scope for the "contrariousness" of its "psychic reality." Unleashing Spenser's dramatic energy in this way meant intensifying his allegorical strategies for rendering mental action. Such a plan could be accomplished, several critics began to argue, by replacing what Cullen calls the "symbolic" character of Spenser's allegory (xxi), that emblematic representation of mind that Hazlitt saw in the outlines of Mammon's cave, with the kind of descriptive/reflective format that Beattie had established. Description or story, presented on a literal level, followed by poignant contemplation of its significance (exactly what Beattie had done in *The Minstrel*), seemed a more direct way of penetrating the core of the heart than fashioning a symbolic geography of mental action. It was a refinement that naturally coalesced with the growing vogue for the simpler, more pathetic Spenserianism that Beattie had established. One could even argue that Spenser himself, as one reviewer of *Psyche* claimed, had furnished numerous examples of this humanized form of allegory. Dissatisfied with the "war between [the] . . . direct and typical significa-

---

fanciful visions of a romantic Spain—a land of "Legends and vision, prophecy and sign / Where wonders wild of Arabesque combine / With Gothic imagery of darker shade" (I, 103–5)—and realistic portraits of Napoleon's devastating Spanish campaign. Thomas Dermody's "The Pleasures of Poesy" (1807) struggles to locate those "Pleasures" alternately in fantasy or reality.

tion" of Spenser's conventional allegory, in Redcrosse's fight with the dragon for example, this reviewer promoted instead Spenser's own version of the descriptive/reflective style in episodes like Redcrosse's battle with Sansjoy. "[T]he poetical effectiveness" of that story, he argued, "is thus far altogether independent of its didactic tendency, . . . [and we] neglect [its] emblematical character . . . [to] surrender our minds to the belief of [its] actual and literal truth" ("Mrs. Tighe's Psyche" 472–77). Sustained and moving reflection on the moral or emotional significance of such events then follows; in this particular case, Spenser goes on to contemplate the great sufferings endured by both Redcrosse and Sansjoy.[23] Expanding this Spenserian "option" to a central position in the allegory became a standard revisionary strategy urged upon all those who would seek to improve on the original. Those poets, wrote the same reviewer of *Psyche,* could redeem Spenser's innate human sympathies from his allegorical abstractions by "com[ing] home to our bosom with some intimate and touching sentiment" extracted from his "picturesque" description. They may thus "sweetly lead us from the excitements of gorgeous description or perplexed action into the tranquil recesses of contemplation" (472–74).[24]

Bringing this format "home to our bosom" specifically meant contemplating the psychic battle of realism and ideality that so many of Spenser's followers now found to make up the most "intimate and touching sentiment" of his allegory. Here, with Beattie's practice of humanizing that allegory as an example, there seemed a special precedent for improving on Spenser's method of "speak[ing] to the heart" about the issues that mattered the most (*R* part B, 1:401). To "[w]ash [one's] hands" of the emblematical character of his allegory and extend its descriptive/reflective character along Beattie's lines struck several reviewers as the most effective way to intensify his "sentimental cast" and his "intimate" understanding of the heart's divisions (*R* part B, 2:566; "Mrs. Tighe's Psyche" 474). It should therefore come as no surprise to find many of the major Spenserian

23. Numerous Romantic reviewers of Spenserian poetry commented on the intermingling of description and reflection in this allegorical practice. It was especially noteworthy, claimed one critic, for "interweav[ing] sentiment and description." It splendidly combined, wrote another, "the descriptive and the sentimental" (*R* part B, 1:150; part B, 2:706).

24. Another reviewer felt that the contemporary Spenserian poet should cultivate "[t]hat mellow richness of description . . . which gives eyes to the imagination, accompanied by those allusions and reflections which make inanimate nature speak to the heart . . . " (*R* part B, 1:401).

poems of early Romanticism closely following Beattie's program for dramatizing "the progress of genius." Several works in Spenserian stanzas, like John Finlay's *Wallace* (1802), Charles Lloyd's *Oswald* (1795), and Richard Polwhele's *The Minstrel* (1814), were presented as direct sequels to Beattie's poem. But a number of less obviously *Minstrel*-like Spenserian poems appeared, which substantially adopted Beattie's descriptive/reflective method for dramatizing the conflict between realism and ideality. In *The Female Vagrant*, for instance, Wordsworth consistently follows natural descriptions, like the portrait of a calm sea in "its hour of rest," with sustained meditations on the dichotomy between ideal peace and real human suffering. Hence the wandering female of his poem compares her agonizing experience of military conflict with the ideal tranquillity of the restful sea:

> Ah! how unlike those later terrific sleeps!
> And groan, that rage of racking famine spoke,
> When looks inhuman dwelt on festering heaps!
> The breathing pestilence that rose like smoke!
> The shriek that from the distant battle broke!
> The mind's dire earthquake, and the pallid host
> Driven by the bomb's incessant thunder-stroke
> To loathesome vaults, where heart-sick anguish toss'd,
> Hope died, and fear itself in agony was lost!
>   (lines 145–53)

The action of Campbell's *Gertrude of Wyoming* is similarly interrupted for long reflections on the difference between war-torn European experience and the idyllic life of Gertrude among the "sweet scenes" of pastoral Pennsylvania. In some cases, this kind of scenario came even closer to Beattie's by tracing the maturation of a poet as he wanders through various types of natural landscapes and reflects on their significance for his own divided creative consciousness. Thus Richard Polwhele, in his cumbersomely titled but psychologically engaging Spenserian work, *The Influence of Local Attachment with Respect to Hope* (1791), records his own responses to nature in lengthy reflections about his conflict between "dull realities" and those "air-bright forms" of the imagination that he associates with his own childhood experience (VI, 16–18).

In adapting Spenser's allegorical duality to their own situation, the Romantics also radicalized his politics both to give him a more palatable social consciousness and to intensify his drama of the mind

in conflict. Behind this important revisionary maneuver lay their inclination to stress his political sufferings rather than his courtly obe-
dience. That bias moved some of them to drop the eighteenth-century
convention of a patriotic Spenserian art and cultivate instead the
more subversive, dissatisfied element of Spenser's political experience, a discontent that of course greatly appealed to the revolutionary sentiments of the young Wordsworth, Coleridge, and many of
their contemporaries. Such dissenting politics, they discovered,
could also nicely elaborate the tension of reality and ideality they
were now locating at the center of Spenser's art. They recognized
that Spenser's own complaints, at the end of Book 6 of *The Faerie
Queene* for instance, usually contrast the poet's ideal creative situation with the inhibiting conditions imposed upon him by court-
lyrealpolitik. Wordsworth and Campbell transformed this kind of
complaint into a more thoroughgoing revolutionary attack on government oppression, a strategy also designed to advance their poems'
basic oppositions of realism and ideality. Campbell shows in *Gertrude
of Wyoming,* for instance, how England's vicious colonial policy of
enlisting Indians to fight its war against America is responsible for
the disruption of Gertrude's idyllic paradise. This critique of England's militant imperialism was so severe, in fact, that reviewers of
the poem frequently condemned Campbell for traitorous inclinations. Wordsworth deserved similar indictments for *The Female Vagrant,* which blames England's foreign wars and its conscription laws
for the destruction of ideal, familial harmony and the poisoning of
innocent minds. This radical branch of the Romantics' developing
Spenserianism was most significant for making Spenser's politically
conservative art and personality unexpectedly amenable, in some
ways even inspiring, for their own increasingly subversive poetics.
    Not all of the period's early Spenserian work centered on the re-
curring dynamics of mental conflict. Indeed, as I shall shortly explain, a quite different, much more conservative form of adaptation
came to dominate early Romantic Spenserianism. Neither did all
those works that did portray the mind's duality follow Beattie's precedent for stylistic simplicity and psychological directness. Tighe cultivated an ornate poetic style and worked out a highly symbolical
allegory in *Psyche,* for instance, bringing the heroine of her poem to
such emblematic locations as the "Island of Indifference" and into
conflict with such traditionally Spenserian allegorical figures as
"Chastity," "Purity," "Patience," "Spleen," and "the Blatant Beast" of
"Slander." Yet enough of the early Romantics' adaptations did follow the Beattiesque paradigm to give Spenserian poetics a new char-

acter of duality "brought home" simply and movingly to the reader's own experience of mental doubling in the modern world.

This strategy of extending what was perceived to be an under-developed part of Spenser's achievement may have only continued the basic trend of eighteenth-century revisionism. But the part cho-sen for intensification—his psychological complexity instead of his moral didacticism—offered what we would now consider a much richer field of possibilities for adaptation. Perhaps even more signifi-cantly, the writers who explored that field assumed that bringing the spirit of Spenser's interiority into the modern world meant funda-mentally changing the format of his poetry, not just tidying up its dress in the manner of the eighteenth-century imitators. Thus they completely dispensed with the old practice of "continuing" *The Faerie Queene* in "newly discovered cantos." Instead of trying to be just like Spenser (only more refined), they sought to transform what they saw as his essential spirit into a radically different, modern form. It is common for twentieth-century readers to conclude that poems like *Gertrude of Wyoming*, except for the stanza, have nothing to do with Spenser.[25] Not only do such responses fail to recognize these works' deep affinities with Spenser's "mental space," they also overlook the benefit, indeed the great requisite for a successful revisionary art, of reformulating that "space" into such a different, modernized shape. Blake knew that it was not enough to straighten up Milton's clothes. Instead one had to cast off his mortal garments and redeem his eter-nal portion into a completely different mold. The same was true for Spenser. Only by dismantling and transforming his appearance could the Romantics bring what they thought to be his eternal linea-ments into their own poetics. In the special focus of that integration, they went beyond the old necessity of reinforcing his moralism and gave an entirely new character of importance to his "inscape." The result may not have been great art. Sentimentality, especially in Campbell's case, sunk most of the period's early Spenserian poems. Yet those works did produce a strikingly new concept of Spenserian adaptation that helped condition Romanticism's overall poetics of self-analysis, providing one important basis for Coleridge's more complex self-debates in his conversation poems and for Words-worth's more sophisticated descriptive/reflective story of the pro-gress of genius, *The Prelude*. More specifically, these experimental poems and the critical foundation supporting them inspired the second-generation Romantics to reformulate Spenserian duality still

25. See Wasserman, *Elizabethan Poetry* 138.

more complexly and incorporate it much more substantially into
their own art.

IV

Spenserianism may have deeply informed the poetics of the early
Romantics in a general way. But it did not emerge as a dominant
force in the period's most sophisticated poems, probably because the
bias toward simplicity and sentimentality precluded a direct or extensive use of it in works as complex as Wordsworthian epic or
Blakean visionary prophecy.[26] Among the leading epic poems of the
younger Romantics, however, Spenserianism becomes essential. It
provides the stanza for Byron in *Childe Harold's Pilgrimage* and Shelley in *The Revolt of Islam* (1817), the central questing motif for Keats
in *Endymion* (1817), and the dynamic of mental doubling that under-
pins all three poems. That dynamic also plays a major role in two of
the most complicated lyrics of later Romanticism, both written in
Spenserian stanzas, Keats's *The Eve of St. Agnes* (1819) and Shelley's
Adonais (1821). Beyond these obvious examples, the same generation's minor poets were just as thoroughly immersed in Spenserian
dualism. John Hamilton Reynolds composed his longest and most
important poem, *The Romance of Youth,* as a drama in Spenserian
stanzas about the mind's division between reality and fantasy. Leigh
Hunt, as I have argued elsewhere ("Leigh Hunt and Romantic
Spenserianism"), spent much of his long career shaping his own poetic identity in terms of a Spenserian conflict between imaginative
escapism and intellectual responsibility. Clearly the younger Romantics were both following their immediate predecessors' special inclination toward Spenserian duality and making a significant advance
at the same time.

   What made for this new surge had as much to do with the limitations as the breakthroughs of early Romantic Spenserianism. Its simplicity began to appear so reductive, for instance, as to encourage
the younger Romantics to fashion a more complex type of Spenserian art. Wordsworth's association of Spenserianism with the plain
speech of the *Lyrical Ballads,* in particular, seemed a mistaken subordination of the stylistic opulence for which Spenser had become so

---

26. Wordsworth even advised against Spenserianism for a long poem because of
what he thought to be its inability to sustain epic action (*Letters* 3:268).

renowned among the Romantics. Notwithstanding the Lake School's "decision to the contrary," Hazlitt argued in 1817, Spenser's language and style is characterized by "a paste of rich and honeyed words, like the candied coat of the auricula; a glittering tissue of quaint conceits and sparkling metaphors, crusting over the rough stalk of homely thoughts" (*R* part A, 2:494). But even more significant to those revaluating Spenser's reception was a powerful and deadeningly conservative strain of moralism that came to dominate the Romantics' early Spenserian poetry.

What most seriously contradicts our traditional reading of Romantic Spenserianism, and what proved most troublesome for Keats's generation, was the tendency of the period's early writers to honor Spenser's orthodox morality above everything else in his art, even his "inscape." Here, they were not so much following a subtle Neoclassical strategy for "taming" his genius; that maneuver was no longer applicable to their new aesthetic situation. Instead, many of them were absorbing from that strategy and the numerous didactic poems it produced a rather conventional bias toward Spenser's moralism. Reminding readers of his edifying instruction, at least, was one of the most direct and defensible ways of countering all those complaints about his dullness that were alienating so many readers in the late eighteenth century. Thus instead of killing off the eighteenth century's didactic Spenser, as we have commonly believed them to have done, the early Romantics actually preserved and reinforced his conservative reputation as England's chief moral poet. Todd introduced him on the variorum title page, in fact, as "The Moral Poet." Aikin began a biography of him by claiming that his "works breathe a fervent spirit of piety and morality" (8). He was frequently classified by critics and poets as one of "the best moral writers" (Boyd xxi); an "unrivalled" teacher, Wordsworth said, of "virtue," "prudence," and "sacred wisdom" (*Critical Opinions* 361; *The White Doe of Rylstone*, line 18). Wordsworth was even said to "love" Spenser primarily because of the "earnestness and devotedness" of his "moral . . . genius" (*Critical Opinions* 361; *Prose Works* 2:20). Coleridge went so far as to declare that "Above all, a deep moral earnestness" distinguishes Spenser's art (*Literary Remains* 97). That claim was echoed by numerous reviewers of Spenserian poems, criticism, and editions, who also commended the moral glosses of eighteenth-century Spenserian commentators like Upton and Hughes.[27] A traditional eighteenth-century idea of Spenser as "The Moral Poet" was

27. See "Todd's Edition of Spenser's Works" 412; *R* part B, 1:400.

thus emerging as one of the leading elements of the early Romantics' Spenserianism. At the same time, popular critics such as Percival Stockdale were also recommending for study and emulation the didactic sections of eighteenth-century Spenserian imitations like Thomson's *The Castle of Indolence* (2:127–30).

It was a body of highly moralistic poems based on these models, not luxurious or even interiorized adaptations, that actually surfaced as the most common form of Spenserian poetry among the early Romantics. A juvenile Leigh Hunt, for instance, wrote a widely read didactic poem in Spenserian stanzas modeled on the second, moralistic canto of Thomson's *The Castle of Indolence* and appropriately titled *The Palace of Pleasure* (1802). Chandos Leigh, little known today but one of Romanticism's most prolific Spenserian poets, wrote a series of imitations in support of "Religion, order, law, the triple cord / Of states" (lines 100–101). Charles Lloyd did the same in numerous imitations with such titles as "Lines to a Brother and Sister, Written Soon After Recovery from Sickness" (1799) and "Stanzas on the Difficulty with Which, in Youth, We Bring Home to Our Habitual Consciousness, the Idea of Death" (1823). In *The Woodman's Tale* Henry Boyd devoted three hundred Spenserian stanzas to the dangers of alcoholism. Sir James Bland Burges, in *Richard the First*, incredibly wrote nearly two thousand Spenserian stanzas about the follies of ambition. Such pietism would persist throughout the next two decades of Spenserian poetry, with Southey still earnestly churning out hundreds of Spenserian stanzas on religion and patriotism for his 1825 narrative, *A Tale of Paraguay*. Clearly, the Romantics were serious, and deadly dull, about the moral center of their Spenserianism.

This sermonizing attitude was precisely the problem, as Hazlitt, Hunt, and several of the more gifted younger Romantics began to realize. Reforming popular misperceptions and prejudices about poetry was something of a mission to both Hunt and Hazlitt, and Spenser's case must have seemed in particular need of redemption. While the beauty of his craft and its psychological depth had become appreciated as never before, most readers were feeling crushed under the avalanche of Spenserian moralism. Their understandable exasperation, as Hazlitt and Hunt both argued, was responsible for a growing popular resistance to the early Romantics' Spenserianism and to Spenser himself. Evidence of such a backlash was not hard to find. Periodical critics were beginning to complain about Spenser's "monstrous allegories" and the "pedantic manner" of his modern followers (*R* part B, 5:2291; 1:450). One reviewer even declared that the "Spenserian school" had been quite "shut out" from "popular reading" (*R* part B, 2:566). In response to such a mounting bias, Hazlitt lamented that Spenser had become "little known to the ordinary run of English readers" because people are "afraid of the allegory, as if they thought it would bite them" (*Complete Works* 10:73; *Lectures* 38). Hunt thought that Spenser was being "excluded" from the general readership because of fears that "he wrote a good deal of allegory" (*Autobiography* 151; *Imagination and Fancy* 49). To think of Spenser as "The Moral Poet," it appeared, could very well mean consigning him to the shelves. Thus it seemed that, all together, these moralizing tendencies were both killing off the recent rise of Spenserian poetics and fostering a distorted idea of Spenser's own stylistic and intellectual tedium. The best countering strategy, Hunt and Hazlitt agreed, lay in temporarily diminishing the importance of his thought while building up a revitalized passion for what had always been the most accessible and compelling feature of his art, his "Poetical Copia."

Many of the Romantics' most fervent accolades to his beauty and their sensational claims for his luxury over his ideas were delivered in this particular context, reflecting the immediate dynamics of their evolving literary culture more than the naive biases of their leading critics. Hunt was far from unsympathetic to Spenser's "virtue" and "prudence," writing Spenserian stanzas against vice in his youth and completing a long Spenserian allegory on worldly vanity, *The Shewe of Faire Seeming* (1858), shortly before his death. Hazlitt, as we have seen, was sensitive to what he called the "visionary medium" of Spenser's intellectual world (*Lectures* 42). When he elevated Spenser's beauty above his thought, therefore, he was only responding to a particular situation in which heavy-handed moralism like Southey's was overburdening modern Spenserian poetry and threatening to deny Spenser a popular following. "Mr. Southey says of Spenser," Hazlitt argued,

> "Yet not more sweet / Than pure was he, and not more pure than wise;" . . . The love of beauty, however, and not of truth, is the moving principle of his [Spenser's] mind. . . . [S]ome people will say . . . they cannot understand . . . [him] on account of the allegory. . . . This is very idle. If they do not meddle with the allegory, the allegory will not meddle with them. . . . For instance, when Britomart, seated amidst the young warriors, lets fall her hair and discovers her sex, is it

necessary to know the part she plays in the allegory, to understand the beauty of the . . . [scene]? (*Lectures* 35, 38, 40)

Hunt was thinking of this specific passage, and its way of replying to
the Spenserian moralists, when he raised some of his most controversial and exclusive paeans to Spenser's beauty. It was in response
to those who "objected" to Spenser's tiresome allegory that he
claimed,

> as to allegory . . . in Spenser's hands it became such an em-
> bodiment of poetry itself, that its objectors really deserve no
> better answer than has been given by Mr. Hazlitt, who asks, if
> they thought the allegory would "bite them." . . . Spenser's
> great characteristic is poetic luxury. . . . His allegory itself is
> but one part allegory, and nine parts beauty and enjoyment;
> sometimes an excess of flesh and blood. . . . Spenser is the
> farthest removed from the ordinary cares and haunts of the
> world of all the poets that ever wrote, except perhaps Ovid;
> and this, which is the reason why mere men of business and
> the world do not like him, constitutes his most bewitching
> charm. (*Imagination and Fancy* 50–51)

This is the statement of a man who wrote numerous Spenserian
stanzas, in both youth and old age, precisely about the ways of the
world. Instead of singling out Hunt's extravagance as a sign of Romanticism's blindness to Spenser's complexity, we should thus read
his argument as an expression of the period's ongoing debate about
how best to appreciate the full variety of Spenser's achievement.

That debate ultimately highlighted for the younger Romantics
Spenser's most significant relation to their own poetics. By focusing
so acutely on his radical extremes—his moralism versus his sensuousness—critics like Hunt and Hazlitt came to recognize in him a
more powerful and pervasive duality of mind than their immediate
predecessors had been able to appreciate. Their own deeper immersion in his contraries made him seem all the more relevant to what
was also becoming for them a more intense experience of the divided consciousness at the heart of Romanticism. Wordsworth's generation had already conditioned them to associate Spenserian poetics
with psychological depth and, more specifically, with mental doubling. To a certain extent, then, we may read their interest in
Spenser's dualism as a natural continuation of those emerging
trends. But where Spenserian duality remained a limited feature of

first-generation Romantic art, and one that was always qualified by
other ways of reading Spenser, it developed into a controlling force
in English poetry when illuminated by the new debate about
Spenser's dramatically different influence on his moral and his voluptuous readers. That debate, with its special focus on his own inclinations toward duty and indulgence, began to make it appear as
never before that at the center of Spenser's art, beneath the moralism, the beauty, the pathos, and the simplicity, lay a fundamental,
all-enveloping conflict between his mixed commitments to aesthetic
luxury and intellectual responsibility.

Hence dichotomous readings of him as both a poet of thought and
beauty, caught between two poles, began to shape the dominant
form of second-generation Romantic Spenserianism, one in which
his own duality of vision became his central point of relation to the
poetics of modern experience. Hazlitt, for instance, commended his
profound insight into "the truth of human passion" (*Lectures* 43) in
the same essay that proclaimed his "love of beauty" over "truth."
Hunt approvingly quoted Wordsworth on Spenser's "highest moral
truths" ("English Poetry" 754) at the same time that he read *The
Faerie Queene* luxuriously, in order "to shut myself away . . . from
care and sorrow" ("Annotations of Todd's Spenser" 7:250). Campbell, who was mostly concerned with Spenserian sentimentality in
1805, wrote in 1819 about his preference for "the magic of
[Spenser's] . . . colouring" to the clouds of his allegory while also
stressing "the form and symmetry of truth" in "his moral meaning"
(*Specimens of the British Poets* 126–31). Not at all contradictory, these
comments locate the part of Spenser where the Romantics, eventually and in their most insightful moments, found themselves: what
Hunt called his "piquancy of contrast" (*Literary Criticism* 442) and
Hazlitt identified as his "splendid chiaro-scuro" (*Lectures* 42).

This capacious dualism became the focal point of the younger Romantics' theorizing on Spenser and Spenserian poetics. Whereas
early Romantic criticism remained undeveloped in its concept of
Spenserian duality, with some critics like Aikin even feeling puzzled
by Spenser's "intermingling the ideas of reality with those of fiction"
(13), Hazlitt recognized that such doubleness constituted Spenser's
genius and his ultimate relevance for the present age. "The two
worlds of reality and of fiction," he thus characterized Spenser's
breadth of vision, "are poised on the wings of his imagination. . . .
[He balances equally] the extremes of sensuality or refinement" (*Lectures* 35). Hunt expanded, "Nothing is more striking in Spenser than
the astonishing variety of his pictures, and the rapidity with which

he passes from one kind to another. . . . an extraordinary mixture of light and darkness—of the sublime and the sordid. . . . No man, by seeing one thing exquisitely, saw further into its opposite than he did. . . . [He is] at once sacred and seductive" (*Literary Criticism* 427, 435, 443; "English Poetry" 749). Hunt was particularly drawn to the mixed lighting effect caused by Una's radiant face in the dark woods, which "made a sunshine in the shadie place" (1.3.4). And he singled out a passage in *The Ruines of Time,* marking it in both his Spenser texts, whose terseness of contrast struck him as the prime embodiment of Spenser's duality, the description of the bittersweet elegy sung by Sidney's sister: "Sorrowing tempered with deare delight . . . O sad joy made of mourning and annoy" (lines 319, 322). Thus when Giamatti speaks of "the grand patterns, the alternatives of day and night, dark and light" in Spenser's universe (69), or when MacCaffrey hits on the term "chiaroscuro" to characterize the double vision at its core (398), we should realize that many of our most innovative readings of Spenserian poetics actually restate what were common assumptions for the younger Romantics.

For them, indeed, such a dichotomous vision meant that Spenser was not simply ambivalent about his morals, but that he spoke to the present most forcefully as a poet of psychological complexity who looked deeply into the doubleness of all experience. From the perspective of Hazlitt's generation, Spenser's depiction of Doubt—who "had a double face, / Th'one forward looking, th'other backeward bent, / Therein resembling *Ianus* auncient" (*FQ,* 4.10.12)—thus seemed, indeed, like a self-portrait. That reading was not so innovative in its substance—Thomson had suggested something akin to it decades earlier—as in its impact as the younger Romantics' central way of thinking about Spenser's relevance to a sophisticated, modern poetics. The significance of this breakthrough may be measured by the way each of the leading second-generation poets felt inspired not only to write a major Spenserian narrative but to make it reenact in some substantial manner the kind of mental drama now thought to be fundamentally embodied in Spenser's divided world of truth and beauty. What enabled them to integrate that drama into their own art so much more thoroughly than their Romantic predecessors had done, however, was not simply their deeper sensitivity to it. Because their attention was focused so closely on its dynamic of interior debate, they also discovered that Spenser often seemed to need help in his attempts to resolve it. And their strategies of correction entailed a basic reformulation of Spenserian allegory that proved instrumental in the working out of their own aesthetic mission.

The leading second-generation poets all felt that Spenser had limited his experience of mental doubling by clinging to a secure but reductive philosophy, an "official morality." Re-creating his allegory thus meant delving beneath its overt body of ideas to recover and intensify the mental doubling embedded within. Such a corrective response carried the obvious benefits of improvement and independence we have seen emerging as the primary goals of the history of Spenserianism. What made the case different for the second-generation Romantics, however, was their discovery that correcting Spenser's duality could help them resolve their own. Unlocking his vision, finally, became not just a matter of exposing his vulnerabilities but also an important means of self-purification, what Blake learned in wrestling with Milton and the process that Bloom characterizes as one of the most enabling "ratios" of poetic revisionism.[28]

Hunt's ongoing reformulation of the Janus-like vision in Spenserian allegory, for instance, played a major role in the working out of his own mature, double-sided outlook on experience. Hunt carried out a lifelong revision of Spenserian allegory in an ongoing effort to resolve his own deep divisions between aestheticism and intellectual responsibility.[29] Throughout most of his long literary career Hunt felt "bound" to confer "moral benefit[s]," yet he constantly wished to abandon his tasks as a teacher-critic in order to luxuriate in the "luminous enjoyment" and "perpetual solace" of literary beauty (*Poetical Works* xxvi; *Autobiography* 420). No one he read seemed to embody this same division so much as Spenser, in whose allegory he found constant tension between moral responsibility and poetic luxury. But in order to make this identification, Hunt felt he had to redeem the mental drama of Spenser's allegory from the philosophical context enshrouding it. Hence the *real* drama of episodes like the Bower of Bliss, the eternal truth hidden beneath the overt moral about vice's false allure, entails Spenser's tremendous battle as a passionate worshiper of beauty against his own sense of intellectual obligations. In such interior dramas, Hunt argued, Spenser repeatedly leads us toward scenes of instruction only to "turn his back upon everything real . . . however he may pretend to bear it in mind; and to give himself up to the dreams of books, or romances, of mythology, of whatsoever is remote from the prose of

---

28. Bloom discusses such acts of revisionary self-purgation in his chapter on "Askesis or Purgation and Solipsism," showing how Wordsworth and Keats, for instance, re-create themselves in addressing Milton (*The Anxiety of Influence* 123–28).

29. For a more extensive treatment of Hunt's response to Spenser, see my "Leigh Hunt and Romantic Spenserianism."

human affairs" (*Literary Criticism* 420). Such a personal interpretation
of Spenser's allegory amounted to no less than Hunt's reading himself into the drama. In thus projecting his own conflict onto Spenser,
or recovering it as the eternal portion of the allegory, he found that
he might correct what he felt to be his own cumbersome sense of
intellectual duty by criticizing Spenser's "official morality." Thus
when he lamented, "It is painful to see how humble . . . [Spenser]
thinks himself bound to speak" in deference to social obligations and
"moral purposes" ("Annotations of Todd's Spenser" I:lxiv), he was
also chastising himself for feeling "bound" to confer "moral benefit."
And when he imagined what Spenser had always secretly desired—
to abandon moral responsibility and indulge in the "superfluities" of
poetic "luxury" (*Literary Criticism* 442)—he was also trying to work
out his own creative salvation as a poet freed from what he called the
"market" of worldly affairs (*Autobiography* 438).

   This deeply personal way of redeeming the true drama of
Spenser's allegory inspired Hunt, in the end, to strike a mature equipoise between the competing claims of truth and beauty. He eventually came to believe that Spenser had, in his most insightful moments, balanced those claims by combining a deep pathos for "poor
human nature," expressed in the psychodrama of such "ghastly re-
alit[ies]" as the Despair and Malbecco episodes, with a provision of
solace in the luxury of his aesthetic pleasure (*Literary Criticism* 442).
At rare moments, like the juxtaposition of the House of Care sequence with the mock-heroic fight of the "mond" brothers, Spenser's
two worlds of what Hunt called gravity and gaiety seemed balanced
in this profound form of "piquant contrast." We have already seen
how Hunt found the most stunning example of such mental "chiaroscuro" in the bittersweet elegy sung by Sidney's sister, an insight
that would have a great impact on Shelley. For Hunt, this poetry of
"sorrowing" and "delight" ultimately constituted the essence of
Spenser's genius, which he characterized as "sacred and seductive"
("English Poetry" 749). Yet such an essence, like the capacious spirit
Hunt wished to release in his own art, also seemed shrouded in the
veil of a formal philosophy. To extract it from that veil and transform it into the dominant force of Spenser's poetry was to reshape
himself, as well, into a poet of "sorrowing" and "delight." This redeemed Spenser did, indeed, become the muse of Hunt's creativity
in his final major poem, an allegory in Spenserian stanzas titled *The
Shewe of Faire Seeming*. It concludes with Sidney's sister, that image of
Spenser in ideal form, singing her bittersweet elegy, a lovely "grief-
taught" lyric, while her face interchanges "gay" and "grave" looks

(lines 343–69). Her divided outlook embodies everything that Hunt had learned from Spenser about the duality of experience and everything that he finally aspired to in his own art.

That Hunt's redemptive experience with Spenser was shared by many of the younger Romantics suggests the formative influence Spenserian duality was coming to exert on modern poetics. Indeed, the various strategies that the younger Romantics developed for reformulating it as a means of working out their own creative salvation may constitute their most significant contribution to our current understanding of Spenser. The central debate of much Spenser scholarship today involves the very same questioning of Spenser's provisionality, his "unending dialectical struggle" (Cheney 243), that so deeply engaged the younger Romantics. There has been a recent backlash in Spenser scholarship against the prolific discourse on his open-endedness, represented by works whose titles—*The Unity of the Faerie Queene* (Horton), *The Spider and the Bee: The Artistry of Spenser's Fairy Queene* (Dundas)—indicate the persistence today of Upton's desire to find completion in Spenser's poetry. Still, the new mainline tradition developed by Alpers, Williams, Cheney, Giamatti, and Mac-Caffrey has conditioned us in the late twentieth century to think of Spenserian poetics as fundamentally dichotomous and indeterminate. Each of its "self constituting act[s]," Goldberg quotes Stephen Greenblatt, "is haunted by inadequacy and loss" (2). The "provisionality" of its strategies, DeNeef adds, engenders a psychology torn by "the conflicting urges to close and to open, to declare and to suggest, to prescribe and to offer" (102, 14). The pressing question now is just how far Spenser goes in the conditional form of pilgrimaging that he carries out in the face of his passionate desire for certitude and completion.

Cheney, DeNeef, and Goldberg find his indeterminacy both rich and inexhaustible. Spenser refuses to reduce experience to "any neat conceptual pattern," Cheney argues (247); he demands, DeNeef asserts, that his readers resist "closure" (176). *The Faerie Queene*, Goldberg concludes, is "a fractured—and fracturing text" (xiv). Yet many of the most sensitive readers of Spenser's "provisionality," like Williams, MacCaffrey, and Giamatti, emphasize his inclination to rest on or at least to contemplate, however briefly and inconclusively, what Keats would call the "seeming sure points of Reasoning" in his philosophy (*LJK* 1:282). In the "last resort," Williams argues, he appeals to "the eternal stability of bright heaven" (232). Standing at the intersection of "visible actuality" and "invisible transcendence," Mac-Caffrey concludes, he would have us fix our vision on "a timeless invisible mode of being" (395), what Giamatti calls "the single and abiding visionary core" of his experience (75). Deeply immersed in the world of mutability yet pulled ineluctably toward "that great Sabbaoth God" (*FQ*, 7.8.1) is just how the younger Romantics saw Spenser. Their readings of his divided stance, and their attempts to work out their own poetics by correcting what they found to be the limitations of his philosophy—the "prison of his allegory" as Gleckner puts it (*Blake and Spenser* 138)—thus anticipate and help illuminate our own deepest inquiries into the nature of his mental questing. How they confronted those questions in their own time created, by the second decade of the nineteenth century, the best conditions ever for a Spenserian poetics. The immediate result was the first truly compelling epic in the history of Spenserian revisionism, *Childe Harold's Pilgrimage.*

V

It is customary for scholars of *Childe Harold's Pilgrimage,* most of whom are primarily concerned with its revolutionary character, to dismiss the significance of its Spenserian origins. Its debts to eighteenth-century Spenserian imitators like Beattie and Thomson, though acknowledged, are generally thought to be superficial (Storey 23; Martin 13–17; Trueblood 49). Similar claims are often made about its relation to Spenser, which most recent critics of the poem limit to the superficial costuming of its archaisms and its nine-line stanzas. Typically suspicious of such resemblances in a poem that seems to differ so radically from Spenser's model, Philip Martin thus concludes that "it is necessary to dispense with the notion that *Childe Harold* is modelled on, inspired by, or even usefully comparable to Spenser's poetry" (13). Michael Vicario has recently warned, however, that "to ignore the tradition of eighteenth-century Spenserian imitation" behind *Childe Harold's Pilgrimage* is to narrow one's understanding of the poem's strategies and its impact on Byron's younger contemporaries (103). The same is true of ignoring Spenser's role in the poem's composition. Byron was reading Vicesimus Knox's *Elegant Extracts,* which includes numerous passages from *The Faerie Queene* and Spenser's eighteenth-century imitators, as he began work on *Childe Harold's Pilgrimage.* He was quite clear, moreover, about his debts to both *The Faerie Queene* and its eighteenth-century progeny, invoking Thomson and Beattie in his preface and presenting the manuscript of *Childe Harold's Pilgrimage* to his publisher as a long poem "in Spenser's measure" (quoted in McGann 96; Shilstone 15–18). By the early nineteenth century, as we have seen, writing "in Spenser's measure" meant assuming certain structural and thematic paradigms within which the action of the poem transpires. Vicario has noted a number of these recognizable characteristics, locating their origins in the Spenserian tradition of Beattie and Thomson.[30] His most significant insight is that Byron's narrative pivots like Beattie's and Thomson's between "realism" and "romance ideals" in a central "dialectic of imagination and historical fact" (116, 123). We could add that Byron specifically follows Beattie's peripatetic motif, his quasi-autobiographical scheme of the growth of creative consciousness, and his descriptive/reflective style of allegory in order to elaborate this controlling drama of a poetic psyche torn between what the narrator of *Childe Harold's Pilgrimage* calls "fairy-land" and "strong reality" (IV, 50–51). In the preface to *Childe Harold's Pilgrimage*, moreover, Byron clearly acknowledges that Beattie's duality helped inspire and sustain the mental dynamics of his own poem. The "variety" of Beattie's mental theater, he claims, gives him the "authority" to attempt "similar variations in the following composition" (5). He would have found another important "authority" for such "variations" in Knox's selections from *The Faerie Queene*, which were grouped under the contrasting headings of "Sacred" and "Lyrical" sequences. One thinks inevitably of Hunt's "sacred and seductive" Spenser.[31]

What makes *Childe Harold's Pilgrimage*, in the terms of Byron's preface, an "experimental" work (3) that both incorporates and transforms the history of Spenserian duality is its method of acting

---

30. King has also detailed Byron's significant debts to Beattie ("Beattie and Byron: A Study in Augustan Satire and Romantic Vision").

31. Reviewers of *Childe Harold's Pilgrimage* were quick to focus on the "whirling gulf," as its narrator put it, of the poem's interior divisions. Hazlitt characterized the narrative as "an indigestion of the mind . . . distracted, restless, labouring, foaming, sparkling . . . " (*R* part B, 5:2336). And that "restless indigestion," to many readers, seemed borne out of the mental turbulence of the Spenserian tradition. The poem's dramatic style, began one reviewer, grew out of a long line of poets in the Spenserian line and surpassed them all, perhaps "even Spenser himself." "Childe Harold," declared another, "gave new language and meaning to the Spenserian [style]." And Jeffrey concluded that none of Spenser's imitators had so successfully availed themselves . . . of the style of Spenser" (*R* part B, 2:837; 3:1731, 1797). However we may read *Childe Harold's Pilgrimage* today, Byron and most of his contemporaries clearly thought of it as the latest, and arguably the most sophisticated contribution to the history of Spenserian revisionism.

out poetically the kind of revisionary Spenserian criticism beginning
to appear in the second decade of the nineteenth century. The limited amount of scholarship on *Childe Harold's Pilgrimage* and Spenserianism, especially Vicario's work, generally focuses on Byron's reaction to the eighteenth-century Spenserians. But as much as he may
have owed to Thomson and Beattie, not to mention Campbell and
the early Romantic Spenserian poets, he ultimately re-created their
tradition by going back to Spenser's own psychodrama and correcting its limitations in the manner of Hunt and Hazlitt. The drama of
that revisionism, similar to Hunt's lifelong Spenserian experience,
played a major role in the shaping of Byron's mature vision of doubleness and fragmentation. It was an outlook, immortalized as many
recent critics have noted in the central motif of the ever-changing
sea of *Childe Harold's Pilgrimage*, that Byron wrought out of Spenser's
dilemma and sustained as the inspiring force behind much of his
own later poetry.

On various stylistic, structural, and thematic levels of *Childe
Harold's Pilgrimage*, Byron confronts Spenser so much more directly
than had earlier imitators and redeems his duality with such greater
complexity that the force of his "significant allusions" may be considered one of the poem's strongest unifying energies.[32] He announces
this deep engagement with Spenser in the most fundamental way, by
giving his poem the full title of *Childe Harold's Pilgrimage*, which, as
nearly all its early reviewers observed, declares a basic link with the
tradition of chivalric quest poetry headed by Spenser. As a young
pilgrim, defined as a "childe" or an unproven knight of the Middle
Ages, Harold is much closer in his stated role to Spenser's chivalric
questers than Beattie's wandering minstrel or Thomson's indolent
bard. And though young, sojourning knights had often appeared in
more conventional eighteenth-century Spenserian poems, none of
them had followed the specific pathways of Spenser's pilgrimages so
closely as Harold. As little as the wayward Harold may resemble vir-

32. Recognizing the strategies of Spenserian revisionism in *Childe Harold's Pilgrimage*
can help answer some of the important questions that continue to rankle in scholarship on the poem: the relation of its stylistic "infelicity" (Gleckner, *Byron and the Ruins*
297) and "wildness" (Martin 98), particularly in its awkward archaisms (Rutherford
26–27), to its thematic content; the connection, or lack thereof, between its original
conception and the shifting narrative, stylistic, and thematic lines along which it develops (McGann 85; Gleckner, *Byron and the Ruins* 40; Martin 106; Storey 80); and the
degree to which it can be considered a revolutionary work of art that initiates a completely new tradition of confessional and philosophical poetry in "Romantic and
post-Romantic art" (McGann 105), the tradition "not so much that of Spenser . . . as it
is that of Eliot and Yeats, Joyce and Faulkner" (Gleckner, *Byron and the Ruins* 271).

tuous questers like Redcrosse or Guyon, his journey, which pushes him back and forth between nostalgic sentimentality and the bloody realities of Napoleonic Europe, drives him straight into the conflict of "actuality" and "transcendence" that the Romantics were finding at the heart of Spenser's allegory. His passage by the sweet "haven" of Calypso's isle, for instance, where he learns to "beware" of idle fantasies and confront the facts of "mortal" danger (II, 253–70), makes him strikingly like Guyon struggling in Phaedria's boat or sailing with the Palmer through the treacherous straits of the Perilous Sea. That reincarnation of Spenser's "poetry of ambivalence" (Fletcher 228) is also meant, however, as a correction, and one that Byron elaborates throughout *Childe Harold's Pilgrimage* to help work out his own modern poetics.

Harold does not pursue a determinate course like Guyon toward a specified moral goal; more like Edwin in *The Minstrel,* he wanders randomly through the mental labyrinths of creative division. Yet Edwin eventually finds a resting point in the truth of philosophy, whereas Harold's quest is described at the outset as a "weary pilgrimage" with no "fix'd . . . goal" (I, 85, 328). Nearly every symbol he encounters, like the Portugese religious icons that ironically emphasize the sinister reality of crime, reveals the doubleness of experience instead of any ultimate truth. This dichotomous vision "beset[s] his entire progress," Vicario argues (114), deepening in intensity rather than coalescing in the kind of resolution that terminates the allegories of Beattie, Thomson, and ultimately, one could argue, of Spenser himself. Harold, and the narrator who eventually takes over his journey, can neither dispense with idealism nor wholeheartedly embrace realism. In the end, and here I disagree with Vicario's claims about Byron's "total synthesis of fact and imagination" (125), the contention of truth and beauty persists more fiercely than ever. Just as the narrator discovers in Rome's Apollonian statuary a "dream of love" whose "eternal glory" outlasts "Time" and the "tinge of years," he turns to contemplate "forms which live and suffer" in the perennial ebb and flow of "Destruction's mass" (IV, 1450–76). This is a pilgrimage, like the voyage of another tormented "Childe" in Browning's poem, that proceeds with multiple elaborations toward an enigma instead of a revelation. And the "shrine" of half-knowledge it finally reaches is represented by that famous concluding image of the restless, rolling "deep and dark blue ocean" (IV, 1603).

Byron's increasing embrace of this enigma at the core of experience, which culminates in his final image of sporting on the billows of the sea, not only subverts the resting points of philosophy where Beattie and Thomson docked, it also corrects what he sees as the fundamental limitations of Spenser's own pilgrimage. What Byron calls the "one [truth] that was" of Spenser's traditional faith becomes transformed into the "thousand images" of a broken mirror that reflect the ambiguity of nineteenth-century experience (III, 291). Put another way, Spenser's underlying sense of reality's equivocations becomes redeemed from his narrow insistence on "one" truth. That transformation was so important for Byron's own creative maturation because it entailed a personal exorcism of limiting fixations within his own psyche. In the opening chapter of *Fiery Dust*, Jerome McGann discusses at some length Byron's early sentimentalism and his persisting nostalgia for the romantic ideals of his youth, for something like "one" truth. Vicario shows how his continual efforts to jettison that nostalgia in early poems like "To Romance" suggest by their very repetitiveness his difficulty in making the transition from idealism to "poetic maturity" (110). In *Childe Harold's Pilgrimage*, Vicario continues, he was still fighting that struggle (111). Correcting Spenser's philosophical certitude, and redeeming the duality that it veils, thus became to Byron a means of casting out his own idealism, or deepening his own conviction of the discontinuity of experience. To study that process in action is to understand how he learned in *Childe Harold's Pilgrimage* the lesson that Hunt spent a lifetime working out.

Byron meant to shape the indeterminate vision of his epic by dramatizing the collapse of antiquated systems of truth into the fractured shards of modern experience, and he found an effective means of carrying out that strategy by juxtaposing Spenser's chivalric universe with the modern world. There was a precedent for this contrast in *The Minstrel*, but Byron goes much farther than Beattie in highlighting the incongruities and their implications for a modern poetics. Having summoned up the medieval background of *The Faerie Queene* with his chivalric title, he elaborates that context by situating Harold in his father's "vast and venerable pile" as he prepares to set sail on a "pilgrimage" to "Paynim shores." Byron also makes extensive use of Spenser's archaic language and what his preface designates as Spenser's "old structure of versification" (4) to reinforce the Gothic foundations of this pilgrimage:

> Whilome in Albion's isle there dwelt a youth,
> Who ne in virtue's ways did take delight;
> But spent his days in riot most uncouth,

And vex'd with mirth the drowsy ear of Night.
Ah, me! in sooth he was a shameless wight,
Sore given to revel and ungodly glee;
Few earthly things found favour in his sight
Save concubines and carnal companie,
And flaunting wassailers of high and low degree.
(I, 10–18)

This antique style, coupled with the poem's medieval title, its archaic subtitle—"A Romaunt"—and its opening context of Spenserian pilgrimage, led contemporary readers to expect what one called an "assortment of chivalrous tales," an approximation we might say of *The Faerie Queene* (*R* part B, 1:396). Some had praise for such an "introduction of old words" and the "semblance of antiquity" it created (*R* part B, 4:1731). But most were baffled by the shocking contrast of that antique "semblance" with the body of the poem, a rather unholy pilgrimage conducted by a wastrel through decidedly modern, unchivalric landscapes of Napoleonic warfare. The "puzzle" for critics was and has been ever since, as one contemporary reviewer put it, how "to account for those portentious [chivalric beginnings] . . . of a poem, the subject of which is certainly neither chastity, nor valor, nor truth, nor fairies, nor damsels . . . but the narration of a modern tourist" (*R* part B, 1:396). McGann suggests a deliberate parody in Byron's archaisms, meant to mock the self-righteous "piosity" of Regency society (56–63). But the self-conscious awkwardness seems also designed to expose the inapplicability of Spenser's style and his vision (in their unredeemed forms, that is) to modern experience. Hence the poem's stylistic incongruities punctuate its central contrast—elaborated in such recurrent themes as the corruption of Harold's noble lineage, the decay of chivalry and religious institutions, the look of fallen paradise in the Cintra landscape—between the obsolescent "one" truth of Spenser's universe and the "thousand" fragments of the modern world. Correcting the fallen part of Spenser through this subversive deployment of his narrative and linguistic patterns thus helps Byron work out his own more radical vision of experience and the poetics of its articulation.

The same holds true of his engagement with Spenser's allegory and stylistic opulence. In one of his most significant innovations, Byron turns the contrast between Spenser's traditional style and the simplified form of modern Spenserianism into a formal component of his ongoing drama about an old order giving way to the fragments of the present. Many parts of the early cantos of *Childe Harold's Pilgrimage*, like the following catalogue of beauties in the portrait of Cintra, struck contemporary reviewers as the closest approximation ever of Spenser's descriptive and prosodic luxury:

> The horrid crags, by toppling convent crown'd,
> The cork-trees hoar that clothe the shaggy steep,
> The mountain moss by scorching skies imbrown'd,
> The sunken glen, whose sunless shrubs must weep,
> The tender azure of the unruffled deep,
> The orange tints that gild the greenest bough,
> The torrents that from cliff to valley leap,
> The vine on high, the willow branch below,
> Mix'd in one mighty scene, with varied beauty glow.
> (I, 243–51)

These passages also contain the kind of traditional allegorical figures to be found throughout Spenser's poetry. As Harold travels through Portugal and Spain, for instance, he frequently encounters such personages as "Folly," "Policy," "Scorn," "wanton Wealth," and "bloated Ease." Many of these characters range themselves against "Chivalry," the "ancient goddess" (I, 406), in what appears to develop as a conventional allegorical fight between vices and virtues. Amid this mixture of luxurious beauty and traditional, or as Cullen would call it, "naive" allegory (105), Spenser had rarely looked more like himself.

Yet it is all wrong, as Byron makes clear, for a narrative about the political and philosophical complexities of modern Europe. The Iberian Peninsula was neither a bower of bliss nor an abstract allegorical landscape; it was a strategic center of military and political maneuverings. The inappropriateness of a luxurious Spenserian style for this context becomes obvious when Byron switches to the simple and direct formats of recent Spenserian imitations like Campbell's and Wordsworth's, which we recall had always been associated with a liberal political realism. Thus he describes the marshaling of the allied forces against Napoleon's armies:

> Three hosts combine to offer sacrifice;
> Three tongues prefer strange orisons on high;
> Three gaudy standards flout the pale blue skies;
> The shouts are France, Spain, Albion, Victory!
> The foe, the victim, and the fond ally

That fights for all, but ever fights in vain,
Are met—as if at home they could not die—
(I, 441–47)

Spenser's "naive" allegory also has little place in a realistic sequence
like this. Thus "Chivalry" loses all of her allegorical accoutrements—
her "thirsty lance" and "crimson plumage"—and turns into the signs
and instruments of modern warfare—"the smoke of blazing bolts"
and the "engine's roar" (I, 407–10). Yet the very association of
"Chivalry" with field artillery seems awkward, if not absurd, an allegorical encumbrance as obsolescent as the philosophy embedded in
Spenser's own chivalric allegory. Hence Byron displaces that conventional allegory with the descriptive/reflective style of modern Spenserianism. Immediately after his description of the gathered armies,
he pauses to reflect on the sham of military glory in a wrenching,
subversive manner exclusively appropriate for the modern form of
Spenserianism: "There shall they rot—Ambition's honour'd fools! /
Yes, Honour decks the turf that wraps their clay! / Vain Sophistry!"
(I, 450–52). Taken by themselves, these passages could fit comfortably within numerous early Romantic Spenserian poems about modern experience. Indeed, the same criticism levelled at Byron's Spenserian colleagues, that their style was like "mere prose" (R part B,
2:693), was also directed at these realistic sequences of Childe Harold's
Pilgrimage. But they do not simply present, as in other early Romantic Spenserian poems, a modern perspective on experience. Rather,
as part of the central tension of Childe Harold's Pilgrimage, they dramatize the birth of modern vision out of a conflict with older ways of
seeing.

This strategy actually makes a plus out of that old vexation of
Spenserian revision: how to wed Spenser's original formats to a
modern style without falling into awkwardness and contradiction.
Awkwardness and contradiction are just what Byron wants, at least
in the beginning of Childe Harold's Pilgrimage. For the later cantos, he
finds even more sophisticated ways of refining Spenser's vision. The
leap forward in style that most readers of Childe Harold's Pilgrimage
notice between cantos 2 and 3 owes a great deal to several key refinements in Byron's Spenserianism. In the later cantos he resorts
much more extensively and with much greater complexity to
Spenser's own allegorical and prosodic strategies for dramatizing the
mind's conflicts. Instead of contrasting those mechanisms with a

modern style, he extends or deepens their intrinsic rhythms of duality. This new kind of adaptation, by strengthening what is already manifest in Spenser instead of grafting onto him a foreign modernism, becomes the first effective poetic example of the second-generation Romantics' most complex form of Spenserian revisionism.[33]

Central to this new poetics is Byron's sustained effort to deepen the "inscape" of Spenser's allegory. In the last two cantos of *Childe Harold's Pilgrimage*, he virtually dispenses with those deliberately awkward contrasts between conventional Spenserian allegory and the modern descriptive/reflective style. A style more suitable to his overall practice of redeeming Spenser's eternal portion, he now discovers, lies in extending Spenser's own allegorical drama of the mind's debate with itself. The Rhine river valley sequence at the beginning of canto 3 is apposite. It functions as an elaborate revision of the Bower of Bliss episode, intensifying the specific dynamics of realism and ideality that Byron and most of the younger Romantics were finding at the core of Spenser's allegory.[34] The interpolated lyric in this passage, reminiscent of the incantatory songs chanted in Acrasia's bower, celebrates the Rhine valley as an "enchanted" place of withdrawal from worldly suffering. This "paradise," like Acrasia's, is inhabited by lovely maidens randomly strewing flowers and smiles. All the "thousand turns" of the river disclose, like every new prospect in the Bower of Bliss, "[s]ome fresher beauty varying round." The narrator's overwhelming desire, like the urge that threatens to divert Guyon from his quest, is to forsake his "weary pilgrimage" and "dwell delighted here" in this haven of sweet repose (III, 496–535). But like the beauty of Acrasia's bower, the luxury of this "enchanted ground" proves deceptive, for beneath the facade of tranquil bliss lurk numerous signs of danger. The Rhine valley's romantic monuments to chivalry also strike the narrator as emblems of human cruelty enshrined at the heart of this supposed bower of

33. Gleckner's characterization of Blake's revisionary reading of Spenser in the *Faerie Queene* illustration resembles the way I am characterizing the second-generation Romantics' most advanced form of Spenserian revisionism. The painting may be seen as "a revelation of the fundamental imaginative truth of Spenser's vision that is obdurately obscured by the spectre's 'selfhood' of his moral-allegorical vehicle" (*Blake and Spenser* 223).

34. It is revealing to note that Gleckner finds Byron instinctively coupling his own poetic landscapes of mental division with Spenser's Bower of Bliss (*Blake and Spenser* 86).

bliss: "Beneath these battlements, within those walls, / Power dwelt amidst her passions . . . And many a tower for some fair mischief won, / Saw the discoloured Rhine beneath its ruin run" (III, 424–41). Faced with such contrasting impressions of the Rhine valley, the narrator cannot indulge his fantasy of a retreat into solitude; instead, like Guyon, he presses on in his quest.

In reproducing the allegory of Guyon's experience, however, Byron also complicates its interior contraries. Spenser's Bower of Bliss allegory, as complex as the Romantics thought it to be in psychological terms, finally reduces to the moral consideration of vice's false allure contrasted with the true substance of virtue. Though many Spenser scholars remain uneasy with Guyon's intemperate destruction of the bower, there is little dispute about the episode's uncompromising verdict on the evils of sensuous excess. Byron removes this entire moral context and makes the underlying mental tension between real and ideal experience his primary concern. He also disrupts the conclusiveness of Spenser's ending, or rather intensifies the sense of uneasiness at the close of Guyon's mission, in order to present the more equivocal nature of psychological questing in the modern world. To work out this destabilization of Spenser's moral base, he modifies one of the basic structures of allegorical conflict in *The Faerie Queene.*

Spenser's war of truth and appearance centers in illusions of beauty juxtaposed against the underlying foulness of those masters of deception who fabricate them, such as Acrasia, Duessa, Archimago, and Busyrane. Neither the facade nor the substance is ultimately desirable. The drama of the allegory focuses instead on the struggle to distinguish between the two and choose another, ulterior level of experience; for instance, the virtue represented by Guyon's mentor, the Palmer. In Byron's modern allegory, fact and appearance become morally neutral, the products of realistic and imaginative perception, which are equally desirable and endlessly competitive. Amid this battle of true contraries, the outer ground of some sort of mediating truth disappears. Byron's Rhine maidens, for instance, are not sirens who deceive and destroy but the preservers of a genuinely attractive "enchanted ground" of the imagination. The ideal they represent is not invalidated but rather qualified by the historical reality of war that informs the Rhine landscape. On the other hand, that reality, though painful, does not appear as the disgusting nether parts of a Duessa, to be shunned at all costs. It is, rather, the wide field of events—sewn with all the mingled sorrow, nobility, squalor, and joy recounted throughout *Childe Harold's Pilgrimage*—that "wanderers o'er Eternity" must traverse in struggling to comprehend the full range of human experience. Neither that struggle nor the swerve away from it into ideal oblivion is negated; and there is no Palmer to offer some ultimate reality outside of these alternatives. Instead, the narrator of *Childe Harold's Pilgrimage,* like the speaker at the end of Keats's nightingale ode, finds himself divided between two worlds in the Rhine valley, bidding an "Adieu" to enchantment that is finally "a vain adieu" because "There can be no farewell" (III, 572–73), no settling the contention of the real and the ideal. It is as if a redeemed Acrasia, desirable in both her extremes, has become the tutelary genius of Byron's allegory. This is what Gleckner calls "antiallegorical allegory" (*Blake and Spenser* 270), in which Spenser's doubling vision is purged from the error of his absolutism to help Byron articulate his own "vigorous skepticism" (McGann 40).

The part of this revisionary allegory that made the greatest impact on Keats and Shelley is Byron's reformulation of Spenser's mutability myth. With the narrator of canto 4 wandering through the monumental fragments of ancient Italy and contemplating the power of "Time, the avenger" (IV, 1162), the entire narrative becomes a protracted meditation on the ruins of time. Byron's pageant of Roman ruins obviously looks back to the decline of worldly cities in Spenser's own *The Ruines of Time* and *Ruines of Rome* (the latter a translation of du Bellay). More specifically, its continuous reminders of historical flux recall Mutabilitie's procession of change at the end of *The Faerie Queene.* Like the speakers in Spenser's poems, moreover, Byron's narrator is divided between his anguish over the "tickle" state of human affairs and his hope for a transcendent ideal impervious to the shock of change. Yet however deeply Spenser grieves for the fragile condition of all "liuing wights," who are "Still tost, and turned, with continuall change" (7.7.21), he eventually finds a qualified solace in that permanent, divine ground beyond the ever-revolving sphere of human affairs. His Nature silences Mutabilitie by appealing eschatologically to the "time . . . that all shall changed bee, / And thenceforth, none no more change shall see" (7.7.59). Hence God's steadfast "pillours of Eternity," "contrayr to Mutabilitie" and upon which "all shall rest eternally" (7.8.2), emerge as the ultimate ground of reality at the end of the *Mutabilitie Cantos.* Byron typically removes this theological focus, bringing the entire debate between permanence and change into the psychodramatic context of realistic and idealistic perception. He also makes this new debate much more ambiguous in its outcome by dramatizing the narrator's intense yearning for a resting point like Spenser's that he can never attain. Instead, he continuously swerves back and forth between the "tickle" world and the "pillours of Eternity."[35]

The ideal of Love, for instance, strikes the narrator as a beautiful seraph, constant throughout history and free from the taint of corruption. But he instantly qualifies his own idealism as the "false creation" of a fevered mind, an "unreach'd Paradise of our despair" (IV, 1090–96), and he returns to the fact of our withering from youth with an ever "unslaked" thirst for such a "Paradise" (IV, 1109). Then it is the Pantheon, and the spiritual idealism it embodies, that seems to shiver "Time's scythe" (IV, 1312). But the narrator's enthusiasm quickly fades into a sober meditation on Eve's disastrous progeny and the bitter reality of blasted hopes, endless change, and inevitable corruption that it represents. The spiritual sublimity of St. Peter's dome inspires more "hopes of immortality," however, which are followed by a different set of "hopes" in the eternity of art. Apollonian statuary beams with a "ray of immortality . . . And Time himself hath hallowed it, nor laid / One ringlet in the dust" (IV, 1457–66). Yet even at the height of this paean to immortal monuments of mind, the narrator comes back to Harold's decay and the history of "Destruction's mass" with which it has always been associated (IV, 1476). These irresolute swings between mutability and eternity, reality and idealism, thus persist to the very end of Childe Harold's Pilgrimage, acting out Byron's most pointed revision of Spenser's mutability myth. Mutability becomes in Childe Harold's Pilgrimage not one part of a dialogue with eternity, a part eventually made subordinate in Spenser's system, but the absolute ground of experience, the basic condition of the modern mind divided between polar extremes. Thus God's "pillours of Eternity" in The Faerie Queene, the foundation of reality for Spenser, become the "arch" and "pillar" of ever-changing "Time" in Childe Harold's Pilgrimage (IV, 986–87). And Spenser's one comparison of Mutabilitie to "th'Ocean [that] moueth still" provides the metaphor of flux that dominates the famous ending of Childe Harold's Pilgrimage, in which the narrator hails the endlessly shifting sea: "Roll on, thou deep and dark blue

---

35. Gleckner senses great sadness in Spenser's inability to uplift himself into that eternity to which he aspires, a limitation of vision that Blake severely reproved (Blake and Spenser 281). The point for Byron, however, was the error of placing a final trust in even such a provisional vision of certitude.

ocean—roll!" (IV, 1603). Lifting that metaphor out of Spenser and giving it new prominence is something like redeeming Mutabilitie, along with Acrasia, as the true heroines of *The Faerie Queene* and the muses of Byron's indeterminate vision.[36]

To help carry out such an antiallegorical recovery of those muses, Byron also extends the prosodic aspects of Spenser's duality. In the last two cantos of *Childe Harold's Pilgrimage,* he drops Spenser's archaic language and dispenses with the awkward stylistic contrasts of the early cantos in order to intensify metrical tensions that are inherent throughout *The Faerie Queene* and central to the *Mutabilitie Cantos.* As his contemporaries were growing more sensitive to the psychodramatic effects of those tensions, Byron was also learning how Spenser specifically likes to "mingle," in his own words, "sterne sounds" with "soft delights" (7.6.37) to punctuate his ongoing swerves between realism and ideality in the *Mutabilitie Cantos.* The metrics of those cantos shifts between harmony and discord, for instance, as the conflict between Mutabilitie and Nature's eternal providence wears on. When Nature first appears, the mellifluous rhythms of the poetry manifest the idealism that inspires her final prophecy of God's "great Sabbaoth":

> And all the earth far vnderneath her feete
> Was dight with flowres, that voluntary grew
> Out of the ground, and sent forth odours sweet;
> Tenne thousand mores of sundry sent and hew,
> That might delight the smell, or please the view:
> The which, the Nymphes, from all the brooks thereby
> Had gathered, which they at her footstoole threw;
> That richer seem'd then any tapestry,
> That Princes bowres adorne with painted imagery.
>
> (7.7.10)

This enchanting "harmoniee . . . that pleasing is to liuing eare"— what sounded to Yeats like "bars of gold thrown ringing upon one another" (*Essays* 379)—contrasts with the fractured rhythms and cacophonous sounds that accompany Mutabilitie's assertion of her ever whirling reign of temporal flux:

> Therein the changes infinite beholde,
> Which to her creatures euery minute chaunce;

36. Byron's revisionism here anticipates Williams's perception that the water imagery of Book 4 of *The Faerie Queene* makes up one of the most sustained and dramatic embodiments of Spenser's sensitivity to the flux and ambiguities of experience (81).

> Now, boyling hot: streight, friezing deadly cold:
> Now, faire sun-shine, that makes all skip and daunce:
> Streight, bitter storms and balefull countenance,
> That makes them all to shiuer and to shake:
> Rayne, hayle, and snowe do pay them sad penance.
>   (7.7.23)

Byron cultivates a similar form of prosodic contrast to reinforce his own dualities of mind. But in order to dramatize his more problematic experience of mental division, he resorts much more frequently to the metrical ruptures of Spenser's harsher style while greatly intensifying their disjointed effects.

After the soothing melodies, for instance, of the narrator's momentary reflections on the harmonious sounds of night, "As I now hear them, in the fading light / Dim o'er the bird of darkness' native site" (IV, 949–50), his poetry becomes fragmented as he returns to the chaotic history of human impermanence:

> There is the moral of all human tales;
> 'Tis but the same rehearsal of the past,
> First Freedom, and then Glory—when that fails,
> Wealth, vice, corruption,—barbarism at last.
> And History, with all her volumes vast,
> Hath but *one* page,—'tis better written here,
> Where gorgeous Tyranny had thus amass'd
> All treasures, all delights, that eye or ear,
> Heart, soul could seek, tongue ask—Away with words! draw near,
>
> Admire, exult—despise—laugh, weep—for here
> There is such matter for all feeling—Man!
> Thou pendulum betwixt a smile and tear
>   (IV, 964–75)

The early reviewers of *Childe Harold's Pilgrimage* celebrated what they alternately called Byron's "melodious," "smooth," "harmonious," "sweet" style (*R* part B, 1:110; 2:544, 706; 3:1272). But they were irritated by his frequent recurrence to this cacophony, this "too frequent struggling of one stanza into one or more which follow it" (*R* part B, 5:2183), which seemed wholly inappropriate for a Spenserian poem. Our focus on the prosody of Mutabilitie's argument, however, shows that Spenser gave Byron all the rudiments for such a difficult style and its pointed antithesis to ringing gold bars. Byron only radicalizes Spenser's example, increasing the number of his internal stops, running the syntax across stanzaic boundaries that he never violates, and generally making such disruptive patterns a much more common part of the modern psychodrama of *Childe Harold's Pilgrimage*. The overall effect is not simply to qualify Spenser's idealism but to magnify and complicate his drama of self-debate. It is a stylistic way of redeeming Mutabilitie. Several perceptive reviewers understood this transformation, noting how Byron's fractured metrics enable him to "think aloud," or to express the "play and pliability" of a turbulent mind (*R* part B, 1:450). Such a free "license" with Spenser's stanza, as Sir Walter Scott approvingly put it, does not simply address the old question of how to combine traditional and modern Spenserian forms.[37] It produces the first effective poetic style for carrying out the Romantics' new idea of extending Spenser's innate duality into a modern vision of experience.

It was Byron's overall strategy for intensifying the discords of Spenser's universe that ultimately showed the younger Romantics how much could be gained from unlocking the duality of that not so antique world. One hundred years of Spenserian history was culminating around the second decade of the nineteenth century, independently of Byron, in an unprecedented confidence about the manageability and the contemporaneity of Spenserian adaptation. Nonetheless, it seems reasonable to suggest that the breakthrough innovations of *Childe Harold's Pilgrimage,* in particular, created the most fruitful conditions ever for a revisionary Spenserianism. Despite the ongoing controversy about the general merit of Byron's epic, there was no disputing its ascendancy as the era's single most popular poem and its most widely acclaimed form of Spenserian adaptation. Many reviewers of *Childe Harold's Pilgrimage,* moreover, were presenting it as the supreme example ever of Spenserian poetics, arguably a significant improvement even on *The Faerie Queene*. "[P]erhaps not even Spenser himself," ventured one admirer, "has been so successful as Lord Byron in the management of this struc-

---

37. Scott, in defending Byron's shifts between metrical fluidity and discord, argued that "the occasional roughness of the verse corresponded with the . . . mental suffering which it expresses. . . . Many of the stanzas, considered separately from the rest, might be objected to as involved, harsh, and overflowing into each other beyond the usual license of the Spenser stanza. But considering the various matter of which the poet had to treat . . . considering also that the effect of the general harmony is, as in music, improved by the judicious introduction of discords wherewith it is contrasted, we cannot join with those who state this occasional harshness as an objection to Lord Byron's poetry" (*R* part B, 5:2055).

ture of verse." "[P]erhaps" not even Spenser could be "excepted," claimed another, from those predecessors whom Byron surpassed "in the same path of poetry" (*R* part B, 4:1731; 1:450). This vigorous endorsement of Byron's revisionism inspired the rise of a distinctive Spenserian poetics, centering around the example of *Childe Harold's Pilgrimage*, which now became immensely popular in England's literary culture. Scott in *Don Roderick*, Reynolds in *The Romance of Youth*, Clare in *The Triumphs of Time* (1824–32), Peacock in *Ahrimanes* (1813–15), and Hood in *The Two Swans* (1824), all composed Byronic-Spenserian allegories about mental growth and division. These works, many of them unfinished fragments, reinforced one of the vital lessons of *Childe Harold's Pilgrimage*: that Spenser's achievement, rooted in division and incompletion, is pliant, accessible, and highly appropriate for a modern poetics of self-debate and discontinuity.

As that evolving poetics began to reshape ideas of epic poetry, giving rise, as Thomas McFarland (*Romanticism and the Forms of Ruin*), Marjorie Levinson, and Anne Mellor argue, to monumental epic fragments like *The Prelude, Don Juan*, and Keats's *Hyperion* poems, this reading of Spenser's fractured muse became increasingly significant. It suggested how his example could facilitate the Romantics' new strategies for making epic and thus guide their overall effort to re-create the Renaissance. Moreover, Byron's sustained elaboration of Spenser's conflicts enhanced greatly that image of a vulnerable "Brother" of a poet that the Romantics had been enthusiastically building up from the eighteenth-century Spenserian tradition. This new but characteristic conflation of his adaptability and his doubleness made him so attractive that Romantic epic poetry, for a short time at least, became closely intertwined with Byron's Spenserian revisionism; Reynolds in *The Romance of Youth*, for instance, and Peacock in *Ahrimanes* produced Byronic-Spenserian epics that became particularly important for Keats and Shelley.[38] To appreciate

---

38. Reynolds, who composed *The Romance of Youth* while his close friend Keats was beginning *Endymion*, made his theme the maturing artist's division between reality and imagination. (For a longer discussion of the impact of *The Romance of Youth* on Keats, see Leonidas M. Jones 101–7.) "The world of imagination is darkened by the shadow of the world of reality," Reynolds writes in a preface. "It was the Author's intention to have shown how ruthlessly discontent and a connexion with the world mar all the beauty and bloom of youth" (32). His semiautobiographical poet-figure chases a dream maiden, a "Fay-queen" in a "shell car" (lines 632, 696) through various scenes of magical beauty whose pictorial enchantment is complemented by the voluptuous lyricism noted above. He longs to join her by repudiating the "fetters of his mortal

fully how much the idea of Spenserian epic began intriguing the Romantics as *Childe Harold's Pilgrimage* appeared in its various installments, we need only consult their opinions about the relative merits of following Milton or Spenser.

Milton, as we have seen, was still overwhelmingly considered the first great epic poet. But when it came to choosing whom to emulate, the difference between Milton's austerity and Spenser's accessibility dominated the conversation. Reynolds, for instance, preferred Spenser's "dreaming innocence" to Milton's "enormous" sublimity (*Letters* 100). Hunt, writing to Lamb, favored Spenser's balmy remoteness—"which wraps you wherever you are / In a bow'r of seclusion beneath a sweet star"—over Milton's exalted manner ("Epistle to Charles Lamb," lines 31–32). And Wordsworth, noting how one can trace Spenser's "affectionate spirit" in all that he writes, concluded that he was much "gentler" than the "exalted being" that Mil-

---

state, / Which chain'd him to the earth" (lines 665–66). But he must finally renounce her for a real world, presented in harsh images and grating cadences, that he so disdains as to break off his narrative before the promised canto about his exploits in the human sphere. The poem concludes with a lament, fittingly reinforced by the entire work's fragmentary status, about a modern world dominated by change and unfulfillment: "We are eternal piners after change; / Ah, woe is me! we never are content" (lines 687–88). Certainly no *Childe Harold's Pilgrimage*, Reynolds's poem nevertheless displays many of the narrative, thematic, stylistic, and psychological features that Byron had learned to adapt from Spenser; in this capacity it became an important influence on Keats's first epic poem, *Endymion*.

Peacock's two short cantos and long prose outline of a projected epic in Spenserian stanzas, *Ahrimanes*, performed a similar role for the composition of Shelley's Spenserian epic, *The Revolt of Islam*. In its debts to Byron and its pronounced independence from his model, *Ahrimanes* helped Shelley toward a significant extension of Byron's Spenserian art. Peacock uses allegory, mythology, and narrative action much more elaborately than Byron. In this respect, *Ahrimanes* more directly recalls the eighteenth-century dream-vision imitations of Spenser, though its Eastern mythology provides a new, radical transformation of Spenser's Christian outlook on mutability and divine permanence. Its two protagonists embark on a mythic quest whose turbulent events show how transcendental powers, derived from Zoroastrian mythology, will ultimately displace human change and strife with unity and permanence. But this journey, through Eastern settings reminiscent of Byron's, also stimulates reflections, in the Byronic manner, on contemporary themes similar to the concerns of *Childe Harold's Pilgrimage*: political despotism, indirectly connected with the recent plight of Napoleonic Europe, is condemned; and conflicts of reality and illusion beset one of the main characters, Kelasris, whose "dreams . . . Fade in the vast reality of pain" (II, 94). "Refl[ections] on instability of things," as Peacock notes in his prose outline (430), were to figure prominently in the work's uncompleted sections; and the mental growth of his two main characters, as they confront these difficulties, was to control the entire narrative.

ton was (*Critical Opinions* 265). Landor pinpointed why an affectionate Spenser could be more appealing than an exalted Milton when
he described his boyhood reading of both poets and thus characterized the Romantics' instinctive and contrasting reception of them:
"Spenser shed over me his sunny dreams . . . the fare / Of Milton
was for boyhood too austere" (lines 11–14). Spenser, of course,
brought much more to the Romantics than "sunny dreams" and "affectionate" tenderness. But we can see that by the second decade of
the nineteenth century what he did bring came to them easily and
more readily than what Milton offered, both for its profound psychological relevance and for its flexible adaptability.

The sense that Spenser might be an ideal muse for the second
Renaissance probably lies behind the Romantics' preoccupation with
his own talent for re-creating the literary past. And here they also
had a strong precedent in eighteenth-century Spenserian theory to
build upon. Spenser's frequent incorporation of prior models often
reminded Hazlitt, for instance, of his own age's difficulty in reformulating the cultural past. Spenser "has in some measure borrowed
the plan of his poem (and a number of distinct narratives) from
Ariosto," he argued, "but he has engrafted upon it an exuberance of
fancy, and an endless voluptuousness of sentiment, which are not to
be found in the Italian writer. Farther . . . there is an originality,
richness, and variety in his allegorical passages and fictions, which
almost vies with the splendour of the ancient mythology." This
"freedom and copiousness" of innovative borrowing, Hazlitt continued, seemed quite "contrary" to the diffident and self-conscious "eti-
quette of modern literature" (*Lectures* 35, 19). Hunt felt that
Spenser's revisionism not only exemplified but could also help
bridge that gap between the innovative energies of past and present.
Free of Neoclassicism's uneasiness about mixing pagan and sacred
traditions, Hunt went beyond his eighteenth-century predecessors in
championing Spenser's spectacular gift for absorbing the "infusions
sweete" of the past. One of Spenser's most notable characteristics, he
argued, is a genius for "mixing up all creeds and mythologies" of
prior cultures with his own beliefs and passions (*Imagination and
Fancy* 51). Such a strength, Hunt claimed on many other occasions,
was sadly lacking in nineteenth-century verse, but Spenser was ide-
ally situated to help restore it. His generous experience of poetic
"infusions" offered an encouraging precedent of cultural transmission for those who would follow his example and reformulate his
own achievement in their efforts to build a second Renaissance.

With these attitudes on the rise, it became increasingly common for poets and critics to emphasize the unique possibilities for success in Spenserian adaptation. Jeffrey felt that Campbell's *Gertrude of Wyoming* "in many places" excelled even "the finer parts of Spenser" (*Contributions* 347). His sentiment was echoed by a critic in the *Quarterly Review*, who found Tighe equalling Spenser's "finest" passages ("Mrs. Tighe's *Psyche*" 478). Another critic was delighted to conclude that no other type of poetic adaptation could claim "so many successful poems" ("Chalmers's English Poets" 72). Hogg placed his own *Mador of the Moor* (1816) among this group, claiming that it surpassed Spenser and all his followers in providing "a new specimen of this stanza in its proper harmony" (lii). Although few reviewers seconded Hogg, we have seen how serious they were about heaping such encomia on Byron: "[P]erhaps not even Spenser himself" had done so well. As they were so enthusiastic about these precedents for successful adaptation, many critics were understandably eager to recommend Spenserian adaptation to the young poets of second-generation Romanticism. Take Spenser for your "master," advised one writer in the *Quarterly Review* ("Chalmers's English Poets" 72), for "no poet," Reynolds elaborated, "has ever failed" in his style (quoted in Leonidas F. Jones 102). All young artists, Hunt proselytized, "ought in an especial manner to love and study Spenser as their poet" (*Literary Criticism* 421). Even Wordsworth, despite some serious misgivings about Spenser's stanza, told an aspiring poet about the special often "overlooked" benefits of Spenserian art (*Letters* 4:284).

Never in the history of Spenserianism had such a message been delivered so forcefully. And all this was developing just as Keats and Shelley were being born into poetry. It is no coincidence, therefore, that Spenser presided formatively over both their creative maturations, or that they became arguably the greatest poets ever in the history of Spenserianism. To appreciate their ascendancy, however, we also need to consider how and why they surpassed their great tutor in Spenserian poetics, Byron. After *Childe Harold's Pilgrimage*, Byron never went back to Spenser's stanza or to the kind of revisionary Spenserian psychodrama he had pioneered. He was even known to pretend general ignorance of Spenser while claiming, much to the astonishment of Hunt, that he could "see little or no merit in Spenser" (*Critical Heritage: Byron* 302). It may be right to say that his discovery of his true voice in the *ottava rima* of *Don Juan* steered him away from a Spenserian style. But such a disingenuous and hyperbolical denial of familiarity with the poet who had helped him so much in *Childe Harold's Pilgrimage* suggests that something about his revisionism bothered him. A clue to that uneasiness lies in his 1814 comment to Thomas Moore, made between the composition of cantos 2 and 3 of *Childe Harold's Pilgrimage,* about the awkwardness of the Spenserian stanza in a long poem. Even though "it is the measure most after my own heart," he told Moore, it seemed "perhaps too slow . . . for narrative" (*Letters and Journals* 4:13). This sounds like the common complaint about Spenser's diffuseness and the tedium of his repetitive stanza in a long poem. We may suspect, however, that such criticism had as much to do with the difficulty of sustaining his metrical and allegorical complexity throughout a long narrative. The problems of diffuseness or tedium, as Beattie had concluded, lay more with Spenser's followers.[39] And Byron was no exception.

Byron's difficulties are suggested by his unexpected recourse in the later parts of *Childe Harold's Pilgrimage* to the simplified prosody and the free-flowing habits of reflection common to early Romantic Spenserianism. That more reductive form of adaptation, at odds with the growing sophistication of his Spenserianism, fills up significant portions of cantos 3 and 4, as in contemplative stanzas like the following:

> And thus I am absorb'd, and this is life:
> I look upon the peopled desert past,
> As on a place of agony and strife,
> Where, for some sin, to Sorrow I was cast,
> To act and suffer, but remount at last
> With a fresh pinion; which I feel to spring,
> Though young, yet waxing vigorous, as the blast
> Which it would cope with, on delighted wing,
> Spurning the clay-cold bonds which round our being cling.
>
>   (III, 689–97)

This simpler way of telling the mental history of *Childe Harold's Pilgrimage* continues until Byron interrupts to say "But this is not my theme" (III, 716). Indeed, as we have seen, it is not the main theme

---

39. Even those who criticized the tedium of Spenser's stanza in a long poem, like Wordsworth, acknowledged that Spenser had little trouble with that problem in extended sequences like the Bower of Bliss episode (*Prose Works* 2:220). And nearly everyone agreed, as Hunt put it, that despite occasional flats in *The Faerie Queene* stanza after stanza comes pouring forth in endless, prolific beauty (*Literary Criticism* 451).

or the high poetics of cantos 3 and 4. Yet its recurring presence suggests that Byron, like Thomson and Beattie before him, found it difficult if not impossible to maintain a complex Spenserian style throughout dozens, even hundreds, of stanzas. Byron's more complicated revisionary innovations, moreover, must have made this obstacle seem all the more insurmountable. Declaring Spenser to have "little or no merit" and moving on to a different, less densely packed style was one way of reacting. Keats and Shelley would run square into the same obstacle, the one persisting and ever-increasing dilemma at the heart of Spenserian revisionism. But they would have to find another, more effective solution to it before they could stand in front of everyone, even Byron, within the crowded pantheon of Spenserian poets.

KEATS
AND
SPENSER

PART 2

A Less Haughty Muse 3

It was the *Faery Queen* that awakened his genius. In Spenser's faery land he was enchanted, breathed in a new world, and became another being; till, enamoured of the stanza, he attempted to imitate it, and succeeded. . . . When his soul arose into poetry, it was [thus] imbued" (*KC* 2:55–56). Charles Brown's description of Keats's birth into poetry and his sustaining inspiration thus memorialized Spenser's most profound impact on any poet up to the nineteenth century. Brown was not always accurate in his recollections of Keats, but he was not exaggerating here. An adolescent Keats first experienced the thrill of poetry when reading Spenser with Charles Cowden Clarke in 1814. That event inspired his first poetic composition, a short lyric in Spenserian stanzas. His early poetry teemed with Spenserian echoes, allusions, and direct quotations. He affixed a motto from Spenser to the title page of his first poetic volume (*Poems*, 1817). And his first major work, *Endymion*, took the shape of a Spenserian quest romance.

We still have much to learn about what so drew him to Spenser. It is not enough to echo with Joan Grundy the common consensus of Keats scholars that he was moved by an irresistible affinity to Spenser's sensuousness ("Keats and the Elizabethans"). Such a claim is certainly valid; perhaps no poet, as Yeats suggested (*Essays* 370), has relished Spenser's beauty with such instinctive passion as Keats. But our concentration on only this part of his relationship with Spenser has led us to believe—as Grundy (4), Finney (323), and many others have concluded—that his maturing descent into the bitter realities of experience drove him to abandon Spenser, whom he always associated with a transfixing but ultimately superficial loveliness. A more comprehensive account of his conversation with Spenser will show, however, that it was much more complicated from the beginning, that it deepened in complexity as he matured, and that it continued as a valuable source of inspiration and support to the very end of his life, when he shaped his last poetry out of a substantial reading of *The Faerie Queene*.

Keats's consuming interest in Spenser can only be fully understood within the particular contexts of Romantic Spenserianism that
were unfolding as he matured. He was quite familiar with this background from an early age, avidly imbibing Spenserian poetry (by
Thomson, Beattie, Tighe, Campbell, Wordsworth, and Byron) and
recent Spenser criticism (mainly by Hunt and Hazlitt) throughout
his poetic apprenticeship. These influences refined his raw love for
Spenser's beauty into a studied appreciation of Spenserian duality,
which he incorporated with developing complexity into his own
Spenserian art. But Keats's earliest fascination with Spenser
stemmed from the Romantics' earnest promotion of him as the gentle
giant who could steer the moderns through the perils of the second
Renaissance. Keats's responsiveness to that idea of a welcoming master gave him the courage to venture into poetry and remained a
steadying ground of inspiration throughout the trials of his poetic
career. To comprehend the basis of his relationship with Spenser,
therefore, we must first assess his nascent poetic aspirations, his
early concerns about the literary past, and his view of Spenser's particular role in that tradition.

I

Miriam Allott, Stuart Sperry, and W. J. Bate have taught us to appreciate Keats's early verse, whatever its aesthetic limitations, for anticipating the major concerns of his mature poetry. We have yet to
notice, however, its rudimentary form of the confrontation with
great precursors that eventually became a dominant feature in his
later work and what Bloom calls one of the direst struggles ever with
the Covering Cherub of poetic tradition (*Poetry and Repression* 113).
Keats's mature remarks on the vexations of poetic influence rank
among Romanticism's most poignant expressions of its quandary
with the first Renaissance: "the Cliff of Poesy towers above me"; "I
have been very idle lately, very averse to writing . . . from the over-
powering idea of our dead poets"; "I have but lately stood on my
guard against Milton. Life to him would be death to me" (*LJK* 1:139;
2:212). The origin of these anxieties can be traced in Keats's earliest
writings.[1] So can the beginnings of both his mature passion to over-

---

1. This claim must qualify Bate's impression that Keats, in his early poems, is

come them and his realization that the age's new confidence about Spenserianism might help him the most.

Keats's early verse, as many of his commentators have noted, is self-consciously a poetry about the intense desire to write great poetry. The figure of Apollo, "great God of Bards," dominates these works as the spirit to whom Keats prays for his own "heavenly birth" into the company of eternal poets ("Ode to Apollo," line 47). His imagination turns frequently to young figures of chivalry, like Calidore, whose eagerness for fame embodies his own "ambitious heat" as an aspiring boy-poet (*Calidore*, lines 127–28). This burning desire for greatness sustains the narrative of his first long poems, verse epistles that proclaim his "mad ambition" to "hold lofty converse with after times" through verses of his own making ("To My Brother George," lines 72–73, 110). *Sleep and Poetry*, his first substantial work, even presents a lengthy outline of his plan to "be among the English Poets after my death" (lines 96–162; *LJK* 1:394). Such aspirations were certainly not uncommon among English poets before Keats. But their overriding intensity was singular, part of the same unique, somewhat "mad" inclination that drove Byron, Keats, and Shelley to the unheard-of extreme of attempting epic poems in their early twenties. This precipitous desire for epic accomplishment could have only grown out of the spirit of an age that declared itself the second Renaissance of English poetry. The ideal of realizing that title so molded the aspirations of Romanticism's younger poets as to make its speedy fulfillment one of the basic conditions of poetic election. To write like his great ancestors seemed to Keats, from the very beginning, the measure of his poetic identity.

It would have been asking much of any aspiring poet to remain undaunted by such a formidable test; but escaping self-doubt was virtually impossible when so many critical authorities were warning about the threat of being dwarfed by those giants from antiquity. Keats's first stirrings toward poetic fame, in fact, thrust him into direct contact with at least two of the period's most eloquent spokesmen on its problematic relation to the past: Hunt, whose vision of Apollo vanishing from modern England he read in *The Feast of the Poets* (1811), and Hazlitt, whose caution to "husband enthusiasm" about the present he heard in the famous 1818 lecture "On the Living Poets" (*Lectures* 145). It is probable, moreover, that Keats's early familiarity with Hunt's *Examiner* and the periodical press at large

---

relatively unaware of the burden of poetic influence and the general Romantic debate about poetic tradition (*John Keats* 105).

exposed him to the many elaborations of these concerns that were pervading London's literary circles.

The extent of Keats's preoccupation with the subject may be traced in the habitual anxiousness of his approaches to poetic fore-bears, particularly those from the English Renaissance, throughout his early verse. Even though he had read little in those "realms of gold," he grew accustomed from early on to look at them as intimi-dating heights in relation to his own meager talent. He expressed this attitude as a "reverence" (Sleep and Poetry, line 273) habitually associated with stern, threatening images of the esteemed masters and abject portraits of the worshipful modern poet. Hence one of his earliest poems, "Ode to Apollo", depicts Milton and Shakespeare as dreadful gods wielding a power that subdues more than inspires. An "awful silence" precedes Milton's "lofty strain," whose "thunders" disturb the peace of heaven (lines 18–23). Shakespeare, the "mas-ter," pours forth a "terrific band" of passions, whose "tyrant tem-per[s]" power his art (lines 24–29). A sonnet of 1816 similarly pre-sents Milton's "stern form," which looms "before my mind" ("Oh! how I love," line 11). All of Milton's formidable compeers seem to "intrude . . . in throngs before my mind" in another sonnet of the same year ("How many bards," line 6).[2] The "rude" strength of the past in the Elgin Marbles actually threatens to suffocate the modern poet, bringing "round the heart" a "most dizzy pain" ("On Seeing the Elgin Marbles," lines 10–11). These various images of primor-dial, bewildering force coalesced in Keats's first great vision of the past's rule over the present. The power of its poetry appeared to him in 1816 as a tremendous planet of "convoluting sound," whose eternal harmonies distort and overwhelm the "small range" of "the present strength of manhood" (Sleep and Poetry, lines 162–81).

"Reverence" of this uneasy sort carried with it a sense of feeble-ness, expressed throughout Keats's early work whenever he contem-plated his own "mad" attempts to speak articulately within the din of that planetary utterance. In the 1816 "Induction" to Calidore, he wonders openly at his own "strange pretense" in such an endeavor

2. Gleckner, focusing on the way Keats characterizes the echoes of the past as a "pleasing chime," finds the sound of tradition in "How many bards" reassuring, even invigorating for Keats ("Keats's 'How Many Bards'"). But Keats's particular way of describing his reception of those sounds, which "intrude" on him, should at least make us suspicious about his ambivalence to their achievement. What Gleckner reads as the Spenserian allusiveness of the sonnet ("Keats's 'How Many Bards'" 17), as I intend to suggest, may come more as desire for relief from the pressures of the past than an unconditional embrace of all the thronging dead.

("Specimen of an Induction," line 64). He often fellowed such pretentious ambitions with images of disease, impotence, and catastrophic failure. The sight of the Elgin Marbles, for instance, prompts a yearning for "godlike hardship" but ultimately leaves him feeling "Like a sick eagle looking at the sky" ("On Seeing the Elgin Marbles," lines 4–5). In one of his first longer compositions, his wishes to "venture on the stream of rhyme" provoke images of a broken vessel: "With shatter'd boat, oar snapt, and canvass rent, / I slowly sail" ("To Charles Cowden Clarke," lines 16–18). And at a critical point in his most detailed early outline of creative aspiration, he associates the convulsive power of tradition first with his "reverence" and then with the enforced shattering of his own wild ambition:

> Will not some say that I presumptuously
> Have spoken. . . .
> That whining boyhood should with reverence bow
> Ere the dread thunderbolt could reach? . . .
> . . . let me like a madman run
> Over some precipice; let the hot sun
> Melt my Dedalian wings, and drive me down
> Convuls'd and headlong!
> (*Sleep and Poetry*, lines 270–304)

Recognizing the depth of these Icarian anxieties, which only increased as Keats went on, can help us understand why he turned to Spenser so enthusiastically at the start of his career and returned again and again as he matured. He very much needed reassurance that his "presumptuous" desire to walk with his great forebears was not foolhardy and self-destructive. His contemporaries were telling him that Spenser was the one poet among the thronging dead who could offer that encouragement. How much their advice meant to him may be measured by the way he absorbed their specific comments about Spenser's mildness, flexibility, and beneficence to fledgling disciples.

Shortly after his first exposure to Spenser, Keats began reading contemporary Spenserian poets and critics who urged him to focus on Spenser's special status as a friendly presence among threatening giants. *Childe Harold's Pilgrimage* taught him to "reverence" Spenser's greatness, but its melancholy strains also made him think of "soft Pity," "tenderness," and "sweetly sad" melodies as the main characteristics of Spenserian art ("To Lord Byron," lines 1–3). He learned from Hunt to concentrate on specific examples of those qualities in

The Faerie Queene, marking his own copy of the epic to coincide with Hunt's enthusiasm for such tender and delicate scenes as Archimago's "little lowly Hermitage," the sprightly dance of plumage on Arthur's "loftie crest," and the radiance of Una's meek but beautiful face, which "made a sunshine in the shadie place."[3] Keats's early reception of Spenser was thoroughly conditioned by this popular idea of what Wordsworth called "the gentle affectionate spirit of the man" (*Critical Opinions* 265). Keats especially relished, for instance, Spenser's expressions of romantic tenderness, often quoting the marriage hymns and adapting for his 1816 verse epistle "To My Brother George" (lines 81–88) Colin Clout's paean to love poetry in *Colin Clout's Come Home Againe* (lines 640–44). He singled out for Clarke's attention "Belphoebe in a brook" and "lovely Una in a leafy nook" ("To Charles Cowden Clarke," lines 35–36). Even Britomart, that chaste and formidable warrior, appeared most notable for her emotional vulnerability. The "rich melodies" and "gentle" pathos of her love for Artegall seemed to possess "magical powers to bless, and to soothe" ("On Receiving a Curious Shell," lines 11, 20; "Hadst thou liv'd," line 54). Thus attentive to Spenser's soothing graces, Keats felt that reading *The Faerie Queene* was like dallying by "Mulla's stream," fondling "the maidens with the breasts of cream" ("To Charles Cowden Clarke," lines 33–34). The significance of this overall impression of Spenser's rare gentleness is apparent in the "Ode to Apollo," where Keats ranks him with the great eternals of the Renaissance but passes with relief to his "Enchantment soft" after confronting Shakespeare's "tyrant temper" and Milton's "lofty strain" (lines 34–35).

Whenever Keats's thoughts turned anxiously upon those more disturbing presences, he tended to seek out Spenser for assistance. As early as 1815, for instance, he complained of the "niggard" modern muse and immediately thought of Spenserian mildness, recalling the description of Una's face as "a sun-shine in a shady place" ("To George Felton Mathew," line 75). That recollection enlivened his

---

3. Keats used Hughes's six-volume Spenser edition (1715) for his early reading of Spenser. Only the first volume of his set is extant. It is located at Harvard's Houghton Library. His markings of that volume have been recorded by Lau ("Further Corrections") and Lowell. Keats also owned a copy of the 1679 edition of Spenser's works, which he never marked. I will refer later to his possible use of a copy of *The Poetical Works of Edmund Spenser* (1778) in John Bell's *The Poets of Great Britian.* This set is now at the Keats House Library in Hampstead.

hope for poetic achievement in modern times, which he then associated with Una's removing her veil to expose a radiant countenance. When one year later he contemplated the "intrusion" of all the bards that "gild the lapses of time" ("How many bards," lines 1, 5), he instinctively hoped that Spenser could help him understand and dissolve the threat (Gleckner, "Keats's 'How Many Bards'" 17). In the "rude vnruliment" of a Spenserian sea storm (*FQ*, 4.9.23) he heard the "disturbance rude" (line 7) of all those elder bards who encroach upon the present. More important, he found the "pleasing . . . harmonee" of Spenser's delightful "musicke" (*FQ*, 2.12.70) reassuring him that the voice of the past could reach him as a kind influence, a "pleasing chime" (line 8). Spenser's way of making a sunshine in the shady places of his psyche became increasingly significant to Keats as he felt the pressures of literary tradition mounting. By 1816 he was already contemplating a major poem, loosely planned in epic terms. Quite understandably, his identification with Icarus had never been stronger. His choice to frame this work as a Spenserian romance, based on Calidore's legend, thus seems hardly coincidental. Indeed, it came out of a direct appeal to the figure he had learned to rely on the most when his deepest insecurities surfaced.

Such an appeal was central to his encounters with Spenser throughout 1816. His readings of *The Faerie Queene* at that time, for instance, focused on examples of beneficent inspiration, especially noted for their contrast with disabling influences. He underlined Spenser's plea for Cupid, as muse, to lay aside his mean disposition for a kinder aspect: "Lay now thy deadly Heben Bowe apart, / And with thy Mother mild come to mine ayd" (1.Prologue.3). He also marked Spenser's earnest call, at the outset of Redcrosse's climactic battle with the dragon, for the muses to soften their dreadful impact and gently assist at this crisis in the narrative:

> O gently come into my feeble Breast,
> Come gently, but not with that mighty Rage,
> Where-with the Martial Troops thou dost infest,
>
> . . . .
>
> But now a while let down that haughty String,
> And to my Tunes thy second Tenor raise,
> That I this Man of God his godly Arms may blaze.
>
> (1.11.6)

Keats specifically underlined the phrase "let down that haughty String." It must have seemed a fitting gloss for his impression of the way Spenser always approached him; the poet of "Enchantment soft" had performed just such a kindness by following Milton's "lofty strain" in the "Ode to Apollo" with his own "softly breath[ing]" lyre.

How much Keats relied on Spenser to "let down that haughty String" may be judged by the progress of his *Calidore* narrative. At a key moment in his "Induction" to the poem, when insecurity threatens to overwhelm him, he spontaneously turns to Spenser's encouragement:

> Spenser! thy brows are arched, open, kind,
> And come like a clear sun-rise to my mind;
> And always does my heart with pleasure dance,
> When I think on thy noble countenance:
> Where never yet was ought more earthly seen
> Than the pure freshness of thy laurels green.
> Therefore, great bard, I not so fearfully
> Call on thy gentle spirit to hover nigh
> My daring steps . . .
>
>   ("Specimen," lines 49–57)

All of the main features of Keats's special affiliation with Spenser surface in this passage: his sense of a "daring" competition with the literary past; his feeling of Spenser's high rank, as a "great bard," in that tradition; his impressions of Spenser's "gentle spirit," associated with soft brows instead of austere glares, and the easy patronage that it offers. Being able to call on this bard "not so fearfully" was so important to Keats that he memorialized it as part of the *Calidore* allegory in 1816.

Calidore is a young knight "burning" with ambition for chivalric glory, Keats's recurrent allegory for his own "mad" poetic ambition.[4] As Calidore approaches a castle, presented as the seat of chivalric or, following the allegory, poetic knowledge, he receives a hearty welcome from an established knight, Sir Gondibert. The correspondence between Keats's earlier portrait of Spenser as a benevolent teacher and this description of Gondibert's kindly tutelage is unmistakeable:

---

4. Keats calls himself "a Calidore" in "Woman! when I behold thee" (line 12). For a lengthy discussion of Keats's idea of himself as "a Calidore," see Stepanik.

> . . . [Sir Gondibert] with a step of grace
> Came up,—a courtly smile upon his face,
> And mailed hand held out, ready to greet
> The large-eyed wonder and ambitious heat
> Of the aspiring boy; who . . . often turned his head
> To admire the visor arched so gracefully
> Over a knightly brow . . .
>   (*Calidore,* lines 124–31)

If we consider the martial imagery that pervaded Romanticism's debate about poetic tradition, we may appreciate the significance of
this brief allegory and what it implies about Spenser's role in that
tradition. A mighty bard fully equipped for the shock of poetic competition, Spenser could put off his fierceness, lift his visor to reveal a
soft brow, and generously smile on his followers. Keats counted on
that greeting so much that he illustrated the title page of his first
poetic volume (*Poems,* 1817) with what might be a portrait of a benevolent, fatherly Spenser, the muse of his earliest creative en-
deavors (Fig. 4).[5]

This is not to say, however, that Keats sailed on blithely throughout his career in the certitude of Spenser's genial influence. His
early conception of Spenser in the "Induction" to *Calidore* betrays
some distress about the master's guidance. Spenser's face seems
open and generous, but his brows are arched, perhaps, Keats later
worries, in surprise or anger at the young poet's "strange pretence."
The invocation ends with Keats thinking about a "startled" and
"jealous" Spenser instead of a generous one. Indeed, as Keats pro-
gressed with his Spenserian art, he found the task not always easy
and the teacher not always compliant. He gradually became aware of
Spenser's limitations, moreover, and the need, as the Romantics understood it, to redeem him. But much as he came to modify his
reading of Spenser, and "husband" some of his naive "enthusiasm,"

---

5. Keats scholars always used to take this illustration as a portrait of Spenser.
Sperry has persuasively argued, however, that it is actually a portrait of Shakespeare
("Richard Woodhouse" 120–21, 128). Even if Sperry is right, though, we should note
that Keats gave the impression of introducing his volume with a Spenser portrait.
While Woodhouse privately associated it with Shakespeare, most of the volume's early
reviewers looked upon it as a head of Spenser put there to announce Keats's intimate
identification with the author of *The Faerie Queene.* Whether Keats thought it represented Shakespeare or Spenser, a question we can never settle absolutely, seems less
relevant to my point than the fact that he created a situation in which his fellow
feeling with Spenser was made prominent.

Poems,

BY

JOHN KEATS.

" What more felicity can fall to creature,
" Than to enjoy delight with liberty."
Fate of the Butterfly.—SPENSER.

LONDON:

PRINTED FOR

C. & J. OLLIER, 3, WELBECK STREET,

CAVENDISH SQUARE.

1817.

Fig. 4.   Title page of Keats's *Poems* (1817). (By permission of the Newberry Library)

his early impression of that generous smile remained a crucial source of reassurance throughout his participation in the second Renaissance. Again and again, it brought him back to Spenser for special assistance in building that second temple. As his thinking matured, it also helped inspire and sustain the increasing sophistication of his Spenserian revisionism.

II

Notwithstanding the unique inspiration of this less "haughty" muse, there was another significant factor in Keats's early attachment to Spenser. From the time Keats first began thinking of himself as a poet, the support of England's current writers meant as much to him as the imagined approval of its old bards. Becoming a part of London's literary circles was another important means of validating his election as a poet. In many of his early works, for instance, he constructs his creative identity in terms of his association with established writers like Byron and Hunt. We have seen how appreciation of Spenser's beauty, his playfulness, and his geniality had become a special unifying principle among writers as diverse as Wordsworth, Coleridge, Lamb, Southey, Byron, Hazlitt, and Hunt. To share their appreciation of Spenser meant staking a certain vicarious claim to membership in their circles. It took Keats some time before he could fully appreciate what they were saying about Spenser's doubleness. But he understood their comments about his beauty and gentleness from the beginning and set about appropriating those ideas with a zeal that had as much to do with the embrace of contemporaries like Hunt as with the kinship of Spenser.

Keats's first responses to Spenser made up the stuff of literary legend. By late adolescence, his literary knowledge was limited and he had yet to write a poem. Then, probably in 1814, he discovered the *Epithalamion* under Clarke's guidance. Something in it made him curious about Spenser, and he requested the loan of Clarke's *Faerie Queene*. Immediately he "breathed" in Spenser's art "like a new world," "ramped" through it "like a young horse turned into a spring meadow," hoisted himself up to look "burly and dominant" in sympathy with the grand scale of Spenserian images like the "sea-shouldering whales" of the Perilous Sea, and thus became a poet himself (*KC* 2:55, 148–49; Clarke 126). The dramatic accounts by Clarke and Brown of this experience have encouraged Keats's modern critics to make equally breathless points about his spontaneous infatuation and "spiritual kinship" with Spenser's sensuousness (Stepanik 7). Much as he may have instinctively loved Spenser's beauty, however, his first reactions were deeply conditioned by his desire to share what his contemporaries were feeling about it.

This is most evident in the case of Leigh Hunt. Keats's early idolization of Hunt and his passion to join Hunt's coterie are well known. That he displayed his Spenserian credentials as an entrée to that circle was evident to reviewers of his early poems, who noticed how obviously he imitated Hunt's idea of Spenserian poetry and even Hunt's affected way of dressing like Spenser (quoted in Schwartz 78, 158–59; *KC* 2:58). This was neither the moral Spenser that Hunt revived in *The Palace of Pleasure* nor the dualistic Spenser that he re-created in *The Shewe of Faire Seeming*. Rather, it was "the Poet's Poet" of beauty whom he was then sensationalizing with a verve that would have been likely to capture Keats's attention. Clarke's very choice of the *Epithalamion* for Keats's perusal suggests how much the influence of Hunt's luxurious Spenser was at work here. The selection may have been random, but it probably arose from the new excitement about Spenser's opulence that Hunt was helping to provoke. Hunt certainly encouraged Clarke to envision Spenser's universe as a "gorgeous world" of beauty (*KC* 2:148). He was also prone to celebrate the rich pageantry, the musical virtuosity, and the voluptuous feminine beauty of the *Epithalamion* as one of the most dense manifestations of that "gorgeous world." He was speaking regularly at this time with Clarke, who often came to see him in prison, where he was incarcerated for political libel and busy regaling his frequent visitors with loquacious discourses on what he called at the time Spenser's "sweet . . . seclusion" ("Epistle to Lamb," line 32). These sessions probably moved Clarke to select the *Epithalamion* for Keats; certainly, they informed the way he presented Spenser to his younger friend. Keats felt all along that Clarke's instruction on Spenser's luxury derived from his "sweet forest walks" with Hunt ("To Charles Cowden Clarke," line 42). Yet even without Clarke, Keats knew from reading *The Examiner*, which often featured short quotations of "Beautiful sequestered" Spenserian scenes, how much Hunt adored Spenser's blissful bowers. And by 1814 he had probably read Hunt's remarks in *The Feast of the Poets* about the many "specimens of almost every beauty of writing" in Spenser's art (69–70).

When Keats asked to see *The Faerie Queene*, then, he was prepared to love what Clarke, paraphrasing Hunt, called "the general beauty of the composition" (125). Thus it is hardly coincidental that his first reactions to the epic read like a gloss of Hunt's criticism on Spenserian enchantment. Like Hunt, for instance, he was most excited by the transporting effects of Spenser's magical descriptions. The "painter of the poets," as Hunt called him, whose images bring us "to a quarter in which no sin of reality is heard," was precisely the Spenser that engaged Keats (*Literary Criticism* 421, 456). It was "the gorgeousness of the imagery" in Spenser's "world of unreality," Clarke recalled, that "appeared most to delight him." And that delight came from his own impression of being called by Spenser's beauty into "his own world of imagination" (*KC* 2:148–49).[6] Keats also shared Hunt's appreciation of the more specific effects of Spenserian language and versification in such enchantment. He thanked Clarke for exposing him to the same trance of sound in Spenser that Hunt loved, which he located in "Spenserian vowels that elope with ease, / And float along like birds o'er summer seas" ("To Charles Cowden Clarke," lines 56–57). He also learned from Hunt exactly how those Spenserian vowels elope with ease: from the "modulation" of vowel sounds, the shifting accentuation of syllables, and the "variety of pauses" in the nine-line stanza (*Imagination and Fancy* 56–57). Hunt found these features, especially the "variety of pauses," best represented in Spenser's description of Archimago's hermitage, which he thus marked during his incarceration:

> A little lowly hermitage it was //
> Down in a dale, // hard by a forest's side, //
> Far from resort of people // that did pass
> In travel to and fro: // a little wide //
> There was a holy chapel edified, //
> Wherein the hermit duly wont to say
> His holy things // each morn and eventide;
> Thereby a crystal stream did gently play //
> Which from a sacred fountain welled forth alway.
>
> (1.1.34)[7]

Hunt's impression of this stanza's modulated sounds and rhythms was so powerful that years later, for his Spenser chapter in *Imagination and Fancy* (1844), he quoted the stanza, marked out the pauses,

---

6. Brown, recounting what he had learned from others who knew Keats as an adolescent, emphasized the same point in his account of Keats's first response to Spenser: "[I]t was the Fairy Queen that awakened his genius. In Spenser's fairy land he was enchanted, breathed in a new world and became another being" (*KC* 2:55).

7. Hunt made these markings in his copy of Todd's Spenser.

and explained their function (56–57). During his own early readings of Spenser, Keats underlined the same stanza in his copy of Hughes and broke his underlining to note the effect of the same pauses.

Hunt also taught Keats how to read *The Faerie Queene* as a gallery of discrete, gorgeous pictures. Preferring to hoard Spenser's isolated beauties instead of following his narratives, Keats openly linked this eclectic way of reading Spenser with Hunt's way of lingering over "Beautiful sequestered scenes." One of his earliest sonnets applauds, among Hunt's chief talents, his gift for errant, sensitive wanderings through Spenser's gallery of riches: "In Spenser's halls he strayed, and bowers fair, / Culling enchanted flowers" ("Written on the Day That Mr. Leigh Hunt Left Prison," lines 9–10). Keats was known, in his own first reading of Spenser, to make just such a progress through *The Faerie Queene,* though with perhaps less delicacy and more boyish glee. Clarke recalled his "ramping" through Spenser's epic, pausing to dwell on captivating episodes of descriptive beauty—"culling enchanted flowers"—instead of following the path of Spenser's narrative and allegorical designs. Indeed nowhere, among the records of Keats's first experience with Spenser, is there any sign of his interest in Spenser's thought or his story. "If you go to him for a story," Hunt wrote, "you will be disappointed. . . . [You should not] read him continuously; but more or less, and as an enchanted stream 'to dip into'" (*Imagination and Fancy* 49–50). The young Keats proved one of the most avid Spenserian "dippers" that Hunt could hope to find.

Keats knew all along how closely he was following Hunt and what that discipleship was meant to prove. For he often celebrated in his early poetry an imaginary friendship with Hunt based on their mutual love of Spenserian enchantment. His sonnet "Written on the Day That Mr. Leigh Hunt Left Prison" affirms that friendship, for instance, by sympathizing with Hunt's love of Spenser's "bowers fair." In his verse epistle "To My Brother George," he claims an intimacy with Hunt founded in their special love of Spenser's charms; his own poetic ideal of shaping a magical world of fancy, he tells George, was learned from Hunt, who had it in turn from Spenser (lines 24–25). The "Induction" to *Calidore* presents this shared passion for Spenserian fancy as the basis of his unique friendship with Hunt, who thus embraces him as a worthy disciple to be recommended to Spenser: "he [Hunt] will speak, / And tell thee [Spenser] that my prayer is very meek" (lines 61–62). Keats was so eager to affirm this Spenserian bond with Hunt that he even had Clarke personally deliver to Hunt his sonnet honoring their mutual love of Spenser's "enchanted flowers."

The full strength of this desire to participate in Hunt's Spenseri- ✔
anism may be judged by the way it inspired and informed Keats's
first poetic composition, his 1814 "Imitation of Spenser," a short,
lyrical fragment consisting of four Spenserian stanzas. Keats's critics
generally find this poem following eighteenth-century imitators like
Thomson and Beattie instead of Spenser (Allott 3–4). Keats probably knew *The Castle of Indolence* and *The Minstrel* by 1814, and his own
Spenserian imitation certainly repeats some of their linguistic and
prosodic tendencies. But its prominent features much more closely
resemble the kind of gorgeous, morally lax Spenser he associated
with Hunt. Considering the thoroughness with which he re-creates
that idea of "the Poet's Poet," it would be more fitting to name his
first attempt at poetry, "Imitation of Leigh Hunt's Spenser." In detailing the "wonders" of a "verdant," secluded bower (Hunt's favorite kind of image in *The Faerie Queene*) Keats makes just the kind of
enchanted stream "to dip into" that Hunt urged his readers to seek
in Spenser. Or, to use another common Huntian metaphor, he
shapes a fanciful gallery portrait, as if one of a series of transporting
pictures that could be extracted from a long, richly adorned narrative like *The Faerie Queene*. Indeed, the poem's beginning adverb,
"Now," implies an overarching narrative temporarily suspended for
this exclusive indulgence in the romance of a blissful bower; a
"Beautiful sequestered scene," we might call it, that closely resembles
the details of that Spenserian retreat so loved by Hunt, Archimago's
hermitage. Such a fragment of unreal beauty excludes any narrative,
moral, or psychological structure. Instead, verses and images are
loosely connected with the recurrent conjunction "and" as Keats's
eye randomly strays across various objects of beauty. Those objects
together conspire to charm the "romantic eye" with one glimpse of a
lovely dream, a static world of ideal unreality in which the sky "never
lowers":

> Now Morning from her orient chamber came,
> And her first footsteps touch'd a verdant hill,
> Crowning its lawny crest with amber flame,
> Silv'ring the untainted gushes of its rill;
> Which, pure from mossy beds, did down distill,
> And after parting beds of simple flowers,
> By many streams a little lake did fill,
> Which round its marge reflected woven bowers,
> And, in its middle space, a sky that never lowers.
>
> (lines 1–9)

Keats expands this transporting dream in the next three stanzas to depict just the kind of watery delights, including a fay who drifts voluptuously, that Hunt relished in the splashing fountains, shaded pools, and half-naked bathing "Damzelles" of the Bower of Bliss.

The prosodic strategies of Keats's imitation, whatever their technical limitations, reveal just how carefully he tried to embrace Hunt's theories about Spenserian enchantment. Specifically following Hunt's points about caesural variation and vowel shifts as the stylistic basis for Spenser's enchantment, Keats produces a series of prosodic effects that look like an exercise Hunt might have set for aspiring Spenserian poets. In the first stanza, for instance, he modulates the long "o" of "Morning" and "orient" to the long "a" of "chamber" and "came," which he then varies to the short "a" of "And," "verdant," "amber," followed by the short "i" of "Silv'ring," "its," "rill," "Which," "did," "distill." These modulations of sound are complemented by a "variety of pauses" designed to approximate, as the following diagram suggests, the pattern of stops in the very stanza about Archimago's hermitage that Hunt presented as a model of Spenser's rhythmical charm:

> Now Morning from her orient chamber came, //
> And her first footsteps // touch'd a verdant hill, //
> Crowning its lawny crest // with amber flame, //
> Silv'ring the untainted gushes // of its rill; //
> Which, // pure from mossy beds, // did down distill,
> And after parting beds // of simple flowers,
> By many streams // a little lake did fill,
> Which round its marge reflected woven bowers, //
> And, // in its middle space, // a sky that never lowers.

As rudimentary as these exercises may seem, the effort that went into them suggests how much it meant for Keats to forge a tentative affiliation with Hunt and thus a poetic identity for himself through his Spenserian poetics. Joining Hunt's community of poets through a shared intimacy with Spenser hence gave a special accent to his joy with Spenser's less "haughty" muse.

We may now suspect that it was Keats's deep desire for these interrelated intimacies with the past and the present that made him so fascinated with Spenser as he began to make himself into a poet. We can also trace several important results developing from the venture of his "Imitation," above and beyond the questionable aesthetic merit of the poem. It enabled Keats to associate his first impression of poetic identity and community with Spenser, a step that would draw him back to Spenser again and again whenever he felt that identity being threatened in the future. There were already signs of how much Spenser might help him bolster his particular sense of himself as a contributor to the second Renaissance. His elevation of beauty over thought in the "Imitation" carried out a kind of "improvement" of Spenser, at least in his eyes, which could only inspire confidence about future, more complicated revisions. He was also learning from Hunt that working in this way with a cooperative guide like Spenser held out much more promise of success than any attempt to follow the likes of those more formidable bards who intruded on his early poetry; it would not be much later, in the "Induction" to *Calidore,* when he would proclaim himself privy to Hunt's special knowledge of Spenser's beneficence ("Specimen," lines 60–65). He was also beginning to learn from Spenser how to develop and express his new poetic identity. The Huntian love of Spenser's sensuousness that he consolidated in the "Imitation" would become a profound inspiration for his mature poetry of "Flora and the country green." Moreover, his early impression of the fragmentary or gallery-like character of Spenserian poetics would prove instrumental, several years later, to his mature formulation of a poetry of divided consciousness.

Keats's close association of Spenser and Hunt, nonetheless, proved a double-edged tool. Distancing himself from Spenser became one way to detach himself from Hunt when their relationship soured. It would also become apparent to him that some distance from Spenser was necessary on aesthetic grounds. Easy as it may have been to produce Spenserian stanzas in the "Imitation," the experience taught Keats how difficult it was to craft a Spenserian style that did not sound forced and obsolescent. He was quite aware of this by 1817, when he placed the "Imitation" among his awkward juvenilia. Still, from the beginning, Spenser had established himself in Keats's psyche as an enabler. One of the most important tasks of later years would be to determine how, with all the opportunities and obstacles he presented, this "gentle spirit" might best serve a modern poetics.

III

Throughout the next two years, Keats's idea of Spenser evolved along the lines set forth in his first impressions. He frequently praised Spenser's gorgeous world of imagination and, as his concerns with literary tradition developed, he expressed growing pleasure in Spenser's mildness and accessibility. In 1816, however, this course radically changed. It was then that Keats began to sense the superficiality of his early love for Spenserian enchantment. Wondering about the aesthetic validity of Spenser's remoteness, he also came to appreciate Spenserian duality and its relevance to his own poetry. That discovery made him begin to think of Spenserian allegory as a poetics for expressing his own struggle toward an epic vision of modern experience. At twenty-one, he started work on a long Spenserian allegory designed as a psychodrama of that struggle. Such a dramatic step forward came out of his new exposure to Romanticism's more complex theories of Spenserian art.[8]

This process began with his move to London in the autumn of 1815. There he expanded his reading considerably, made the acquaintance of other young poets, and immersed himself in the capital's literary life and its current enthusiasm about an Elizabethan revival. He now made a conscious effort to cultivate the Elizabethan poets and distance himself from the eighteenth-century writers he had been previously following (Finney 1:87). This phase of growth and revaluation brought him, in particular, to Hunt's more complex ideas of Spenserian allegory and dualism. By the early part of 1816, Hunt had begun to air these attitudes more openly. He was using allegory, obviously indebted to Spenser, for his influential satire *The Descent of Liberty*. And in his popular chivalric romance, *The Story of Rimini*, which was strongly associated with Spenser in its medieval pageants and luscious bowers, Hunt performed an extensive adaptation of the Spenserian dualism of truth and beauty that was becoming so important to him. He paused frequently in his narrative to indulge his idea of Spenser's descriptive gorgeousness. But he gave the poem a dramatic center by contrasting the ideal love of Dante's lovers Paulo and Francesca, which develops in remote bowers of bliss, with the sociopolitical realities that intrude upon and eventually destroy their romance. Hunt's elaboration of this conflict makes Spenser's "chiaroscuro" the controlling focus of a short epic, four cantos long. Keats had certainly not grown beyond liking the luxurious Spenserian beauties that permeated *The Story of Rimini*. He called the poem a "sweet tale . . . a bower for . . . [the] spirit" ("On *The Story of Rimini*," lines 3, 12). But he was also learning to appreci-

---

8. To recognize Keats's deeper understanding of Spenser's allegory of psychic division, which began late in 1816, is to qualify our common assumptions about his exclusive infatuation with Spenserian enchantment and his indifference to allegory before the composition of *Endymion* (R. S. White 18; Bate, *John Keats* 172).

ate its Spenserian dualisms. Even more important than its luxury, he declared, was its tendency to evoke both a "smile" and a "tear" ("On *The Story of Rimini*," line 10), which is precisely how Hunt characterized Spenserian duality.[9] Keats's appreciation of such "piquancy of contrast" in Spenser must have deepened considerably when he actually entered Hunt's circle in 1816 and came into contact with many of those, like Hazlitt, Reynolds, and Shelley, who were joining Hunt in the new conversation about Spenserian dualism.

We can trace Keats's reassessment of Spenser most specifically in his markings of Hughes's edition of *The Faerie Queene*. He acquired this text in 1816 and probably began highlighting passages in it at once. His amoral love of Spenser's ornate beauty clearly persisted, with scenes like the portrait of Duessa's rich attire—"A goodly Lady clad in scarlet Red, / Purfled with Gold and Pearl of rich assay" (1.2.13)—heavily underlined. A large share of Keats's markings, however, bear out his new interest in Spenser's doubling psychodrama. Instead of just "ramping" through Spenserian fragments of beauty, he now kept a steady eye on narrative, allegorical, and thematic continuity. He marked nearly every page in Hughes's text, conducting something like Hunt's more complicated "regular reading" of *The Faerie Queene* and focusing his attention on many of the same conflicts between truth and beauty that fascinated Hunt.

Spenser's sensitivity to the agonizing disjunction between dreams and reality particularly intrigued him. He underlined and put marginal strokes alongside the long sequence describing Archimago's "false Dream" and the great woe it brings to Redcrosse and Una (1.1.39–55). He similarly marked Fradubio's account of his fatal infatuation with the illusory beauty that Duessa fabricates to beguile him (1.2.30–45). Moreover, he noted an episode whose doubleness Hunt often commended, Arthur's story about his beautiful dream of Gloriana and his bitter sorrow upon its sudden dissolution (1.9.15). Keats also underlined one of the main images that Hunt looked to as representative of Spenser's mental "chiaroscuro," Una's unveiling of her radiant face in a shadowy bower (1.3.4). This is the same image Keats had just presented in his 1815 verse epistle "To George Felton Mathew" (line 75) as a fitting emblem for the activity of the modern muse. However deeply he still felt attached to "the wonders of an isle," he was obviously learning to develop an even stronger admiration of Spenser's talent for seeing into the opposites of things.

---

9. For a more detailed discussion of Hunt's way of characterizing Spenser's doubleness in these terms, see my "Leigh Hunt and Romantic Spenserianism" (131).

That shift in priorities was also giving Keats a profound appreciation of the poignance of Spenser's insight into suffering, as manifested in his more literal renderings of mortal frailty. Composing the
"humanity" of his vision, as Alpers puts it (*Poetry* 314), this ongoing
revelation of the ills our flesh is heir to would become increasingly
important to Keats's own sense of artistic mission. He felt particularly moved, for example, by Una's anxieties and Redcrosse's despair, marking numerous descriptions of Una's tears—"Then 'gan
she wail and weep" (1.2.7)—and Redcrosse's decay—his "feeble
Thighs" and "pined corse" (1.8.40). He both underlined and put
marginal strokes against Spenser's own lament for their sufferings:
"I . . . Feel my Heart pierc'd with so great Agony, / When such I see,
that all for pity I could die" (1.3.1). And with the most distinct mark
in all of his Spenser annotations, a double underline, he singled out
a phrase that must have seemed the perfect gloss for the new way
that Spenser came to him: "with Tydings from the Heart" (1.9.51).
As Keats now saw it, Spenser's descents into the mind's war with
itself had taught him, anticipating Wordsworth, to think deeply into
the human heart. Keats would not forget his "Tydings" when that
kind of thinking became the great empowering agent for his own
poetry.

Receiving Spenser in this new way entailed something like the revisionism that Hunt, Byron, Hazlitt, and others were now advocat-
ing. It meant redeeming Spenser's mental drama from his moral
concerns as a means of working out one's own creative salvation.
Keats was learning to appreciate that kind of revisionism in Byron's
poetry, no longer praising *Childe Harold's Pilgrimage* for its melancholy enchantment but instead for its tremendous mental turmoil—
"Strange thunders from the potency of song" (*Sleep and Poetry,* lines
230–35).[10] With Byron's war of realism and ideality thundering in
his ears, he must have also begun to suspect that such a new Spenserian poetics could help him manage his own developing conflict
between a poetry of truth and beauty. For at the same time that he
was marking *The Faerie Queene,* giving preeminence to its psychodrama of the heart's division, he began to revise the Bower of Bliss
and Calidore episodes for an extended quest poem, a new Calidore
story, about his own experience of that dilemma. Just as Byron corrected himself by faulting Spenser, Keats now learned that revision-

10. Keats had reservations, of course, about Byron's personality and his general
poetic habits, and his ambivalence intensified as he matured. For a sustained discussion of his complicated response to Byron, see Lau ("Keats and Byron") and Hirst.

ism could help him cast out what he was growing to consider his greatest aesthetic liability: the sentimentality and exclusive sensuousness of his earliest poetry. At this stage, though, he was not quite certain how to shape his specific corrections of Spenser into the building blocks of his own creative maturation. Still, his decision to take on such a substantial task in his first extended narrative tells us how much he found Spenserian allegory dovetailing with his own mental history and, of equal importance, how confident he was about tailoring Spenser's less "haughty" muse to his own poetry.

"Lo! I must tell a tale of chivalry," he repeats, with obvious frustration, three times in the "Induction" to *Calidore*. "Chivalry," as we have seen, is synonymous with artistic maturity in Keats's early poetry. His recurring and unacted-upon imperative thus pinpoints the central tension of the Calidore sequence, a burning yet unfulfilled desire to abandon the luxurious Spenserianism of his early days for a poetry of mental action. That conflict, presented in a form loosely resembling the psychodrama of truth and beauty in the Bower of Bliss episode, controls the entire "Induction." Just as Guyon is initially dazzled by the splendors of Acrasia's bower, Keats at first immerses himself in Spenserian dreaminess and contemplates "Archimago's wand" because of its "graceful" power to "charm" (lines 4, 7). His imagination, like an Archimagan wand, plays across several images of medieval enchantment: a procession of knights bedecked with "large white plumes," a "sweet" and "trembling" maiden, a secluded pond rich in "mossiness," and the "grandeur" of a jousting tournament (lines 13–30). This former ideal, however, quickly proves dissatisfying, which moves him to act as a Palmer to himself and exclaim: "No, no! this is far off:—Then how shall I / Revive the dying notes of minstrelsy" (lines 31–32). But Keats finds it difficult to produce a more complex art, and he quickly falls back, like Guyon lingering before the nymphs, to the comfortable familiarity of romantic enchantment, the "splendour" of bright lances, magnificent banners, colorful shields, and "Light-footed damsels" (lines 32–44). Again, however, he admits the superficiality of this fantasy and repeats the still-unanswered imperative, "Yet must I tell a tale of chivalry" (line 45). That hope is never realized; neither is the conflict of warring poetics resolved. Keats returns at the close of the "Induction" to the "flowers" and "shade" of Spenserian bowers (line 67). But in the very act of carrying out these oscillations, he does in fact "tell a tale of chivalry"—the kind of Spenserian chivalry that he now interpreted as interior mental warfare. In fact, his particular way of telling that tale performs a rudimentary correction of Spenser's alle-

gory, casting off the moral veil of the Bower of Bliss episode to extend its inner psychodrama of creative division. It was no doubt
Keats's realization of how closely he was coming to those "Tydings
from the Heart," and not without taking certain liberties, that moved
him at this point to address Spenser with both the intimacy and the
anxiousness of his direct invocation.[11]

That appeal inspired Keats in the narrative proper of *Calidore* to
attempt a more complex revision of the mental drama in Spenserian
allegory. He introduces the poem as a reworking of Spenser with the
conventional eighteenth-century ploy of presenting it as a continuation of an unfinished *Faerie Queene* narrative, in this case the legend
of Calidore. But in actually shaping out his narrative, he follows the
more progressive revisionary strategies of recent Spenserianism. He
probably chose the Calidore legend as backdrop for the same reason
that Byron selected the Bower of Bliss, because it concentrates
Spenser's concern with the competing claims of realism and fantasy.
More frequently than any of the other narratives in *The Faerie
Queene,* the story of Calidore features young characters dallying to
their peril in bowery retreats, divided between their responsibilities
for action in the world and their desire for the bliss of luxurious
solitude.[12] These allegories, of course, seemed overly schematic to
the Romantics. Vice gains the upper hand, the Blatant Beast invades
the bower, when moral watchfulness is relaxed. But just as Byron
redeems the psychological dynamics from this scenario, Keats turns
the bower motif of Calidore's legend into a drama of creative consciousness. Following Byron, and Beattie as well, he arranges that
drama as a pilgrimage of his own creative growth beyond the bowers
of luxurious fantasy that had captivated his youthful imagination.

Keats's gravitation to the Calidore legend also suggests his awareness that redeeming Spenser's allegory in such a way had important
implications for his own experience at this crossroad in his creative
development. The central episode of Calidore's quest in *The Faerie
Queene,* his vision of Colin Clout and the dancing graces on Mount
Acidale (6.10.5–31), would have struck Keats as an allegory of the
creative psyche engaged in a developmental struggle not unlike his

11. Morris Dickstein discusses Keats's progression to this more complicated use of
the bower allegory in *Endymion,* contrasting it with the naive celebration of the bower
in his earlier poetry (31–35, 95, 103). That progression, I would add, began as early
as the Calidore sequence.

12. Cheney has looked to Book 6 of *The Faerie Queene,* and its memorable drama of
Calidore's intrusion on the poet's vision, as a centerpiece of Spenser's ongoing conflict
between actuality and ideality (2, 17).

own. Calidore's disruption of Colin Clout's song, which is marked in the copy of *The Faerie Queene* that Keats probably used near the end of his life, was interpreted by Hunt as an allegory of Spenser's movement beyond pastoral poetry to epic composition (Kucich, "'A Lamentable Lay'" 128). That personal drama would have appeared strikingly relevant to the Keats of 1816, who was striving to pass "the realm . . . Of Flora and Old Pan" for a "nobler" poetry about "the agonies, the strife / Of human hearts (*Sleep and Poetry*, lines 101–2, 123–25). Yet there is a more "official" dimension to Calidore's act, entailing his ultimate rejection of pastoral sports for moral duties in the sphere of worldly action. In assuming this responsible position, Calidore actually becomes a foe to poetry, dispersing the graces and silencing their muse. To Keats, who was conditioned to regard Spenser's moral compulsions as "a drawback on the poetry" (Hazlitt, *Complete Works* 11:490), this part of Calidore's allegory must have demanded correction, for it seemed to present a repudiation of poetic experience, a withdrawal from the complexities of mental division for the comforts of philosophy. Those particular comforts held little appeal for Keats, yet he was struggling with his own form of creative withdrawal; and his swerves between Flora's realm and the strife of human hearts would have encouraged him to identify with Calidore's state of self-division. To reeducate Calidore in the ways of the heart thus became a means of correcting Spenser's moralism that could also strengthen Keats's resolve to progress beyond enchantment into psychodrama.

The first step in his revisionary procedure is to make Calidore a young, unproven knight. In *The Faerie Queene* Calidore is "full stout and tall . . . well approved in batteilous affray" (6.1.2). But Keats introduces him as "Young Calidore . . . paddling o'er the lake / His healthful spirit eager and awake" (lines 1–2). This change reinforces the personal dimension of the allegory, with Calidore appearing very much like the young Keats, who had formerly likened himself to Calidore. Keats punctuates this reference to his own burning aspirations with his allusion to the young, untried Redcrosse, who first appears in *The Faerie Queene*, eager for experience, with the famous line, "A Gentle Knight was pricking on the plaine." This conflation of Calidore and the inexperienced Redcrosse is highly strategic, for it suggests that Calidore is less experienced and more misguided than he appears to be in *The Faerie Queene*. Like Spenser, he needs to be reeducated, transformed from a Christian warrior into a poet-hero.

To carry out this new program of learning, Keats pursues his initial link between Calidore and Redcrosse's experience, the latter being the most sustained educational history in *The Faerie Queene*. He rewrites the story of Redcrosse's spiritual growth as a drama of creative conflict in order to refit Calidore as a poet-figure torn between truth and beauty. Like Redcrosse in Errour's den and then unarmed in a bower with Duessa, his Calidore strays into various bowers that falsely allure: first a secluded, verdurous island reminiscent of the setting of the "Imitation of Spenser," "this sweet spot of earth . . . [t]he bowery shore" (line 26); then a fantasy bower of the mind as Calidore sinks into a reverie over several beautiful maidens, "All the soft luxury . . . Fair as some wonder out of fairy land" (lines 92–94). Also like Redcrosse, Calidore is rescued from these lapses by stronger and wiser figures. Arthur saves Redcrosse from Orgoglio's dungeon by sounding the trumpet that unmasks the illusions of evil, and Redcrosse is finally restored to spiritual health in the House of Holinesse by a hermit, Heauenly Contemplation, deeply schooled in the ways of Christian virtue. Keats's Calidore is similarly jolted from his bowery lassitude by a trumpet's call (line 55) and is summoned from his romantic dream by an older knight, "like something from beyond / His present being" (lines 100–101), who takes him into a castle for instruction in chivalric lore. Although Keats thus depends on the Redcrosse narrative in fashioning his creative autobiography, to tell his own story properly he also has to liberate the psychological truths from the moralism of Spenser's allegory. Hence his bowers are not indicators of moral decay or confusion, like Spenser's, but emblems of his own overindulgent sentimentality. Calidore's tutor is not a spiritual doctor, like Redcrosse's Heauenly Contemplation, but a teacher of chivalric or, within the structure of Keats's personal allegory, poetic craft. Calidore finally enters a seat of poetic learning, associated with Apollo's board, not a temple of spiritual regeneration like the House of Holinesse where Redcrosse is restored.[13] He would presumably have emerged, if Keats had continued the poem, looking more like the Colin Clout of poetic intricacy than the warrior Calidore who grapples with the Blatant Beast in Book 6 of *The Faerie Queene*. Colin, in this scenario, might have reversed the scene on Mount Acidale and made Calidore throw down his weapons, take off the armor hidden under his shepherd's weeds, and honor the dancing graces.

But Keats did not finish *Calidore*, and we must ask why he aborts

---

13. Notably, Keats left the House of Holinesse sequence unmarked in his copy of Hughes's Spenser.

this revisionary pattern in midline. One obvious explanation is that his correction of Spenser was not pushing him beyond the sentimental style of the "Imitation." Instead of making that style one component of the allegory's overall tension between fantasy and reality, Keats finds himself overrelying on it, resorting to it exclusively for lengthy passages. Siding with Colin Clout could also mean reverting to an overindulgent pastoralism. It takes some fifty-five lines of the following type of descriptive luxury, for instance, before Calidore can finally wrench himself away from his bower of bliss:

> fir trees grow around,
> Aye dropping their hard fruit upon the ground.
> The little chapel with the cross above
> Upholding wreaths of ivy; the white dove,
> That on the window spreads its feathers light,
> And seems from purple clouds to wing its flight.
> Green tufted islands casting their soft shades
> Across the lake; sequestered leafy glades,
> That through the dimness of their twilight show
> Large dock leaves, spiral foxgloves, or the glow
> Of the wild cat's eyes . . .
> (lines 40–50)

The sheer excess of beauty here belies its purported function of counterpointing the call to action in an allegorical drama of conflicting desires. It signifies an awkward regression, instead, to the enchantment of the "Imitation," and its excessive perpetuation in *Calidore* subverts every attempt to develop the poem's allegorical design. After Calidore is summoned by the trumpet, for instance, the narrative slips back into a distractingly long portrait of "Delicious sounds" and "soft luxury." It is Keats's apparent frustration with these lapses, we may suspect, that prompts him to abort the poem in the midst of its gorgeous excess.

Although Keats's general inexperience in sustaining long poems contributes to this problem, limitations in his revisionary methods are more specifically responsible for his breakdown. Byron and Hunt, we recall, were learning to improve themselves by projecting their flaws onto Spenser and correcting his version of their own excesses. Although Keats begins now to associate his creative growth with his improvement of Spenser, his specific corrections of Spenser's moralism are rather conventional—for the Romantics, that is—and not constructively attuned to his own creative situation. Despite his general identification with the moral conflicts of Spenser's Calidore, his own problem is not so much an inhibiting compulsion toward didacticism, like Hunt's, as an overindulgence in idealistic fantasy. Hence making Spenser less of a moralist and more of a poet, as ideologically sound as it may have been for the Romantics' revisionary Spenserianism, does little to help Keats out of his own particular dilemma. This inexperience in the strategies of Spenserian adaptation also shows up in his stylistic innovations. Instead of extending Spenser's stylistic tensions in a way that would help unencumber himself, as Byron was learning to do in *Childe Harold's Pilgrimage*, he turns to a foreign style completely unrelated to the Spenserian tradition: Hunt's loose, run-on couplets from *The Story of Rimini*. That decision does not allow him to respond to Spenser in any way that might help correct his own flaws. It is also likely, as many commentators have noted, that Hunt's diffuse manner only encouraged his natural proclivity toward stylistic and imaginative excess.

He certainly had much to learn yet about Spenserian revisionism. Yet the experience of *Calidore* was constructive in several important ways. It must have showed him, above all, how relevant Spenser's dichotomy of truth and beauty was to his own situation, and how much he needed help in working out that tension. It also reassured him, despite his difficulties with the poem, of Spenser's ability to render that help with generosity. Even near the breakdown of the narrative, he could imagine Spenser as Sir Gondibert, benevolently reaching out to him. The fact that he had aborted the poem did not seem to cause him great distress, moreover, because Spenserian narratives and the mental experience they dramatized, as everyone agreed, were intrinsically fractured. He could thus give it a prominent place in *Poems* (1817) and confidently introduce it as a fragment by titling it *Calidore: A Fragment*. He would never feel so easy about failing to complete a Miltonic narrative. As important and nonthreatening as a Spenserian poetics must have seemed to him, however, he was also learning that a more complicated revisionary scenario was necessary to make it function well for him. Working out that strategy, he was beginning to think, might be the best step toward making himself "a Calidore," a mature poet.

What Keats learned from *Calidore* is especially significant if we consider the date of its composition. Editors have always dated it February or March of 1816, on the basis of its obvious relation to Hunt's recently published *The Story of Rimini*. Yet in the late summer of 1816, Keats was still exclusively following his early ideal of Spenser's enchantment. In August, he wrote to his brother of the "gay apparel" and the fantastic "portal" of Spenserian "trance[s]" ("To My Brother George," lines 25–30). He told Clarke in September about those floating Spenserian vowels and the maidens "with the breasts of cream." It is difficult to imagine him speaking single-mindedly about this luxury while carrying out a major revaluation of Spenser's interiority in *Calidore* and in his careful markings of the Hughes text. It would make more sense, therefore, to place this re-assessment and the composition of *Calidore* in the autumn of 1816, during the excitement of his first meetings with Hunt. They would have provided the best opportunity for him to learn about Hunt's subtler notions of Spenser. We may observe Hunt's direct influence on the psychodrama of *Calidore* in his careful attention to the manuscript of the poem, which he marked to single out several passages that dramatize conflicts of illusion and reality.[14] That manuscript exchange suggests that the entire poem took shape sometime late in 1816 as a way of cementing the association with Hunt that Keats had been fostering for some time through Spenserian poetry.

If we assume this date of composition, then we may suspect that much of what Keats was learning about Spenserian poetics conditioned his early thoughts about his first epic poem, *Endymion*. During the winter of 1816–17, he became a full-fledged member of London's literary scene, learning firsthand that his age was demanding the epic achievement expected of a second Renaissance and discovering how much creative uneasiness such a stern requisite had imposed. His reading of Wordsworth's argument in Book 4 of *The Excursion* for the relevance of classical mythology, which he recalled when he met the older poet in 1817, encouraged him to consider writing an epic modernization of classical myth. It also suggested the great difficulty of such an endeavor. By December 1816, Keats was planning an epic along these lines and writing about the anxieties it was causing him. Thus in "I stood tip-toe upon a little hill," he surveys a wide range of mythological subjects and confronts the enormous burden of retelling them in an original way. "Was there a Poet born?" he asks, who could perform such a deed. It seemed beyond his own means, at least for the present moment, as he thus leaves the question dangling and abruptly ends the poem: "but now no more, / My wand'ring spirit must no further soar" (lines 241–42). In the

14. Stillinger records Hunt's annotations of the *Calidore* manuscript (*Poems of John Keats* 549).

face of these qualms, however, he continued his search for a relevant mythological theme. The story of Diana and Endymion seemed particularly apposite in its central conflicts between dreams and reality, which he highlighted in the closing sections of "I stood tip-toe"—a poem he sometimes referred to as "Endymion."

Probably not long after he had written *Calidore*, we may thus conclude, Keats was planning an epic adaptation of the Endymion legend that would address his divisions between realistic and imaginative experience. And he was deeply worried about his qualifications for the task. It is possible that his choice of Endymion's tale was guided by his recollection of Spenser's references to it in *Epithalamion*.[15] It is even more likely that his reconsiderations of Spenser in the winter of 1816–17 addressed his specific concerns about the writing of *Endymion*. His recent experience with *Calidore* had immersed him in the very kind of psychological allegory that he was planning for *Endymion*. It had also confirmed the tolerant guidance that Spenser would bestow on the "ambitious heat" of an eager but nervous young poet with epic aspirations. Moreover, it had suggested that a more complex revisionary Spenserianism might be an effective tool for settling his creative indiscipline and fulfilling those aspirations. The priority that these considerations assumed in his mind during the early months of 1817 can be traced in his preparation of *Poems* for publication.

His arrangement of the volume's contents, selected from his writings of the previous three years, encapsulates the progress of his Spenserianism over that span and reveals the central role he envisioned for Spenser in his immediate future. He relegated the "Imitation," for instance, to a group of short lyrics designated as juvenile efforts while placing *Calidore* among his longer, more advanced works. The title page of the volume actually suggests how the Spenserian poetics of *Calidore* could be improved. It features a motto, two lines from Spenser's *Muiopotmos*, that performs the kind of self-corrective revisionism missing from *Calidore:* "What more felicity can fall to creature, / Than to enjoy delight with liberty." These lines describe the joyous flight of Spenser's butterfly, Clarion. Wandering in "riotous excesse" throughout a flower garden, Clarion falls prey to a spider whom he negligently overlooks. Spenser is emphatic

---

15. As an indication of how Keats was interrelating his thoughts about Spenser and the proposed epic, we should note that he underlined a passage in *The Faerie Queene* that could be taken as a gloss for Endymion's final decision: Spenser's reference to Odysseus' refusal of godhead in favor of pursuing his mortal love (1.3.21).

about the moral of this allegory, warning against "wauering wit," "unstaid desire," and "riotous suffisaunce"—all terms that Keats might have deemed appropriate characterizations of his own creative extravagance. Yet the two lines he chose to quote express some ambivalence about Clarion's indulgence. For a moment, Spenser acknowledges the great "delight" of such "felicitie" at the same time that he implies its danger with the ominous word "fall." By giving priority to that ambivalence as a gloss for his own poems, Keats reinterpreted *Muiopotmos* as an allegory of the poet's division between what Spenser calls "desire" and "gouernaunce," between beauty and responsibility.[16] Even more significantly, he brought out Spenser's submerged instinct to engage in the ambiguity of that conflict instead of shying away from it into the righteousness of what Gleckner calls "ideological desiderata" (*Blake and Spenser* 269). For Keats to redeem Spenser's duality in this manner was to correct his own instinct to retreat, even though he was more likely to withdraw into enchantment than morality, and to strengthen his own engagement with the mind's divisions. We may read the motto to *Poems*, therefore, as less a preparation for the works in that volume than a promise of a new form of self-corrective revisionism. And smiling on the promise of that title page is the benevolent portrait associated with Spenser, who came to Keats like "a clear sun-rise" and made his heart "with pleasure dance" as he strode forth into the forbidding landscape of epic poetry.

IV

Since the first appearance of *Endymion* in 1818, critics have disputed the meaning and coherence of its allegory. Many, including most of its first reviewers, have even doubted the presence of any allegorical structure in the poem.[17] Most readers would now support Sperry's argument for a controlling allegory about the mind's division between ideal and real experience. But little effort has been made to link that allegory to Spenser in any substantial way. Major questions still persist, moreover, about its specific mental dynamics, its relation to Keats's own psychological history, and the clarity of his effort to

16. Bloom has noted a similar focus on creative division in Shelley's reading of *Muiopotmos* (*Shelley's Mythmaking* 149–59).

17. Sperry provides a useful summary of critical attitudes toward the question of allegory in *Endymion* (*Keats the Poet* 90–95).

dramatize and resolve its conflicts. Without claiming that *Endymion* is an exclusively Spenserian poem—for Keats was already demonstrating the assimilative dexterity that prevents us from easily categorizing any of his major works—I wish to suggest that our recognition of its Spenserian origins can help answer these questions. Keats may have been testing his creative powers generally in *Endymion*, leaping headlong into the sea, but in some important particulars he was building on the experience of *Calidore* as a way of carrying out that "test of Invention." What he continued to learn about Spenserian revisionism determined many of the strengths and weaknesses of *Endymion*.

That specific education directed much of his creative growth in the important months that followed *Calidore*. His deepening impression of Spenser's genial instruction was one of the strongest conditioning factors in his evolving plans for *Endymion*. As he began to prepare for the task ahead, his instinctive nervousness about poetic tradition escalated dramatically. He was immersing himself in England's Renaissance literature, particularly the works of Shakespeare and Milton, and developing his first informed appreciation of their astonishing power. He read and quoted Shakespeare throughout the spring of 1817 with a breathless admiration that moved him to proclaim, sounding very much like Dryden on Milton, "Shakespeare is enough for us—" (*LJK* 1:143). Several months later he began his mature assessment of Milton, in which *Paradise Lost* struck him "every day" as more of a "wonder" (*LJK* 2:139, 146). This new depth of admiration could prove stirring at times: he fancied Shakespeare his "presider" and felt his heart "distend with Pride" at the prospect of soaring in Milton's company (*LJK* 1:142; 2:146). But the leading habit of mind it provoked, at least throughout 1817, was the impulse to contrast his own paltry achievements with such an awesome tradition. Thus he first conceived of *Endymion* as a "test of Invention" specifically measured against the standards of the old poets. Its theme, he admitted just before commencing work, was less significant—"one bare circumstance"—than its tenuous claim to a place among the monumental poems of England's literary tradition. "Did our great Poets ever write short Pieces?" he asked in explaining his chief motives for writing an epic (*LJK* 1:170). Given the enormous respect he was acquiring for those "great Poets," we might expect him, with no theme and little experience in anything but short lyrics, verse epistles, and fragmentary narratives, to have been daunted by the titanic manner in which he was presenting the task to himself.

It should come as no surprise, then, to find him delivering a string of comments about his own age's mediocrity before the grandeur of the past. His remarks tended to rephrase the claims of a steady decline from the Renaissance—a dwindling into the present's last act—that were dominating the current debate about literary tradition. The "Invention" of "our great Poets," he feared as he began his own epic "test" against that high measure, seemed "of late Years" to have been lost (*LJK* 1:170). Near the close of *Endymion,* he still felt that the muse of his native land had won its "full accomplishment" in the Renaissance: "The thing is done" (IV, 17–18). Or, put another way at the midpoint of his composition, "the count / Of mighty Poets is made up; the scroll / Is folded by the Muses" (II, 723–25). It was this body of apprehensions, shadowing every step of his epic trial, that informed his more famous comparison of modern and old poets to petty "Elector[s] of Hanover" versus "Emperors of vast Provinces" (*LJK* 1:224). That distinction, made after the completion of *Endymion,* could provoke a spirited desire to greet the genius of Renaissance bards: "Let us have the old Poets" (*LJK* 1:225). But it also located *Endymion* among the petty states, a hard judgment that troubled him throughout his epic risk.

Keats voiced these worries with a regularity that neared obsession. The "Cliff of Poesy Towers above me," he confided shortly after beginning *Endymion.* "[T]ruth is I have been in such a state of Mind as to read over my Lines and hate them" (*LJK* 1:141). The "high Idea I have of poetical fame," he added about the same time, "makes me think I see it towering to [*sic*] high above me" (*LJK* 1:169). Only the "mighty ones" of the past, he stopped to admit in one of the early sections of *Endymion,* could "tell" the tale in a satisfactory way (II, 249–54). Toward the end of *Endymion,* this very thought left him overwhelmed with "despondency," too paralyzed even to beseech the "Great Muse" of his native land for assistance: "But then I thought on poets gone, / And could not pray:—nor could I now—so on / I move to the end in lowliness of heart" (IV, 27–29). He did move on to the end, but his "lowliness of heart" made him wonder, at least temporarily, about ever trying another "test" against such an impossible standard. What he said about Shakespeare as he completed *Endymion* could have been applied, with all of its sobering tautological absoluteness, to all of the "mighty ones" put together: "He has left nothing to say about nothing or any thing" (*LJK* 1:189).

Spenser, however, had left something to say and wanted others to say it. That was a tremendous consolation to Keats as he agonized over the prospect of adding anything to the "full accomplishment" of the past. Just before starting *Endymion,* he was complaining about his nervousness, being "all in a Tremble," and the "depressions," "irregularities," "turmoil and anxiety" that were tormenting him (*LJK* 1:132–33, 141–42). He admitted the provocation of all this unrest to Hunt: "[A]t last the Idea [of becoming a poet] has grown so monstrously beyond my seeming Power of attainment that the other day I nearly consented with myself to drop into a Phaeton" (*LJK* 1:139). He tried to make light of this "narvus" despondency, but there was no gainsaying the feverish anxiety of what he called "this continual burning of thought." It was when it became particularly acute—"this Morning . . . I am nearly as bad again"—that he "opened Spencer" (*LJK* 1:133).

What he found, and probably not by accident, was an encouraging passage in *The Faerie Queene* on poetic ambition (1.5.1). He underlined it in the Hughes text and quoted it in a letter to Reynolds:

> "The noble Heart that harbors vertuous thought,
> And is with Child of glorious great intent,
> Can never rest, until it forth have brought
> Th' eternal Brood of Glory Excellent—"
> (*LJK* 1:134)

Receiving that assurance, which must have reminded him of the way Spenser helped him in *Calidore,* eased his worries for the moment. He immediately felt an onrush of confidence and declared, "I shall forthwith begin my Endymion" (*LJK* 1:134). About the same time, as Gleckner has argued ("Keats's 'How Many Bards'" 18), he was remembering the "pleasing" Spenserian influence from "How many bards" to reassure himself about his own artistic potentials, which he affirmed with the images of creative amplitude in "On the Sea." A short time later, when a new bout of "anxiety" and "lowness of Spirits" interrupted his work, he felt comforted again by Spenser's kindness, or more specifically by the Shenstonian playfulness of spirit that had become associated with Spenser's art. Writing to his publishers for a cash advance, Keats conceived of "a nice little Alegorical [*sic*] Poem called 'the Dun' Where we would have the Castle of Carelessness—the Draw Bridge of Credit—Sir Novelty Fashion'[s] expedition against the City of Taylors—&c &c." This digression on the sportiveness of Spenserian allegorizing helped rejuvenate him. For he began to feel "set . . . forward," despite his recent troubles (*LJK* 1:146).

He thanked Spenser just as he had in *Calidore,* only now with greater sophistication, by working his gratitude into the allegory of

Endymion. At a crucial turning point in Book 3, he conflated Endymion's self-doubts with his own creative anxieties and brought a Spenser-like figure in for help. Traveling under the sea, Endymion feels disheartened by the wreckage of sunken ships and wishes to abandon his quest. His despair blends into Keats's own fears of poetic unfitness when he glances upon "mouldering scrolls," reminiscent of the muses' folded scroll that had darkened Keats's hopes. They are, like those early productions of England's giant sons of genius, "Writ in the tongue of heaven, by those souls / Who first were on the earth" (III, 129–31). Endymion then asks for "kind influence" from the heavens, recalling Keats's own plea in the book's invocation for "the gentlier-mightiest" influence of the gods (III, 43), a neologism strikingly applicable to Keats's idea of Spenser's unique role as a benefactor among the mighty dead. At this critical juncture Endymion meets Glaucus, a mythological character featured in Spenser's own underwater episode at the House of Proteus (*FQ*, 4.11.13), who becomes the instrument to set the young wanderer forward. His appearance bears an uncanny resemblance to the portrait of Spenser in the "Induction" to *Calidore*, and the manner of his encounter with Endymion, like the happy meeting between Keats and Spenser/Gondibert, recalls the benevolent, enabling way that Spenser came to Keats throughout the Calidore sequence (III, 187–314).

Glaucus is a "hoary," majestic, "care-worn" sage, resembling both the popular Romantic image of a nobly suffering Spenser and Keats's particular depiction of Spenser's "noble countenance" in the "Induction" to *Calidore*. Just as Spenser is "startled unaware" by Keats's aspiration in the "Induction," Glaucus is roused suddenly "as from a trance" by Endymion's intrusion. Both Glaucus and Spenser respond to their young applicants with a generosity rendered in quite similar terms. Spenser's brows are "arched, open, kind." Glaucus's "snow-white brows / Went arching up" as he looks upon Endymion with "kind eyes." Spenser's whole aura seems to smile on Keats, while Glaucus lets a smile play round his lips upon sight of Endymion. Such a welcome greeting encourages Keats to respond "not so fearfully," just as it urges Endymion to "[b]e not afraid." It also makes Keats's heart "with pleasure dance" and moves Endymion's heart to play "dancingly." A restorative bond develops between Glaucus and Endymion, like the one between Keats and Spenser, with one key exception. Endymion returns the kindness, after first dreading Glaucus's aged look, by reviving him from oblivion. This act, if we continue the parallel with the Keats/Spenser dynamic, can be read as Keats's own rehabilitation of Spenser in the revisionism of *Endymion*. By saving Glaucus, Endymion corrects his own antihuman idealism and thus prepares himself for the completion of his quest in his union with the Indian maiden. Redeeming a benevolent guide, therefore, inspires his own maturation from bowers of bliss to the complex regions of the human heart, which is precisely the scenario Keats was trying to work out in his revision of Spenser. His confidence about the success of that enterprise seems hinted by his changing Glaucus from a father-figure, in an early draft, to the "friend" and "brother" of the poem's final version. Going "forward . . . side by side," Glaucus and Endymion, Spenser and Keats, are not Oedipal competitors but loving colleagues—"twin brothers," Keats has Endymion exclaim (III, 713)—engaged in a mutual process of bettering themselves. We need only recall Wordsworth's addressing Spenser as "Brother, Englishman, and Friend" to remember how much that concept of Spenser's role in poetic transmission could mean to the Romantics.

Everything Keats was learning about the fitness of such a "Friend" to lead him into epic poetry was being confirmed by his immediate peers. Reynolds was at work on the Spenserian autobiography of creative growth, *The Romance of Youth,* which Keats often associated with his own project. He asked Reynolds about the progress of that poem in the very letter that announced his own Spenserian ambitions for *Endymion*. At the same time, he was very much concerned with Shelley's Spenserian epic, *The Revolt of Islam.* The two young poets toyed with rivalry, well aware that each was engaged in epic poems at least somewhat similar in nature and format. Both were also familiar with the breakthrough Spenserian innovations of *Childe Harold's Pilgrimage,* canto 3, and they probably knew that Byron was working on the fourth, most complex canto of what was at once the age's most popular poem and its greatest Spenserian work yet. Nearly all poets of importance, it must have seemed, were walking "side by side" with Spenser, working out their own poetics through their conversation with him. To join that procession, the message was made clear in the summer of 1817, was one of the best ways to unfold and augment the "scroll" of "mighty poets."[18]

The extent to which Keats consciously took such a step in *Endymion* may be judged by his appropriation of the most progressive

18. Leon Waldoff has recently labeled Spenser "the presiding spirit" of *Endymion,* though he does not investigate the kind of mental relationships between the two poets that I am about to discuss (*Keats and the Silent Work of Imagination* 43).

allegorical and narrative patterns of current Spenserian poetics. He does not write in nine-line stanzas, for reasons I will take up later, but he frames the general contours of his psychodrama after the most advanced branch of Romantic Spenserianism. He follows the principal narrative strategy of Beattie and Byron, for example, grounding the action of his poem in the travels and education of a young pilgrim. That quest, also like Beattie's and Byron's, bears an obvious relation to the author's own mental history. Endymion is conscious of his "boy-hood" (I, 881) and eager to mature, the over-riding theme of Keats's early career and the same autobiographical record that Beattie, Byron, Shelley, and Reynolds chart in their Spenserian poems. While Endymion is not so obviously a minstrel as Beattie's hero, he is a visionary poet-figure like Byron's Harold, Shelley's Laon, and Reynolds's "youngster boy" (*The Romance of Youth*, line 1). His pilgrimage, then, is a poet's quest, and it brings him into the same fundamental conflict between truth and beauty that so deeply engaged Keats, along with those other Spenserian heroes and their creators.[19] In Endymion's pursuit of the visionary goddess who perpetually dissolves into the cold light of reality, we can thus trace the major dialectic of Romantic Spenserianism. Endymion's inability to resolve that struggle also follows the experience of his immediate predecessors. Like Edwin, Endymion is a "wanderer" (II, 434) with no fixed direction for his steps or his thoughts. And, more like Harold, his "way" is often "lost" (II, 656). His journey is, in a phrase that Byron might have leapt upon as a motto for his own work, a "torture-pilgrimage" (III, 524). In handling the allegory of that torturous voyage, moreover, Keats pursues the kind of advanced, self-purifying revisionism that he was learning from Byron and which we

19. The allegorical strategies of Tighe's Spenserian epic, *Psyche*, also help Keats shape his own pilgrimage of the mind. Like Endymion, Tighe's Psyche travels through fantastic landscapes of the imagination in a series of strange voyages clearly meant to express mental growth allegorically. On another level, Endymion's visionary flights recall the dream-vision motif of one important strand of eighteenth-century Spenserian imitation. Like the protagonists of Denton's *House of Superstition*, Jones's *Palace of Fortune*, Darwin's *Temple of Nature*, and Hunt's *Palace of Pleasure*, Endymion is carried to strange locations where he gains new perspectives on human relations. Frequently, he is trained by visionary goddesses, Venus and Cynthia, reminiscent of similar instructresses in the eighteenth-century tradition of Spenserian dream visions. *Endymion*, of course, dispenses with the conventional didacticism of the earlier works, but its narrative and allegorical frameworks still depend structurally on their example. Keats was familiar with Darwin's and Hunt's poetry and, considering the popularity of Spenserian dream visions in the nineteenth century, he probably knew other examples of the form.

have already seen him work into the Glaucus episode. He may aspire
to many different goals in the writing of *Endymion*. But clearly one of
his chief objects is to extend the Spenserian allegory of *Calidore* in
such a way as to explore and deepen the complexity of his own poetic consciousness.[20]

That process centers in Keats's refinement of the central bower
motif in *Calidore*, an improvement through which he comes closer to
Spenser's allegorical strategies while also transforming them more
radically. Still trying to exorcise the sentimental indulgences of his
youth, he secularizes Spenser's bower allegory once again to clarify
the mistake of locking one's mind in enchantment. He is more emphatic about that point, however, integrating Spenser's allegory so as
to present a more graphic illustration of the error of such a disengagement from reality. Where the Bower of Bliss allegory exposes
the horror of vice and its distorting effects on forsaken characters
like Grille, Keats details the disastrous outcome of idealistic extremism and stresses the need to embrace real experience. *Endymion's*

---

20. Keats's specific handling of Phoebe and the dream sequences in his new myth
supplies further evidence of his conscious decision to base much of his poem upon
Spenserian foundations. His own mythmaking relies heavily on Spenserian sources, as
Allott has noted, but it looks back, of course, to a variety of other models: Tooke's
Pantheon, Lempriere's *Classical Dictionary*, Spence's *Polymetis*, Ovid's *Metamorphosis*, and
Drayton's *The Man in the Moone*, among others. However, his particular renderings of
Phoebe and her association with visionary dreams, key points in the drama of his
narrative, depend primarily on Spenser's example in the *Epithalamion*. The first
Spenserian piece he had ever read, and one that lived brightly in his imagination
throughout his life, the *Epithalamion* was often in his thoughts during the composition
of *Endymion*. He specifically quoted its lines on the sunset—"Hast thee O fayrest
Planet to thy home / Within the Westerne fome" (282–83)—to Reynolds's sisters (*LJK*
1:158). Its descriptions of Phoebe's beauty and lovers' "deluding dreames" (line 338)
struck him as particularly fitting for some of the more memorable, visionary sequences in his own poem. His first description of Phoebe, for instance, recalls both
the lines quoted above and Spenser's conflation of Phoebe and his own blushing
bride. Spenser details the "yellow locks lyke golden wyre," the "perle" ornaments, and
the "abashed . . . blush" that make his bride seem like "[s]ome angell . . . Lyke Phoebe
. . . Clad all in white" (lines 148–66). Remembering the lines on Apollo's "Westerne
fome," Keats compares Phoebe's hair to the "western sun" and then catalogues her
"golden hair," her "pearl round ears," and "Blush-tinted cheeks" (I, 609–19). During
another visionary sequence later in the poem, he again depicts her "golden hair" and
repeats Spenser's plea for Phoebe to withold her envy of his human lover (lines 372–
82). Keats's Endymion similarly "'gan crave / Forgiveness" (IV, 451–52) from his
goddess for loving a mortal woman. In his great moment of revelation, when he
regrets his loving "a nothing," a false dream that made him the dupe of "phantoms"
(IV, 629–38), Endymion rephrases Spenser's outcry against "deluding dreames,"
"charmes," "evil sprights," and "things that be not" (lines 338–44).

first vision of Diana takes place in a gorgeous bower, which turns into a nightmarish landscape when reality intrudes upon it (I, 682–86). His second vision also occurs in a "deep hollow," and its failure to conform with the reality he awakes to similarly brings a heavy "sorrow" that "[c]lings cruelly" to his mind (I, 906–17). His third vision, experienced in a secluded grotto, results in the same "empty folly" and "chain of grief" (I, 960–81). This pattern of imaginative breakdowns in delusive bowers recurs throughout *Endymion,* most notably in the Glaucus episode of Book 3. Like the enchanted knight of Acrasia's bower, Glaucus succumbs to the "fierce temptation" of a blissful dream experience in Circe's "twilight bower."[21] When he awakens to Circe's true deformity, his "specious heaven" becomes a "real hell" (III, 417–76). The lethal folly of poetic enchantment, replacing the unmasked vulgarity of evil in Spenser's deceptive gardens, thus becomes a major new focus in Keats's revisionism.

His greater familiarity with Spenser's allegorical strategies also enables him to deepen that focus by appropriating the subtle danger signs that punctuate Spenserian bowers. Nearly every delight in the Bower of Bliss, as even the most aesthetically inclined Romantic followers of Spenser well knew, contains some insidious betrayal of its artifice. The gorgeously sculptured branches over one of Acrasia's gates, for instance, are constricted like serpents in "wanton" and "intricate" or deceptive "wreathings" (1.12.53). The fountain of "richest substaunce" is "over-wrought" with a "wanton" excess of "imageree" (1.12.60). The "Infinit streames" welling out of the fountain are shown to "fall," always an ominous word in a garden of temptation (1.12.62). Keats had not bothered with such details in *Calidore,* whose verdurous retreats indicate no traces of a lurking serpent. He fills the bowers of *Endymion,* however, with the kind of intricate details that betray the falseness of Acrasia's pleasure spot. Like the knight who is beguiled by Acrasia, for instance, Endymion falls into a "trance" with Diana, his senses "dazzled" and his eyes "veil[ed]" (I, 585–604). The "deep hollow" in which his second vision occurs is shadowed by "darkening boughs" and "ragged brows," which, like the artfully sculpted branches in the Bower of Bliss, threaten to enclose and smother (I, 863–64). Endymion's third bower reminds him of Echo's cave, a disturbing association with that deity, Narcissus, who is hopelessly trammeled in an impossible love not unlike Endymion's. All of these passages duplicate the strategy if not always the

---

21. Waldoff claims that Keats "modeled Circe on Spenser's Acrasia" (*Keats and the Silent Work of Imagination* 56).

specific details of Spenser's bower allegories, but they do so to punctuate Keats's basic revision of the Spenserian paradigm. The insidious enchantments of *Endymion* represent the seductions of artistic
imagination, not libidinous desire.

Keats emphasizes that difference in a yet more specific transformation of one episode in *The Faerie Queene,* the tale of Fradubio. He
knew this story well, having previously marked in his copy of
Hughes's Spenser the specific passage where Fradubio, enthralled
with Duessa's beauty, catches her in a secluded place revealing her
true deformity:

> I chaunst to see her in her proper Hew,
> Bathing her self in Origane and Thyme:
> A filthy foul old Woman I did view,
> That ever to have touch'd her, I did dearly rew.
> (1.2.40)

Glaucus is betrayed by Circe's "specious heaven" until, like Fradubio
with Duessa, he inadvertently glimpses her "deformities" through "a
thorny brake" (III, 493–503). Where Fradubio's indiscretion provokes the enmity of Duessa, Glaucus's error brings down the wrath
of Circe. But in Glaucus's case, the error is psychological, not moral,
arising from his excessive idealism rather than the blindness to vice
that ensnares Fradubio. It is this kind of detailed "significant allusion" to Spenser's allegorical paradigms that enables Keats to explore the dangerous excesses of his own psyche as thoroughly as he
does in *Endymion.*

But transforming Spenser's moralism in this way only repeats with
greater sophistication the *Calidore* experience of *recognizing* liabilities.
To *cast them out,* Keats goes one step further into the kind of advanced revisionism that makes redeeming Spenser, as Endymion res-
cues Glaucus, an integral part of saving onself. That self-purification
involves his new sympathy for Spenser's double vision and his growing association of Spenser's penchant for moral absolutes with his
own instinct to withdraw into the unconditional comforts of enchantment. Keats realizes now that to cleanse Spenser of his need for certainty, and thus redeem his core of dualism, is to begin a related
effort to overcome his own imaginative regressiveness and
strengthen the duality of vision in himself. *Endymion* is begun with
that particular strategy in mind.

In his opening description of pastoral Latmos, for instance, Keats associates poetic enchantment with old religious verities. That coupling manifests the equation he now draws between Spenser's theological liabilities and his own creative ones, both of which he presents as antiquated creeds incompatible with a world of contradiction and uncertain meaning. Latmos is a favored land of "o'er-hanging boughs," rural dance, and song of "ebon-tipped flutes," all of which calls to mind Keats's bowery world of enchantment. It is also a place of comforting but obsolescent moral and religious certitudes—"old piety," "Time's sweet first-fruits," "minstrel memories of times gone by"— which belong to "buried days" and are "Not of these days" (I, 130, 321, 435; II, 7, 830). Those outworn values refer directly, of course, to the pagan beliefs of Classical Greece. But with Keats so concerned about literary tradition in *Endymion*, and so specifically bent on modernizing Spenser's values, his preoccupation with "times gone by" would also seem deeply implicated with the obsolescence of Spenser's "old piety." Neither that piety nor the enchantment of Latmos, however, can resolve the "lurking trouble" of self-division that Endymion experiences. Where Spenser's faith makes him drop the ambiguity of his bower episodes, and Keats's own early aestheticism makes him retreat from the tension between truth and beauty, Endymion finds it impossible to sort out his bower experiences. He remains perpetually divided between the beauty of his visions and their potential falseness. Even in the end, when he continues to yearn for an ideal solitude—"A hermit young, I'll live in mossy cave" (IV, 860)—he simultaneously gives up his visionary goddess and vows "no more of dreaming" (IV, 669). By thus replacing Spenser's old certitudes with a situation of duality, Keats also liberates himself from his own naive enchantment to engage in that intersection of actuality and transcendence.

In carrying out this strategy, Keats corrects the moralism of several specific Spenserian episodes and gradually comes to recognize, much to his own benefit, the duality of vision locked within them. His revisions consistently reverse Spenser's characteristic progression from human to divine orders, deepening in the process his own sympathy for the complexities of human experience. This pattern is most evident in one of the more obviously Spenserian sequences of *Endymion*, Endymion's subterranean retracing of Guyon's adventures in Mammon's cave. Endymion's education in the contradictions and the values of the flesh is opposite to Guyon's ascent toward the divine. The imagery that punctuates his training correspondingly subverts the allegorical design of the imagery in Guyon's adventure.

Guyon is tempted from his spiritual pursuit of temperance by material wealth and carnal pleasure, whose venal implications are betrayed in the cave's overwrought beauty:

> That houses forme within was rude and strong,
> Like an huge cave, hewne out of rocky clift,
> From whose rough vaut the ragged breaches hong,
> Embost with massy gold of glorious gift,
> And with rich metall loaded every rift,
> That heavy ruine they did seeme to threat
>   (2.7.28)

Endymion's underground voyage takes him through similar caverns lined with "veins of gold" that form "eternal eventides of gems." But where Spenser uses such imagery to expose the world's glittering insubstantiality, Keats links it positively with Endymion's descent into the confusing but fecund world of experience. Both the strange contradictions of the human heart and Endymion's personal rehabilitation in learning to embrace them are visualized in the resplendent elements he views at each new bend in his education. After learning the value of selfless love from Venus and Adonis, for instance, he feels "assured / Of happy times" and beholds this strange, attractive scene:

> So, with unusual gladness, on he hies
> Through caves, and palaces of mottled ore,
> Gold dome, and crystal wall and turquois floor,
> Black polish'd porticos of awful shade . . .
>   (II, 593–96)

A similar vision of elemental brilliance—"Large honey-combs of green . . . all bestrown / With golden moss" (II, 667–71)—accompanies his commitment to "earthward" sympathies under Cybele's direction. Rescuing Mammon in this way, which Keats would recall several years later in an important letter to Shelley, directly rebuts Spenser's championship of transcendent verities and, by association, Keats's own naive enthusiasm for poetic enchantment. It thereby confirms his new determination to plunge into the labyrinth of the human heart. In celebrating Mammon's power as a genius of human complexity, it also suggests Spenser's latent aptitude for double vision and his ability, if purged from his limitations, to guide Keats in that descent.

Keats's impression of Spenser's aptitude for this special task becomes clarified as he redeems the "earthward" sympathies in Spenser's mutability myth. He certainly means Endymion's experience of change in the bower of Venus and Adonis to recall the treatment of mutability in Spenser's Garden of Adonis (*FQ*, 3.6.29–52). Allott (178–79) and Dickstein (103–5) have noted his obvious attempt to re-create the details of the Spenserian scene.[22] The relation he establishes between the two bowers, however, is finally designed to punctuate the differences in their central allegories of mutability while revealing the deep truths shrouded within Spenser's philosophy. Where Spenser's episode looks upward to the divine order that enfolds and transcends all mortal beauty, Keats's looks downward on the virtues of transitory human love. The physical delights of Spenser's bower, much as they are to be honored, are all passing, part of an eternal process of mutability characterized by Adonis's cyclical existence—"All be he subiect to mortalitie. / Yet is eterne in mutabilitie" (3.6.47). This stressing of the eternal quality of sublunary change directs attention to the permanence of the divine order, to the directives for the garden's operation, which are "spoken by th'Almightie lord" (3.6.34). Keats's allegory, in contrast, fixes attention on the sensuous union between Venus and Adonis as a supreme ideal in itself. Adonis's "Apollonian" beauty and Venus's "diverse passion," registered in her panting bosom and dilating nostrils, recommend a materialism inimical to the eternal priorities of Spenser's myth. And Venus's sorrowful devotion to the injured Adonis, forming the longest part of Keats's sequence, promotes the very kind of love for human frailty that Spenser would transcend. All this teaches Endymion to immerse himself in mutable form at the expense of substance—the opposite of Spenser's message—and he speeds on his journey into the human heart with Venus's blessing. Spenser's Mutabilitie, in a scenario not unlike her transmogrifying passage into canto 4 of *Childe Harold's Pilgrimage,* thus becomes redeemed as the heroine and the muse of Keats's epic. It is no doubt with that specific transformation in mind that Keats takes the procession of

22. Like Spenser's garden, which is protected by "the thickest couert . . . of shadie boughes" (3.6.43–44), Keats's retreat is "embowered high" by a wall of myrtle trees (II, 389). Its sweet incense similarly recalls the "dainty odours, & most sweet delight" of Spenser's scene (3.6.43). Its beauty is most graphically rendered in a catalogue of flowers—ivy, woodbine, convolvulus, clematis (II, 409–18)—much like the list of flowers that emphasizes the beauty of Spenser's garden, "yuie," "Eglantine," "Caprisole" (3.6.44). These flowers also make up the bed of Adonis as they do in Spenser's garden.

Neptune's entourage at Proteus's underwater palace (4.11.8–53), one of Spenser's primary sites of flux and "shifting appearances" (Williams 117), as a general model for his own climactic narration of Neptune's wedding procession at the end of Endymion's submarine voyage.[23]

A much more specific revision of one moment in the Bower of Bliss episode suggests how much it meant for Keats's creative future to unlock Spenser's vision in this way. In his travels Endymion meets a provocative fountain nymph who, revealing her breasts while she begins to "plait and twist / Her ringlets round her fingers" (II, 102–3), recalls the wanton nymphs who bathe in Acrasia's fountain and nearly seduce Guyon away from his spiritual mission. Hunt utterly sympathized with Guyon's deviation, calling it "the loveliest thing of the kind . . . that ever was painted" (*Imagination and Fancy* 90), and felt that Spenser was actually divided between making his moral and dallying with his gorgeous creations. Keats finds something here even more compelling than Spenserian duality when he turns Spenser's temptresses into a congenial spirit who "gladden[s]" Endymion's way by teaching him about the "gentle bosom" of love (II, 121, 127). That change not only emphasizes the drama of the heart's "bosom" that Spenser ultimately shadows in a veil of moralism, it also redeems the poignant experience of mingled joy and sorrow at the core of that drama.

We have seen how Hunt's interest in the pathos of Spenser's "chiaroscuro" made a deep impression on Keats. What Hunt later characterized as the interpenetration of the "grave" and "gay" in Spenserian duality (*The Shewe of Faire Seeming*, line 366), became more specifically important to Keats as he carried out his psychodrama of the heart's "gentle bosom" in *Endymion*. He had already noted in his Hughes text many expressions of that form of pathos among the characters of *The Faerie Queene*: Arthur's impression of the "World's Delight" intermixed with a "Sea of Sorrows" (1.7.39); Una torn by love and sorrow for the missing Redcrosse, her "Wound" fed with "fresh renewed Bale" (1.7.28); Odysseus pining for love of Penelope in his "long wandering" trials (1.3.21). The poignance of this interplay between what Spenser himself calls "Sweet" and "Sour" (1.3.30)—another phrasing of opposites underlined in the Hughes text—struck Keats as one of the most profound revelations of Spenserian interiority. To detach it from Spenser's moralism and

---

23. The episode at Proteus's house is marked extensively in the last copy of *The Faerie Queene* that Keats may have used, which I discuss in chapter 4.

escalate its prominence in his own work became a regular feature of his revisionism in *Endymion*.

Endymion's first division between reality and dreams, for instance, makes him think of pleasure's quick transformation into pain, which "[c]lings cruelly to us" (I, 906–7). The "sweet grief" (I, 939) he hears in a murmuring brook corresponds with his own experience of the heart's division. Diana sympathizes with that dichotomy, lamenting over her inability to unite Endymion's mortality with her own divine sphere: "woe! woe! Is grief contain'd / In the very deeps of pleasure, my sole life?" (II, 823–24). Glaucus similarly finds his travel between mortal and divine realms a "task of joy and grief" (III, 702). These recurring contrasts of joy and grief become so important to the allegory of Endymion's mental pilgrimage that they eventually receive a hymn of their own, the "Ode to Sorrow." Sung by the Indian maid, herself an embodiment of reality's conflict with the ideal, the ode is a sustained witness to sorrow's close neighborhood with "Heart's lightness" (IV, 146–290). Like the questers of *The Faerie Queene*, whom Williams finds "caught in the world's ambiguities" (117), the main characters of *Endymion* all feel that interplay along their pulses and register in their "pallid" and "wan" looks of "woe" the emblems or "Tydings" of the self-divided heart (III, 79–80, 104–7; IV, 764–65). But where Spenser often subordinates those "Tydings" to philosophical considerations in the end—the pathos of Una's betrothal feast gives way to a sustained contemplation of the heavenly kingdom— Keats makes them the focal point of his allegory. Redeeming Spenser's gift for thinking into the human heart thus helps Keats toward the most poignant truths of the heart's "fierce dispute" with itself. To burn through those truths, uncovering the presence of Melancholy in the very temple of Delight, would become one of the driving energies of his mature poetry.

Much as the conversation with Spenser in *Endymion* thus assists Keats, it does not preclude the glaring stylistic and narrative lapses that most readers of the work quickly recognize. We may attribute much of its awkwardness to problems in Keats's Spenserianism. He suffers, first of all, from the main difficulty faced by all Spenserian poets up to Byron, that of sustaining the richness of Spenser's style and the complexity of his psychodrama throughout a long poem. Critics of *Endymion* have always complained of the diffuseness of its allegory, attributing it to Keats's poetic immaturity. But the problem has as much to do with the difficulty of laboring extensively in Spenserian form, which had undone many a poet more experienced than Keats. This hardship also explains the stylistic infelicities and excesses of *Endymion*; if Keats felt apprehensive about using Spenser's stanza in *Calidore*, he is certainly put off by its demands when he begins contemplating the projected four thousand lines of *Endymion*. Hunt's run-on couplets once again prove an easier form to manage. But using them encourages the stylistic laxness for which Hunt has often been criticized and distances the poem—with the exception of a few colorful archaisms like "raft," "fray," "raught," "disparted," "scuds"—from Spenser's opulence and complexity of style. If *Endymion* teaches Keats how much Spenser could contribute to a modern poetics, it also confirms what Wordsworth was saying about the burden of wielding Spenserianism through a long poem.

There was another problem with following Spenser in a long poem, which was beginning to change Keats's whole way of thinking about Spenserian narrative and epic poetry generally. One of the great thrusts of Romantic epic was to replace the Christian ethos of Renaissance precursor poems with a modern ontology. Various re-formulations of Milton's system were attempted: Wordsworth's song of himself in *The Prelude*, Blake's purgatory experience of prophetic election in *Milton*, Keats's own theory of cultural progress in *Hyperion*. With Spenser, as we have seen, this endeavor meant dismantling his central vision of those divine "pillours of Eternity" upon which all experience rests. But instead of replacing that vision with another, more progressive system, the Romantics chose instead to extend or intensify his indeterminate hoverings between alternate modes of vision. Yet it is the divine ground in *The Faerie Queene*, as most of his twentieth-century commentators agree, that ultimately sustains and gives meaning to the ongoing dualities of every quest in the poem. "Life is full of 'double senses,'" Williams summarizes, "by which the purpose of fate is worked out" (81). By replacing that "purpose" with indeterminacy, the Romantics took away one of the principal foundations for the epic scale of Spenser's pilgrimages. The "official" Spenser could approach "hints" of a complete epic vision, as MacCaffrey would say (394), but the redeemed Spenser of duality could yield only fragments of insight. Keats must sense this problem by the end of *Endymion* when he tries awkwardly to conflate the real and visionary maidens, closing his epic with an "official" ethos instead of a persisting Spenserian dualism. But such an ending, of course, clashes with the poem's dichotomous vision and finally rings false. To shape a revisionary Spenserian poetics of "double senses," Keats was thus learning, might mean to turn one's back on epic poetry, or to reconceive the whole Romantic enterprise of building epic monuments.

Amid all these new questions, one old personal problem added to Keats's complications. However much he may open himself in *Endymion* to the interplay of real and ideal experience, he still remains ✓ overattached to the kind of Spenserian enchantment that had disrupted *Calidore*. Notwithstanding his efforts to break free of that dependence, the old method was comfortably familiar and its luxurious descriptions help fill out large sections of the narrative; but those excesses also cloud the poem's psychodrama in a welter of excrescent detail. The allegory of Endymion thus becomes as much a drama of Keats's own creative regression as a story of his artistic maturation.[24] His description of the bower in which Endymion recounts his dream visions, for instance, loses its allegorical implications of misplaced ideals when it degenerates into the reductive adornments of *Calidore*. Allott notes the regressive imagery and phrasing in this sequence (138):

> they came to where these streamlets fall,
> With mingled bubblings and a gentle rush,
> Into a river, clear, brimful, and flush,
> With crystal mocking of the trees and sky.
> A little shallop, floating there hard by,
> Pointed its beak over the fringed bank;
> And soon it lightly dipt and rose, and sank,
> And dipt again, with the young couple's weight,—
> Peona guiding, through the water straight,
> Towards a bowery island opposite
> (I, 419–28)

The disruptive recurrence of these passages suggests that Keats still needs to cast out, or at least control, his overdependence on Spenser's enchantment before he can produce a disciplined Spenserian poetics or, in a broader sense, think successfully into the human heart.

His sensitivity to this problem and the new difficulties he was locating in Spenserian art helps explain the major shift in his response to Spenser after *Endymion*. His awareness of the regressive qualities of *Endymion* (what he called its "mawkishness" [*The Poems of John Keats* 103]) made him determined to break free of all the negative influences of his youth, especially those connected with his love of

24. Bate calls this "allegory manqué" (*John Keats* 174).

enchantment. He deliberately distanced himself from Hunt.[25] He
also thought it wise to put off Spenser for the moment, partly because so much of his own enthusiasm for romance was bound up
with Spenser's and partly because he was not yet sure how to make
Spenserian revisionism work in a sustained way. Thus when he bade
farewell to "golden-tongued Romance" and the "Fair plumed syren"
of enchantment in the Lear sonnet of January 1818, he was not, as a
number of critics assume, declaring a final break with Spenser.[26]
Rather, he was announcing a pause in their conversation in order to
reconsider the problems and capitalize on the advantages of their
relationship. The focus of those revaluations became clear in another sonnet ("Spenser, a jealous honorer of thine") written several
days after the Lear poem and dedicated to Spenser. In it, Keats hints
some disdain for those who, like one part of himself, prefer to wrap
themselves exclusively in Spenser's remoteness—"deep in thy mid-
most trees"—without any conception of his full complexity. He also
confesses a present unfitness for the task of engaging with Spenser
on that more complex level, and he hopes for the steady maturation
to undertake such an endeavor in riper years:

> Spenser, a jealous honorer of thine,
> A forester deep in thy midmost trees,
> Did last eve ask my promise to refine
> Some English that might strive thine ear to please.
> But Elfin-Poet, 'tis impossible
> For an inhabitant of wintry earth
> To rise like Phoebus with a golden quell,

25. After the completion of *Endymion*, he determined to absent himself from Hunt's
coterie. "I will not mix with that most vulgar of all crowds," he told Haydon, "the
literary" (*LJK* 2:43). He removed Hunt's name from his personal list of the "three
things to rejoice at in this Age" (*LJK* 1:203). And he flatly declared that "I will cut all
this—I will have no more of . . . Hunt in particular" (*LJK* 1:224). His frustration with
the Spenserian enchantment he associated with Hunt is particularly evident in his
anger with Hunt's suggestions that he make *Endymion* more sentimental: "Hunt says
the conversation [between Endymion and Peona] is unnatural and too high-flown. . . .
Says it should be simple forgetting do ye mind, that they are both overshadowed by a
Supernatural Power, & of force could not speak like Franchesca in the Rimini. He
must first prove that Caliban's poetry is unnatural,—This with me completely over-
turns his objections" (*LJK* 1:213).
26. From 1818 onward, this argument runs, Spenser was consigned to the pretty
baubles of nonage. "*The Faerie Queene*," Grundy representatively argues, "appears to
be merely or primarily a sensuous pattern . . . ultimately discarded for a poetry of
power" ("Keats and the Elizabethans" 12, 19). Helen Vendler is one of the few recent
critics to argue for Keats's persisting indebtedness to Spenser, claiming instead that
"Spenser's influence [on Keats] . . . is a lifelong one" (316).

Fire-wing'd, and make a morning in his mirth:
It is impossible to escape from toil
O' the sudden, and receive thy spiriting:—
The flower must drink the nature of the soil
Before it can put forth its blossoming.
Be with me in the summer days, and I
Will for thine honor and his pleasure try.

In its outline of a projected Spenserianism, this sonnet reveals both the striking changes and the continuity in Keats's developing ideas of Spenserian poetics from *Calidore* to *Endymion*. It indicates, on the one hand, everything he had learned about the complexity of trying to grow anew in Spenser's soil. Such an effort no longer seems a simple matter of proceeding with a vague sense of Spenser's approval, easily "receiving a spiriting" as Keats had felt in *Calidore*. To follow Spenser now presents several specific advantages and difficulties. Extending the Spenserian duality of "mirth" and, if we hear the pun, "mourning," and everything that dichotomy implies about the modern psyche, promises to raise a new phoenix of poetry out of the ashes of the Renaissance. That metaphor of burning purgation, together with the images of toil and drinking deeply from the earth, announces the primary knowledge of the heart's pulse to be illuminated by such a rebirth of poetry. Yet the major questions of how to sustain Spenser's mental and stylistic complexity and how to harmonize his indeterminate vision with an epic poetics remain. The resolve to grapple with these questions informs Keats's metaphor of drinking deeply from a new soil, turning over a new set of considerations, before issuing a fresh blossom.

It was now all much more complicated and forbidding than it had seemed at the outset of *Calidore*. Yet that Keats had come this far so relatively early in his career reminds us of the special enabling conditions of second-generation Romantic Spenserianism, which would continue to see him through this new stage. His perception of Spenser's mildness remained intact, despite his concerns about the obstacles ahead. He could still say "Be with me" with a qualified confidence that he would never feel toward any of Spenser's giant peers. Moreover, he now had the experience, as he began his creative maturity, to know how much was at stake in "being with" Spenser and what problems had to be solved in order to make their partnership successful. Keats's continuing efforts to refine that relationship would eventually help bring him to where he could also "be among" all "the English Poets."

So Continuing Long 4

I n his 1817 sonnet "Milton and Spenser," John Hamilton Reynolds addresses these lines to Keats's friend Benjamin Bailey: "We are both lovers of the poets old! / But Milton hath your heart,—and Spenser mine;—" (lines 1–2). Well aware that Bailey and Keats were together absorbed with Milton in the autumn of that year, Reynolds must have also sensed his poem's applicability to Keats. He knew about Keats's growing preoccupation with Milton, which was rapidly developing into the passionate contemplation of Milton's genius that pervaded Keats's letters of the next two years. Reynolds also noted how Spenserian prosody, diction, and thematic motifs were dropping out of Keats's poetry. By February 1818 he was wondering about Keats's possible apostasy from Spenser and begged a sign of continued devotion, only to receive the ambiguous reply of Keats's sonnet "Spenser, a jealous honorer of thine." But that statement, as we have seen, only announced a hiatus for Keats to reconsider his conversation with Spenser and all the great bards of the past, a pause to "get Wisdom" through a "continual drinking of Knowledge" and "looking into new countries" before attempting any new poetic experiments (*LJK* 1:271, 239). Enlarging his vision of the old poets' "vast provinces" meant "looking into" Milton's kingdom with special interest (*LJK* 1:224). The drama of that encounter has understandably captivated our attention, but it has also tempted us to forget at times Keats's resolution to wait like a "receptive" flower taking "hints from every noble insect that favors us with a visit" (*LJK* 1:232). Spenser was certainly one of those noble visitors, and the hints he offered not only differed from Milton's but, in vital contrast, arrived with more favor.

Spenser was never far out of mind throughout this "gradual ripening of the intellect" (*LJK* 1:214), and his vistations often seemed uplifting. Keats alluded to Spenser's poetry throughout 1818 and recalled Thomson's *The Castle of Indolence* as he began the great odes of 1819. By the autumn of 1819 he was seriously considering a poem on Leicester's history, with the obvious model of Spenser's *The Ruines of Time* before him (*LJK* 2:234). He also told Joseph Severn,

on his trip to Italy, that one of his greatest poetic ambitions was to
write an allegorical work about Una (*KC* 1:267). While contemplating these projects, he was producing long Spenserian narratives—
The Eve of St. Agnes and *The Jealousies*—along with shorter lyrics on
Spenserian topics, including "La Belle Dame Sans Merci" and the
nine-line stanza on Artegall and the Giant, his last poetic composition. He also turned to Spenser for comfort during his last days in
England, marking his favorite passages from *The Faerie Queene* (*LJK*
1:241, 362; 2:17, 78, 93, 232). All this implies more than a passing
interest in or nostalgia for the favorite poet of his salad days. His
mature thirst for knowledge clearly included a new desire for
Spenser, who indeed provided much of the sustenance for the great
creative journey he was now undertaking.

I

We have seen how Keats came away from *Endymion* with a profound
respect for Spenser's thinking into the human heart and its divisions.
To "get Wisdom," as Keats saw it in 1818, meant martyring himself
to that task. "'Knowledge is Sorrow,'" he declared, quoting Byron,
"and I go on to say that 'Sorrow is Wisdom'" (*LJK* 1:279). Such was
to be the wisdom of his mature poetry. Thus he determined to
"sharpen . . . [his] vision into the heart" by exploring a world "full of
Misery and Heartbreak, Pain, Sickness and oppression." Wordsworth seemed the only fit Virgil among the moderns to guide him
along the "dark passages" of the heart (*LJK* 1:281). Among the old
poets, Milton appeared saddled with a deficient "anxiety for Humanity" in his absorption with theology (*LJK* 1:278). Shakespeare
certainly qualified as a "mighty Poet of the human Heart" who had
memorably rendered "the fierce dispute / Betwixt damnation and
impassioned clay" (*LJK* 1:278; 2:115). But Spenser, though he
lacked the phenomenal range of Shakespeare's understanding,
seemed to have surpassed all the English poets in the sensitivity with
which he plumbed the heart's sorrows. Two centuries of writers before Keats had agreed on one of the most compelling features of his
art: not philosophy, not luxury, not even didacticism, but what Coleridge called a tender strain of "melancholy grace . . . diffused over
all his compositions" (*Coleridge's Miscellaneous Criticism* 143). Such a
core of sorrow, Keats began to realize, presented one of the richest
poetic veins of the kind of wisdom he now wished to bring into his
own art.

The new "hints" that he received from Spenser consistently addressed and deepened his own most poignant experience of the heart's conflict. He might have been contemplating Spenser's Irish hardships when he visited Ireland in the summer of 1818. Certainly the trip made him associate Ireland's miserable living conditions with the ubiquitous grief of Spenser's poetic world. "What a tremendous difficulty is the improvement of the condition of such people," he lamented. Then he remembered the Spenserian lines on ambition that had meant so much to him at the beginning of *Endymion*. Only now they seemed associated with a despair, probably not unfamiliar to Spenser, about doing much good under the burden of the world's misery: "I cannot conceive how a mind 'with child' of Philanthropy could gra[s]p at possibility—with me it is absolute despair" (*LJK* 1:321). Several months earlier, Spenser's anguish over such a world of baffling negations had helped inspire Keats's own famous vision of the "eternal" strife and destruction at the core of mental experience. Writing to Reynolds about that awful tumult, he remembers Spenser's Perilous Sea and the "sea-shouldring Whales" that had once delighted him (*LJK* 1:259–63). But he can now only see in Spenser's seascape the monstrous nightmares of a mind besieged with ominous threats:

> Most vgly shapes, and horrible aspects,
> . . . .
> The dreadfull Fish, that hath deseru'd the name
> Of Death, and like him lookes in dreadfull hew,
> The griesly Wasserman, that makes his game
> The flying ships with swiftnesse to pursew,
> . . . .
> All these, and thousand thousands more,
> And more deformed Monsters thousand fold,
> With dreadfull noise, and hollow rombling rore,
> Came rushing in the fomy waves enrold,
> Which seem'd to fly for feare, them to behold.
> (2.12.23–25)

Transfixed by that tumultuous scene, Keats brings its imagery of devouring sea maws into his own haunting vision of the psyche's fierce conflicts:[1]

1. Horton characterizes this passage in the psychological terms of Keats's re-creation of it: "The imponderable sea becomes a suggestive symbol for obscure, threatening devastations. . . . The dark vastness of the sea [is] . . . a mythic and geographic zone

> . . . but I saw
> Too far into the sea; where every maw
> The greater on the less feeds evermore:—
> But I saw too distinct into the core
> Of an eternal fierce destruction,
> And so from happiness I far was gone.
> Still am I sick of it. . . .
> Still do I that most fierce destruction see,
> The shark at savage prey.
> ("Dear Reynolds, as last night I lay in bed,"
> lines 93–103)

As Keats went on plumbing the depths of Spenser's gulf of sorrow, he found more and more of himself there. In Spenser's description of the shivering January, "Yet did he quake and quiver like to quell, / And blowe his nayles to warm them if he may: / For they were numbed" (*FQ*, 7.7.42), he must have recognized signs of the consumption that began to afflict him during the winter of 1819. It was a memorable recognition, for he worked those features of decay into his opening portrait of the Beadsman in *The Eve of St. Agnes*: "Numb were the Beadsman's fingers, while he told / His rosary" (lines 5–6). Several months later he also found in Arthur's dream of Gloriana, which he had previously marked in Hughes's text, the imagery to express his own experience of the thralldom of love and the painful difference between romantic ideals and hard reality. Arthur's grief-stricken awareness of the disappearance of his dream maiden is encapsulated in the distinct image of the "pressed Grass where she had lyen" (1.9.15). Similary, the withered sedge of "La Belle Dame Sans Merci" registers the knight's anguished sense of losing his "fairy's child." Later that year, when all of Keats's personal ambitions seemed doomed to incompletion under the threat of imminent death, he felt that Spenser's Cave of Despair summed up his bitterness (*LJK* 2:232). In his last days, nothing seemed to embody his own impression of the bittersweet "playing of different Natures with Joy and Sorrow" (*LJK* 1:219) so profoundly as Spenser's dichotomous vision. One of the most striking emblems of that contrary vision, the coupling of Displeasure and Pleasance during the Masque of Cupid, is marked in the copy of *The Faerie Queene* that Keats probably used in his last months. Displeasure and Pleasance march to-

---

where inner terrors may be consigned and objectified" (136, 138). Williams also reads the episode as an evocation of "the mind's sea . . . our inner ocean" (71).

gether, one carrying "An angry Waspe" the other "an hony-lady Bee" (3.12.18).

Keats could not have missed the appropriateness of that emblem for the poetics of duality he was mapping out in 1818. With self-conscious determination, he was transforming his early bias toward enchantment into a mature equipoise between the competing claims of romance and realism. Comparing imagination to Adam's dream in his famous analogy, he proclaimed its "truth" (*LJK* 1:185). A poetry of Romance thus seemed "a fine thing," and Fancy was to be untethered: "Ever let the Fancy roam . . . Oh, sweet Fancy! let her loose" (*LJK* 1:253; "Ode to Fancy," lines 1, 67). Yet Fancy's truth had to be counterpointed with an undersong of the heart's suffering. A "complex" art, he declared, must be "imaginative and at the same time careful of its fruits," carefully working out "a parallel of breast and head" (*LJK* 1:187, 277). That balance became the dominant subject of his 1818 lyrics, presented variously as a "terrible division" between body and soul ("God of the meridian," line 6), a "Double-lived" existence among Elysian delights and mortal "passions" ("Bards of passion and of mirth," lines 33–40), or the "Dancing music" of "Muses bright and Muses pale" ("Welcome joy, and welcome sorrow," lines 18–20).[2] Eager to find literary examples of such a dance of the muses, he juxtaposed Godwin's "patient study of the human heart" with Scott's romance (*LJK* 2:25). He also imitated Milton's poetic coupling, *L'Allegro* and *Il Penseroso*, in "Welcome joy, and welcome sorrow." But no one was so well equipped to lead him in that dance of opposites as the poet of the wasp and the bee. If Keats had forgotten anything about his long experience in Spenserian dualism, he was reminded of its relevance to his own situation in Hazlitt's famous lecture on Spenser. It was at the Surrey Institute in the spring of 1818 that Hazlitt characterized Spenser's poetic universe as the "two worlds of reality and of fiction . . . poised on the wings of his imagination."[3]

2. The question of Keats's stance toward the dialectic of realism and imagination has been central in the last two decades of scholarship on his poetry. Stillinger, in his landmark study, *The Hoodwinking of Madeline*, has conditioned a generation of scholars to recognize Keats's subversive and qualifying strategies against the imaginative idealism that drives so much of his poetic experience. More recently, however, critics like Leon Waldoff have begun to initiate a major revaluation of Keats's ongoing efforts to integrate the competing claims of reality and imagination, to stand balanced in that "intersection" of "actuality" and "transcendence" that MacCaffrey associates with Spenser. Waldoff provides a useful summary and extension of the sustained critical debate about Keats's attitude toward such an "intersection" in his opening chapter of *Keats and The Silent Work of Imagination* (1–31).

3. Keats arrived late for the lecture, but he often met with Hazlitt and went over

It did not take Keats long to recognize that Hazlitt's point confirmed what he had already suspected about Spenser's unique relation to his own developing poetics of "breast and head." Throughout
the spring of 1818, he turned to Spenser as an important resource to
help him articulate that poetics. Writing to Reynolds, for instance,
he referred to Acrasia's *carpe diem* song, which Hazlitt had quoted, as
a succinct expression of the delicate balance between the real and
the ideal. It represents, he claimed, the "honey" of ideal bliss, yet its
theme of transience also points to the "bitters" of worldly suffering
(*LJK* 1:370). In his verse epistle to Reynolds, "Dear Reynolds, as last
night I lay in bed", he relies on Spenserian motifs to make a more
elaborate point about the blended truths of imagination and reality.
The first half of the poem depicts a magical castle, which is modeled
on Claude's *The Enchanted Castle* but also recalls a typical Spenserian
scene of enchantment in its "mossy" landscape, its "fays and elves,"
and its neighboring "enchanted spring" and "clear lake" with "little
isles." Keats was probably thinking of Busyrane's castle in particular.[4]
Like that edifice, Keats's enchanted castle allures with a supernatural
beauty that conceals dangers within. Intriguing magical forces cause
ghostly flappings of doors and windows in both castles: the doors of
Keats's castle "all look as if they oped themselves, / The windows as if
latch'd by fayes and elves" (lines 49–50); the doors and "yron
wicket" of Busyrane's castle also fly open magically to reveal gaudy
interiors (3.12.3, 29). But the secret power behind this magic, in
both castles, is treacherous. The "vile Enchaunter" Busyrane carries
out his evil plots against Amoret within the attractive veil of his fantastic castle. A "Lapland witch" designs Keats's "Enchanted Castle"
and builds it with the help of "many a mason-devil." Keats contrasts
this ambiguous fairy world with the grim Spenserian vision of a devouring sea that we have already examined, but he does not endorse
either image. Instead he wavers between the two, seeking refuge in
"new romance" at the conclusion yet unable to dismiss those "horrid
moods." In the fashion of what he was coming to see as Spenser's
characteristic genius, his imagination balances the two worlds of fiction and reality on its wings.

It is in this balance that the Busyrane episode seems particularly
apposite. Its Masque of Cupid features an extended sequence of discordant contrasts peaking in the dance of Displeasure and Pleas-

---

the manuscript versions of the Surrey talks. By May 1818 he was reading the published versions of Hazlitt's lectures.

4. The Spenser edition that Keats probably used in his last readings of *The Faerie
Queene* bears extensive markings of the episode in Busyrane's castle.

ance that so resembles the dynamics of realism and ideality. Apollo, for instance, is depicted in Busyrane's tapestry as both a "faire" god and "a cowheard vile," foully disguised for love of Isse. Rugged and "brackish" Neptune also appears out of character as a "Steare" gobbling fodder, debased for love of woman. Such discordant images anticipate the assembly of Cupid's masque, in which numerous allegorical figures representative of inimical emotions march together: Fear and Hope; Cruelty and Grace; Displeasure and Pleasance (3.11–12). That weird procession, and the discords that it features, winds its way throughout Keats's epistle to Reynolds. The poem begins with a grouping of masquelike figures, "all disjointed" in their opposing tendencies to "vex and please." In a facetious version of Cupid's masque, they hold lofty ideals in tension with mundane realities: "Alexander with his night-cap on— / Old Socrates a-tying his cravat" (lines 8–9). This tension becomes more disturbing as the epistle proceeds and Keats envisions, like Britomart spying the odd assembly of characters in Busyrane's haunt, looks of "love and hate . . . smiles and frowns" in the enchanted castle (lines 38–39). Keats already knew that Spenser had not always been able to sustain this poise of opposites, and he was not very comfortable with it himself. For now, he rejected Britomart's final destruction of Busyrane's illusions and left his own fierce dispute between reality and enchantment open-ended. But it was a disturbing indeterminacy, with the "lore of good and ill" or romance and realism lost in "a sort of purgatory blind" that Keats would eventually feel compelled to resolve (lines 75, 80).[5] Still, there was no doubt that penetrating more deeply into Spenser's universe of duality was helping him shape his own poetic world.

In the normal pattern of influence dynamics, increasing appreciation of a forebear's depth can provoke mounting anxieties about going so far oneself. This was true of Keats's relation with Milton, who, as Hazlitt observed, threatens more and more to devour you as you come closer to him (quoted in Wittreich, *The Romantics on Milton* 381). With Spenser, however, Keats found a refreshing contrast. His growing familiarity with Spenser's dualism only reinforced his early sense of his old master's unique gentleness and pliability. The more he learned about the pathos of Spenser's insights into human conflict, the more certain he was of his teacher's tenderness and benevo-

5. Goldberg has argued, however, that even the certitudes at the end of the Busyrane episode are qualified by Spenser's revisions of the close of Book 3, in which the union of Amoret and Scudamour is forestalled, oppositions and tensions sustained (1–3).

lence. Spenser's drama of the heart's division did not intimidate followers in the awesome manner of Shakespeare's burning passion or Milton's soaring philosophy. Rather it came as a mild, poignant lament for human suffering, much as the dove's song gently sympathizes with Timias's grief in a passage from *The Faerie Queene* that Keats especially admired:

> Shee sitting by him as on ground he lay,
> Her mournefull notes full piteously did frame,
> And thereof made a lamentable lay,
> So sensibly compyld, that in the same
> Him seemed oft he heard his owne right name.
>
> (4.8.4)

As Timias makes "this gentle bird" his "Companion" in sorrow, Keats adopted the muse of a gentle Spenser as the "Companion" of his descent into the heart, that voyage of conception in which the two, like Timias and the dove, "so continued long" (4.8.5).

Keats would never again feel quite the elation over Spenser's generous arrival that he had experienced in *Calidore*. He had learned now to recognize the difficulty of walking with even so patient a "Companion" as Spenser. Yet his sense of relaxation in Spenser's company, especially following more severe engagements with Milton and Shakespeare, can be measured in the carefree spirit of his Spenserian activities throughout 1818 and 1819. Walking through Scotland in the summer of 1818, he described his formidably accoutred traveling companion, Charles Brown, as a parodic Redcrosse Knight. Several months later, he joked about his own pride by linking it to Braggadocchio's and compared Reynolds's literary subterfuge, in parodying Wordsworth, to Archimago's wiles (*LJK* 1:362; 2:17, 93). In 1819, he lampooned Brown's austere habits with several parodic Spenserian stanzas ("Character of C. B."), compared his own mental condition to the pleasant lassitude of *The Castle of Indolence* (*LJK* 2:78), and produced an ebullient social satire, *The Jealousies*, in the vein of Spenserian farce. These playful encounters, occurring just as Keats began to feel his greatest distress about the towering cliffs of poesy, suggest how much he continued to rely on the refreshing comfort of Spenser's companionship. It even became instinctive for him to return to Spenser for replenishment immediately after a debilitating encounter with Milton.

Keats's relationship with Spenser was helping him so much, in fact, that he began to conceive of it as an allegory of his overall creative development. As his self-imposed task of "getting Wisdom" reached a crucial juncture in the spring of 1818, he began to map out a new path for his art and thought of his future as a poet in terms of his ongoing interaction with Spenser. It was an instructive relationship for him, but not one without disagreement. Plotting out his new creative mission, he conceptualized it as a self-corrective re- vision of Spenser's thinking into the human heart. Keats had always taken great interest in Spenser's self-conscious way of recording his own poetic aspirations. But he also felt that Spenser had sometimes gone astray in planning out those ambitions, repudiating his identity as a "mighty Poet of the human Heart" to think of himself as a mor- alist. In the Hughes text of *The Faerie Queene*, for instance, Keats marked with obvious approval Spenser's characterization of himself as a poet "heart pierced" with "dear Compassion of Mind" (1.3.1). Yet he also observed how Spenser had seemingly renounced that identity at the beginning of *The Faerie Queene* by declaring his inten- tion to "moralize my Song" (1.1.1). To discipline his own reflexive withdrawal from "dear Compassion" and thrust himself into the pierced heart was the basic principle of Keats's mature aesthetics. Because he so closely associated both his interiority and his form of escapism with Spenser's, there was hardly a more fitting way to artic- ulate this project than to present it as an allegory of his corrective response to Spenser's moralizing retreat from the heart.

As Keats reordered his priorities in the spring of 1818, subor- dinating Milton's abstract philosophizing to Wordsworth's "mar- tyr[ing] himself to the human heart" (*LJK* 1:278–79), he found Wordsworth providing a specific incentive for composing that alle- gory out of Spenser's own materials. Keats had known for some time that much of Wordsworth's immersion in "life's ordinary woes" (*The White Doe of Rylstone*, line 54), especially in his Spenserian poetry, had come out of a corrective extension of Spenser's own "mental processes." Wordsworth had even conceived of narratives of mental growth in terms of modified Spenserian quest allegory (*Prose Works* 2:20). That precedent encouraged Keats to think of his new Words- worthian voyage through the heart's "Mansion of Many Apart- ments" as an improvement on a recurrent type of quest in *The Faerie Queene* that had always fascinated him: the journey through a myste- rious house or castle in which explorers must sort out a baffling mixture of reality and illusion. In this scenario, characters like Red- crosse at the House of Pride, Arthur at Orgoglio's prison, Britomart and Redcrosse at the Castle Joyeous, or Guyon in Mammon's subter- ranean palace, enter complicated buildings in various states of immaturity and confusion. They progress through labyrinthine apartments where discordant appearances provoke and reflect their own divisions between gorgeous ideals and the substance of reality. Often glittering facades will at first confuse the voyagers' insight and intoxicate their senses. As they gradually explore dark recesses and inner corridors, Arthur stumbling through the darkness of Orgoglio's dungeon or Redcrosse tripping on the bones of the dead at the "priuie Posterne" of the House of Pride, the complex truths of experience become evident. Redcrosse learns the treacherous malignity of pride, Guyon the self-destructiveness of overindulgence, Arthur the futility of ignorance, Britomart the subtlety of concupiscence. Keats had already been encouraged by Thomson's *Castle of Indolence* to contemplate the relation of the House of Pride sequence to his own mental state. He had marked the passage in his Hughes text and borrowed its quest motif for Calidore's entrance into the castle of poetic knowledge. Now he found that he could adapt that same motif for a more sophisticated allegory about his own creative education as a corrective response to Spenser's model.

Like Spenser's immature pilgrims, the young poet enters the "Mansion of Many Apartments" where he becomes dazzled at first "with the light and the atmosphere" of the mansion's outer rooms. This experience first delights him and, like Redcrosse in the voluptuous antechambers of the Castle Joyeous, he sees "nothing but pleasant wonders, and . . . think[s] of delaying there for ever in delight." But just as Spenser's heroes pass hesitantly into the shadowy interior of their houses, Keats's maturing poet moves deeper into the "dark passages" of "the heart and nature of Man." Like Spenser's enlightened characters, he then becomes convinced "that the World is full of Misery and Heartbreak, Pain, Sickness and oppression" (*LJK* 1:281).

Up to this point, Keats's imaginative autobiography reads like an allegory of what Spenser had been teaching him all along about exploring the ambiguities at the core of experience. Indeed, Keats's allegory is probably the richest metaphorical characterization ever of just the kind of exploratory inwardness that Spenser scholars find so notable throughout *The Faerie Queene* and particularly in its journeys into houses of the mind.[6] But the standard conclusion to those voy-

---

6. Alpers, for instance, describes episodes like the passage through Busyrane's castle as "a series of speaking pictures that creates our psychological experience as it unfolds . . . [bringing about] the intensification of our involvement as we move further into Busyrane's palace" (*Poetry* 14–15). Williams finds such episodes mental "lab-

ages, as Keats sees it, reveals where the teacher was misleading and in need of correction. Spenser's explorations habitually end with a spiritual revelation, in which the ambiguities of experience are resolved in a vision of some ultimate truth. Redcrosse's trials in the House of Pride finally lead to his spiritual renewal in the House of Holinesse and his vision of the New Jerusalem. The insight of Spenser's characters always remains limited, their questing perpetual as long as they inhabit this temporal world. But they are bequeathed glimpses of eternal truth as a result of their descents into experience, and they usually leave dark castles with a clarified, if still imperfect, apprehension of providence.[7] To Keats, that movement toward closure, Williams's "clear vision," must have seemed like his own step backward into enchantment, as if Redcrosse's eschatological vision did not appear all that different psychologically from his entranced gaze upon Duessa in a remote bower. When Keats envisions the culmination of his own progress through the "Mansion of Many Apartments," he pointedly leaves the journey incomplete and darkens the revelation that concludes Spenser's quests: "We see not the ballance of good and evil. We are in a Mist—*We* are now in that state—We feel the 'burden of the Mystery'" (*LJK* 1:281). It is the burden of modern doubt, which cannot be transcended, Keats would argue, in the manner of Spenser's tentative ascents beyond the mist of this world's confusion. Indeed, the "Genius" of modern poetry, Keats goes on, must be "explorative of those dark Passages," not on the wing beyond them. Redcrosse might have learned much more had he stayed in the House of Pride.

Correcting Spenser's preference for the light thus became deeply

---

yrinths" in which the psyche "explore[s] experience" and "the inscrutable doubleness of things" (81, 85, 225). It is especially striking, in considering Keats's allegory as a brilliant illustration for these contemporary readings of Spenser's exploratory poetics, to find some recent characterizations of the manner in which Spenser "merely glimpse[s] the truths he seeks to unearth" (Quilligan 136)—the same metaphor of half-seeing that is so quintessentially Keatsian in the "Mansion of Many Apartments" allegory.

7. Fletcher explains that "the 'houses' and 'castles' of *The Faerie Queene*" provide in the end a center of truth "which is preminently the zone of the sacred, the zone of absolute reality" (211). Williams describes this progression from half-seeing to certainty in terms that Keats would have found particularly revelatory of Spenser's error in trying to rest at last in "absolute reality." Behind "a life of tension and flux," she writes, is "the 'Sabaoth's sight' of wholly clear vision, when we shall no longer see 'like an image in a glass'" (225). For Keats, resisting what seemed like the false allure of "wholly clear vision" to see "like an image in a glass" appeared to be the only honest way of greeting experience.

intertwined with Keats's resolution to purify his own "Genius" and explore "those dark Passages" himself. It is probably no coincidence that just as he thought of surpassing Spenser he made the ongoing association with Wordsworth in this passage more specific, quoting "Tintern Abbey." Wordsworth's appearance as a sensitive, less threatening alternative to Milton must have reminded him of Spenser's similar role as a contrasting figure to Milton who allowed, even welcomed, his followers to take such freedoms with his example.

To put all this into artistic form would mean building a Spenserian poetics out of the allegorical revisionism that clarified Keats's personal mission. It was not long until he began to think of life as "a continual allegory" and poetry as an extended interpretation of it (*LJK* 2:67). By April 1818, Hazlitt was promoting Spenser's vibrant allegorical pictorialism as the "finest thing" in his art (*Lectures* 38). At about the same time, Keats could have learned from canto 4 of *Childe Harold's Pilgrimage* how much Byron was profiting from sustained reformulations of those speaking pictures. In his epistle to Reynolds, Keats was already experimenting with a similar practice. Yet he had also learned from the "slipshod" *Endymion* that making substantial poetry out of such a demanding procedure was no easy matter (*LJK* 1:374). There was no doubt in his mind that those who had gone before him, even Byron, had fallen into diffuseness and sentimentality. Although he had once delighted in Beattie, Tighe, and Campbell, he could now "see through" them, finding in them "nothing . . . or weakness" (*LJK* 2:18, 243). He frowned upon Byron's maudlin selfhood in *Childe Harold's Pilgrimage*, finding "the whole of anybody's life & opinions" a laborious subject for poetry (*LJK:* 1:225). He would have liked to forget all about the "mawkishness" of his own *Endymion*. Yet another long Spenserian poem must have seemed out of the question.

Keats was determined, though, to make an epic poem, the only way to validate his new claim to maturity and membership in the second Renaissance. He also knew that rewriting *Paradise Lost* had become the central test for the Romantics' aspirations about cultural renewal. "We have no Milton," he declared in the autumn of 1818 (*LJK* 1:396), and his protracted thinking about the challenges and problems of Miltonic epic now culminated in a resolution to fill that gap with an epic poem that would displace what he called Milton's "divine philosophy" with a modern, secular cosmology (*LJK* 1:281). As another way of updating Milton, he also meant to follow Wordsworth's pathway into the heart and humanize the abstractions of Milton's vision. If there was any thought of incorporating Spenser into that humanizing enterprise, it could only have been peripheral. The demands of trying to do so much with Milton were so monumental as to absorb all his energies and turn the writing of *Hyperion* into virtually a line-by-line contest against Milton's specter, with each episode of his first two books responding directly to parallel sequences in the opening books of *Paradise Lost*. Laboring to supplant Milton must have given Keats something like the feeling Coleridge characterized as struggling to push a stone out from beneath a pyramid, which may very well account for the ponderous, agonizing movements of his own titans. It is a wonder, as Bate remarks, "how he ever managed to do it" so well (*John Keats* 392), producing what is generally considered to be the best blank verse in English since Milton. Instead of repeating what has been said about Keats's accomplishments in *Hyperion*, however, I wish to turn to his own feelings of the enormity of the struggle and what may have caused him to abandon the narrative.

It is generally believed that beyond the debilitating effects of his brother's recent death the most significant factor in Keats's suspension of *Hyperion* was the exhaustive burden of sustaining Milton's dense poetic style. A feeling of enervation pervades his statements about the hardship of going on with the task, of "bearing the burthen of a long poem" in a Miltonic vein. In late December 1818, he complained about not being able to "get into" that "vein" again. The weight of composition "came upon me and I could not get on." By February, he was still finding it difficult to get into "cue for writing" and hoped "for the sp[r]ing to rouse me up a little." By March he had to admit that he was "not exactly on the road to an epic poem," and soon after he gave up the project altogether (*LJK* 2:26, 12, 15, 62). What drained him so much had as much to do with the inherent contradictions in his epic plan as with the suffocating pressure that Milton seemed to exert on his imagination.

Those contradictions are most apparent in Keats's attempt to present an epic philosophy through Oceanus's central speech about the march of progress. Oceanus's cosmography, as Bate points out (*John Keats* 400–401), was both dissatisfying to Keats and inimical to one of the major thrusts of his recent intellectual development. Such a systematic mode of philosophizing may have been necessary to displace Milton's vision and consolidate his own epic outlook. But it had also become alien to his doubling experience of reality and his growing skepticism about "the truth of any of my speculations" (*LJK* 1:243). This meant, as Sperry argues (*Keats the Poet* 196), that not only did Milton present an intimidating front but the whole concept of Miltonic epic was beginning to seem intractable. On both counts, the recent experience left Keats feeling dispirited and "dumb," even though he would return to Milton later (*LJK* 2:43). This is the effect that made him so eager to "open Spencer" once again in the winter of 1819, both for Spenser's refreshing benevolence and his ability to offer instead of an epic vision a "play of double senses" that was becoming, whatever its limitations, more and more compatible with Keats's own way of seeing things.

It was just now, moreover, that Byron's revisionary dealings with Mutabilitie in the last canto of *Childe Harold's Pilgrimage* gave Keats a valuable model for deepening Spenser's indeterminacy along the lines of the "Mansion of Many Apartments" episode. Byron's example also suggested a way of solving those central problems of sustaining a complicated Spenserian poetics and integrating it with a skeptical vision of experience. Despite the length of *Childe Harold's Pilgrimage,* the entire work increasingly took on the appearance of a poetic fragment, especially in the disjunctive contemplation of the ruins of time that make up its final canto. The Spenserian fragment poem, of course, had been around for some time and Beattie had even tried to validate it. What made Byron's use of the form so different, however, was his confidence about its theoretical justification and his extremity in carrying out the most intensive structural fracturing of Spenser's vision ever. Transforming *The Faerie Queene,* already monumental in its incompleteness, into an even more broken fragment thus struck Keats as the best way to bring Spenser into the misty corridors of modern experience. Moreover, he began to suspect that compressing such a fragment into a truncated form, producing an elliptical drama of the mind's division as opposed to Byron's discursive pilgrimaging, could most effectively advance this dismantlement and reconfiguration of Spenser's intended wholeness. To contract Spenser's comprehensive or "diffuse" narrative (*LJK* 2:157) could not only punctuate a modern fracturing of his universe but also make possible, at last, the concentration of Spenserian strengths that so many of his imitators, including Byron, had sacrificed in their long works. Short Spenserian poems like Shenstone's had appeared successfully before, but their authors had never been able to claim the intellectual justification now available to Keats. For the first time in the history of Spenserianism, it was now possible to engage in a fragment poem without any qualms about the seriousness or intellectual validity of the enterprise. Also for the first time in that history, a

poet had emerged with the lyrical gift to exploit fully the special
advantages of working in a compact Spenserian form.

II

Keats's frustration with Milton's intractability brought him back to
Spenser and moved him to act on these possibilities when, in early
1819, he wrote a medieval romance in Spenserian stanzas, *The Eve of
St. Agnes*. The abortive experience with *Hyperion* had just provoked
his most severe worries ever about the impossibility of matching up
to England's "dead poets." He spoke about "the burthen of a long
poem" and found himself "smok[ing] more and more my own insuf-
ficiency" (*LJK* 2:26, 33). Richard Woodhouse provides a telling record of the extremity of this self-doubt. Replying to a letter from
Keats about the futility of modern poetic achievement, he tried to
calm his young friend's apprehensions that "there was now nothing
original to be written in poetry; that its riches were already exhausted,—& all its beauties forestalled—& That you should consequently, write no more" (*LJK* 1:380–82). Woodhouse claimed all
that was not true, and Keats replied that he was not so troubled as
he seemed. Yet he remained locked on the subject of the moderns'
doubtful place "among the English poets," particularly bothered by
the fact that Milton's "gormandizing" intellect had left "the shore [of
knowledge] . . . all bare" for succeeding generations (*LJK* 1:255).
With his long-standing qualms about a closed tradition reaching this
critical point, his turning to Spenser, who had always been the one to
allay those fears, was the most natural thing for him to do.

It has often been thought that he took up *The Eve of St. Agnes* as a
brief escape from hardship into a Spenserian bower of luxury, a
pause to distance himself from the tragedy of his brother Tom's recent death and the disappointment of the *Hyperion* experience before returning to more serious work (Bate, *John Keats* 66). But we
have seen that he had been seeking more than escapism or even
simply reassurance from Spenser all along. However much he may
have been looking now for those kind brows of his old master, his
reaching out also came from his desire to act on the ideas he had
been entertaining for some time about a compact Spenserian allegory. It was his new recognition of how that revisionary poetics
could be embodied in an elliptical pictorialism, an antiallegorical al-

legory of densely juxtaposed pictures of the mind, that finally enabled him to take such a step.

In December 1818, he began to study Renaissance prints and
paintings that reminded him of the struggle between truth and
beauty in Spenser's own pictures. He was struck, for instance, by the
contrast between the psychological depth of Raphael's cartoons and
the sentimentality of Guido's religious art: "A year ago I could not
understand in the slightest degree Raphael's cartoons—now I begin
to read them a little—and how did I lea[r]n to do so? By seeing
something done in quite an opposite spirit—I mean a picture of
Guido's in which all the Saints, instead of that heroic simplicity and
unaffected grandeur which they inherit from Raphael, had each of
them both in countenance and gesture all the canting, solemn melo-
dramatic mawkishness of Mackenzie's father Nicholas—" (*LJK* 2:19).
Instead of simply dismissing Guido's superficiality, Keats found
something valuable in the contrast of these two painterly styles. The
distinction between them probably brought to mind Hazlitt's recent
point about the "dazzling minuteness" with which Spenser had created so many dramatic paintings of the "two worlds of reality and
fiction" (*Lectures* 35). The "chiaroscuro" Keats saw in Guido and
Raphael must have also reminded him of the tension between enchantment and reality in his own Spenserian revisionism, for he
made the same equation between religious idealism and sentimentality that had previously moved him to associate Spenser's extremism with his own. He even criticized Guido's idealism with the same
word—"mawkishness"—that he had once applied to the undis-
ciplined enchantment of *Endymion*.

As he thought more deeply about these visual dichotomies and
their relation to his own art, his gaze focused on Spenser more directly. He was intrigued by a print of an early Renaissance painting
whose central allegory of pleasure versus damnation bears a striking
resemblance to the Spenserian castle allegory he associated with his
own creative history. The painting, identified by Gittings (*John Keats*
280–81) as *The Triumph of Death* in Conte Carlo Lasinio's *Pitture a
fresco del Campo Santo di Pisa* (1812), depicts a procession of revelling
medieval courtiers. Their entertainment is disrupted by a troup of
grotesque demons, who threaten to carry them off to join other
damned corpses (Fig. 5). This scenario obviously resembles the central conflict between enchanting facade and evil substance in
Spenser's castle allegory. Indeed, the painting makes a perfect gloss
to episodes like the House of Pride and Mammon's cave, in which
monstrous demons threaten to devour unsuspecting pilgrims, and

Fig. 5. *The Triumph of Death*, from Carlo Lasinio's *Pitture a fresco del Campo Santo di Pisa* (1812). (By permission of the Newberry Library)

the bones of the damned lie just behind luxurious banqueting halls. Keats was alert to such an application, describing the contrasts of *The Triumph of Death* in terms of the same kind of dualism that he found at the center of Spenser's allegory. The overall scene is "Full of Romance," he explained, "and the most tender feeling—magnificence of draperies beyond any I ever saw not excepting Raphael's." But at the same time, it abounds with the "Grotesque to a curious pitch." Yet the tension of both perspectives ultimately makes up "a fine whole—even finer to me than more accomplish'd works—as there was left so much room for Imagination" (*LJK* 2:19). That "fine whole," as Keats saw it—perhaps thinking of the ambivalent phrase describing Amoret's recovery, "perfect hole" (*FQ*, 3.12.38), that Goldberg reads as an apt motto for Spenser's doubling psyche (3)—encompasses the same dualistic perspective through which Spenserian allegory opens up into the complex "whole" of experience. Keats extended that perspective by dropping the moralism of *The Triumph of Death* and reinterpreting it as a drama of mental division. The "room for Imagination" he discovered in it was thus very similar to the same space for a deeper, less ideological probing of the heart that he found left unexplored in Spenser's allegory. Hence *The Triumph of Death* became, in Keats's reading, rather like a succinct, highly complex pictorial frame of the Spenserian allegory that he was transforming into a creative autobiography of growth and self-purgation.

That amazing insight moved Keats to refine his overall conception of Spenserian revisionism and its application to his personal creative history. Reconstructing the dense mental paintings, or frames, of Spenser's castle allegory now seemed a promising way to carry out his own descent into the "Mansion of Many Apartments." If Gittings is right to find *The Triumph of Death* a major inspiration for *The Eve of St. Agnes*, then we must suspect that Keats meant to build much of the poem around this new revisionary strategy. Such an intention offered rich possibilities for restricting Spenser's moralism while heightening his relevance to Keats's modern poetic experience. To think of Spenser's castle allegory as a concise series of pictures like the various panels of *The Triumph of Death* was tantamount to casting off its prosaic didacticism, its conclusive authorial digressions on vice and virtue, in order to concentrate on the mental drama of truth and beauty recorded in what Hamilton calls its "mosaic" of pictures (214). That "entrelacement" of contrasting pictures of the mind, where "meaning resides in the interrelation of them all" (Williams 234), is one of the strongest vehicles of psychological allegory that Spenser scholars like Hamilton, Tuve (363), and Williams (234) find in *The Faerie Queene*. Keats's extension of such "entrelacement" in the antiallegorical tableaux of *The Eve of St. Agnes* became, in turn, one of his most effective mechanisms for exploring the dark labyrinth of the heart's conflict.[8] It was a form of adaptation that also added a special value to his use of the Spenserian stanza. Where the stanza had always been considered awkward in a long poem because it encourages a discontinuous string of enclosed pictures, it became quite appropriate for the kind of compact "mosaic" that Keats wished to shape out of the diffuse narrative of *The Faerie Queene*.[9] Writing in Spenser's stanza was therefore not simply a facile way of making a bond with him, but an integral part of the entire process of paring his vision—and, by extension, Keats's own—into a "fine whole."[10]

Although *The Eve of St. Agnes* follows a distinct narrative line, its pictorialism has always made the strongest impression on admirers.[11] The poem reads like a series of painted windows, each framed by the hexameter closure of Spenser's stanza. Those panes resemble the panels of *The Triumph of Death,* all contributing to the effect of one tapestrylike picture, the poem itself. The psychodramatic pattern of that tapestry closely resembles the design of Spenser's castle allegory, in which the pleasures of enchantment clash with the bitter truths of reality. Where Spenser first brings Redcrosse and Britomart into the luxurious outer apartments of the Castle Joyeous, for instance, Keats paints a sumptuous antechamber:

8. Stillinger has conditioned us to think of *The Eve of St. Agnes* as one of Keats's most elaborate dramatizations of the mind's "conflict between actuality and the ideal" (*The Hoodwinking of Madeline* 92). For a summary of the prodigious amount of critical elaborations and qualifications of his reading, see my "The Spenserian Versification of Keats's *The Eve of St. Agnes*."

9. Bate notes how Keats found the stanza attractive now because it "[t]empts poetic narrative toward tableau" (*John Keats* 440).

10. Despite the outpouring of recent studies of the psychological depth of *The Eve of St. Agnes*, there has been little effort to examine how much Keats's conversation with Spenser helped him shape out the poem's interior universe. Sperry's conclusion is representative: "*The Eve of St. Agnes* lacks the larger unity and cohesiveness that characterizes Spenser's world" (*Keats the Poet* 201).

11. The question has been whether its magnificent drapery should be viewed as the gorgeous gallery of paintings that Rosetti loved in *The Eve of St. Agnes* or as the vehicle for, in Sperry's phrase, "an exceptionally subtle study of the psychology of the imagination" (*Keats the Poet* 202).

Soon, up aloft,
The silver, snarling trumpets 'gan to chide:
The level chambers, ready with their pride,
Were glowing to receive a thousand guests:
The carved angels, ever eager-eyed,
Star'd, where upon their heads the cornice rests,
With hair blown back, and wings put cross-wise on their breasts.

At length burst in the argent revelry,
With plume, tiara, and all rich array,
Numerous as shadows haunting fairily
The brain, new stuff'd in youth with triumphs gay
Of old romance.
(lines 30–41)

Like Redcrosse lapped in the luxury of a gorgeous couch, we are partly "Hoodwink'd" along with Madeline by the overwhelming splendor of the scene's "faery fancy." As Keats penetrates further into the castle's interior, like Spenser carrying Britomart into her sleeping chamber in the Castle Joyeous, he paints an even more seductive world of soft delight. Madeline rests "In blanched linen, smooth, and lavender'd" while Porphyro arranges round her

candied apple, quince, and plum, and gourd;
With jellies soother than the creamy curd,
And lucent syrops, tinct with cinnamon;
Manna and dates, in argosy transferr'd
From Fez; and spiced dainties, every one,
From silken Samarcand to cedar'd Lebanon.
(lines 263–70)

In the manner of Spenser's paradigm, however, a more disturbing truth emerges within these interior reaches of the castle. Porphyro, somewhat like "crafty" Malecasta sneaking into Britomart's bedchamber, intrudes on Madeline's enchantment with the guile of a seducer. Madeline, compared to the raped Philomela, calls him a "traitor." As the poem's romantic veil gives way to this disturbing realism, Keats's painting becomes just as gruesome as Spenser's developing allegory. Where Redcrosse steps upon the bones of the dead as he escapes from the House of Pride's illusions, Keats summons up a series of monstrous images: the Baron's dream of "witch, and demon, and large coffin-worm"; Angela "palsy-twitch'd, with meagre face deform"; the Beadsman unburied in his "ashes cold." From the beginning to the end of *The Eve of St. Agnes*, Keats thus weaves together a Spenserian "entrelacement" of beauty and truth to fashion a dramatic picture of the mind's ongoing swerves between enchantment and realism.

He also learns from Spenser how to paint those contrasts into a single panel of his allegory. Spenser's description of Malecasta's "great chamber," for example, both honors and questions its voluptuousness:

> But for to tell the sumptuous aray
> Of that great chamber, should be labour lost:
> For liuing wit, I weene, cannot display
> The royall riches and exceeding cost,
> Of euery pillour and of euery post;
> Which all of purest bullion framed were,
> And with great pearles and pretious stones embost,
> That the bright glister of their beames cleare
> Did sparckle forth great light, and glorious did appeare.
>   (3.1.32)

The intoxicating splendor of this room betrays various hints of excess and misdirection. An unexpected reference to "labour" at the beginning of the description, for instance, implies the presence of a manufactured, perhaps overlabored beauty. Such an implication is deepened by the repetitions of "great" and "euery," which make the room's ornamentation seem redundant, artificially fabricated. The "bright glister" and "great light" of so many "pretious stones" also seems excessive, "exceeding" the measure of genuine beauty and thus only "appear[ing]" glorious. Spenser further suggests this false illumination with the couplet rhyme of "beames cleare . . . glorious did *appeare*" (my italics). Several imperfect, eye rhymes—cost/post, were/cleare—add to the subtle feeling of disproportion that qualifies the enchantment of this chamber.

Keats brings the same kind of ambiguity into his voluptuous portraiture of the "sumptuous aray" of Madeline's castle. His description of her casement window has been compared to Spenser's "opulence" of coloring (Allott 466). But it also re-creates the dichotomous perspective that is basic to the pictorialism of Spenser's castle alle-

gory. Like the appearance of Malecasta's chamber, Madeline's casement window entrances the observer with a rich assemblage of
shapes and colors:

A casement high and triple-arch'd there was,
All garlanded with carven imag'ries
Of fruits, and flowers, and bunches of knot-grass,
And diamonded with panes of quaint device,
Innumerable of stains and splendid dyes,
As are the tiger-moth's deep-damask'd wings;
And in the midst, 'mong thousand heraldries,
And twilight saints, and dim emblazonings,
A shielded scrutcheon blush'd with blood of queens and kings.

(lines 208–16)

Also like Spenser's example, however, this picture contains numerous qualifications of its beauty. The "carven imag'ries" recall the
"carved angels" of the poem's opening lines, whose lustful appearance now intrudes on the romantic etherialism of Madeline's bedchamber. The appearance of "knot-grass," generally found in waste
ground, further disturbs the aura of enchantment in Keats's painting. His grouping of images with negative connotations—"panes,"
"stains," "dyes," "blood"—creates a double effect of beauty and suffering. Finally, a series of off-rhymes—was/grass, imag'ries/device,
device/dyes—disturbs the perfect idealism of Madeline's world in the
manner of Spenser's own discordant echoes. The total effect of these
qualifiers is to shape a picture of divided impressions whose ambiguity, like the tensions in Spenser's tableaux, represents the mind's
oscillation between romance and reality.

We have seen, however, that Keats's new form of revisionism also
intensifies Spenser's contrasts, making the allegory more open-
ended and less didactic as a way of correcting his own youthful penchant for idealistic absolutes. He accomplishes this partly by diminishing his narrator's role in the psychodrama. Unlike Spenser, who
pauses at times to reflect on the moral of his stories, the narrator of
The Eve of St. Agnes has little to say by way of interpretation. His only
commentary comes through his painting, and even then it is both
sparse and inconclusive.[12] He momentarily commends the romance

---

12. Michael Ragussis is particularly concerned with the elusive role of the narrator
in *The Eve of St. Agnes*.

of Porphyro's meeting with Angela, for instance, when he introduces "young Porphyro, with heart on fire" praying for the aid of saints just as Angela comes magically along "with ivory-headed wand" to help him. The narrator's delight with this enchantment quickly dissolves, however, when he focuses on Angela's "palsied hand." The deeper he takes us into the castle, the darker these pictorial ambiguities grow, until finally, at the end of the poem, we are left with a visual enigma instead of the kind of authorial gloss that culminates and resolves Spenser's allegory. The lovers flee into what appears as both a dreamscape—"They glide, like phantoms" into an "elfinstorm from faery land"—and a brutal world of coldness, suffering, and death in which Angela and the Beadsman expire. Like the mysterious gates of the Baron's castle that open weirdly onto this uncertain terrain, the psychodrama of *The Eve of St. Agnes* yields only an enigmatic picture of those "dark Passages" of the mind. Spenser's continuous and conclusive allegory thus reemerges as a fragmentary picture, or a compressed tapestry of antiallegorical allegory made up of calculated glimpses into the "mist" of the human heart.

The conciseness of *The Eve of St. Agnes* serves an important aesthetic purpose as well, enabling Keats to sustain complex allegorical patterns throughout the poem while avoiding the diffuseness that had become so characteristic of Romantic Spenserian poems. It also helps him orchestrate one of the Romantics' most successful integrations of allegorical and prosodic revisionism in their Spenserian poems. Keats had always been intrigued by the relation of stylistic and mental tension in Spenser, associating "Spenserian vowels that elope with ease" with ideals of enchantment and the tumultuous rhythms of the Despair episode with psychological realism.[13] His metrical experimentation in *The Eve of St. Agnes* suggests that he was also sensitive to Byron's way of intensifying Spenser's stylistic contrasts in order to punctuate the deeper competition of realism and ideality in *Childe Harold's Pilgrimage*. Where Byron's revisionism had lapsed amid the demands of a long narrative, however, Keats is able to heighten Spenser's oppositions with greater control while maintaining a more disciplined correspondence between allegorical and prosodic dichotomies in his much shorter poem. Just as he sharpens

---

13. In "The Spenserian Versification of Keats's *The Eve of St. Agnes*," I discuss Keats's fascination with the prosodic virtuosity of the Despair passage (104). He marked lengthy sections of the episode in the Hughes text.

the conflicts of Spenser's allegorical tapestry, so he winds Spenser's different rhythms into a much more mingled yarn. Instead of progressing, as Spenser habitually does, from indolent melody to a vigorous discord, he fuses both rhythms in a sustained tension that reinforces the ongoing ambiguities of *The Eve of St. Agnes.*

In the first stanza alone, for instance, the gruff opening so reminiscent of Spenser's vigorous style—"St. Agnes' Eve—Ah, bitter chill it was! / The owl, for all his feathers, was a-cold"—quickly clashes with what Spenser himself might have called the "delitious harmony" of the verses on the Beadsman: "his frosted breath, / Like pious incense from a censer old / Seem'd taking flight for heaven, without a death" (lines 1–2, 6–8). These polar styles collide most dramatically during the bedroom sequence, when the dynamic between idealism and reality grows fiercest. Here the voluptuous rhythms associated with Madeline's charmed sleep—"The lustrous salvers in the moonlight gleam; / Broad golden fringe upon the carpet lies" (lines 284–85)—contend with the staccato cadence of Porphyro's attempt to wake her into a reality that she is not at all prepared to embrace: "He ceased—she panted quick—and suddenly / Her blue affrayed eyes wide open shone" (lines 295–96). Contrary to the pattern of Spenser's model, this tension never finds resolution. The final sequence of Keats's poem echoes Una's urgent call for action during the Despair episode—"Arise, Sir Knight arise" (1.9.53)—while relapsing into the incantatory rhythms of enchantment. Thus Porphyro cries out to Madeline: "Arise—arise! The morning is at hand" (line 345). But their subsequent escape is rendered in the luxurious sibilants and flowing rhythms of Spenser's opulent style:

> The arras, rich with horseman, hawk, and hound,
> Flutter'd in the besieging wind's uproar;
> And the long carpets rose along the gusty floor.
>
> They glide, like phantoms, into the wide hall;
> Like phantoms, to the iron porch, they glide.
> (lines 358–62)

Metrically as well as psychologically, Keats's closing stanzas thus make up a conclusion in which nothing is concluded. The stylistic innovations here, like Byron's, do not so much cast a foreign mantle on Spenser as deepen and intensify metrical clashes essential to his poetics. Because of the compactness of *The Eve of St. Agnes,* these stylistic extensions of Spenser's native manner also complement

Keats's revisionary allegory with a consistent succinctness that evaded Byron.[14] This condensed heightening of Spenser's own allegorical and stylistic duality makes *The Eve of St. Agnes* one of the few Romantic poems that seems both quintessentially Spenserian and utterly modern at the same time, the foremost goal of every type of revisionary Spenserianism. While Keats refines and perfects many established strategies to reach that goal, he also introduces one brilliant stylistic innovation of his own that revolutionized the process of bringing Spenser into the modern world. Although he uses some archaic lan-

14. The care that Keats took to shape and sustain this prosodic flux can be measured in his revisions of one key instance of mental oscillation. (My discussions of the manuscript revisions of *The Eve of St. Agnes* follow Stillinger's transcription in his edition of Keats's poetry.) The narrator's first impression of Porphyro's secret design comes with a melodious rhythm indicative of his desire to idealize the seduction of Madeline:

> But soon his eyes grew brilliant, when she [Angela] told
> His lady's purpose; and he scarce could brook
> Tears, at the thought of those enchantments cold,
> And Madeline asleep in lap of legends old.
>
> Sudden a thought came like a full-blown rose,
> Flushing his brow, and in his pained heart
> Made purple riot. . . .
>   (lines 132–38)

At the word "strategem," however, the narrator adopts a more realistic interpretation of Porphyro's motives and his style becomes abrupt:

>   then doth he propose
> A strategem, that makes the beldame start:
> "A cruel man and impious thou art:
> Sweet lady, let her pray, and sleep, and dream
> Alone with her good angels, far apart
> From wicked men like thee. Go, go!—I deem
> Thou canst not surely be the same that thou didst seem."
>   (lines 138–44)

Keats carefully revises this sequence to accentuate its metrical tensions and the drama of a divided mind that they enact. To create a more incantatory rhythm for Porphyro's entry, he alters the original hexameter line, "Sweet Madeline asleep amongst those legends old," to this final version, "And Madeline asleep in lap of legends old." The change drops the original spondee of "Sweet Madeline" for a more flowing pentameter rhythm while enhancing the line's play of alliteration and assonance. Keats alters the next stanza's opening line for similar purposes, revising it three times as follows:

guage in *The Eve of St. Agnes,* he avoids obvious Spenserian words and expletives that would make the poem artificially imitative in the eighteenth-century manner.[15] Yet while the diction of *The Eve of St. Agnes* seems rather modern, its linguistic opulence has led many readers to label it one of the closest approximations ever of Spenser's rich style. What enables Keats to make the language of *The Eve of St. Agnes* appear so Spenserian and yet appropriate for the nineteenth century is his adaptation of Spenser's past participle.

Sudden a thought more rosy than the rose
Sudden a rosy thought more rosy than the rose
Sudden a thought came full blown like a rose
Sudden a thought came like a full-blown rose

Although the first two attempts are obviously banal, they reveal Keats's wish to produce a mood of enchantment. His simile comparing a thought to a blown rose achieves this effect more successfully. The minor change in the final version nicely balances the syntax of the simile—a thought came / a full-blown rose—to fashion the metrical evenness of Spenserian harmony.

In the more anxious part of this episode, Keats works just as carefully to deepen the rhythmical turbulence of passages like Una's rescue of Redcrosse. Angela's expletive "Go, go!" originally read "O Christ." The change is partially intended to appease conservative readers. But more significantly, Keats also wishes to sharpen the metrical abruptness of Angela's speech with the sudden halts and the gruff consonance of the final version. He accompanies this prosodic roughness with deliberately formed cacophony, rejecting the fairly euphonious original line—"Thou canst not surely be the same as thou didst seem"—for the discordant "that thou" collocation of the revised version—"Thou canst not surely be the same that thou didst seem." Similar changes, both toward fuller mellifluousness and harsher dissonance, recur throughout Keats's manuscript revisions.

15. He uses Spenserian diction, but with restraint, and his selections focus on luxurious words that are not so obviously associated with Spenser's antique language: "frayed," "eremite," "vermeil." Just as characteristically Spenserian as "wight," "weet," or "carle," this diction had not been standard fare in Spenserian imitations and thus lives in *The Eve of St. Agnes* as a remote but not egregiously outmoded language. Keats also ranges throughout the Elizabethans for an older vocabulary not at all constricted to Spenser's domain. Thus words like "cates," "dainties," "beldame," "amort," and "tinct" help conjure up an old world of enchantment without imposing the distraction of a blatantly artificial Spenserian style. Archaic uses of the third-person singular verb—"saith," "riseth," "returneth"—produce a similar impression. These strategies are all the more effective because of Keats's careful balancing of voluptuous language against his rougher style. This tension both staves off any potential excess of luxury and highlights by contrast the rare luster of the poem's mellifluousness. The gorgeous ornamentation of Madeline's bedchamber is thus controlled and heightened by the counterpointing mundane, unmelodious style of Porphyro's secret intrusion: "And 'tween the curtains [he] peeped, where, lo!—how fast she slept" (line 252). The poem's only plain Spenserian archaism comes in an ironic context: Angela's cynical laugh at romance, "I've mickle time to grieve'" (line 126).

Much of the stylistic euphony of *The Faerie Queene* depends on Spenser's manipulation of the past participle, which he uses both to integrate stanzas with a sweeping rhythmical flow and, as an adjective, to infuse individual lines with energy and balance. He often situates the past participle, for instance, at the beginning of a verse to gather the pentameter flow of the preceding line into a forceful trochaic phrase. The rhythm of the first line is thus wrapped into the next; it pauses, and then proceeds in a varied but harmonious cadence. Hazlitt must have sensed the action of this pattern when he likened the flow of Spenser's verses to the infinitely varied pitch of ocean waves, a rhythm well exemplified in the following passages:

> A goodly Lady clad in scarlet red,
> Purfled with gold and pearle of rich assay.
> (1.2.13)

> Yet goodly court he made still to his Dame,
> Pourd out in loosnesse on the grassy grownd.
> (1.7.7)

> So fashioned a Porch with rare deuice,
> Archt ouer head with an embracing vine.
> (2.12.53)

Spenser complements this undulating rhythm by using the past participle adjectively within individual lines to balance and energize them. In these examples, participial adjectives create a polysyllabic evenness or "tinkling," as Cowley heard it (*C* 186), in the pentameter line and give substantive phrases the energy of verbs: "Without regard of armes and dreaded fight" (1.2.3); "Now when the rosy-fingred Morning faire" (1.2.7); "And next her wrinkled skin rough sackcloth wore" (1.3.14).

Keats studied these participial forms carefully, marking in the Hughes text nearly all of the examples I have just quoted and many other similar passages. To duplicate Spenser's opulent style in *The Eve of St. Agnes,* he actively incorporates both Spenserian uses of the past participle. The following past participles at the start of verse lines, for instance, weave stanzas together and invigorate individual lines in Spenser's typical manner:

> her maiden eyes divine,
> Fix'd on the floor, saw many a sweeping train.
> (lines 57–58)

'Mid looks of love, defiance, hate, and scorn,
Hoodwink'd with faery fancy; all amort.
(lines 69–70)

Beside the portal doors,
Buttress'd from moonlight, stands he.
(lines 76–77)

Keats also uses many participial adjectives to create Spenserian effects of balance and energy. It is their presence in the following lines
that helps make *The Eve of St. Agnes* so evocative of Spenserian harmonies:

The sculptur'd dead, on each side, seemed to freeze
(line 14)

Flatter'd to tears this aged man and poor
(line 21)

Upon the honey'd middle of the night
(line 49)

A casement high and triple-arch'd there was
(line 208)

This last, famous line specifically recalls the "Archt" porch fashioned
with "rare deuice" in the Bower of Bliss. The echo is quite appropriate, for the intricate beauty of Keats's stanzas is fashioned with the
same "rare deuice" of participial form that helps make the luxury of
the Bower of Bliss unforgettable.

Much as Keats uses Spenserian participles to produce such antique
beauty, he also modifies the form to carry Spenser's luxury into the
modern world. The past participles of *The Eve of St. Agnes* actually
function to intensify Spenser's dualism in a highly compressed format. As a verb form that combines process and stasis, freezing action
in a past that is ever continuous and completed at the same time, the
past participle embodies the intersection of flux and permanence,
mutability and ideality, that Keats takes over from Spenser throughout *The Eve of St. Agnes*. It is a highly compressed rhetorical form of
duality that Keats would use with increasing frequency in his last
lyrics. In "To Autumn", for instance, one of his densest gatherings
of this form, the motion of natural cycles seems fixed in a state of
suspended action: "moss'd cottage trees," "half-reap'd furrow,"

"soft-lifted hair," "barred clouds." Similar effects may be found in *The Faerie Queene*, but not nearly as often as in *The Eve of St. Agnes*, which features them in nearly every stanza. Keats's more frequent reliance on the form amounts to a rhetorical intensification of Spenser's duality, as if Spenser's occasional recourse to a rhetoric of duality becomes transformed into the standard language of *The Eve of St. Agnes*. The compression with which Keats thus uses the participial form both to replicate Spenser's beauty and modernize it helps explain why the style and vision of *The Eve of St. Agnes* seem at once so quintessentially Spenserian and so much a part of the nineteenth century. Within the narrow space of a verb, we may conclude, Keats encapsulates the entire revisionary program by which *The Eve of St. Agnes* becomes the first successful oxymoron in the history of Spenserianism—a modern Spenserian poem. That experience places Keats in the very center of his labyrinthine "Mansion of Many Apartments" and gives him a voice to articulate what he finds there during his annus mirabilis of 1819.

III

Keats maintained his conversation with Spenser throughout the great year of 1819, during which he consistently practiced, modified, and extended the revisionary strategies of *The Eve of St. Agnes*. One reason his continuing Spenserianism usually goes overlooked, however, is that he did not produce any more sustained poetic responses to Spenser—not, at least, until he began *The Jealousies* near the end of 1819. We may attribute this shift in emphasis to the independence of manner and the stunning dexterity of borrowing that Keats developed in this year. He would never again compose a major work in the vein of any one single precursor; even his longer works that rely extensively on specific models, such as *The Fall of Hyperion* in its recasting of Dante and Milton, resist exclusive affiliation with one source. Yet there was probably another reason why Keats did not go on immediately to attempt any more extensive reconstructions of Spenser. He had learned by now to turn to his old mentor and companion in times of crisis and painful self-evaluation. That need would arise soon enough, with his struggles in *The Fall of Hyperion* and during the torturous final months of his life. For now, however, fresh from the encouraging success of *The Eve of St. Agnes*, he was eager to experiment with different modes, which is why I do not intend to examine the long narratives or the odes of 1819 in elabo-

rate detail. To say they are not indebted to his Spenserian experience, though, would be a mistake. Indeed, we cannot fully appreciate the complexity of those breakthrough works without recognizing
how the revisionary strategies of *The Eve of St. Agnes* help shape their
general themes, their narrative structures, their stylistic patterns,
and, above all, their psychodynamics.

It is a commonplace of Keats criticism that his ongoing conflict of
realism and ideality makes up the dramatic center of his 1819
poems. It is not so obvious to note how that conflict, though developing out of a wide variety of experiences, came into his mature
poetry through the conduit of his recent Spenserianism. The fact
that it so often acquires a Spenserian resonance in the odes, for instance—with the contrast between "magic casements" and "fairy
lands forlorn" in the "Ode to a Nightingale"; or the encounter in
"Ode to Psyche" between those two lovers, Cupid and Psyche, whom
Keats always associated with *The Faerie Queene*[16]—suggests that his
recent Spenserianism played a major role in focusing the interiority
of his 1819 works. The same experience was equally influential in
shaping the stylistic advances that articulated that mental situation so
memorably. Keats's intensification of Spenserian prosody and pictorialism alerted him, in a broad sense, to the moderns' crucial need to
become "Misers of sound and syllable." We must "'load every rift' of
. . . [our] subject with ore" (*LJK* 2:323), he told Shelley, quoting the
Cave of Mammon episode in an obvious recollection of his own recent loading of Spenser's rifts. That enriching compression of
Spenser's style generally helped inspire the great condensation of
phrasing for which the 1819 works, especially the odes, are so noteworthy. It also revealed various practical methods for so hoarding
energy, all of which Keats vigorously executed throughout the 1819
poems: the condensed pictorial representation of mental conflict
through open-ended or antiallegorical allegory; the highly focused
psychodrama of an exploratory voyage through enigmatic houses;
the increased deployment of past participles to express the duality of
arrested motion; and a preference for short poems, whose elliptical
brevity encapsulates the fractured experience of modern vision
while ensuring compactness of style. This final lesson entailed one of
Spenser's most salutary contributions, though an indirect one, to

16. In the copy of *The Faerie Queene* that Keats may have used in his last months,
Spenser's famous portrait of Cupid and Psyche in the Garden of Adonis (3.6.50) is
marked. Wolfson finds "Ode to Psyche" echoing the contraries of *Amoretti* 77 (*The
Questioning Presence* 305–6).

Keats's developing poetics. In the past Keats had always discounted the ultimate value of the short lyric, using it chiefly as a stepping-stone to what he deemed greater projects in the epic genre. Now, certainly in part as a result of his revaluation of Spenser, he began to consider lyrical and dramatic poetry as the best formal vehicles for a self-questioning modern poetics. The immediate result of that redirection of energies, the 1819 odes, was enough alone to place him among the English poets.

The single most important outgrowth of his recent experience with Spenser, however, was his inclination throughout 1819 toward the revisionary pictorialism of the allegory in *The Eve of St. Agnes.*[17] *The Fall of Hyperion*, for instance, features a series of pictures quite similar in their visual details and their psychological implications to the allegory of the "Mansion of Many Apartments" and its poetical manifestation in the tapestry of *The Eve of St. Agnes.* The dreamer finds himself initially enchanted by a sumptuous feast. Then, like the poet at Keats's mansion or the narrator entering Madeline's castle, he moves into a complicated edifice where he begins to experience human suffering. Passing from this "antichamber" of his dream, he then proceeds to the labyrinth of Hyperion's interior rooms. There, like Keats's poet clouded in a mist or his narrator in *The Eve of St. Agnes* encountering the dualities of Madeline's bed-

---

17. This is not to say, however, that he utterly stopped using the allegorical forms of Spenserian dualism that had made up such an important part of his earlier poetry. Vendler notes how extensively the 1819 odes transform the kind of Spenserian allegorical representations of mutability that had figured so largely in *Endymion* (88, 205–7, 242–43). "La Belle Dame Sans Merci" features a condensed form of the dream-vision motif of *Endymion*. The specific details of its brief allegory, where a "knight at arms" awakens from his dreamed dalliance with a fairy maiden to find himself alone on "the cold hill's side" (lines 1, 44), recall Arthur's story of waking from his dream of "lovely Blandishment" with Gloriana, "Queen of Faires," to find "her place devoid, / And nought but pressed Grass where she had lyen" (1.9.15)—a passage that Keats underlined in his copy of Hughes's edition of *The Faerie Queene*. Even the words of the fairy's song in "La Belle Dame Sans Merci," "And sure in language strange she said— / 'I love thee true'" (lines 27–28), echo Gloriana's plea to Arthur: "Most goodly Glee and lovely Blandishment / She to me made, and bade me love her dear" (1.9.14). In the typical pattern of Keats's Spenserian revisionism, the psychodrama of "La Belle Dame Sans Merci" is much more ambiguous than the mental experience of Arthur's story. Arthur is unhappy at the disappearance of his dream lover and unsure if his vision is true. But he vows to press on in his search for Gloriana, convinced that what he saw partakes of the "divine" and is somehow attainable. Keats's knight-at-arms wanders aimlessly in despair, enthralled by a vision that he cannot hope to translate into reality.

chamber, he witnesses the titans' fall into human limitation and sees deeper into the pain and contradiction of experience. As in the allegories of Keats's mansion and *The Eve of St. Agnes*, moreover, this final step brings none of the illumination that comes at the end of Spenser's episodes. Moneta, who bears in her contrariety many resemblances to the veiled, hermaphroditic Venus whose blessing Scudamour beseeches (*FQ*, 4.10.40–41), reveals in her eyes a profound vision of sorrow and mutability. But where Venus grants Scudamour's wish and, in effect, enables him to complete his quest for Amoret (a provisional finality, of course, that Spenser eventually dismantles), Moneta discloses in her eyes a "blank splendour" that hints at no resolution to the immense sufferings and contradictions her visionary look embodies.

In *Lamia* Keats adapts Tighe's version of the Spenserian castle in her Psyche allegory, despite his claim to "see through" her weakness (*LJK* 2:18), probably because she orchestrates her drama of enchantment and realism through the interaction of two characters, Cupid and Psyche, whose descent into the heart's "Mansion of Many Apartments" resembles the voyages of his own similarly opposed pair of lovers, Lycius and Lamia.[18]

If we consider how integrally Keats associated such ambiguous

18. Weller provides a detailed study of correspondences in the poetry of Keats and Tighe. Tighe begins her sequence in the characteristic Spenserian manner, introducing Psyche to the dazzling enchantments of the outer halls of Cupid's abode:

> Increasing wonder filled her ravished soul,
> For now the pompous portals opened *wide*,
> There, pausing oft, with timid foot she stole
> Through halls high domed, enriched with sculptured pride,
> While gay saloons appeared on either side
> In splendid vista opening to her sight. . . .
> The amethyst was there of violet hue,
> And there the topaz shed its golden ray,
> The chrysoberyl, and the sapphire blue,
> As the clear azure of a sunny day.
> (I, 397–409)

Keats follows this specific example of the Spenserian pattern for the psychodrama of truth and beauty in *Lamia*, bringing the enchanted Lycius, like the young-minded poet of his own "Mansion of Many Apartments," to a similar external chamber of delights. The "ample span / Of the wide doors" to Lamia's palace open like Cupid's "portals wide" to disclose the luster of marbled architecture that also seems brighter than, as Tighe puts it, "the beams of heaven" (I, 405):

pictures of the mind with the Spenserian revisionism of *The Eve of St. Agnes*, we may also find his conversation with Spenser responsible for an allegorical methodology even more basic to the later poems. We have seen how Keats learned in *The Eve of St. Agnes* to darken the "clear vision" of Spenser's allegories by dropping their conclusive authorial glosses. Such a lesson also suggested to him, however, that a still more sophisticated way to complicate the procedures of Spenserian allegory would be, instead of dropping those instructive commentaries, to replace their assertiveness with open-ended questions about the enigma of the allegory. The result was a kind of self-questioning allegory, a more forcefully interrogative version of the Spenserian pictures of *The Eve of St. Agnes*. This new form of anti-allegorical allegory recurs throughout the 1819 poems. The odes, for instance, can be read as dramatic meditations on such pictures,

> they had arrived before
> A pillar'd porch, with lofty portal door,
> Where hung a silver lamp, whose phosphor glow
> Reflected in the slabbed steps below,
> Mild as a star in water; for so new,
> And so unsullied was the marble hue,
> So through the crystal polish, liquid fine,
> Ran the dark veins, that none but feet divine
> Could e're have touch'd there.
>   (I, 378–86)

Tighe's description of Cupid's festival, in which "melodious music" invisibly prepares the "splendid banquet" (I, 424–25), similarly provides a model for Lamia's sumptuous banquet, during which "haunting music" (II, 122) is the magical force that lays out the table. Tighe's continuation of the Spenserian sequence, in which this enchantment gives way to a darker reality, proves just as useful to Keats. She makes all of Cupid's illusions vanish in order to dramatize Psyche's painful descent into real experience: "Dread horror seizes on her sinking heart, / A mortal chillness shudders at her breast, / Her soul shrinks fainting from death's icy dart" (II, 244–46). Lamia's enchantment similarly disintegrates in the cold light of reality, and like Psyche she turns pale and frigid: "pale . . . [her hand] lay upon the rosy couch: / 'Twas icy . . . all was blight; / Lamia, no longer fair, there sat a deadly white" (II, 250–76). Keats's adaptation of this pattern from *Psyche* is finally not that different from his revisionary handling of Spenser. To deepen his own vision into the dark passages of the heart, he finds it necessary to "see through" and correct Tighe's repetition of Spenser's ideological errors. Where she has Psyche learn a conventional moral about temptation and virtuous wedlock, *Lamia*, like *The Eve of St. Agnes* and *The Fall of Hyperion*, yields no ultimate illumination amid its dark corridors of the mind. Lamia's enchanted palace remains both an artifice and a genuine ideal. The exposure of its illusions is both clarifying and disastrous.

as if they verbalize the ambiguous interpretations that are left implicit in the tapestry of *The Eve of St. Agnes*. "Ode to Psyche" begins with a vision or a portrait of Cupid and Psyche embracing in the kind of scene that Spenser loved to allegorize, which is then followed by the narrator's uncertain attempt to comprehend that picture. Similarly in the "Ode on Indolence," whose dreamlike figures resemble the ghostly participants of the Masque of Cupid, the speaker observes "three figures" passing before him like images painted "on a marble urn" and then struggles irresolutely to identify their meaning and value. The narrator of "Ode on a Grecian Urn," in the most well-known instance of this pattern, turns over various interpretations of a design figured on a vase only to arrive at Keats's most famous conundrum, "'Beauty is truth, truth beauty.'" This same kind of questioning informs *The Fall of Hyperion*, whose narrator views a temple evocative of hidden meaning like so many of Spenser's allegorical structures and then wonders how to interpet it. Moneta's beaming eyes provide their own form of allegory—the story of the titans' war—which the narrator must also struggle to comprehend. We would not call any of these poems "Spenserian." Yet our recognition of such patterns of indeterminacy and their roots in *The Eve of St. Agnes* can help us see how many of the principal strategies of Keats's mature, self-questioning poetics grow out of his Spenserian experience. Our familiarity with that line of development may also deepen our overall understanding of the range of his duality in the 1819 works. To know that the figures on the urn in "Ode on Indolence" recall the participants in the Masque of Cupid, for instance, is to comprehend the entire poem not so much as a meditation on love or ambition as a dramatic response to what Keats always considered a profound site of contrariety in *The Faerie Queene*.

How much Keats attributed his ongoing elaborations of the second Renaissance to these Spenserian "incentives to conversation," indeed, how much he continued to honor Spenser's enabling inspiration in spite of its errors, may be suggested by his recreation of Venus as Moneta. When Scudamour sees Venus smiling with "amiable grace" at his "offence" and favoring his "pretence," he feels "emboldened with more confidence" to carry out his mission (4.10.56). The parallel with Keats's first reception of Spenser's "kind" grace, which gave him the confidence to carry on with his own strange "pretence," is unmistakable. Integrating Spenser and Venus with the figure of Moneta, in an amazingly dextrous collocation of "significant allusions," thus makes the "benignant light" that Moneta beams down on the questing poet-figure of *The Fall of Hyperion* a beaconlike testament to how much Spenser had guided Keats all along in his "strange pretence" to "be among the English Poets." The élan of so translating what is a rather comical Spenserian scene—Venus laughs coquettishly at Scudamour's amorous impatience—into one of the severest moments in all of Keats's poetry may represent the most stunning example ever of Spenser's capacity to enkindle joy among those latecomers caught up in the dire contentions of poetic revisionism.[19]

IV

If we assume that by the summer of 1819 Keats had thoroughly incorporated these compact forms of Spenserianism into his overall creative endeavor, then we might feel at a loss to explain *The Jealousies*. Composed in Spenserian stanzas and set in an elfin fairyland, it is clearly located within the tradition of Spenserian poetry. Yet in its narrative diffuseness it seems to retreat completely from all of Keats's recent Spenserian advances. As a rambling burlesque on contemporary politics and mores, it appears to owe more to the works of Pope, Swift, and Byron. Brown was puzzled by its "startling contradictions" and Keats's lack of interest in them as he ploughed ahead, according to Brown, "chiefly for amusement" (*KC* 2:99). Readers ever since have regarded the poem as a confused foray "outside Keats's range" and thus "one of his weakest performances" (Allott 702).

Keats's apparent indifference to the work has left his critics generally disinclined to spend much time with it, beyond tracing its allusions to contemporary political and literary figures. Yet Keats seemed genuinely interested in its quality, despite the cavalier stance he sometimes adopted toward it. He expressed wishes to improve it for publication, and he often spoke of resuming composition after sickness forced him to put it aside in what he always considered, as late as August 1820, a temporary hiatus (*LJK* 2:268, 289, 299, 328).

19. Vendler persuasively argues for Keats's recollection of the androgynous Nature of the *Mutabilitie Cantos* in his portrait of Moneta (205–8). If we accept her claim, we may see an even more complicated twist to Keats's honoring of Spenserian influence here. Nature subordinates Mutabilitie to Spenser's religious ideals of transcendent permanence. For Keats, then, to turn Nature's transcendentalism into Venus's coquettish, endless doubling, is to highlight the revisionary troping at the heart of the special intimacy with Spenser he was celebrating.

Clearly, no matter how slight the work may have appeared to him, there was something in it that he cared about. If we regard it seriously in its Spenserian context, we may find it actually extending and qualifying the revisionism of *The Eve of St. Agnes*. We may also find that its new position toward Spenserianism reflects a change in Keats's overall aesthetics that we have tended to overlook because of its development after what we now consider his last important works.

Toward the end of 1819, Keats was growing dissatisfied with the abstractness of his Spenserian strategies and his creative production in general. His allegorical mechanisms, however much they may have humanized Spenser's vision, began to seem heavily formalized, even inimical to the sensitive tracing of the heart's pulses that had become the purported mission of his art. Moreover, the very focus on mental duality that came out of his Spenserianism, much as it may have energized his poetry, started to appear excessively self-absorbed and therefore at odds with the sweeping exploration of human experience that was the ideal of negative capability.[20] His moves in the summer of 1819 toward a more realistic and objective poetry are well documented: the attempt at a Drydenesque worldliness in *Lamia*, the cultivation of Shakespearean passions for *Otho the Great* and *King Stephen*, the gripping embrace of human suffering in *The Fall of Hyperion*. Less obvious is the difficulty he encountered in reformulating practices that had made a major contribution to the drama of the 1819 poems. Unable to part with them easily—"I have been endeavouring to persuade myself to untether Fancy"—yet feeling "more at home amongst Men and women," he found himself in a quandary. "I and myself cannot agree about this at all" (*LJK* 2:234). One solution, which had worked before in the Lear sonnet, was to exorcise perceived excesses by swinging to their opposite. It would have been unlikely for Keats to reject completely the Spenserian forms of mental drama that had become so important to his craft. Yet for a time it must have seemed necessary to cast them aside, or substantially transform them in order to reach what had surfaced as his new and greatest ambition: the writing of "a few fine Plays" in Shakespeare's tradition.[21]

---

20. Wolfson summarizes a line of critical responses, mostly negative, to the growing selfhood and emotionality of Keats's later poetry ("Composition and 'Unrest'" 53–60).

21. Wolfson defends the last lyrics by showing how they extend many of the formal and mental contraries that had sustained Keats's great poetry of 1818–19 up to the ode "To Autumn" ("Composition and 'Unrest'"). Rather than dispute this claim, for

We can trace this reorientation most clearly in a new kind of Spenserianism that he began to develop late in 1819. He wished to attempt a new poem, for instance, that would drop the stylistic "colouring" and the allegorical "drapery" of *The Eve of St. Agnes* for a more straightforward display of "Character and Sentiment" (*LJK* 2:234). With such an intention in mind, he began to reconceive Spenser, or rather to place a new emphasis on that part of Spenser which the early Romantics had taught him to appreciate long ago: his pathos as a poet who wrote about "Men and women" in his role of political writer and deep thinker into human frailty. Keats thus felt particularly interested in adapting his sad lament for Leicester's hardships in *The Ruines of Time* and his commiseration with Una's patiently endured sorrows (*LJK* 2:234; *KC* 1:267). It was not so easy, though, to steer away from the dualities of Spenser's allegory for this more Shakespearean kind of art. Keats never began those projects. Instead he set about revising *The Eve of St. Agnes* to erase some of its "colouring" and supply what he termed in defending his revisions more "Character" (*LJK* 2:163), as if an act of exorcism was required before embarking in the new direction.

The extremity of this self-correction suggests how hard it was to curtail Spenserian "drapery." Instead of simply toning down his Spenserian "colouring," Keats adds a touch of vulgar realism, "pettish disgust" Woodhouse called it (*LJK* 2:163), that makes a burlesque of the poem's psychodrama. Porphyro is made to encroach upon Madeline's breast, like the seductive villain of a Gothic potboiler, while panting into her "burning ear." And the sober original version of the deaths of Angela and the Beadsman is replaced with this piece of Byronic cynicism:

> Angela went off
> Twitch'd with the Palsy; and with face deform
> The beadsman stiffen'd, 'twixt a sigh and laugh
> Ta'en sudden from his beads by one weak little cough.[22]

Not so much of a calculated move to enhance the quality of his con-

---

her evidence is compelling, I wish to present Keats's final acts of self-correction as yet another dimension of the contraries that Wolfson emphasizes. His last revaluation of himself entails the kind of questioning of his own inwardness that Wolfson finds carried out in the formal conflicts of his final lyrics.

22. Stillinger records these emendations in his edition of Keats's poems. On Woodhouse's advice, they were kept out of the published text.

clusion, this change seems more like Keats's flailing out against a personal excess he cannot subdue. The rodomontade that Woodhouse heard in Keats's defense of the revision is another sign of that tendency to overcompensate for a fixation on interior conflicts too closely related to his own psyche.

Our recognition of this problem can show us how *The Jealousies* is not at all an anomoly in Keats's creative evolution but a part of the last major development in his Spenserian theory and his general aesthetics. Indulging in long, rather flaccid narratives like *Otho the Great* and *The Jealousies* during his last months of composition was but another form of overreacting against what now looked like excessive self-preoccupation in the mental drama of his recent works. Ludolph's Gothic rantings in *Otho the Great,* the hyperbolic voice of self-division that he is constantly urged to restrain, may be read as a type of self-parody; that is, Keats's satire on his own self-absorbed experience with mental conflict. His concern to limit that experience is behind the severe condemnation of self-divided poetic dreamers in *The Fall of Hyperion.* The poet of the 1819 odes might be considered a bold explorer into the contradictions of the human heart, but he could also be viewed as a fevered, "dreaming thing"—as Moneta reprimands him—cut off from the hearts of fellow mortals by his own obsessive conflicts. This may be why the narrator of "Ode on Indolence" refuses to follow those figures who represent, among other things, the center of contrariety in the Masque of Cupid. The self-reproaches of *The Fall of Hyperion* are directed at Keats's own relentless participation in such a masque. Yet the burdens and limitations of the way he fashions that epic criticism of himself also provide the impetus for a different kind of self-correction in *The Jealousies.*

The structure of *The Fall of Hyperion* actually reduplicates the very self-division it is meant to resolve, and it foments this internal conflict in the face of two of Keats's most imposing and self-confident precursors: Milton and Dante. As an allegorical vision, *The Fall of Hyperion* aspires to the prophetic insight of Keats's strongest forebears. But this same visionary format must have struck him, on some level, as antithetical to the kind of humanizing perspective he wished to impose on the earlier *Hyperion.* Thus while he fabricates an elaborate allegorical framework, he also tries to de-Miltonize or simplify the poem's diction.[23] Such divided impulses are closely linked with the very fevered conflicts of mind the poem is meant to transcend.

---

23. Allott notes this contradiction and points out many examples in her running annotations of *The Fall of Hyperion.*

Always his own best critic, Keats must have seen the irony. Not surprisingly, he began brooding once again on Milton's superior confidence of purpose.

Although the aesthetic issues were now somewhat different, the psychological situation paralleled the conditions that drove Keats to abandon *Hyperion*. As he reexperienced in Milton's company the conflicting sensations of reverence and intimidation, he went into a defensive crouch and looked for ways to subvert Milton's authority. He told both Reynolds and Bailey, while refitting *Hyperion* into a vision, how "the Paradise lost becomes a greater wonder." It seemed the "most remarkable Production of the world." Yet its lofty style—written in "the vein of art"—struck him as "a corruption of our language" (*LJK:* 2:139, 146, 212). This criticism may seem to betray his old nervousness about Milton's dominant power, which is still more obvious in his blustering claim about Chatterton's linguistic superiority to Milton (*LJK* 2:212). Such a rash comparison was part of a defensive strategy to belittle Milton by forcing him into an association, an unfavorable one at that, with the less threatening Chatterton. The anxiety of rivaling Milton that was at the bottom of these measures surfaced openly when Keats declared, in what Bloom calls the motto of Romanticism's influence dilemma: "I have but lately stood on my guard against Milton. Life to him would be death to me" (*LJK* 2:212). A self-corrective poetics, it would seem, could not be carried out in a Miltonic vein.

But there might be other ways. "I wish to devote myself to another sensation," Keats went on (*LJK* 2:212). Spenser had rescued him from Milton once before. Now, in the scenario that had become the pattern of his relations with the English Renaissance, he shifted from Milton to a different, less pressured Spenserian handling of the same aesthetic and psychological conflicts. The facility with which he reeled out stanza after stanza of *The Jealousies* suggests just how relaxing it was to return to Spenser once again, as if he now experienced the very kind of emboldening pleasure that he had chronicled in his portrait of Moneta. We may even read the excursive frivolity of *The Jealousies* as a sustained *jeu d'esprit* on the soothing effect of Spenser's companionship. Yet there are also serious aesthetic strategies beneath the poem's surface banter. Through its awkward allegory, Keats plays out the self-corrective impulse of *The Fall of Hyperion*, without the inhibitions that had previously beleaguered him and in a format that proves even more conducive to his own concerns in late 1819. He combines his recent patterns of Spenserian revisionism with a pastiche of Byronic satire, Popean mock-heroism, and eighteenth-century Spenserian parody in a farcical alliance that critiques his preoccupation with his own fevered divisions.[24]

Such a critique arises from a much more elaborate version of the way he parodies the psychodrama of realism and ideality in his revisions of *The Eve of St. Agnes*. He establishes the basis for a similar drama of mind in *The Jealousies* by grounding his narrative in conflicts between the different orders of action in fairyland and the human world. This paradigm obviously recalls the doubling experience of Spenserian characters like Arthur whose travels between England and the realm of "faery" depict allegories of the mind's division between reality and enchantment. But this psychodramatic apparatus is dismantled in Keats's poem by the same kind of worldly cynicism that travesties the scene of interiority in *The Eve of St. Agnes* revisions. His fairy king and queen, Elfinan and Bellanaine—like the sylphs of *The Rape of the Lock,* the characters of *Don Juan,* or the lowlife figures of such Spenserian parodies as Pope's "The Alley"— enmesh themselves in the political and sexual imbroglios of mortal affairs. Their motivation for action, like the power that moves so many of Byron's high-speaking characters, is concupiscence. They both love humans "smooth as shades" while despising the "mere shade" of a fairy lover (line 9). With that concern governing the action of *The Jealousies,* the poem's allegorical scenario of mental conflict degenerates into a bedroom farce. It is probably significant in this respect that Keats's narrative reverses the direction of Spenser's quests, shifting the action from fairyland to the real world that Elfinan seeks out instead of following Arthur's path from England to Gloriana's kingdom. Such a reversal drives home Keats's rejection of allegorical experience in *The Jealousies* and his refusal to engage in the kind of self-reflexive psychodrama that makes up the stuff of questing toward distant ideals in Romantic Spenserianism. That he uses one part of the Spenserian background, the parodic line, to qualify this mainstream tradition is equally significant. Such a maneuver is symbolic of the way he was critiquing himself, bringing his own inclination to self-parody against some of the major thrusts of his 1819 poetics.

Keats applies that parodic impulse to his own creative situation

24. Bate (*John Keats* 624), Gittings (*The Mask of Keats* 117), and Brogan (299) note the element of self-parody in *The Jealousies*. Ridley compares that parody to the revisions of *The Eve of St. Agnes* (179). Gittings (*The Mask of Keats* 142) finds the poem deeply concerned with the very chiaroscuro of "light and shade" (142) that had played such a central role in *The Eve of St. Agnes*. None of these readings attempts, however, to show how *The Jealousies* makes a sustained comment on Keats's prior Spenserianism.

most pointedly in scenes of great pictorial virtuosity, the type of elaborate panel-making that carries the weight of his allegorical complexity in *The Eve of St. Agnes*. These passages are consistently interrupted and their potential for psychodrama subverted by the low, colloquial style of *The Eve of St. Agnes* revisions. Passages like the following description of a holiday crowd, for instance, approach Keats's most sophisticated Spenserian manner:

> Legions of holiday; bright standards waved,
> And fluttering ensigns emulously craved
> Our minute's glance; a busy thunderous roar
> From square to square among the buildings raved,
> As when the sea, at flow, gluts up once more
> The craggy hollowness of a wild-reefed shore.
>
> (lines 733–38)

In its contrast of a magical "holiday" scene with a reference to the undulating sea, that famous image of mutability in *Childe Harold's Pilgrimage* and a frequent symbol of temporal impermanence in Keats's own poetry, this picture offers hints of the allegorical clashes between realism and enchantment in Keats's earlier Spenserian painting.[25] But those hints are quickly wiped out by the kind of burlesque raillery common to Spenserian parodies like "The Alley:"

> Powder'd bag-wigs and ruffy-tuffy heads
> Of cinder wenches meet and soil each other;
> Toe crush'd with heel ill-natured fighting breeds,
> Frill-rumpling elbows brew up many a bother,
> And fists in the short ribs keep up the yell and pother.
>
> (lines 770–74)

The contrast here seems quite different from Keats's earlier notion of combining grotesque and sentimental styles to dramatize mental conflict. Rather the parodic vulgarity of the rabble scene, more like the coarseness of *The Eve of St. Agnes* revisions, undercuts entirely the poem's movement toward psychodramatic complexity. The painter of *The Eve of St. Agnes* is thus replaced by a buffoon of a poet who would have been right at home in "The Alley." Such a poet actually stumbles into the court rout of *The Jealousies* to sing a "pro-

---

25. In echoing "On the Sea," this passage particularly recalls Keats's aspirations in that sonnet toward a Spenserian amplitude of style and depth of psychology.

thalamion," not in Spenser's eloquent manner but "with [a] rhyming clack" that produces what Keats calls elsewhere "tit-bits for Phoebus" (line 777). It is as if one part of the Spenserian tradition rushes in to make a mockery of the poetic opulence and the mental interiority that had become central to Keats's mature Spenserianism. Such carving of Apollo's bounty into "tit-bits for Phoebus" is just how Keats rather uneasily tried to correct himself in his last months as a poet.

The self-parody of *The Jealousies*, like the cynicism of *The Eve of St. Agnes* revisions, would never produce a satisfying poetics. It reveals Keats's discomfort with himself more than anything else, which is probably why it could get out of control in the awkward excesses of works like *Otho the Great* and *The Jealousies*. Nevertheless, like so many of Keats's experiments, it helped to exorcise liabilities and push him forward, in this case away from a self-absorbed inwardness toward a poetics more deeply immersed in the sufferings of others. That step also entailed yet a different, more comfortable kind of engagement with Spenser, who in his special gift for pathos seemed especially fit to preside over the sensitive and restorative poetics that Moneta prescribes. Keats was already reconsidering the importance of Spenserian pathos, intending with his Leicester and Una plans to adapt Spenser's political realism and emotional sensitivity for such a new, more penetrating drama of the human heart. The raillery of *The Jealousies*, moreover, reinforced his lifelong sense of companionship with an easy master whose persisting "life" did not mean "death" to Keats because he could be refit, "toyed with" as Shenstone would say, and assumed into the voice of a modern song. Keats spent much of his last months in Spenser's company, absorbing him one final time to carry out this last variation in their ever-evolving dialogue.

V

During his last months of intense intellectual activity, the summer of 1820, Keats thought about Spenser more than any other poet from the literary past. He read extensively in *The Faerie Queene*, marked numerous passages from it, quoted it in his letters, and wrote one short Spenserian poem that was, in fact his last poetic composition. His reimmersion in *The Faerie Queene* amounted to a last and substantial revaluation of how Spenser could best speak to the modern world. Though Keats would always remain fascinated with Spenserian duality, no matter how much he needed at times to distance himself from it,[26] his primary attention focused now on the interconnected areas of Spenser's political experience and his emotional poignance. Where the old master had once guided Keats into the labyrinth of mental division, he now came as the sorrowing poet of loss, hardship, and the breaking of the spirit, who led the way into the deep core of human suffering. Keats had been exposed to Spenser's sympathy for human heartaches many times before, but perhaps it was the magnitude of his own sufferings in his last months that fully sensitized him to this side of Spenser. It seemed that everywhere he looked in The Faerie Queene now he found a reflection of his own understanding of the human condition as beset with pain, sickness, and death. That discovery amounted to a unique reading of Spenser as a Shakespearean poet of human passion, who may have meant even more than Shakespeare in these last days because of his exceeding compassion for the human fragility that Keats now experienced so deeply along his own pulses. It is a reading that can add much to our own understanding of that "literal" level of suffering in The Faerie Queene that has moved so many of its recent commentators to honor the "pathos" of its "human characters" (MacCaffrey 408), who in their "sufferer's syndrome" (Crompton 119) must endure "the 'weake state of sad afflicted man'" (Berger, Allegorical Temper 127). Keats may be able to tell us so much about that Spenserian "state" because he finally absorbed in the depths of his heart, and perhaps with greater poignance than any other reader of Spenser, the "modest revelation" of The Faerie Queene, as Berger puts it, that "fraile" humanity "is ordained to wander 'on the foam / Of perilous seas, in faery lands forlorn'" (240).

Like Keats's earlier reformulations of Spenser, such a reading also meant correcting perceived limitations, in this case the stylistic embellishments, aristocratical prejudices, and moral absolutism that had limited, to a certain extent, Spenser's empathy for frail human nature. Keats may have been correcting some of his own limitations here. He seemed more concerned, however, with the general ideal of freeing himself from any interferences with his own sensitivity to human weakness, which is precisely what he meant to accomplish by harmonizing Spenser's core of emotionality with his own voice.

---

26. The markings in the Spenser volumes he may have used focus often on examples of Spenserian duality—the contrasts in the Masque of Cupid, for instance, or the contrast of "sweet life" and "inly deep" pain that Timias experiences at the hands of Belphoebe (3.5.34).

His famous letter to Shelley of August 1820 suggests how much this last rehabilitation of Spenser helped him define that voice. Responding to Shelley's *The Cenci*, he criticizes modern artists for grasping after a "purpose" and he politely censured the "magnanimity" of Shelley's work, or its lack of concentrated detail. The rhetorical excess and moralistic "purpose" of *The Cenci*, he suggests, are hindrances to the "dramatic effect" of its passions. To illustrate his point more graphically, Keats rewrites one of his favorite Spenserian episodes, the Cave of Mammon. He argues that an "*artist*," as opposed to a writer with a purpose, "must serve Mammon—he must have 'self-concentration' selfishness perhaps. You I am sure will forgive me for sincerely remarking that you might curb your magnanimity and be more of an artist, and 'load every rift' of your subject with ore" (*LJK* 2:322–23). This reference to Mammon's cave instructs Shelley by redeeming Spenser's heart from his moral thinking and his stylistic preoccupations. We have seen that Mammon's cave, where "rich metall loaded every rifte" (2.7.28), abounds with lavish ornamentation that Spenser is at great pains both to relish and to condemn on moral grounds. The episode also features, though less obviously, a sensitive probing of what Spenser calls "this fraile life of man" (2.7.65) in the "endlesse" wailings of the damned inhabitants of the Garden of Proserpina and the final collapse of Guyon, whose "vitall powres gan wexe both weake and wan, / For want of food, and slepe" (2.7.65). In rereading the entire episode, Keats associates Spenser's "rich metall" with the "dramatic effect" of these sequences and recommends a more condensed portrayal of the "fraile life" they document. Such a correction thus purifies Spenser's emotional center from his moralism, his aestheticism, and even his inward division between the two. That redemption of his empathy for the "enfeebled spright" allows Keats to tell Shelley what it means to be "more of an artist."

Shortly before writing to Shelley, Keats memorialized in a poem this resurrection of the modern artist from Spenser's ashes. It is his last poetic composition, a single Spenserian stanza about the encounter between Artegall and the Giant in Book 5 of *The Faerie Queene*. Keats seeks to deepen the humanity of that episode as well, rescuing Spenser's sympathy for the oppressed from his aristocratical prejudices. The Giant is a crude, unlearned champion of democracy, who wishes to abolish privilege and draw "all the wealth of rich men to the poore" (5.2.38). In his opposition to "Tyrants" and his sympathy for the suffering masses, the Giant must have seemed to Keats at one with Spenser's own tenderness. From a nineteenth-century liberal's perspective, however, it must have also appeared as though such kindness was eventually sacrificed to aristocratical bigotry and moral absolutism. Spenser has Artegall, the spokesman for aristocracy, defend privilege as a manifestation of natural hierarchies created by God. When the Giant resists this argument, Artegall instructs his servant, Talus, to hurl the brutish proponent of equality into the sea. Keats deplores the ideology here but appreciates the buried sympathies for human suffering, which even touches momentarily on the Giant's frailty: "So downe the cliffe the wretched Gyant tumbled . . . His timbered bones all broken rudely rumbled" (5.2.50).[27] For his own poem, Keats redeems that sensitivity by staging a rematch in which the Giant, strengthened by a progressive education, defeats his reactionary foes:

> In after time, a sage of mickle lore,
> Yclep'd Typographus, the giant took
> And did refit his limbs as heretofore,
> And made him read in many a learned book,
> And into many a lively legend look;
> Thereby in goodly themes so training him,
> That all his brutishness he quite forsook,
> When, meeting Artegall and Talus grim,
> The one he struck stone blind, the other's eyes wox dim.

The resurrection of this rough Giant, deepened in his sensitivity for the oppressed and schooled to strike down political and moral tyranny, seems no less than a brief allegory of the redemption of Spenser's own innate but limited sympathy for the "weake state of sad afflicted man."[28] A reeducated Spenser, so the allegory implies, gives birth to the "artist" of "after time." If we follow that allegory all the way out, we cannot miss in the playful self-referentiality of "a sage of mickle lore" the refreshing lightness that Keats always felt in his relationship with Spenser. The giant from the past who came to him so

27. This passage is marked in the Spenser volumes that Keats may have used.
28. Keats also could be thinking here of Spenser's and his own potentially extreme fixation on inward dualities. The Giant is obsessed with weighing opposites in his balance, especially the contraries of "right or wrong, the false or else the true" (5.2.44). Spenser certainly does not repudiate that occupation, but rather shows how the Giant is proceeding in a misguided way. The outcome of this preoccupation with measuring opposites, on the part of both Spenser and the Giant, as Keats probably saw it, is a diminishing of sympathy for the common crowd that both the Giant and Artegall try to lead.

often with encouragement could also be instructed generously in a mutual interchange from which Keats's voice as a modern "artist" arose.

Even when that voice was silenced by his last physical and emotional torments, Spenser may have helped Keats shape a poetry that could be felt along the heart's pulses. This last work, a poem of his own heart, brought him into closer contact than ever before with our "enfeebled spright." And it manifested perhaps more dramatically than anything else in the history of Spenserianism how the voice of the past could be redeemed to produce the harmonies of a modern song. It was not anything like a poem, as we conventionally think of poems; rather it was fashioned forth in what appear to be Keats's last markings of *The Faerie Queene,* the recent discovery of which adds an important new dimension to our understanding of the Keats/Spenser dynamic.

During his last months in England, Keats told Fanny Brawne that he was marking his favorite passages in Spenser for her (*LJK* 2:302). Until now, we have assumed that the text he used was lost sometime during the mid-nineteenth century. But new evidence suggests that portions of that text have been resting unnoticed for the last thirty years at the Keats House Library in Hampstead. The books in question, comprising volumes 3–6 of the eight-volume set *The Poetical Works of Edmund Spenser* (1778) in John Bell's *The Poets of Great Britain,* were owned by Charles Brown.[29] Although they bear no significant annotations, they are heavily scored with underlinings and marginal strokes, especially in those sections of *The Faerie Queene* they contain, which is everything after Book 2, canto 10. While we cannot be absolutely certain who made these markings, I have argued elsewhere for the very strong possibility of Keats's hand ("'A Lamentable Lay'"). Rather than restate my argument, I will direct readers to that article and simply summarize here the focal points of the evidence: the passages marked in the Bell text correspond to those parts of *The Faerie Queene* that Keats was known to feel most fond of; they also identify those sections of *The Faerie Queene* that Keats adapted in his own poetry; the eccentricities of style in the Bell markings closely match Keats's characteristic manner of marking his other books (see Figs. 6 and 7); and the dramatic events depicted in the Bell markings bear a striking resemblance to Keats's traumatic experiences with

---

29. The four existing volumes that make up this collection are rebound in two-volume sets, numbered 2 and 3. In 1955 they were sent to Keats House from New Zealand, where Brown took them when he emigrated, by Mrs. Mona Martha Osborne, Brown's granddaughter. The whereabouts of volumes 1, 2, 7, and 8 of Bell's edition, or 1 and 4 of the rebound set, are unknown.

Fanny Brawne in 1820. That last point requires elaboration here. For if we assume that Keats did read and mark the Bell text, then we may find that the passages of *The Faerie Queene* he singled out make up a revisionary Spenserian poem of his own heart and its sympathy for the "weake state of sad afflicted man."

His letters of 1820, written in the throes of his advancing illness and the threat of losing everything dear to him, reveal several particular anxieties and obsessions that are closely related to the passages marked in the Bell text. Forced by his illness to live under the care of friends at Hunt's house, away from Fanny Brawne, Keats frequently expressed deep sorrow over their separation. It was a grief exacerbated by his distrust of her loyalty, which made him fear her being "a little inclined to the Cressid" (*LJK* 2:256). At times, he thought that her devotion to him would cure his illness and he likened her to a spirit from the heavens: "Health is my expected heaven and you are the Houri" (*LJK* 2:270). But the remedy he imagined was never efficacious, and his persisting agonies left him with a grim apprehension of his own irremediable deterioration under the burdens of physical disease, unfulfilled love, and a cruel abbreviation to all his creative hopes. "The very thing which I want to live most for," he told Brown, "will be the great occasion of my death. . . . If I had any chance of recovery, this passion would kill me. Indeed, through the whole of my illness, both at your house and at Kentish Town, this fever has never ceased wearing me out." And to Fanny, he confessed his "suspicions" of her faithfulness and lamented that the entire miserable situation was "doing me to death by inches" (*LJK* 2:345, 352, 292, 303). This preoccupation with his own decline induced a morbidity of temperament, shadowed by the bitter awareness of what he might have written and how he might have loved, that bordered at times on suicide: "God knows how it would have been"; "I do not want to live. . . . I wish this coming night may be my last"; "I should like to die. . . . I am glad there is such a thing as the grave—" (*LJK* 2:304, 312–13, 359).

The pattern of these sorrowful thoughts corresponds provocatively with the general motions of mind in the passages marked for notice throughout the Bell text. A survey of them reveals two thematic issues that are frequently combined dominating the marker's interest: the sorrows of romantic love and the myriad dimensions of human suffering. These episodes of grief pivot so consistently upon concerns that were foremost among Keats's thoughts in 1820 that a reading of them presents something like an imaginative gloss on his emotional and mental life in 1820. For him to have singled them out

XXXIV.

Why didſt thou promiſe ſuch a beauteous day,
And make me travel forth without my cloak,
To let baſe clouds o'ertake me in my way,
Hiding thy bravery in their rotten ſmoke ?
'Tis not enough that through the cloud thou break,
To dry the rain on my ſtorm-beaten face,
For no man well of ſuch a ſalve can ſpeak,
That heals the wound, and cures not the diſgrace :
Nor can thy ſhame give phyſick to my grief;
Though thou repent, yet I have ſtill the loſs :
The offender's ſorrow lends but weak relief
To him that bears the ſtrong offence's croſs.
    Ah ! but thoſe tears are pearl which thy love ſheds,
    And they are rich, and ranſom all ill deeds.

XL.

Next unto him was Neptune pictured,
In his divine resemblance wondrous lyke ;
His face was rugged, and his hoarie hed
Dropped with brackish deaw ; his three-forkt pyke
He stearnly shooke, and therewith fierce did stryke
The raging billowes, that on every syde
They trembling stood, and made a long broad dyke,
That his swift charet might have passage wyde,
Which foure great hippodames did draw, in teme-
                    [wise tyde.

Fig. 6. *Top*: From Keats's copy of *The Poetical Works of William Shakespeare* (1806). Sonnet 34. *Bottom*: From the Keats House copy of Bell's *The Poetical Works of Edmund Spenser* (1778). *The Faerie Queene*, 3.11.40.

VII.

Lo in the orient when the gracious light
Lifts up his burning head, each under eye
Doth homage to his new-appearing fight,
Serving with looks his facred majefty ;
And having climb'd the fteep-up heavenly hill,
Refembling ftrong youth in his middle age,
Yet mortal looks adore his beauty ftill,
Attending on his golden pilgrimage ;
But when from high-moft pitch, with weary car,
Like feeble age, he reeleth from the day,
The eyes, 'fore duteous, now converted are
From his low tract, and look another way :
  So thou, thyfelf out-going in thy noon,
  Unlook'd on dieft, unlefs thou get a fon.

XXXIII.

A teme of dolphins raunged in aray
Drew the smooth charett of sad Cymöent ;
They were all taught by Triton to obay
To the long raynes at her commaundement :
As swifte as swallowes on the waves they went,
That their brode flaggy finnes no fome did reare,
Ne bubling rowndell they behinde them sent ;
The rest of other fishes drawen weare,   [sheare.
Which with their finny oars the swelling sea did

Fig. 7. *Top*: From Keats's copy of *The Poetical Works of William Shakespeare*. Sonnet 7. *Bottom*: From the Keats House copy of Bell's *The Poetical Works of Edmund Spenser*. *The Faerie Queene*, 3.4.33. (By permission of the London Borough of Camden from the Collections of Keats House, Hampstead)

this way suggests the extent to which Spenser's pathos illuminated and helped express his own growing insight into the depths of woe. Suffering of body and mind dominates the passages marked in the Bell text. The following introduction to Book 4, canto 3, distinctly noted with a marginal stroke, could well serve as the basic theme for all of these selections:

> O why doe wretched men so much desire
> To draw their dayes unto the utmost date,
> And doe not rather wish them soone expire
> Knowing the miserie of their estate.
>   (4.3.1)

The Bell markings seem conditioned by a design to prove the truth of this sentiment. They regularly note examples of the "miserie," both physical and emotional, of nearly everyone's "estate" in *The Faerie Queene,* and their focus on suffering centers most often in the kind of lover's anguish that overwhelmed Keats in 1820.

While some instances of love's joy are noted—"that sweete fit, that doth true beautie love" (3.3.1)—examples of its agony predominate. Selected references to Greek mythology, for example, stress the torments that human and divine lovers inflict upon each other: Medea's "furious loving fitt" and Jason's "falsed fayth" (2.12.44); the "bitter balefull stowre" that assailed Venus in her love and grief for the dying Adonis (3.1.34); Apollo "rending his golden heare" for loss of Hyacinth (3.11.37). Within the narrative of Spenser's own chivalric tales, similar torments are marked for special attention: Poeana's "grief entire / For losse of her new love, the hope of her desire" (4.9.13); the misery of Timias who, reft of Belphoebe's love, can find "no ease of griefe nor hope of grace" (4.7.38); and the ongoing sequence that receives the most sustained notice among all these markings, Britomart's agonizing experience in unfulfilled love of a "wounded mind," which brings her "Huge sea of sorrow, and tempestuous griefe" (4.1.7; 3.4.8). Such a persistent focus on the "griefe" of Spenser's lovers is particularly intriguing in its attention to the specific kind of lover's grief that so afflicted Keats in his last months.

He complained most bitterly about the debilitating effects of his jealousy. It is therefore quite revealing to find Spenser's most agonizing portraits of jealously declining lovers noted throughout the Bell text. Marginal strokes, for instance, point out Scudamour's cutting grief when he hears, in graphic detail, about Amoret's purported infidelity: "his heart / Was thrild with inward griefe, as when in chace / The Parthian strikes a stag with shivering dart" (4.1.49). Similar markings highlight Belphoebe's devastating sight of her squire's "soft handling" of another woman, which provokes her lacerating cry, "'Is this the faith?'" (4.7.36). Britomart's tormented distrust of Artegall's faith also receives special attention: "She him condemn'd as trustlesse and untrew" (5.6.5). Among all such selections, particular interest focuses on a long sequence whose potential relevance to Keats's situation is fascinating: Malbecco's self-consuming descent into a miserable abyss of romantic jealousy. Nearly every stanza in this episode is marked, with careful attention given to the verses detailing Malbecco's anguish over Hellenore's desertion and his consequent decay of body and spirit. Watching Hellenore dance with the satyrs, he "grieved sore . . . [and] did his hart with bitter thoughts engore" (3.10.45). Self-tortured by such throes of jealousy, he degenerates physically and mentally in a dramatic metamorphosis punctuated throughout all of its stages by the annotator's marginal strokes:

> But through long anguish, and selfe-murd'ring thought
> He was so wasted and forpined quight,
> That all his substance was consum'd to nought
>
> . . . .
>
> Matter of doubt and dread suspitious,
> That doth with curelesse care consume the hart.
> (3.10.57–59)

The narrator's summary of this episode, with his emphasis on the "selfe-consuming smart" of "Fowle Gealosie," is also marked (3.11.1). Such a preoccupation, on the annotator's part, with these self-consuming smarts of romantic jealousy makes one think inevitably of Keats's frequent lamentations while marking Spenser for Fanny Brawne. "I am tormented day and night," he lashed out at her, by "my jealousies. . . . I am literally worn to death" (LJK 2:275, 303).

We may locate the deep center of Keats's identification with Spenserian examples of love's debilitating effects in a group of markings that highlight scenes of young men decaying hopelessly from unfulfilled romance. Keats finally suspected his own consumptive emaciation to be an incurable product of his thwarted love for Fanny Brawne. It therefore seems remarkable to find several passages noted in the Bell text that depict unhappy young lovers in what appear to be irreversible states of desiccation. One marked sequence, for instance, graphically portrays Timias's physical and mental decay in the misery of his unexpressed love for Belphoebe. His anguish

> 'gan ransack fast
> His inward partes, and all his entrayles wast,
> That neither blood in face, nor life in hart
> It left, but both did quite drye up, and blast.
>   (3.5.48)

Later, when Timias incurs Belphoebe's wrath, his degeneration grows even more severe. This sequence is also marked in the Bell text:

> There he continued in this carefull plight,
> Wretchedly wearing out his youthly yeares,
> Through wilfull penury consumed quight,
> That like a pined ghost he soone appeares.
>   (4.7.41)

Marginal strokes in the Bell text also stress young Marinell's similar enervation ("hart-wounding loue," Spenser calls it) while grieving for his lost Florimell:

> That in short space his wonted chearefull hew
> Gan fade, and lively spirits deaded quight;
> His cheeke-bones raw, and eie-pits hollow grew,
> And brawney armes had lost their knowen might,
> That nothing like himselfe he seem'd in sight.
> Ere long so weake of limbe, and sick of love,
> He woxe, that lenger he note stand upright,
> But to his bed was brought, and layd above,
> Like ruefull ghost, unable once to stir or move.
>   (4.12.20)

These passages are striking in their relevance to Keats's condition not only because of their moving display of the same mental and physical collapse, brought on by love's discontent, that he endured. Their similes of "ruefull" and "pining" ghosts recall the precise figure he used in 1820 to describe his own emaciation. Presenting himself to Brown as a disembodied spirit enervated by disease, thwarted ambition, and unfulfilled love, he spoke of his last months as a "posthumous existence" (LJK 2:359). He would have been hard put to find a literary representation of this state more apt than the three Spenser passages marked in the Bell text.

There was one final heartache of this time that, for the most part, lay too deep for words. It, too, corresponds with a definite pattern of markings in the Bell text. I speak now of Keats's withering sense of human potential and, more specifically, creative promise lopped short by what seemed a whimsical and malicious fate. "God knows," he wondered with mingled regret and bitterness, "how it would have been" (LJK 2:304). The annotator of the Bell text found such a thought, and all of its cruel implications, riveting. He marked numerous passages that together make a powerful statement about the folly of ambition, the fragility of human achievement, and the brevity of fame in this mutable world.

This pattern of markings actually rearranges Spenser's idea of providential order, much as Keats characteristically revised his ideology, to shape a darker, secular vision of the futility of all human struggle against a transient doom. Spenser is deeply sensitive to that capricious fate and its power to undermine our human "hunger" to raise a "famous moniment" of deeds and poetry in "triumph . . . on death" (5.12.1; 2.10.56). But he reassures himself with many providential alternatives to the unsteady nature of human affairs. However, his vision of a transcendent order enveloping worldly change, presented for example in the conclusions of the Mutabilitie Cantos and the Garden of Adonis episode, went unnoticed in the Bell markings. The annotator's different bias moved him to concentrate instead on the mutability of Spenser's world: "[W]icked Time," for instance, "fowly" marring the "glory" of "flowring herbes" in the Garden of Adonis (3.6.39); Agape's encounter with the grisly Fates, who mercilessly cut off human striving with "cursed knife . . . Most wretched men, whose dayes depend on thrids so vaine!" (4.2.48); and Mutabilitie's own climactic portrait of the devastated empire— the "balefull" realm of "changes infinite"—that she rules (7.7.23). The annotator glossed this focus, moreover, by isolating numerous references to man's "tickle" experience from their context within a larger vision of God's redeeming order: "so tickle be the termes of mortall state" (3.4.28); "Such is the weaknesse of all mortall hope, / So tickle is the state of earthly things" (6.3.5); "O weake life! that does leane / On thing so tickle as th'unsteady ayre" (7.7.22). Extracted from their full context, these observations compose a painful motto, quite different from Spenser's final opinion, about human experience as it is portrayed in the Bell markings.

Keats found that modern vision invigorating at times. But his response to it, in moments of bitterness, was not free of suicidal undertones. "I do not wish to live." It should not be surprising at this point to see the annotations in the Bell text locating two instances of suicide in *The Faerie Queene* (2.10.55; 2.12.52).

If we do indeed presume Keats's hand in these markings, then we can find them extending and in a way completing the last stage of his engagement with Spenser. They dramatize a mind cutting through Spenser's moralism, his politics, his aestheticism, even his preoccupation with the "hart diuided," to recover and absorb his feeling for the "miserie" of our "estate." Such a recovery also meant casting off his robe of allegory to unveil the literal signs of human suffering that proliferate throughout *The Faerie Queene* to a degree perhaps never more fully appreciated by anyone before or after Keats. This appropriation of Spenser's self-proclaimed "softened heart" finally enabled Keats to speak, on his own terms and as a modern "artist" should, about the "wounded mind" of "fraile man." "If my health would bear it," he explained in one of his final letters to Fanny, "I could write a Poem which I have in my head, which would be a consolation for people in such a situation as mine" (*LJK* 2:312). He may have inscribed just such a poem throughout the Bell volumes. The passages marked out in them, extracted from *The Faerie Queene* and taken as a collective unit, compose a poem in their own right: the poem of Keats's most poignant thinking into the human heart, given voice through Spenser's compassionate sympathy with a "World of Pains and troubles" (*LJK* 2:102). As much sorrow as that poem may have expressed, the unlocking of his heart did prove a "consolation" for Keats. Marking *The Faerie Queene*, he told Fanny Brawne, "has lightened my time very much. I am much better" (*LJK* 2:302). Such was the uplifting of spirit he always received from his conversation with Spenser.

Never before had that dialogue brought so much out of himself, the echo of the past modulating so plangently into the voice of the present. It was a kind of harmony for which Spenser himself had provided a gloss in that dovelike hymn of sweet companionship that we have seen to characterize Keats's "so continuing long" with him. Timias, "consumed quight . . . like a pined ghost" in his thwarted love for Belphoebe, collapses to moan his "doole" aloud. The nearby dove hears and, moved with "deare compassion" for his smart, she begins to sing in sympathy with his "sad plight." His response to her "mournefull muse," singled out by a marginal stroke in the Bell text, might very well explain the drama of Keats's last reading of Spenser:

Shee sitting by him, as on ground he lay,
Her mournefull notes full piteously did frame,
And thereof made a lamentable lay,
So sensibly compyld, that in the same
Him seemed oft he heard his owne right name.

(4.8.4)

We might conclude that hearing his "owne right name" in Spenser's
song, from the beginning to the end of his career, always had a way
of making Keats "much better" as a poet.

SHELLEY
AND
SPENSER

PART 3

n anti-Christian hater of kings, Shelley would appear to be a natural enemy of that great English champion of monarchy and Protestantism, Edmund Spenser. Yet he read Spenser avidly throughout much of his adulthood, and most of his critics today would agree with Fletcher's claim that he "owes some of his deeper skills to Spenser" (341). I wish to explore the tension of likings and antipathies in Shelley's engagement with Spenser, viewing his response within the context of Keats's Spenserian experience. Shelley's reaction was more contentious, but it also shared many of the special interests and strategies of Keats's Spenserianism. Like Keats, Shelley extended his era's concept of Spenser's unique accessibility and relevance among the giants of the literary past. Although Shelley never reached quite the depth of Keats's anxiety about the shadowing cliffs of poetry, and we may wish to qualify Bloom's pronouncement about his "fears that there are no more palms to be won" (*Map of Misreading* 149), he was as concerned as anybody in his time with the problem of following those he addressed as "the dead Kings of Melody" (*PW* 617). He was also prone from early on to answer that concern with a conviction of Spenser's encouraging influence, which grew for him as well as for Keats into a sustaining inspiration. Extending Spenser's duality, especially in his mutability theme, also became for Shelley an important means of working out his own aesthetic and intellectual contradictions, what Bloom has called his "incurable and involuntary dualism" (*Map of Misreading* 11). Like Keats, Shelley passed through different stages of response on his way toward a deeper appreciation of Spenser's pathos and mental division. Also like Keats, he learned from epic mistakes to handle Spenser's strengths more efficiently in condensed formats. But another part of him was attracted to Spenser's moral zeal and mythological visions of cosmic harmony, however misdirected they may have seemed. As a passionate radical in politics and philosophy, though, Shelley was troubled by Spenser's orthodoxy much more severely than was Keats. Consequently he found bringing Spenser into the modern world more problematic. The pattern of his developing response thus differed from Keats's in some important ways, and it was always punctuated by a contentiousness unlike anything in Keats. That antagonism could grow counterproductive at times, but it was part of the severe contentions of friendship that ultimately pushed Shelley toward a mutual understanding with Spenser. He finally made a reconciliation that helped him formulate a theory of literary influence designed to transform the pressures of the cultural past into the basis of his own mature vision of poetic experience. That vision, however different from Keats's, also received much of its distinctive shape from his "so continuing long" with Spenser.

I

Unlike Keats, Shelley never encountered Spenser during his apprentice years. His juvenilia is also free of the worries about poetic influence that pervade Keats's earliest poetry, largely due to his adolescent isolation from London's literary culture and his relative unfamiliarity with England's Renaissance traditions.[1] But very early on he did come into contact with Spenserian art and its relation to questions of poetic influence. His experience, though quite different from Keats's, served him in the same way of establishing a special rapport with the Spenserian context that proved extremely beneficial in later years. He was concerned from a young age with the difficulty of modernizing England's eighteenth-century literary tradition, and he found that problem exemplified in the mixed appeal and obsolescence of the eighteenth-century Spenserian tradition. His earliest poetic attempts were thus deeply engaged with the crux of updating the Spenserian tradition. It was an education, begun early and developed steadily, that helped make his eventual dealings with Spenser a basic part of his later, more sophisticated engagement with "the dialectics of literary tradition" (Bloom, *Map of Misreading* 38).

By the time Shelley discovered Spenser when he was twenty-one, he had been immersed in the eighteenth-century Spenserian tradi-

---

1. Mary Shelley thus remarked on Shelley's lack of familiarity with Renaissance poets like Spenser in his early years: "Our earliest English poetry was almost unknown to him" (*PW* 837).

tion for some time. His adolescent literary interests centered in recent works about political and social reform. "[M]y opinion," he explained to Elizabeth Hitchner in 1811, "is that all poetical beauty
ought to be subordinated to the inculcated moral" (*LPBS* 1:59). At
the same time, however, he was also delighted with the exotic fictions of Gothic romance. He consequently sought literary models that
combined moral zeal with a flair for the fantastic. Matthew Lewis's
Peter Wilkins, for example, interested him because it provided a supernatural backdrop for its hero's fight against religious tyranny and
social prejudice. Shelley thought about writing a similar novel, which
would integrate romantic adventure with theories of social reform
(*LPBS* 1:25). But he found the most compelling integration of these
features in the dream-vision allegories of the mid-eighteenth-century
tradition of Spenserian poetry.

We have seen how one line of that tradition had produced works
featuring exotic allegorical frameworks for various attacks on social,
political, and ecclesiastical abuses. An immensely popular vogue,
these dream-vision poems were quite accessible to the young Shelley
and, in their combination of moral zeal and supernatural machinery,
well suited to his particular tastes. He read widely in them, wherein
he took much of his earliest poetic inspiration.[2] Yet he also balked at
their conservatism, finding their passionate censure of custom, vice,
hypocrisy, and prejudice underpinned with a Spenserian loyalty to
church and state that was unacceptable to him. Such religious and
political orthodoxy, in fact, struck him as the principal cause of un-
happiness in human history. He remained drawn, however, to the
imaginative formats, the moral energy, and even the particular
themes of social abuse in the mid-eighteenth-century Spenserian
poems. To appropriate these resources while condemning the philosophy that informed them was no easy balance to maintain. The
inherent contradiction here was also at the heart of Romanticism's
more consuming debate with the English Renaissance and its "old
pieties." Shelley's immediate models, however, were not so threatening in their alien philosophies as the "dead Kings" of Renaissance
tradition. Re-creating Mickle and West, though it presented difficulties, was not the same as wrestling with Milton. Instead of dis-

2. There is no specific record of Shelley's reading in the eighteenth-century Spenserian poets. Carlos Baker has already shown, however, in an argument on which I
intend to elaborate, how the style and preoccupations of those poems became regular
features of Shelley's early verse (*Shelley's Major Poetry* 23–28; "Spenser, the Eighteenth
Century and Queen Mab").

heartening Shelley, the problem actually seemed invigorating, and confidently tampering with the Spenserian tradition became one of his earliest ways of conceptualizing the dynamics of poetic revisionism.

His early fascination with eighteenth-century Spenserianism, and the contradictions he experienced in dealing with it, can be traced throughout his juvenilia and most importantly in his first long poem, *Henry and Louisa* (1809), a narrative in Spenserian stanzas about the pernicious social and psychological effects of England's Egyptian campaign.[3] Shelley was not yet ready for an extensive deployment of the dream-vision format, but he did incorporate many of the basic features of the didactic strain of mid-eighteenth-century Spenserian poetry. The rhyme scheme of his opening stanza, for instance— ababbccdde—recalls the ten-line structure of the most common verse form of that tradition, Prior's regularized stanza. Most of the poem's following stanzas, though they conform to the legitimate Spenserian pattern, repeat the measured phrasing of eighteenth-century syntax: "Hope is our tempered lance, faith is our shield; / Conquest or death for these wait on the gory field" (lines 79–80; *The Esdaile Notebook*). The diction of *Henry and Louisa,* moreover, eschews Spenserian archaisms for the kind of Augustan language characteristic of the poems written in Prior's style: "Yet darest thou boast thyself superior.—Thou! / Vile worm! whom lovely woman deigns to bless" (lines 13–14). Shelley's vituperative moralism also recalls the general spirit and many of the particular subjects of his eighteenth-century models. His frequent indictments of war, venality, custom, and religious hypocrisy echo similar denunciations in the Spenserian works of Mickle, Thompson, West, Southey, and Darwin. Moreover, his personifications of virtues and vices—Glory, Reason, Prejudice, Passion, Virtue—reduplicate the naive allegorical landscapes of those predecessors, just as axiomatic morals like the following draw upon their moral rhetoric: "Yet what is this [glory] compared to Woman's love, / Dear Woman's love, the dawn of Virtue's day. / The bliss-inspiring beam, the soul illumining ray?" (lines 59–61).

Much as Shelley thus depended on these Spenserian precursors to conduct his moral teaching, his message jarred against their most

---

3. For other examples of Shelley's juvenile experiments with mid-eighteenth-century Spenserian poems, see "Epithalamium of Francis Ravaillac and Charlotte Corday," "Bigotry's Victim," and "Dares the Lama."

honored values. His story of Henry's journey to Egypt in a mercenary force condemns English imperialism and Christian bigotry.[4] England's church and state, the two bulwarks of eighteenth-century Spenserian moralism, emerge in Shelley's narrative as the main culprits behind mankind's "unbettered misery" (line 10). Mickle, Thompson, and many others had celebrated Britain's military and commercial dominance of the globe. But to Shelley, the Egyptian campaign only carries "Britannia's hired asassins" (line 186) to blight a foreign soil. And where most of the earlier Spenserians had made the Christian basis of their moral systems abundantly clear, Shelley denounces religion as the "hated cause of all the woe / That makes the world this wilderness" (lines 144–45). To highlight these radical shifts of value, Shelley grants his heroine a moral triumph in her pointed defiance of English government and Christian theology. Louisa repudiates the imperialistic aims of Britain's armies; she also prizes "fair Reason" and her human love for Henry above the "joys of Heaven" (lines 53, 95). Her suicide, committed in response to Henry's death, is meant to appear as an act of triumphant virtue that overcomes the prejudices of Christianity. Thus heralding a new age of secular, democratic ideals, Shelley must have sensed the inherent contradiction of preaching a revolutionary message in the poetic structures of an outworn creed.

His uneasiness is apparent in his awkward efforts to break out of the eighteenth-century mold. These attempts often come at the expense of narrative and thematic coherence. He tries to distance himself from his predecessors, for instance, by setting his allegory in a contemporary, realistic context. Instead of Knights of Education fighting their moral battles in timeless fairyscapes, Shelley puts Henry and Louisa into a real battle scene. They function allegorically, as representatives of a radical Shelleyan virtue pitted against orthodox piety, but they are also human figures caught up in the complexities of modern politics and militarism. This departure from conventional allegory to promote a liberal social agenda may help confirm Shelley's progressive stance. Yet at times it is heavy-handed and extreme, reflecting his discomfort with his many close ties to a traditional background. He interrupts the narrative frequently, for

4. The British invaded Egypt in 1807 only to wreak pointless damage while suffering heavy losses. Kenneth Neill Cameron supplies pertinent historical information (266).

example, to deliver long, redundant speeches on his radical values, which assert his revolutionary position at the cost of narrative, thematic, and allegorical continuity. Before the narrative can get under way, Louisa lectures Henry on the virtue of love over glory and power (lines 44–52). Her speech is anticipated by the narrator's attack on glory (lines 25–34) and followed by his repetitive plea for the subordination of power to virtue (lines 53–56). Several stanzas later, he again denounces temporal power in favor of "Virtue's votary" and "dear Love" (lines 148–49). This overstated radicalism seems as much a reflection of Shelley's uneasy desire to distance himself from his conventional model as a product of his naive reforming impetuosity. Even when he curtails some of that zeal in more complex Spenserian works like *Queen Mab* and *The Revolt of Islam*, he still tries to assert himself rather uncomfortably, as we shall see, by lapsing into similar patterns of redundant and hyperbolic digression.

Henry and Louisa is a juvenile work, not to be judged on the same aesthetic level with those later poems. Yet it can help us understand why Shelley became attracted to Spenser and how their relationship was fraught with tension from the beginning. It demonstrates his interest in the moral energy and the imaginative flair of the didactic Spenserian poets of the mid-eighteenth century. Despite the difficulty he encountered in adapting them, he also discovered in *Henry and Louisa* that he could enter Spenserian revisionism with a spirit of confidence. The experience enabled him to produce his first long poem, whatever its technical limitations, and such an accomplishment meant a great deal to him. *Henry and Louisa* "was written when he was sixteen or seventeen," Cameron explains, "but he seems to have felt that it had a special importance in the history of the development of his mind" (261). Somewhat like Keats, then, Shelley grew into poetry conscious of the strides he might take through a Spenserian poetics. That knowledge became a valuable source of inspiration when he discovered what it really meant to try to build a second Renaissance. But he was also conditioned from the beginning to recognize the substantial encumbrances of such a poetics, the manifestations of which in *Henry and Louisa* he came to regret.[5] When he eventually learned to displace the eighteenth-century background with Spenser's own example, he thus carried both a spirit of cautious

---

5. He later apologized for his "deviations" from the Spenserian paradigm (*The Esdaile Notebook* 131).

optimism into that mature encounter and a wariness about his inevitable struggle for independence.

Before he could take that step, however, he needed to discover just how far he could go with the eighteenth-century Spenserians, and his testing yielded in 1812 his first major poem, *Queen Mab*. As he began to contemplate a great philosophical work on social and moral reform, he often thought back to the didactic Spenserian poets of the mid-eighteenth century. His letters of 1810–12 frequently allude to Romantic continuers of their tradition, like Southey and Darwin. Southey's use of the dream-vision motif in *Thalaba* (1801) particularly captured Shelley's imagination and directed him back to the eighteenth-century practitioners of that Spenserian form. He had already made a brief foray in the genre with his "Epithalamium on Charlotte Corday." Now, without any apparent anxiety about literary competition, he began an epic work based on the allegorical structures, patterns of imagery, narrative lines, and thematic concerns of the eighteenth-century Spenserian dream visions.[6] However comfortable he may have felt with a Spenserian poetics, however, his decision against the Spenserian stanza for *Queen Mab* hints at some tension. A number of the eighteenth-century dream visions were composed in non-Spenserian meters, and *Thalaba* was in blank verse. But Shelley had loved the Spenserian stanza throughout his adolescence, experimenting with its possibilities whenever he wrote in the eighteenth-century Spenserian vein. His departure from it now, for his most elaborate venture in that tradition, may suggest the same defensiveness about the conservative thrusts of eighteenth-century Spenserianism that had left him uneasy in *Henry and Louisa*. Having just met Southey in 1811, moreover, he was dismayed with the older man's apostasy from the liberal cause, which must have deepened his reservations about the gulf between his own principles and the values of his most significant poetic guides. Recognizing his ambivalence toward their examples can help us understand how the Spenserian context both authorized and inhibited the composition of *Queen Mab*.

In *Queen Mab*, Shelley draws upon the same moral zeal that fuels the Spenserianism of *Henry and Louisa*. He also practices the same

---

6. W. H. Hildebrand notes that Shelley first attempted a dream-vision poem in his Oxford writings. The recurrence of this motif in his poems of 1810 comes with a more detailed form of borrowing that indicates his increasing familiarity with the didactic techniques of Spenser's eighteenth-century imitators.

kind of social commentary that he had previously taken over from the Spenserian tradition, attacking religious intolerance, political oppression, custom, and avarice. But he now conducts those attacks with a much more conscious eye to his predecessors, carefully framing his invective in the allegorical mechanism of their dream-vision poems. The pattern of events in which Ianthe ascends to Mab's throne and beholds the world's ills is basic to mid-eighteenth-century Spenserian dream visions and their adaptations by later poets like Hunt, Darwin, and Southey. Shelley's readers have cited his inexperience and lack of originality for this heavy dependence on the established paradigm (Baker, "Spenser, the Eighteenth Century and Queen Mab" 83–84). But we may get closer to his intentions if we recognize how he scrupulously borrows from his precursors in order to link himself with the Spenserian tradition, as if that connection would validate his authority as an epic poet and visionary reformer.

The pattern of his allusions to the eighteenth-century background is so obvious as to make his association with that context unmistakable. His heroine, Ianthe, for example, has the same unusual name as Thompson's protagonist in *Sickness*. Mab's glittering palace in the heavens shares many details with the aerial structures in Spenserian poems by Jones, Darwin, Southey, and Hunt (Baker, "Spenser, the Eighteenth Century and Queen Mab" 83–84). Her habit of twirling her wand three times to waken Ianthe's soul (I, 107) repeats the same gesture of goddesses in the Spenserian poems of Hunt (*The Palace of Pleasure* I, 38) and Jones (*The Palace of Fortune*, line 364). Even specific phrases in *Queen Mab* recall word groupings from Shelley's models. Mab and Ianthe, for instance, survey the distant earth from their cosmic perspective, viewing all the "thronging thousands" below as if they were "an anthill's citizens" (II, 99–100). Their vision reproduces a similar image from one of Shelley's favorite Spenserian imitations, Thomson's *The Castle of Indolence*, in which a "magic globe" reveals "all things that do pass / Upon this ant-hill earth" (I, 434–36). This kind of borrowing is even more direct in the most didactic passages of *Queen Mab*. As Mab condemns religious tyranny, for instance, she pictures an allegorical fiend named "Religion" who smiles "Whilst innocent babes writhe on its stubborn spear" (VI, 118). That phrase restates almost verbatim William Thompson's description of a religious tyrant who "smiled at the infant writhing on the sphere" (*Sickness* V, 90). Such deliberate imitations, though far removed from the "significant allusion" of a mature revisionism, serve the purpose of declaring Shelley's collegiality with the zealous reformers of the eighteenth-century Spenserian tradition. The strat-

egy is not unlike Keats's studied incorporation of Hunt's Spenserianism to validate himself as a poet.

Yet such a pronounced identification with his models, as much as
it may have helped Shelley to authorize himself, was also troubling.
While he continued to share the reforming spirit of his predecessors,
his resistance to their Christianity and their imperialism had grown
more passionate than ever. Much more vehemently than *Henry and
Louisa*, *Queen Mab* impugns both systems as the arch-causes of the
world's woe. Christianity's God thus appears as "A vengeful, pitiless,
and almighty fiend . . . hungering for blood" (IV, 211–13). Its purported Savior brings to earth a sword to "satiate with the blood / Of
truth and freedom His malignant soul" (VII, 171–72). Commerce,
and the British imperialism that supports it, acts as Religion's partner
in spreading a "poison-breathing shade," beneath which "No solitary
virtue dares to spring" (V, 44–45). Denouncing these twin fiends,
Mab grants Ianthe prolonged visions of the monstrous destruction
they wreak. Only with the eradication of their baneful influence, she
finally explains, will the promised millennium arrive. Such a thorough subversion of his predecessors' most sacred values must have
left Shelley anxious, as never before, about his equally thorough
adoption of their aesthetic methods. He worried openly about the
obsolescence of *Queen Mab* (*LPBS* 1:557). But more experienced now
as a poet, he was prepared to cut a balance between tradition and
independence through strategic revisions of his models.

His most obvious change in the eighteenth-century model entailed
his displacement of the Christian cosmic order with a secular theory of
universal harmony. Most of the Spenserian vision poems based their
moralism on traditional Christian concepts of God's all-encompassing
order. "[L]et me ever sit and sing," Thompson concludes *Sickness*,
"Thy numerous Godhead," which sparkles in the soul and perme-
ates a universe of order (V, 350–51). These assertions of divine
power, as in Boyse's *The Vision of Patience*, usually stress its dispensa-
tion of just rewards for the virtuous and punishment for the repro-
bate. Shelley follows this paradigm of singing a hymn to an "all-
sufficing Power" (VI, 197), but he devotes his song to a new kind of
"Power." It is Godwinian "Necessity" that rules the world of *Queen
Mab*. Instead of simply celebrating Necessity's reign, however, Shelley also insists upon the falseness of those hymns to deity by his
Christian predecessors. "There is no God!" Mab exclaims (VII, 12).
Necessity, she argues, is an ontological reality in contrast with the
manufactured "God of human error." Though it produces "unvary-
ing harmony" in the world, it is amoral with neither "human sense"

nor "human mind." Unlike the Christian God, it therefore "Requir'st no prayers or praises." Eventually, Mab explains in a direct reversal of the theology of Shelley's precursors, the false idolatry of Christian history will fade into oblivion and Necessity's all-enduring power will be acknowledged as the true "mother of the world" (VI, 197–219). Because Mab's form of articulating these claims thus deliberately repudiates the eighteenth-century Spenserians, the radical vision of *Queen Mab* takes shape, in part, as a calculated attempt to distance Shelley from his most important models.

This revisionary tactic operates more subtly in numerous reversals of eighteenth-century image patterns and thematic motifs. Shelley's millennial vision, for instance, pointedly subverts the theology of corresponding episodes in the Spenserian poems of Denton, Jones, and Boyse. Denton's *House of Superstition* ends with a vision of the "millenary year." It will arrive as compensation for all those Christian martyrs who, maintaining their beleaguered faith in spite of overwhelming persecution, have died "Scorching in flames" (line 124). Shelley's Ahasuerus similarly concludes his speech with a vision of the eventual triumph of truth's "imperishable throne" over falsehood and idolatry. This millennial period will also prove a compensation for the "fierce flame" of oppression that has long scathed the persecuted votaries of truth (VII, 259). Ahasuerus's sufferings, however, are brought on by his own defiant and, in Shelley's eyes, courageous anti-Christianity, the exact position attacked by Denton. His tormentors, moreover, are the very Christian worshipers whom Denton praises; the millennium will come upon their demise, not their vindication.[7]

7. Shelley also rewrites different aspects of the Christian paradise in Boyse's *The Vision of Patience* and Jones's *The Palace of Fortune*. Boyse's dreamer comes, after witnessing much grief and weathering a horrid storm, to a pastoral island of perennial warmth and abundance: "The tempest ceas'd. . . . An island we perceiv'd that stemm'd the flood . . . Where bleating flocks a plenteous herbage found" (lines 151–56). Mab's vision of the millennium portrays mankind as a storm-swept sailor, landing on an island graced with warm climes and fruitful soil: "No storms deform the beaming brow of Heaven. . . . But fruits are ever ripe, flowers ever fair" (VIII, 116–19). Shelley makes this parallel, however, only to subvert his source. Boyse's charmed island represents a Christian state of "Piety" and "holy Truth" (line 248) while the paradise of *Queen Mab* rises upon the grave of such pieties to project the re-created truth of Shelley's secular philosophy. Jones's Christian views of paradise undergo a different kind of transformation in *Queen Mab*. His poem warns against false promises of a worldly Eden. Paradise on earth, according to Christian history, can only emerge at the end of time. Island paradises like the following are thus to be shunned, Jones warns, as devious bowers of bliss that leave the soul "[un]resigned to Heaven":

One of the most dramatic of these reversals, and perhaps the most revelatory of Shelley's uneasy relation with his predecessors, occurs during Ahasuerus's speech. The poem's most vituperative attack on Christianity, it specifically challenges a key episode in Jones's *The Palace of Fortune*. Jones's Queen of Fortune enlists the counsel of a ministering spirit, named "Knowledge," to convince Maia, the poem's mortal protagonist, of the dreadful folly of most human aspirations. The spirit is a severe, elderly man, his visage furrowed with time. He commands great respect, revealing a countenance at once noble, wise, and defiant that glows with the "Darting" energy of "superior grace":

> Grave was his port, yet show'd a bold neglect,
> And filled the young beholder with respect;
> Time's envious hand had plough'd his wrinkled face,
> Yet on those wrinkles sat superior grace;
> Still full of fire appear'd his vivid eye,
> Darting quick beams, and seem'd to pierce the sky.
>
> (lines 321–26)

The spirit explains how he has traversed the globe in search of knowledge, only to find the human sphere governed by "vain wishes" and "weak mind[s]." Wearied by the follies of humanity, he finally turns to "Heaven's laws" and submits his soul "to my Maker's will" (lines 346–54). Shelley gives the spirit of Ahasuerus a role similar to Knowledge's. He is summoned by Mab to bolster Ianthe's confidence in her teachings. Like Knowledge, Ahasuerus is a grave and wearied elderly figure who inspires tremendous respect. His severe countenance testifies to hard-earned wisdom and a firm defiance of

---

> . . . a fair isle . . . where spring eternal reigns. . . .
> Now morning breath'd; the scented air was mild,
> Each meadow blossom'd, and each valley smil'd;
> On every shrub the pearly dew-drops hung,
> On every branch a feather'd warbler sung;
> The cheerful spring her flowery chaplets wove,
> And incense-breathing gales perfum'd the grove.
>
> (lines 415–23)

With some minor alterations of style, this portrait could easily fit into Shelley's millennial vision of "ever-verdant . . . garden-isles" (VIII, 101, 118). But Shelley, in a pointed reply to Jones's illusory Eden, insists on the "truth" of his "visioned bliss" (IX, 79). It exists, or can exist, in the present, not at the end of human history; and it comes into being when humanity *refuses* to resign itself any longer to a Christian heaven.

misfortune. Yet like Knowledge's appearance, it also radiates both vigorous energy and "awful grace":

> His port and mien bore mark of many years,
> And chronicles of untold ancientness
> Were legible within his beamless eye:
> Yet his cheek bore the mark of youth;
> Freshness and vigour knit his manly frame;
> The wisdom of old age was mingled there
> With youth's primaeval dauntlessness;
> . . . . inexpressible woe,
> Chastened by fearless resignation, gave
> An awful grace to his all-speaking brow.
>   (VII, 73–82)

Ahasuerus explains how, like Knowledge, he has endlessly trodden the paths of man only to find vice and folly strewn before him everywhere. At last, also like Knowledge, he has resolved to place his faith in a power beyond the human sphere. But Ahasuerus, Shelley's version of the wandering Jew, has been cursed unjustly by an envious God and wanders in quest of a benevolent alternative to Christianity. His search exposes him not to common human vices but to the evils perpetrated by Christian bigotry. Ahasuerus finally submits himself to Reason's "imperishable throne," built on the prophesied ruins of the very faith recommended by Knowledge.

In rewriting the story of Knowledge, Shelley also recasts specific images to emphasize his antagonism to Jones's theology. Where the "vivid eye" of Knowledge darts "quick beams" that penetrate Heaven's mysteries, Ahasuerus seems blinded by his sufferings, the chronicles of grief "legible" in his "beamless eye." His blindness, however, signifies a renovated vision before which the light of Knowledge's faith grows dim. Like the "eyeless skulls" of his children, murdered by God's wrath, the ledger of woe sketched in Ahasuerus's dark eye indicts the tyrannical myopia of Christian faith. His blindness, moreover, represents an oracular insight that looks beyond Christian history and its record of sorrow toward a new, imminent millennium. Shelley underscores the renovative quality of this vision by contrasting Knowledge's decline in old age with Ahasuerus's potential for youthly renewal. In his aged decline, Knowledge faces the grave: "Twice forty winters tip my beard with snow," he laments, "And age's chilling gusts around me blow" (lines 329–30). As he closes his speech, he admits his own feebleness, longs for his life's end, and finally dies with the hope of entering heaven at last. Ahasuerus, in contrast, bears the mark of youthful vigor in his aged countenance and imagines a future when he will transcend the "wintry storm" of his present misery and liberate himself from the "chilling gusts" of age that plague Knowledge (line 330). As he disappears from the poem, instead of dying like Knowledge into a "sudden cloud" of "thickening darkness" (lines 357–58), his shadow flees fast as the shades of night before "the morning beam" (VII, 271).

This elaborate revisionism shows how much Shelley wishes to distance himself from his precursors. But the very elaborateness of the scheme also betrays some uneasiness about clarifying that distance. After all, no matter how much he tries to disentangle himself from authors like Jones, his basic poetic structures come directly from them. The relentlessness of his revisions thus seems more the outgrowth of his inability to free himself from the embarrassing conventionality of his precursors. That contentious embrace may be responsible for his hyperbolic denunciations of their Christianity. The Ahasuerus sequence, for example, one of the poem's heaviest debts to the eighteenth century, delivers a tirade of nearly two hundred lines that does more to denounce Shelley's models than to advance his redeeming view of human history. Christianity's God is "the vengeful almighty," the "omnipotent Fiend," a "heartless conqueror," a "parish demogogue," a "malignant soul," the "almighty Tyrant," the "wrath[ful] Almighty." Repetitions of this sort occur whenever Shelley attempts to present a millennial horizon, as if his reminders of his untoward debt to the past consistently intrude on his vision of the future. By 1812 Shelley had good cause to despise the religious and governmental institutions that had deprived him of family patronage, a university career, and the affection of his first beloved, Harriet Grove. Yet the extremism of his diatribes, especially when we consider its recurrence in later, more complex poems, suggests other motivations. The "omnipotent Fiend" he so deplores may be as much the restless specter of his own predecessors as the lingering ghost of an outworn creed.

The revisionism of *Queen Mab* certainly does not carry out the kind of self-redemption that we have seen informing Romanticism's more successful Spenserian poems. Yet its effects are far from wholly deleterious. No matter how roughly it works itself out, it does enable Shelley to write the poem, his first significant work, which must have reinforced his early impression that Spenserianism could help him reach important goals. That confidence, gained early on and steadily developing throughout his apprentice years, would prove reassuring when he eventually confronted Spenser and the true giants of the English Renaissance. His recent experience with the eighteenth-century poets, moreover, was actually pushing him in that direction. Not only had they dissatisfied him with their limitations,[8] but they were also preparing him to look onward to Spenser for what they had but dimly shadowed forth: his stylistic dexterity, his allegorical complexity, and, of most significance, his deep concern with mutability. His eighteenth-century imitators were also preoccupied with the "tickle" state of this world, with Jones grounding the entire narrative of *The Palace of Fortune* in the vagaries of temporal fame and Denton focusing his *House of Superstition* on contrasts between the ephemeral rule of sublunary tyrants and "the great sabbatic rest" of the Christian millennium (line 130). This focal point of eighteenth-century Spenserianism probably inspired Shelley to present his "Necessity" as a new alternative to Time's "light-winged footsteps" (IX, 33), and it helped foster the profound engagement with the subject of mutability in his mature art. It also prepared him to embrace Spenser with a particular warmth when he discovered that such things as the *Mutabilitie Cantos* exist.

Much as Shelley's experience with the eighteenth-century Spenserian poets may have readied him for that step, it also provided the basis for some of the major problems in his mature relationship with Spenser. His chafing under the yoke of conservatism would continue when he took on Spenser's counsel, as would his exaggerated reactions against it. He would also find it difficult to abandon the sermonizing habits of his eighteenth-century predecessors when he entered Spenser's subtler world. And his conflicting attractions to the imitators and the original would produce one of the major tensions in his mature Spenserian poetics. Even though he had yet to read Spenser, then, the general parameters of their conversation had already been well established.

II

It was no coincidence, therefore, that Shelley's discovery of England's Renaissance literature in 1813 entailed a special interest in

8. When Shelley rewrote *Queen Mab* as *The Daemon of the World*, he tempered much of his antagonistic language and dropped many of the specific references to the eighteenth-century Spenserian tradition.

Spenser. Traveling to London in the autumn of 1812, he began his detailed acquaintance with the capital's literary world. Many of the figures there who were leading the way of England's second Renaissance—Hunt, Hazlitt, Godwin, Byron, and Keats, among others— became his colleagues within the next several years. Their influence moved him to redress the large gaps in his literary training with an intensive study of England's Renaissance writers. He was encouraged, moreover, to give up his love of minor eighteenth-century poets for a deeper commitment to those older giants whom he eventually addressed as "the great bards of elder time" (*PW* 514). Thus he was made to face squarely the burden of poetic tradition that all his new mentors were talking about. It was their interest in Spenser's unusual relevance and tractability, combined with his own recent experience in manipulating Spenserian traditions, that focused Shelley's attention on the author of *The Faerie Queene*. He began reading Spenser's poetry early in 1813 and deepened his knowledge of its complexities over the next several years, increasingly associating his own poetic ambitions with Spenserianism until, like Keats, he shaped his first mature epic as a sustained revision of *The Faerie Queene*.

Godwin, who became a pivotal guide for him late in 1812, was largely responsible for this new engagement with Renaissance and, more particularly, Spenserian contexts.[9] Shelley's deep absorption with Godwin's social and political theory has been well documented, but we are only beginning to understand Godwin's significant impact on his literary thinking.[10] This influence, at the beginning of their relationship, centered on the contrasts between Renaissance and eighteenth-century literature. For many years Godwin had placed the eighteenth-century poets at the apex of what he thought to be England's continuously progressive cultural history. In the early years of the nineteenth century, however, he met Hazlitt, Lamb, and Coleridge, who persuaded him to recognize the superiority of England's Renaissance achievement. The revaluation struck him as a monumental breakthrough in his intellectual development, nothing less than a mental rebirth that continued to invigorate him for years

9. One cannot overestimate the tremendous influence that Godwin exerted on Shelley at this time. Shelley wrote to Godwin in 1812, shortly before the two met, placing Godwin in the role of parent and moral instructor: "[E]ver may you, like the tenderest and wisest of parents, be on the watch to detect those traits of vice, which yet undiscovered are yet marked on the tablet of my character; so that I pursue undeviatingly the path which you first cleared thro' the wilderness of life" (*LPBS* 1:314).

10. See St. Clair, McCracken, and Hyde.

afterward. About the time he met Shelley, Godwin was still reflecting on the excitement of that moment, which had abated very little in ten years. Thus he recalled in an 1813 journal what it was like to first look into Renaissance realms of gold: "This opened upon me a new field of improvement and pleasure, and engaged me in a course of reading which, from that hour, I have never deserted. . . . [O]n the present occasion a new world was opened to me. It was as if a mighty river had changed its course to water the garden of my mind. . . . What a blessing for a man at forty-three years of age . . . to enter into the lease of a new life, where everything would be fresh, and everything would be young!" (quoted in Paul 356–57). The magnificence of this new world, Godwin quickly came to believe, not only overshadowed the eighteenth-century landscape, it also made the coming of any comparable second Renaissance highly problematic. Where, Godwin asked, in the present or the past, was one to find the "competitors and rivals" of England's great Renaissance poets? Even the minor writers of that era, "any one of which would have done for almost the best man of any other age," made the present seem paltry by comparison (*Life of Chaucer* 392–93).

Whatever sadness Godwin might have felt about that conclusion was qualified by his agreement with those contemporaries who believed that Spenser could help them rebuild the mighty past. Godwin attributed the greatness of the first Renaissance to its power for dramatizing the life of the mind, and he found Spenser's strong execution of that power allowing unusual space for competition. "Those were the times when authors thought," he declared, and their thinking made them deeply "acquainted with whatever . . . human nature is capable of designing and performing" (*LPBS* 1:340–41). Godwin claimed that Spenser was particularly well "acquainted" with the labyrinth of the mind, as demonstrated by the psychodrama of his allegory. The "inscape" of that allegory, we recall Godwin arguing, seemed especially compelling when focused on the tensions of love, acted out by the allegorical strife of such opposite figures as Britomart and Malecasta, Belphoebe and Braggadocchio, Busyrane and Britomart. It was the mental energy of such encounters, Godwin concluded, that earned Spenser a principal seat among "the great bards of elder time." Yet he also found Spenser less intimidating than those other "great bards," mainly because the compassion Spenser brought to the subject of love made him seem unique in his mildness. No doubt influenced by the new Romantic bias toward Spenser's pathos, Godwin felt a pleasurable intimacy with the "gentle Edmund" of soft emotions. He even attempted a brief Spenserian imitation about two lovers, "Inkle and Yariko" (1784), which fea-

tures pastoral descriptions of a "fragrant bow'r" and gentle sentiments of "mirth and joy" felt within a "temple . . . of love" (lines 19–
27; *Four Early Pamphlets*). It might be foolhardy for even "the best
man" of the present to expect to come up to the Renaissance. Yet
there was something about Spenser's gentleness, Godwin believed,
that removed the tension of competition and made it possible to
walk with relative comfort in his footsteps.

These considerations were much in Godwin's thoughts when Shelley came under his wing late in 1812. This new disciple, still absorbed with eighteenth-century Spenserian poets and generally igno-
rant of the Renaissance, must have reminded him of his own
limitations before his great turnabout. It was not long after he met
Shelley that he recalled that event in his journal; he thus must have
been eager, when Shelley requested literary advice in December
1812, to transmit the lesson he had only learned at forty-three. In
one of English literature's great letters of instruction, he told Shelley, first of all, to drop the eighteenth-century poets and their modern continuers: "*You* have what appears to me a false taste in poetry.
You love a perpetual sparkle and glittering, such as are to be found
in Darwin, and Southey, and Scott, and Campbell" (*LPBS* 1:341).
Against these superficial latecomers in the Spenserian tradition,
Godwin recommended the "pregnant sense" of Spenser's own example. He thus presented Shelley with a roster of Elizabethan poets
headed by Spenser: "[W]hat illustrious poets had those times in
Spenser, Drayton, and Daniel!" (*LPBS* 1:341). Godwin associated
their power with the understanding of human nature possessed by
the great historians of the world. He also made it clear that the
"abundance" of their strength made competition nearly unthinkable.
Although he did not mention Spenser's special accessibility, he must
have communicated some sense of it to Shelley, either previously or
soon after his letter of advice; of all the Renaissance poets Godwin
recommended, Spenser was the only one that Shelley immediately
sought out and began reading.

Within days of receiving Godwin's instruction, Shelley ordered a
number of the recommended works, including "Spencers Works
Fairy Queen &c" (*LPBS* 1:342).[11] This was the only poetic volume he
ordered within a long list of historical texts recommended for their

---

11. Baker gives evidence showing that Shelley received the volumes and began
reading Spenser sometime between Christmas 1812 and February 1813 ("Spenser, the
Eighteenth Century and Queen Mab" 95). It is impossible to know which edition of
Spenser that Shelley used now or later, for he never quotes directly from any text.
Silverman suggests Aikin's 1802 edition (30), but his claim is mainly conjecture.

insight into human nature. Spenser's appearance in that list implies that Shelley conceived of him, from the beginning, as Godwin's thinker into the human heart. He began reading *The Faerie Queene*, and probably some of the shorter poems, soon after. During the next several years, he also developed an impression of Spenser's mildness along the lines suggested by Godwin.[12] He came to associate Spenser, for instance, with tender love themes, writing a short 1814 lyric on love's "sweet toil" that begins with a Spenserian stanza (*PW* 523). His passion for Mary Godwin also became associated with Spenser's chivalric tales of love, as he adopted the nickname of "Elfin Knight" in his devotion to her (*PW* 35). This appreciation of Spenser's pathos encouraged something like the kind of intimacy with him that Godwin felt. It could border on impishness, for instance, when Shelley signed "E.K." on the manuscript of "Hymn to Intellectual Beauty," his modern version of Spenser's "Hymne of Heavenly Beautie." Or, it could reflect his serious estimation of Spenser's value as a flexible guide amid an unyielding Renaissance tradition. Walking side by side with Spenser through an epic, he declared in the preface to *The Revolt of Islam*, proved much less intimidating than trying to follow Shakespeare or Milton (*PW* 35). Shelley may never have felt quite the kind of passionate bond with Spenser that continually sustained Keats. But Godwin's instruction did help him share Keats's recognition, as both young men embarked on their adult poetic careers, that Spenser was unusually equipped to guide them into a modern poetry of the mind.

As Spenser's world opened up before Shelley, his idea of the precise form of that guidance began to take shape. Several recurrent Spenserian themes began to intersect with his own intellectual preoccupations, particularly with his growing concern about the debate between realism and ideality that was consuming Romantic literary culture and making up the center of the first long poem of his maturity, *Alastor*. He discovered now that Spenser had anticipated that debate in his treatment of despair, which had become a focal point of Romantic commentary on *The Faerie Queene*. Spenser's Despair episode, as the Romantics understood it, carries out a sustained psychodrama of the mind's quest for transcendent ideals coming into conflict with its apprehension of a bitter reality. That is precisely how Shelley seems to have read the passage, applying it to the clash between the millennial idealism of modern European politics and

12. *The Journals of Mary Shelley* record Shelley's extensive readings of Spenser in 1814, 1815, and 1817 (677).

the crushing reality of despotism's return in the post-revolutionary epoch, "an age of despair" (*PW* 33).[13] His concern with the dualities of Spenserian psychodrama are even more evident in his new concentration on the subject of mutability, which he had already learned to associate with Spenserianism. Between 1813 and 1816 he wrote two lyrics on mutability, incorporating the cadences and phrasings of Mutabilitie's most ringing pronouncements about her rule. Where she sees "all things tost and turned . . . within this wide great Vniuerse" (7.7.56), Shelley laments that "All that is great and all that is strange" passes away "In the boundless realm of unending change" ("On Death," lines 23–24). Her proud rhetorical question, "Wherefore, this lower world who can deny / But to be subiect still to Mutabilitie" (7.7.47), is answered by Shelley's famous conclusion, "Nought may endure but Mutability" ("Mutability," line 16). Such an engagement with Mutabilitie's question reveals how much Spenser's central debate about ideality and temporal experience was concerning Shelley. His conclusive answer, which actually contradicts Nature's final point about divine providence, also suggests where he thinks the orthodox Spenser gets the argument wrong. That secularization of Spenser's episode set the immediate pattern for Shelley's revisionism, which would focus for some time on removing the veil of an "official morality" from the psychodynamics of Spenser's doubling allegory.

Shelley was not able, however, to feel calm or objective about that kind of revisionism. His recent quarrel with the eighteenth-century Spenserian poets was too fresh in his mind;[14] in fact, he was still acting it out during his initial encounters with Spenser. In the winter of 1812–13, he composed a short poem of eight Spenserian stanzas, titled "On Leaving London for Wales."[15] It reads like one of the moral sermons of *Queen Mab*, condemning social vices like custom and hypocrisy in the old didactic style. Yet also like *Queen Mab*, it attacks that centerpiece of eighteenth-century Spenserian politics,

13. Not coincidentally, the subject of despair pervades Shelley's early writings, often in connection with Spenser. Despair's "terrific power," he exclaims in a modified Spenserian stanza of 1810, overwhelms his "ruined soul." "[M]y wayward lot," he writes in a short lyric of 1814, is "cankered" by the chains of despair (*PW* 865, 521).

14. *The Journals of Mary Shelley* list Shelley's persisting interest in Southey and Thomson in 1815 (677, 681), while Shelley's letters of this period often allude to Campbell, Darwin, and Jones (*LPBS* 2:471–72, 477).

15. We cannot be sure whether or not he had read Spenser by the time he composed this poem. A later emendation, in which he included the Spenserian archaism "unholiest rede," leads Cameron to think that he was reading *The Faerie Queene* either during or shortly after the composition of "On Leaving London for Wales" (193).

aristocracy. London is a "miserable city" where "the gloom / Of pen-
ury mingles with the tyrant's pride" (lines 1–2; *The Esdaile Notebook*).
Such persisting enmity to the politics of eighteenth-century Spenserianism could have only prepared Shelley to deplore Spenser's
own strenuous orthodoxy. At this point, he was not ready to sanction
the Romantics' sympathy with Spenser's political hardships. Moreover, his own recent championship of the Irish cause would have left
him appalled at Spenser's well known Irish solutions, whether or not
he read them firsthand in *View of the State of Ireland*. If he shared
some of Keats's grateful sense of Spenser's mailed hand warmly
reaching out, then, he would have also been extremely uneasy about
the chivalric armor in itself, and what it said about Spenser's
loyalties.

The prospect of following such a master was further complicated by Shelley's lingering attachment to the didactic strategies of
eighteenth-century Spenserianism. "On Leaving London for Wales"
takes a step toward the Spenserian dualities of mind that he was
beginning to appreciate, recording his division between "visions" of
"Fancy" and "sad realities" (lines 64–65). Its exploration of that conflict, however, is repeatedly interrupted by moralistic denunciations
of "the mad floods of Despotism" (line 70). Thus, much as the idea
of a revisionary Spenserian psychodrama was intriguing Shelley, it
was complicated, as we may now see in "A Hymn to Intellectual
Beauty," by his resistance to Spenser's orthodoxies and his attachment to different, sometimes antagonistic strains within the Spenserian tradition itself.

Shelley's hymn may owe as much to Platonic as Spenserian backgrounds. But his title declares its close relation to Spenser's "An
Hymne of Heavenly Beautie," and his key substitution of "Intellectual" for "Heavenly" suggests his revisionary approach to Spenser's
faith. The word change also focuses his revisionism on Spenser's debate about ideality by emphasizing Spenser's own treatment of intellectual beauty in the "Hymne." He defines it there as "Sapience," or
the composition of God's mind, which appears as a beautiful woman
whose radiant penetration of the transient human sphere becomes
one of the poem's focal points. Shelley's new title thus highlights
Spenser's concern with the intersection and the discrepancies between mortal and divine experience. In the body of his modern
hymn, Shelley more specifically recasts the mutability theme of
Spenser's "Hymne" as a drama of the mind's swerves between this
world's incessant change and a transcendent order of permanent
beauty. His own interior debate closely follows the mental patterns

of Spenser's poem, which begins with an unsuccessful attempt to apprehend the beauty of God's divine order. Spenser then switches tactics and looks for traces of that beauty in the human world. Finding it "enregistred" in "every nooke" (line 131), he is inspired with the vision of Sapience and hopes to draw his readers to similar encounters with the divine presence. Shelley goes through a parallel tripartite movement toward neighborhood with transcendent power. He initially laments its separation from human experience. Then, "musing deeply on the lot / Of life," he grasps its fleeting reflections in "every form" of the sublunary world "containing thee" (lines 55–56, 82). Inspired to dedicate his powers to its glory, he concludes in hope of kindling similar visions in all of humanity.

To work out the minute details of these mental shifts, Shelley appropriates specific ideas and phrases from "An Hymne of Heavenly Beautie." Struggling to apprehend the "endlesse perfectnesse" of God's "almightie Spright," Spenser wonders how he can "expresse" such an image for the illumination of mankind (lines 8, 104–5). Shelley, similarly struck by the "awful LOVELINESS" of intellectual beauty, also regrets his inability to "express" its glory for the edification of mankind (lines 70–71). Where Spenser tries to define transcendent power as God's "truth, his love, his wisedome, and his blis" (line 110), Shelley associates it with "Love, Hope, and Self-esteem" (line 37). Spenser's conception of God's appearance on earth in shadowy images, seen through "grosse mists . . . As in a looking glasse" (lines 113–15, 140), more obviously informs Shelley's complicated vision of intellectual beauty's inconstant shadow in the world: "The awful shadow of some unseen Power / Floats though unseen among us" (lines 1–2). In a still more apparent connection, Spenser's plea for God to redeem this "darke world" from ignorance (line 137) reappears as Shelley's wish for intellectual beauty to free "This world from its dark slavery" (line 70). The "extasy" of revelation, which makes Spenser "onely thinke" on God's beauty (lines 261–66), also reemerges as Shelley's "ecstasy" in a vision that inspires him to "dedicate my powers / To thee and thine" (lines 60–62). Finally, the tones of a lover's affection in Spenser's portrait of the womanly Sapience, a "soveraine dearling" adorned with "goodly face" (lines 184, 232), echo in Shelley's romantic appeals to intellectual beauty, a "Spirit fair" who "for its grace may be / Dear, and yet dearer for its mystery" (lines 83, 11–12). If the "Hymn to Intellectual Beauty" is Shelley's first step toward a "tentative myth" about transcendental idealism, as Bloom suggests (*Shelley's Mythmaking* 43), it also marks the beginning of Spenser's profound influence on the drama by which

Shelley pursues, questions, and eventually qualifies that great myth-making enterprise.

Much as Shelley thus relies on Spenser's muse to help sustain his own song, he also finds its Christian orientation burdensome. His revisions of "An Hymne of Heavenly Beautie" show him consistently trying to liberate the struggle of mind in Spenser's hymn from its theological moorings. In some cases, subverting the poem's ideology seems a rather straightforward matter. Shelley has little trouble, for instance, reversing the conventionally upward thrust of Spenser's religious vision to establish his own secular perspective. Where Spenser travels from the beasts of the field to the various celestial orders to Sapience and ultimately through her to "that imortall light" of God (line 169), Shelley steadily directs his vision away from the misguided celestial yearnings of his boyhood down to the reflection of transcendent power in "the lot / Of life" (lines 55–56). In place of Spenser's concluding disdain for the dross of "this vile world" (line 299), Shelley honors the presence of his "SPIRIT fair" in "every form" of the same world (lines 82–83). But just as Shelley felt uneasy about following his eighteenth-century models, he cannot be comfortable writing in the vein of an orthodox poet like Spenser, no matter how much he tries to correct Spenser's errors. He is not exactly authorizing himself as he previously did with the eighteenth-century poets, and the tension of his response to Spenser is thus not so severe. Yet he still feels it strongly enough to resist the company of a guide whose values he resents. As before, that discomfort urges him to repudiate such an allegiance, which may explain his extreme insistence on the uncertain or unconventional nature of "Power" and account for the hyperbolic "ecstasy" of his dedication to that very un-Spenserian "Power." It is an even more likely explanation for his passionate denunciation of conventional pieties like Spenser's: "the names of Demon, Ghost, and Heaven, / Remain the records of their vain endeavour, / Frail spells" (lines 27–29). Revisionism of this sort may do less to help Shelley work out his own vision than to express his discontent with the company of Spenser. It also reminds us of his persisting interest in different and sometimes incompatible aspects of the Spenserian tradition, for his antagonism to the "frail spells" of religion seems to come straight out of the moralistic center of his eighteenth-century Spenserianism. As a brief piece of sermonizing, it temporarily interrupts the psychodramatic action of his modern encounter with the dualities of transcendence and actuality. This pattern of likings and antipathies in Shelley's relationship with Spenserianism would soon acquire epic scope in *The Revolt of Islam*.

III

Several decades ago Frederick L. Jones thus pinpointed what he thought to be the most surprising feature of Shelley's epic in Spenserian stanzas: "The astonishing thing is that Shelley's prolonged attention to Spenser should have had almost no influence upon *The Revolt of Islam*" (663). With only slight qualification, this view has prevailed up to the present.[16] One cause of our failure to apprehend Spenser's influence is Shelley's own difficulty with it. He remained divided about his Spenserianism throughout the writing of *The Revolt of Islam* and was reluctant to talk about it afterwards. Yet the fact that he was reading *The Faerie Queene* daily while composing *The Revolt of Islam*, in itself, should alert us to the depth of his interaction with Spenser. Moreover, his very decision to write in nine-line stanzas, as we have seen in the case of so many other poets, meant assimilating certain basic principles of the Spenserian tradition.[17] Venturing an epic in Spenserian stanzas during the second decade of the nineteenth century, as we have also seen, specifically meant incorporating the dualistic aspects of that tradition into the central project of formulating a modern poetics—precisely what Shelley had begun to do in "Hymn to Intellectual Beauty." Now, as he prepared to undertake his first great trial of invention, two developments made him focus his attention on that process of redeeming Spenser's duality: the appearance of canto 3 of *Childe Harold's Pilgrimage*, and his first serious experience with the dilemma of England's literary tradition.

Although Shelley was starting to find much of himself in Spenser's interiority, he was discovering something just as valuable in Spenser's unique relation to the whole question of literary influence. By 1816 he was experiencing, for the first time in a substantial way, apprehensions about the specters of those "dead Kings of Melody."

16. Curran, who calls *The Revolt of Islam* "the most ambitious poem ever conceived in the stanza of Spenser after *The Faerie Queene*," is surprised that "critics have been loath to pinpoint exact sources in Spenser for characters and events in Shelley's epic-romance" ("Spenser and Shelley"). Brian Wilkie, in a response that is characteristic of this lack of critical engagement with the poem's Spenserian dynamics, only says generally that "Shelley's method has something in common with the epic method of Spenser, whose ghost haunts the entire poem" (135).

17. Brian Wilkie argues that Shelley "never in any blatant way invited comparison between his works and those in the orthodox epic canon, though he often did so indirectly" (143). But in the early nineteenth century to write an epic in Spenserian stanzas, and to call attention to that choice, as Shelley did in the original preface to his poem, was certainly to conceive of one's stance in relation to Spenser's achievement.

This apprehension was an inevitable result of his growing sensitivity to the second Renaissance under way all around him and the special pressures it was creating. Those demands were pushing him now to overlook his inexperience and, like Keats, hurry himself in his early twenties into attempting a mature epic within the line of Renaissance tradition. He had recently been encouraging Byron to make such an attempt (*LPBS* 1:348, 507–9), and in 1816 he began to prepare himself for such a monumental labor. He immersed himself in England's great Renaissance writers—Spenser, Shakespeare, Milton, Beaumont, Fletcher, and Jonson—no doubt thinking, just as Keats was, about how he could extend their achievement.[18] Considering the rapidity with which he composed *The Revolt of Islam*, finishing an epic of nearly five thousand lines in six months, he may very well have set the kind of severe time deadlines and length requirements that Keats imposed on himself. That speed of composition may suggest his relative freedom from any creative inhibitions. Yet Keats wrote *Endymion* nearly as fast, the rapid pace as much an outgrowth of his anxieties as a transcendence of them. However we look at it, the scenario was daunting for any poet, let alone one in his early twenties, and certainly demanding enough to provoke what Keats tried to laugh off as "narvous" feelings.

But Shelley had also been trained to recognize the burdens of such a project, and in such a way as to foment any nervousness he might have naturally felt. Godwin had warned him about the difficulty of measuring up to even the minor geniuses of the Renaissance, and the new companionship of men like Hunt, Hazlitt, and Keats was focusing his attention on the many different versions of that warning in the periodical press. Whenever he appraised the current state of England's literary climate, he tended to echo those pronouncements on the culture's anxiety about its inimitable past. He also attributed such cultural distress to the causes most frequently mentioned by his contemporaries. Lamenting the age's "despair" of political reformation, he associated it with the dubious prospects of literary renovation: "This influence has tainted the literature of the age with the hopelessness of the minds from which it flows. . . . Our works of fiction and poetry have been overshadowed by the same infectious gloom" (*PW* 34–35). The present's "gloom" about its own creative limitations, he went on, arises from at least

18. *The Journals of Mary Shelley* record these readings (636, 647, 655–56, 662–63, 673–74, 677). Brian Wilkie writes: "Shelley had fairly immersed himself in epic authors during and just before the period when he wrote *The Revolt*" (123).

three sources: the domineering effect of the spirit of the age, which restricts contemporary poets to the imitation of themselves instead of their greater ancestors; an apprehension of inaptitude to wear the "crown of immortality" that graced Milton and "those mighty intellects" of the English Renaissance; and the proliferation of a massive critical industry to remind aspiring poets of their inferiority (*PW* 35–36). Shelley also spoke of a "gradual, silent change" in things, an awakening from the "trance" of "despair," which inspired him to attempt his poem (*PW* 33–34). But his detailed outline of the age's theories about its own cultural inferiority shows how concerned he was with the difficulty of sparking that revival.

Shelley's uneasiness about his own relation to the past surfaces frequently throughout 1817, often in ways directly connected with the writing of *The Revolt of Islam*. Its preface begins with a self-deprecatory gesture, the bluntness and defensiveness of which seem less a token of customary modesty than a sign of insecurity, like Keats's hyperbolic disclaimers in the original preface of *Endymion:* "The Poem which I now present to the world is an attempt from which I scarcely dare to expect success, and in which a writer of established fame might fail without disgrace" (*PW* 32). This apprehension of unfitness persists throughout the preface, with Shelley anticipating negative critical judgments and apologizing to his more sympathetic readers for failing to meet their expectations (*PW* 33, 35–36). The cause of his diffidence is evident when he defines his relation to his poetic forebears. After denying any fundamental debts to them, he immediately claims his readiness for epic labor and calls witness to a breathless list of achievements: having trodden the Alps, lived under the eye of Mont Blanc, wandered among distant fields, sailed down mighty rivers, witnessed populous cities, observed the theater of war and catastrophe, conversed with living men of genius, sported with danger upon the brinks of precipices, and so on (*PW* 34). Such hyperbole would seem to betray some insecurity about that purported readiness to walk with the giants of the past. Shelley is more candid later in the preface, admitting that in some instances he had "completely failed" to keep up with his precursors (*PW* 35).

Hints of this apprehension surface in the poem's many images of tremendous ruins from a mightier past, one of the most common figures of tradition's ominous power in the Romantic debate about poetic influence. A young Laon, teaching himself revolutionary doctrine (somewhat as the young Shelley apprentices himself to epic tradition), thus discovers a vast ruin—"broken tombs and columns riven"—from which issues the "everlasting wale" of a "sorrowing" echo (lines 754–56). The sorrowful aura of the place seems connected with Laon's sense of neighborhood to "dwellings of a race of mightier men, / And monuments of less ungentle creeds" (lines 759–60). Laon confronts the "scrolls" of those "mightier men" much as Keats encounters the folded scroll of the muses in *Endymion,* wishing that man could become "greater" but feeling his own small presence swept away by "the sway / Of the vast stream of ages" (lines 765–70). His sense of unfitness intensifies when, following the collapse of his revolution, he envisions the "awful ghosts" of the immortal past in the "shattered portal" of a "lone ruin" (lines 2534, 2569–74). This metaphorical pattern and the concerns about the past that inform it offer a special gloss on "Ozymandias," composed in the same year as *The Revolt of Islam.* The "vast" and "collosal wreck," which commands observers to "despair" of rivaling the achievements of the past, is usually seen as an emblem of ironic transience. Nothing remains of Ozymandias's glory but a ruin. Yet given Shelley's preoccupation with the signs of inimitable power in the massive fragments of the past, we may also find Ozymandias's shattered monument suggesting the emptiness of a belated culture: "Nothing beside remains. Round the decay / Of that collosal wreck, boundless and bare / The lone and level sands stretch far away" (lines 12–14).[19] Shelley was not prepared to heed unconditionally Ozymandias's injunction to despair; Laon can hope to be "greater" than his precursors (line 767). Yet Shelley recognized how naturally such a feeling of submissiveness could arise from his self-imposed rivalry of the past, and he consciously took measures to forestall it.

Much of the scenario that made Spenser a propitious guide for Keats in *Endymion* applied to Shelley's situation now, and he was quick to capitalize on the opportunities to allay his despair. His early experience in Spenserian adaptation, notwithstanding his difficulties, provided a degree of confidence with Spenser that he could not feel with any other great Renaissance poet. From *Childe Harold's Pilgrimage,* as we shall see, he was also learning specific guidelines about making Spenser fit a modern context. As he was planning that transformation, he also became more certain of Spenser's faults, or rather of that combination of strengths and weaknesses that had al-

19. One thinks of Bate's discussion of Fuseli's famous drawing of "the artist 'moved by the grandeur' of the past. What is shown of the 'grandeur' of the past is only the gigantic foot of some classical collosus and, above it, a great hand pointing upward. The modern artist cannot touch the hand. He is seated at the pedestal, half-bowed, with his left hand to his forehead, as if in despair. But his right arm is stretched out in a caress, at once affectionate and helpless, over part of the collosal foot" (*Burden* 90).

ways made him seem so attractive to revisionists. Spenser's duality of vision had been a great inspiration for Byron, but he was flawed enough and human enough, Shelley declared, to have become "a poet-laureate," as opposed to "the sacred Milton," who never seemed to stumble in his lofty values (*SP* 295; *PW* 206). Shelley's impression of Spenser's weaknesses and vulnerability even let him sometimes exercise in his Spenserian poems a kind of Shenstonian playfulness with a companionable guide. The dedication to *The Revolt of Islam* begins with a somewhat parodic portrait of Shelley as a Spenserian knight returning from creative wars to deposit the spoils of his poem with Mary, "mine own heart's home" (line 2). There was no doubt about how much Shelley, as the "Elfin Knight," valued this special feeling for Spenser's kind influence. He defends his choice of Spenser's model in *The Revolt of Islam* by plainly distinguishing it from more threatening sources: "I have adopted the stanza of Spenser . . . not because I consider it a finer model of poetic harmony than the blank verse of Shakespeare and Milton, but because in the latter there is no shelter for mediocrity; you must either succeed or fail" (*PW* 35). Shelley may never have approached the "great bards" quite so "fearfully" as Keats did, but he shared Keats's relief about the "shelter" that Spenser offered from their threats of failure. That reassurance was a major factor in his decision to undertake epic labor dressed as a Spenserian knight.

Yet also like Keats, he never would have made such a decision without an equally strong impression of Spenser's capacity to facilitate the mental dynamics of that labor. From canto 3 of *Childe Harold's Pilgrimage*, which Byron composed and published in 1816, Shelley learned how much Spenser could contribute in this important respect. Byron and Shelley were together in Switzerland during the summer of 1816, discussing poetry and philosophy even as canto 3 was being written. Shelley was closely involved in the production of that canto, reading it in manuscript and carrying the final draft copy back to England where he wished to oversee its publication. He was particularly interested in its revolutionary advances over the poem's first two cantos. It "infinitely surpasses" those sections, he claimed, to become "the finest specimen of [Byron's] . . . powers yet exhibited" (*LPBS* 1:493, 557). Part of Shelley's excitement was aroused, as Philip Martin has shown (64–96), by the canto's new Wordsworthian interactions with nature, which his own recent discussions with Byron had inspired. His enthusiasm must have also been triggered, however, by Byron's experimentation with the kind of revisionary Spenserianism he had just been developing for himself.

In canto 3 of *Childe Harold's Pilgrimage,* Byron secularizes Spenserian dichotomies of realism and ideality along the very same lines that Shelley was now planning for his own epic. Byron specifically drops the theology of Spenser's mutability myth and adapts its doubling psychology to the drama of his narrator's inward rehabilitation after the failure of the French Revolution. Instead of withdrawing into Harold's isolationism or the anguish of unsuccessful revolutionaries like Rousseau and Napoleon, the narrator undergoes a gradual renovation of spirit in his communion with nature. His experience introduces him, however, to the conflict between his ideal visions of cosmic harmony and his realistic grasp of political discord. He specifically recognizes this tension in the clash between this world's mutability—the "wretched interchange of wrong for wrong" (III, 660)—and its symbols of eternal ideals—the "icy halls" of the Alps where "throned Eternity" looms secure, "Imperishably pure beyond all things below" (III, 593, 643). Struggling like the narrator of the *Mutabilitie Cantos* to transcend the passing scene of human change and embrace an eternal cosmic unity, the speaker of canto 3 condemns the brutality of European politics and declares that love is the moving principle of "throned Eternity," not Spenser's divine providence. All the beauteous things of earth, he concludes, "here extend, / Mingling, and made by Love, unto one mighty end . . . Into a boundless blessing, which may vie / With the immortal lights, in its eternity" (III, 950–67). "Love," as Shelley would later say himself in *A Defence of Poetry,* is the new "pillour of Eternity" on which all social reform and inward renewal of the spirit must be constructed.

That secularization of the dichotomies in the *Mutabilitie Cantos* was both an inspiration and a blueprint for the kind of Spenserian poetics that Shelley had been envisioning for himself. He had been intrigued for some time, as we have seen, with transferring Spenser's drama of mutability and transcendence to a modern, secular context. He was also thinking of focusing that context, as his lyrics on despair and mutability suggest, in his age's struggle to recover from the disaster of the French Revolution and somehow renew its millennial idealism. Moreover, the specific kind of idealism he wished to regenerate in European culture dovetailed with Byron's concept of love. Amid the incessant change of "this naked world," Cythna declares in *The Revolt of Islam,* love persists to make "a rule and law to ages that survive" (line 3720). Byron had just shown how a secularized Spenserianism could bring together all of these concerns in an epic poem about social renovation and the rehabilitation of the modern psyche. Besides speaking directly to Shelley's aesthetic and intellectual priorities in 1816, that example must have also broken down some of his apprehensions about the potential incompatability of Spenserianism for a modern poetics. How much Byron's example of transforming those Spenserian patterns meant to him may be guessed by his decision to write an epic in Spenserian stanzas about the struggle between despair and idealism, mutability and transcendence, in the aftermath of the French Revolution. Redeeming the psychodynamics of Spenser's mutability myth, we may conclude, became an important means for Shelley to work out his own modern vision of experience.

Byron, of course, was not the only one encouraging Shelley to ground his epic in the kind of Spenserianism that became so important in the second decade of the nineteenth century. Keats was currently structuring *Endymion* in that manner and discussing at least some of his strategies with Shelley. More pointedly, Peacock's recently composed *Ahrimanes* supplied the Zoroastrian model for the opening allegory of *The Revolt of Islam* and suggested how a Spenserian poem about dialectics between good and evil, ideality and dislocation, could become the vehicle for a vision of life in the nineteenth century. But *Childe Harold's Pilgrimage* was particularly important, and not only because it was the most popular of all Romantic Spenserian poems or because Shelley watched over its production so closely. He also found in it a possible solution to his own persisting division between the moral proselytizing of Spenser's eighteenth-century imitators and the psychodynamics of Romantic Spenserianism. One of the major aesthetic conflicts of *Childe Harold's Pilgrimage*, we recall, is its oscillation between a complex Spenserian allegory of mind and the more diffuse descriptive/reflective style of early Romantic Spenserianism. To Shelley, however, that division must have appeared less an aesthetic conflict than a merging of stylistic oppositions similar to his own. No one has ever accused Byron of moralistic zeal, but the reflective passages of *Childe Harold's Pilgrimage*, especially in their comments on political oppression, do share many of the characteristics of Shelley's more formulaic didacticism. Byron's way of switching between them and his pictures of mental debate, then, gave Shelley an authoritative precedent for coupling his own moralistic and psychodynamic Spenserian styles. That precedent was no great model of aesthetic success, and Shelley would have to modify it considerably along with many other important features of Byron's Spenserian art. But it did help him cope with one of the major obstacles to his developing plans for an epic Spenserian poem.[20]

The extent to which Shelley conceives of *The Revolt of Islam* as a Spenserian project is suggested by the deliberate steps he takes to authorize himself as an epic poet through association with his primary model, whom he clearly identifies as Spenser. It is the same kind of validating maneuver he used earlier in the company of the eighteenth-century Spenserians; only now, with more at stake, he is much more adamant about the new identification with Spenser. His initial subtitle for the poem, "A Vision of the Nineteenth Century, *In the Stanza of Spenser*" (italics mine), would have signaled his readers to expect a sustained engagement with Spenser according to Romanticism's revisionary paradigms. His opening simile of epic writing as the chivalric enterprise of "some victor Knight of Faery" (line 3) reinforces that connection, as does his eventual division of the epic into twelve cantos, the traditional number of books in classical epic but more specifically the number of cantos in a book of *The Faerie Queene*. This latter parallel is significant, for Shelley also arranges his narrative to reenact, canto by canto, the story of Book 1 of Spenser's epic.[21] Like Redcrosse and Una, Laon and Cythna pursue justice together, become separated, grow weak in enslavement and isolation, receive moral instruction leading to spiritual rebirth, fight a momentous battle against forces of evil, and finally enjoy a form of nuptual union. These actions even transpire during the same cantos that depict similar events in Book 1 of *The Faerie Queene*. Such sustained allusiveness to *The Faerie Queene* narrative is clearly meant to place Shelley in a direct line going back to Spenser. Yet following Spenser so closely does more than simply reassure or authorize Shelley; it also supplies an important basis for his "Vision" of the nineteenth century.

Shelley may forge that "Vision" out of Byron's example for adapt-

20. Richard Haswell has summarized the many critical complaints that have been raised about what has often been considered the disunified structure of *The Revolt of Islam* (81–82). The poem's divisions, we may suspect, have more do to with Shelley's attraction to differing forms of Spenserian allegory than to any lack of aesthetic design on his part.

21. Both Haswell (84) and Ruff (21) have noted this parallel, but neither one of them finds any sustained controlling pattern in Shelley's borrowings from the first book of *The Faerie Queene*. Ruff does note in passing, however, that Spenser's "chiaroscuro" of light and dark in Book 1 of *The Faerie Queene* may have given Shelley a pattern of imagistic contrasts to sustain throughout the doubling procedures of his own narrative (21).

ing Spenser's dualities to the story of psychic and social regeneration in post-Napoleonic Europe, but he takes a course of his own in carrying out the details of his revision. He specifically recasts Book 1 of *The Faerie Queene,* probably because it features Spenser's most dramatic story of a mental recovery borne out of the conflict of truth and falsehood, ideality and transcience—the interconnected redemptions of both Redcrosse and Una. Shelley drops the theological context of their experience, however, and draws out its psychological core for the basic paradigm of his own modern drama about imaginative redemption from the conflict of mutability and transcendence. Like Una, Cythna is associated with the "radiant stamp" of inviolable truth and virtue (line 1060). Also in the fashion of Una, she stands opposed to "dark Falsehood," which, again like Una, she tirelessly fends off though beleaguered by a host of enemies including her well-meaning but, like Redcrosse, sometimes benighted lover (line 1062). Laon lapses into error and falsehood, like Redcrosse in the House of Pride. He, too, despairs, suffers a withering enervation of body and spirit, and must be educated in another House of Holinesse before he can also apprehend the eternal ideals of another New Jerusalem. Many of Spenser's readers today find the cleavings and reunifications of Redcrosse and Una presenting a psychodrama of mental fragmentation, which progresses through the conflicts of actuality and transcendence toward an integrated vision of divine providence (Lockerd 14; Quilligan 74). Shelley proves himself an adept reader of that interior dynamic in Book 1, and his effort to extract it from Spenser's theology and transform it into the psychodrama of his own protagonists' different kind of inward renewal becomes the dramatic process by which his modern "Vision" takes shape.

To carry out that revisionary process, Shelley reconstructs the intricate patterns of Spenser's mental drama and subtly shifts their theological emphases to psychological ones. His modifications make the story of Redcrosse's pilgrimage toward God's New Jerusalem, in its purified form, a penetrating drama of imaginative renewal leading to a secular millennium in which the conflicts between eternity and the productions of time are finally resolved. Where Redcrosse, for instance, abandons Una because of his own lapse of faith, manifested in his attachment to Duessa's illusions, Laon and Cythna are separated by the political tyranny of Othman and, even more important, by their complicity in the psychology of hatred. Redcrosse and Una fall prisoner to their own spiritual weaknesses, figured in the domination of Sansloy and Orgoglio, but the enslavement of Laon and Cythna results from their repudiation of love for the tyranny of hatred. Laon murders the slave traders and Cythna scorns Othman's temporarily kind advances. Their literal imprisonment, in which they wither and despair like Redcrosse in Orgoglio's dungeon and at the Cave of Despair, thus figures an imaginative fall quite different from the spiritual lapses in the minds of Spenser's lovers. Laon's renewal similarly alters the theological contexts of Redcrosse's redemption. Where Redcrosse is saved from Orgoglio and Despair by Arthur and Una, both representing Christian grace, Laon is freed by a hermit who renews him inwardly by giving him lessons in Godwinian social theory.[22] This hermit, who recalls Spenser's Heauenly Contemplation, inspires Laon with a Shelleyan vision of the social millennium, which replaces the glimpse of the New Jerusalem after Redcrosse's regeneration. Laon's final victory over the forces of evil and delusion constitutes his repudiation of his own hatred, moreover, in contrast to Redcrosse's defeat of the dragon, which affirms his refurbished Christian faith. At every key point along these parallel histories, then, Shelley follows the narrative and mental strategies of Spenser's allegory, modifying them, or deepening their psychological resonance, for his own secular allegory about the intersection of actuality and transcendence. Put another way, he recovers and expands the drama of psychological collapse and renewal that so many Spenser scholars find embedded within Spenser's stories of imprisonment and liberation.

He was also learning how Spenser's "entrelacement" of mental pictures could be similarly modified to illuminate centers of mental conflict, which no doubt inspired his presentation of *The Revolt of Islam* as "a succession of pictures" whose allegorical significance would "illustrate . . . the growth and progress of individual mind" swerving between such poles as "enlighten[ment]" and "ignorance," "love" and "hatred" (*PW* 32). Those "pictures" are consistently made out of the lineaments of Spenser's drawings of mental conflict and rehabilitation. Cythna's imprisonment in the underwater cavern, recalling both the Cave of Despair episode and Florimell's enslavement in Proteus's sea-cave, is apposite. The allegory of Redcrosse's torment in the Despair sequence, which Shelley had already learned to read as a drama of mental swerves between transcendence and reality, now helped him portray the collapse of idealism in Cythna's

---

22. One reviewer of the *The Revolt of Islam* was astute enough to note the Spenserian paradigm here, comparing the hermit to a Spenserian character who talks incongruously like William Godwin (quoted in Newman I. White 139).

"frenzy" of "despair." Like the broken Redcrosse, Cythna is taken, weak in spirits, to a cave where her grief breeds madness. The cave's appearance, inhabited by "ghastly shadows" and a fiendish eagle, resembles some of the most graphic details of Spenser's Cave of Despair, "whereof aye dwelt the ghastly Owle . . . And all about it wandring ghostes did waile and howle" (1.11.33). The horrific landscape, as in Spenser, visualizes the protagonist's collapse into a welter of delusion. But that decay results from Cythna's suppression of her own kindness (Haswell 85–86). It is a mental aberration with definite precedents in Redcrosse's failure to trust Una and the subsequent rigidifying of his own imaginative sympathies. Yet a significant dimension of Redcrosse's fall is his lapse of Christian faith, a part of Spenser's "ideological desiderata" that Shelley finds an encrustation on the living mental drama of his allegory. To redeem that living form and punctuate his own independence from what he saw to be Spenser's limitation, Shelley makes Cythna explain how she has blighted her own surroundings by taking on the obtuseness of hatred. Finding her environment "like mind" (line 3081), she glosses the allegory of the cave that imprisons her: "Thus all things were / Transformed into the agony which I wore / Even as a poisoned robe around my bosom's core" (lines 2962–64).

Shelley uses another part of The Faerie Queene to comment on this departure from Spenser's example, recasting the Florimell allegory in a way that even more pointedly unlocks Spenser's mental dynamics from the prison of his philosophical system.[23] The plights of Florimell and Cythna are similar in many obvious details.[24] Where Florimell endures seven months in Proteus's undersea dungeon, Cythna languishes for seven years in Othman's submarine cave. The tactics of Proteus and Othman are nearly identical: each first tries to win his prisoner's affections through kindness; finding such gentility scorned, each then resorts to violence. Proteus hurls Florimell "Downe in a Dungeon deepe" (3.8.41) at the bottom of the sea, and Othman, receiving only harsh rebukes for his genuine if misguided expressions of love, rapes Cythna before imprisoning her beneath the sea. These parallels actually highlight Shelley's deviation from

23. Florimell's tale was so deeply embedded in Shelley's imagination that he invoked it two years later to describe persons in his household at Florence (*LPBS* 2:125). Hunt, who must have had a lot to say to Shelley about Spenser during all the hours they spent together, was so fond of the character of Florimell that he named one of his daughters after her.
24. Baker has noted the Florimell/Cythna connection in his dissertation, "Spenser and Shelley" (116).

the moral emphases of Spenser's allegory. Spenser lauds Florimell's chaste virtue in her resistance to Proteus: "Eternal thraldome was to her more liefe, / Than losse of chastitie . . . what so my feeble Muse can frame, / Shall be t'advance thy goodly chastitie" (3.8.42–43). Shelley, in contrast, exposes Cythna's resistance to Othman as a sign of her lack of imaginative sympathy. Her performance of what Spenser, seconded by MacCaffrey in one of her rare anti-Romantic readings (268), would call a virtuous deed reveals her own insensitivity to Othman's sincere though confused affection. It is her psychological rigidity that drives him to violence. The allegory of Cythna's imprisonment may thus be seen to portray the mental anguish of a mind temporarily given over to the hatred engendered by philosophies like Spenser's. When she casts off the tyranny of her own selfhood by expressing sympathy for the Nautilus, her prison simply disappears. The allegory of her escape and ensuing visions of universal peace may finally be read as an emblem of Shelley's own ongoing practice of clearing away Spenser's system and redeeming the psychology embedded within it in order to reach his own "Vision" of a rehabilitated century.[25]

Nowhere is that redemption of Spenserian psychodrama more integral to the visionary process of *The Revolt of Islam* than in its final stanzas, which re-create the dualities of that section of *The Faerie Queene* that was always the most important to Shelley, the *Mutabilitie Cantos*. In this reformulation of Spenser's most memorable allegory of the contest between actuality and transcendence, Shelley offers nothing like the pageant of ever-changing time that Spenser provides, or the "Sabaoths sight" of an eternal rest toward which he yearns. But Shelley does present the concluding voyage of Laon's boat as a kind of procession through a landscape of ceaseless change and toward a brief vision of eternal joy in the Temple of the Spirit. The deaths of Laon and Cythna are announced with a speech about the "flood of time" that has left them mouldering (line 4687). They sail three days along a mighty river whose "shapes and shadows" are "changing ever" (line 4748). The landscape around them constantly brings on "New changes"—shifting from forests to meadows to mountains—which remind them of "all mortal change" (lines 4782, 4786). "Morn, noon, and even" come and go like the pageant of days

25. Alpers seems to me to come closest among Spenser scholars to the way Shelley reads the allegory of Florimell's imprisonment and rescue. He explains that "Florimell's rescue comes not through any supranatural agency, but is the direct result of her expressing her love anguish at the beginning of canto twelve" (*Poetry* 121–22).

and hours in Spenser's myth (line 4756). Finally, in the last two
stanzas of the poem, just as a vision of God's "Sabbaoth" emerges in
the last two stanzas of *The Faerie Queene,* Laon and Cythna arrive at
an immutable paradise. The rolling waves of their river wash into a
"windless waveless lake," in which their boat temporarily hangs
"[m]otionless" (lines 4806, 4810). Upon their arrival at their final
resting place, the Temple of the Spirit, their wonderment closes the
poem just as swiftly as Spenser's breathless apprehension of "the pillours of Eternity" concludes the *Mutabilitie Cantos.* From those "pillours," however, Shelley builds a radically different temple of the
psyche, just as he reshapes Spenser's dichotomy between change and
permanence into a completely new kind of equipoise in the mind's
perception of temporal and eternal experience.

His recasting of the Mutabilitie episode entails both a more optimistic view of sublunary experience and a stronger promise of imminent redemption in the human psyche's personal apocalypse. The
figure of Mutabilitie has gone through something of a redemption
in Spenser studies lately, appearing to MacCaffrey, for instance, as a
representation of this world's fecundity and a reminder that the
"good of life is bound up with change" (427). Still, she can appear at
times as a terrifying giantess, whose "changes infinite" also wreak
woe and havoc in the world. Her tyrannical rule over mankind can
be a cause for grievous lamentation and a stimulant for us to fix
hope solely on God's suppression of her power at the end of time. In
The Revolt of Islam, however, the characterization of mutability is unconditionally appealing: "A scene of joy and wonder to behold /
That river's shapes and shadows changing ever" (lines 4747–48).
The contrast punctuates Shelley's theory of a universal harmony informing the rough mutations of the world, like the "Power" of Mont
Blanc's avalanche or the irresistible sweep of the West Wind, which
would be celebrated if understood. Such an understanding in man's
mind, what Wasserman calls an "imaginative apprehension of
Power" (*Shelley* 231), would break down the traditional barriers between temporal and eternal experience, bringing about a paradise
on earth, here and now. Hence, where Spenser can only hope for an
eschatological vision of God's apocalypse, Shelley builds the "pillours
of Eternity," as Blake constructs his Jerusalem, in the present situation of England's green and pleasant land. Those "pillours" actually
stand in the mind of man, for the Temple of the Spirit is not so
much a place or a providential design as it is a condition of mind to
which the narrator of *The Revolt of Islam* travels along with Laon and
Cythna. The pillars of Spenser's myth are thus broken down, or

more precisely, reconstructed in Shelley's epic to hold up a new kind of temple set in a modern landscape of the human imagination. That rebuilding takes place on a stylistic as well as an allegorical level. One of the features of Shelley's psychological landscape that most strongly distinguishes it from the "mental space" of *The Faerie Queene* is the inward dislocation caused by the collapse of once reliable pillars of belief like Spenser's. To dramatize how much more problematic it is for the modern mind to negotiate such a landscape and reach, or even apprehend, any eternal temple of the spirit, Shelley takes over Byron's practice of heightening Spenser's stylistic contrasts between eternity and the "tickle" state of human affairs. In reading *The Faerie Queene*, Shelley had fallen in love with "the brilliancy and magnificence of sound" in Spenser's musical stanzas, "a measure inexpressibly beautiful" (*PW* 35). Like Byron, but with even greater alliterative and assonant virtuosity, he now fashions a modern equivalent of those golden, ringing stanzas to embellish his own scenes of cosmic harmony:

> Till down that mighty stream, dark, calm, and fleet,
> Between a chasm of cedarn mountains riven,
> Chased by the thronging winds whose viewless feet
> As swift as twinkling beams, had, under Heavens,
> From woods and waves wild sounds and odours
>   driven,
> The boat fled visibly—three nights and days,
> Borne like a cloud through morn, and noon, and
>   even,
> We sailed along the winding watery ways
> Of the vast stream, a long and labyrinthine maze.
>   (lines 4738–46)[26]

Shelley also learned from Byron how to counterpoint such euphony with a radically cacophonous style associated with sociopolitical and psychic disruptions:

> The ground in many a little dell
> Was broken, up and down whose steeps befell
> Alternate victory and defeat, and there

26. Contemporary reviewers, many of whom were given to exclusive praise for Spenserian harmonies of style, predictably lauded this kind of versification in *The Revolt of Islam* (quoted in Newman I. White 134).

The combatants with rage most horrible
Strove, and their eyes started with crackling stare,
And impotent their tongues they lolled into the air,

Flaccid and foamy, mad like a dog's hanging;
Want and Moon-madness, and the pest's swift
Bane
When its shafts smite—while yet its bow is twang-
ing—
Have each their mark and sign—some ghastly
stain;
And this was thine, O War!
(lines 2474–84)

This rough style so dominates long sections of the middle cantos on revolutionary violence that no less a passionate admirer of Shelley's craftsmanship than Yeats complained: "The rhythm is varied and troubled, and the lines . . . are broken capriciously" (*Essays* 379). But that is precisely the point, as it is for Byron: to roughen a turbulence already there in Spenser, one that Yeats was not interested in hearing, so as to broaden the gulf between idealism and reality inherent in his own metrical oppositions. The effect is to reinforce that overall strategy of redeeming a core of psychological tension in Spenser's world to make his poetics the instrument of a modern vision.[27]

27. Shelley's manuscript revisions, as recorded by Rogers and Brewe, show how carefully he works to maintain this equipoise of competing styles. He revises many lines of his closing vision, for instance, to enhance the musicality associated with its idealism. His description of the enchanted bower in which Laon awakes originally read as follows:

high above was spread
The emerald heaven of trees of unknown kind,
Whose rare and moonlike blooms . . .
Faint and wavering light upon the fountain shed.
(lines 4608–11)

The last two lines are then smoothed into a more lulling iambic rhythm, whose alliterative phrasing and "harmonious arrangement of . . . pauses"—Shelley's own phrase for the fluid pacing of Spenser's melodious style (*PW* 35)—create the soft witchery of sound in the visionary sequences of *The Revolt of Islam:*

Whose moonlike blooms and bright fruit overhead
A shadow, which was light, upon the waters shed.

Much as this revisionary method helps Shelley fashion "A Vision of the Nineteenth Century," it can also prove a serious burden. To comprehend that strain, we must recognize Shelley's recourse to another way of modernizing Spenser, which was to impose on him the old radical form of eighteenth-century moralizing. Here we may pinpoint the growing conflict in Shelley's dialogue with Spenser. The more deeply he engages in Spenserian allegory throughout *The Revolt of Islam*, the more he feels the need to distance himself from it, which he does by relapsing into the hectoring style of *Queen Mab*. In fact, his didactic sequences often directly gloss his allegories, as if it is necessary to insist on his correction of Spenser's example. This scenario is most evident in the poem's opening canto. Its conflict between snake and eagle, Shelley's most openly allegorical sequence and his most direct adoption of a Spenserian manner, is followed by the visionary woman's long explanation of its meaning. She specifically explains how a conventional allegorical reading of serpent-eagle warfare, the kind of interpretation that Spenser invites for Redcrosse's battle with the dragon at the end of Book 1, does not apply in this case. She makes it clear, in fact, that Spenserian allegory needs to be reversed, for her snake is an embodiment of the spirit of good. Her explanation of the un-Spenserian nature of this allegory actually recalls many of the principal features of Shelley's eighteenth-century Spenserianism. She obviously resembles, while taking the mortal narrator off in a magic boat to a supernatural palace, the visionary goddesses of *Queen Mab* and its precedents. Acting

---

The diction of these passages similarly grows more elaborate and euphonious through various stages of revision. Hence the original introduction of the winged child, "When this had past the winged spirit came . . . And said, I was abashed with fear and shame," becomes the much more opulent "Then the bright child, the plumed Seraph came . . . And said, 'I was disturbed by tremulous shame'" (lines 4657–59). Many other examples could be cited, some lines being reworked as many as five or six times, which reveals the deliberate care that Shelley takes to wed his Spenserian rhyme and vision.

He works just as carefully to impose a fractured style on the realistic scenes of nineteenth-century disruptions. Thus his line on bloodied fields of battle originally runs without any metrical pauses, "A harvest sown with other hopes and [shrifts?]." He then inserts numerous stops for the more fragmented final version, "A harvest sown with other hopes, the while / Far overhead, ships from Propontis keep / A killing rain of fire:—" (lines 2394–96). This kind of change is even more obvious in the scene describing the final separation of Laon and Cythna. "I stood beside her but she saw me not," Laon initially reports. As a more powerful sign of his emotional divisions, this line becomes much more discordant in the revised version, "She saw me not—she heard me not—alone" (line 4225).

like her counterparts in those works, she delivers a long lecture on
human history and moral philosophy. Like Mab's speech, her ser-
mon is a forum for Shelley's own radical theories of reform, which
are now combined with Peacock's Zoroastrianism. This lecture is delivered with Mab's moral earnestness, and it indicts the chief objects
of Mab's tirades: custom, priests, kings, conventional faith, etc. Similar moments that are often even more codified in their didacticism,
such as Cythna's long speech to the slave traders after she escapes
from her prison, typically come right after Shelley's allegorical revisions of Spenser.

Shelley defended these recurring mixtures of psychological and
didactic allegory by calling *The Revolt of Islam* a re-creation of *Queen
Mab* within the context of a human story, a "sad reality" (*LPBS* 2:96).
The transparency of any such unified purpose, however, makes one
question the motivations behind Shelley's plan. It is not hard to see
that the formulaic style of eighteenth-century didacticism is too fundamentally different from Spenserian interiority for a workable co-
existence of the two modes. That Shelley should have even tried to
yoke them together not only tells us that he was still attached to the
strategies of *Queen Mab,* it also suggests that he remained disturbed
about his close affiliation with the conservative Spenser and that he
was anxious to put some distance between himself and the very poet
he depended on the most. Exactly how uneasy Shelley was about
their relationship can be judged by an encounter with Spenser that
probably took place while he was writing *The Revolt of Islam.* Discussing with Peacock the story of Artegall and the Giant, the same passage that bothered Keats, Shelley expressed such indignation with its
conservative moral that Peacock remembered for many years all the
details of his outburst. Like Keats, Shelley sided with the Giant
against the aristocratic privileges and Christian hierarchies that
Spenser commends. But his anger with Spenser was much more severe than Keats's as he implacably positioned himself against such
attitudes. Peacock recalled: "Shelley once pointed out this passage to
me, observing, 'Arthegall argues with the Giant; the Giant has the
better of the argument; Arthegall's iron man knocks him over into
the sea and drowns him. This is the usual way in which power deals
with opinion.' I said, 'That was not the lesson which Spenser intended to convey.' 'Perhaps not,' he said; 'it is the lesson which he
conveys to me. I am of the Giant's faction'" (*LPBS* 2:71). To be of
the Giant's faction could mean to act like Typographus in Keats's
allegory and reeducate or liberalize Spenser, which is what Shelley
attempts to do in the revisionary procedures of *The Revolt of Islam.*

But the fact that Keats's Giant also strikes out at Artegall and Talus, blinding them, suggests that joining the Giant's faction could also mean declaring war on Spenser.

The more conservative Spenser scholars call this anti-Artegallianism "mad obstinacy" on Shelley's part (Horton 188), and they may not be far off. The reality seems to be that Shelley once again felt overburdened by the hostile philosophies of his closest guide and reacted with the same kind of defensive extremism that characterizes *Queen Mab*.[28] Certainly he wished to downplay his association with Spenser by the time he was finished with the poem. He removed the Spenserian subtitle from the final version of *The Revolt of Islam* and went so far in his preface as to disclaim any connection with Spenser. Forgetting about the several hundred Spenserian stanzas that compose his epic, he declared his unwillingness "to tread in the footsteps of any who have preceded me. I have sought to avoid the imitation of any style of language or versification peculiar to the original minds of which it is the character; designing that, even if what I have produced be worthless, it should still be properly my own" (*PW* 34).[29] The same tensions that made Shelley thus deny any contact with Spenser's "original mind," we may suspect, also drove him to punctuate *The Revolt of Islam* with those diatribes against everything that Artegall stood for.[30] Underneath this "obstinacy" we may also find

28. Bloom has called Shelley "the most generous strong poet of the post-Enlightenment . . . in his attitude towards precursors" (*Anxiety of Influence* 151). That claim may be valid for the Shelley of *A Defence of Poetry*, but it does not apply so well to the earlier poet "of the Giant's faction."

29. Jean-Pierre Mileur notes similar evasions and defenses in the preface to *Alastor* (248).

30. We may even trace some of that anxiousness in the minute and sometimes redundant scrupulousness with which Shelley inverts Spenser's allegorical patterns. In modifying the history of Redcrosse, for instance, he incessantly reverses the values of Redcrosse's allegorical battles with serpentine figures of evil. Those reversals begin, as we have seen, with the opening allegory's sinister portrait of the eagle, which Spenser conventionally associates with both Christ and Redcrosse in the battle against the dragon (1.11.34). The sculptured figure on the people's victory statue similarly subverts the values of Redcrosse's Christian warfare. It stands in the posture of St. George, Redcrosse's historical name, trampling a serpent. But the "obscene worm" is called "Faith" (line 2168), meaning specifically the very Christian faith that Redcrosse embodies. Toward the end of *The Revolt of Islam*, Redcrosse's battle against the dragon Errour and its wormy brood undergoes a similar reversal. Like his Spenserian prototype, who is besieged by Errour's "fruitfull cursed spawne of serpents small" (1.1.22), Laon is entrammeled among a horde of serpents representative generally of mistaken opinions, "A couch of snakes, and scorpions, and the fry / Of centipedes and worms"

not simply Shelley's irritation about his debts to the proponent of a distasteful philosophy, but also his apprehension about having the independence of his own vision qualified by Spenser's prior and still culturally potent Christian ethos, his own voice thus "taken over" by a "reservoir of rhetorical power" that John Archer calls "still the main cultural force within European civilization" (265). We might not want to say of Spenser what Bloom claims for Milton, that "Shelley is captured by him" (*Poetry and Repression* 98). But it does seem evident at least that Shelley was flinching under the yoke of a Spenserian system that preceded him, inspired his own mythmaking, and threatened to dominate his creative efforts no matter how much he revised, displaced, or transformed it.

What may have made it so difficult to cast off that mantle was the very way that Shelley went about trying to replace it with his own system. We have seen in the examples of Byron, Hunt, and Keats, that an effective Spenserian revisionism for the Romantics not only corrected Spenser's limitations but redeemed them in ways that helped each poet work out his own aesthetic conflicts. This is not the case in *The Revolt of Islam*. Shelley may have disagreed profoundly with Spenser's philosophy, and he may have rightly understood that redeeming Spenser's "inscape" was the best way to bring him into the nineteenth century. But in modifying Spenser's dichotomous vision, he only changes its terms while continuing what the Romantics felt were its fundamental limitations. Ultimately, he acts on Spenser's own mistaken aspirations when he tries in *The Revolt of Islam* to resolve the conflict of realism and ideality into a final vision of a transcendent, eternal realm. The Temple of the Spirit may look quite different from Spenser's "pillours of Eternity," but the architectural principle is the same.[31] Hence for all his revisionary labor, Shelley preserves the very reluctance to rest in uncertainties and the very insistence on absolute ideals that his peers were criticizing in Spen-

---

(lines 4133–34). But where Spenser's "spawne of serpents" figure religious contentiousness, over which Redcrosse as true Christianity prevails, Shelley's "fry" of "worms" depicts the spirit of Christianity itself, over which the antireligious Laon triumphs. In effect, Redcrosse is thrust into the degrading position of his reptilian foes. None of these turnarounds, taken singly, is inappropriate to Shelley's purposes. But their repetitiveness suggests some discomfort with his efforts to untether himself from an authority on whom he depended.

31. Baker makes a similar point in relation to *Queen Mab*: "In casting down the old idols, Shelley wished only to substitute for them a morality of his own devising" ("Spenser, the Eighteenth Century and Queen Mab" 83).

ser. Instead of deepening Spenser's duality to cast off the lineaments of his own absolutism, he actually perpetuates the major form of error that the Romantics found in Spenser. Like Keats at the end of *Endymion,* Shelley would have to reassess the whole procedure of his revisionism before he could rely on it to help him work out his own creative salvation. That revaluation would push him toward the increasingly skeptical qualification of his early idealism that many current Shelley scholars find to be one of the hallmarks of his most sophisticated poetry.

Contributing to such a development was his growing recognition that a mature Spenserian poetry would have to be compact. For *The Revolt of Islam* taught him the same lesson about the difficulty of maintaining Spenser's style that Keats had learned in *Calidore* and *Endymion.* Shelley now realized that, regardless of personal conflicts with Spenser, the very strain of writing a long poem in his manner dooms the imitator to periodic flats. "I have completely failed," he acknowledged, to keep up such a burden throughout the entire poem (*PW* 35). A fragmentary or elliptically lyrical Spenserianism, he would learn, might be a wiser stylistic choice. Moreover, he would come to suspect, it might be the only kind of Spenserian form appropriate for the new, open-ended art he was just beginning to shape—a poetics that immersed itself in the shards of Byron's fractured mirror instead of trying to edify them into a temple. It was Shelley's good fortune, shared with Keats and abetted by the historical conditions of second-generation Romantic Spenserianism, to reach these conclusions early in his career, and in a way that helped facilitate that more supple poetics toward which he was heading. Though his time was also limited, he was learning enough and early enough to proceed toward his own version of the special harmony that Keats eventually found between Spenser's song and the voice of modern poetic experience.

The Knight of   6
the Shield of Shadow

I

The experience of writing *The Revolt of Islam* helped provoke in 1818 some key changes in Shelley's attitude toward the literary past, which in turn significantly altered his way of thinking about Spenserian revisionism and its relation to the making of a modern poetics. His didactic excesses in *The Revolt of Islam* taught him that the first step toward becoming a legitimate member of the second Renaissance was to eliminate his eighteenth-century moralism, once and for all. In its place, he had to commit himself more strenuously to the interiority of England's first Renaissance and the self-questioning procedures of his own maturing philosophical skepticism.[1] The negative effects of his defensiveness toward Spenser, moreover, left him convinced of the need to approach the old poets with a more receptive spirit, no matter how much some of their values repelled him. It must have seemed like a fresh beginning of sorts, a new dedication to the "imperial spirits" of the past (*PW* 468), which was reinforced by his emigration to Italy in 1818 and consequent exposure to the great traditions of Italian and Greek art. He began constructing a new literary history in his own

1. He also made a general effort now to exorcise the overall didactic impulse that had controlled so much of his poetry up to and including *The Revolt of Islam*. "Didactic poetry is my abhorrence," he exclaimed in the preface to *Prometheus Unbound* (*PW* 207). Claire Clairmont recorded in 1820 that Shelley's "three aversions" were "God Almighty, Lord Chancellor & didactic Poetry" (184). Shelley also constructed a sustained argument in *The Defence of Poetry*, of course, against the limitations of didactic poetry. It was sometime during this evolutionary transition, moreover, that the "incurable and involuntary dualism" that Bloom finds intrinsic in his psychology (*Map of Misreading* 11) began to exert more and more of a controlling force over his poetry. His deepening capacity to entertain contrary perspectives on experience has led Shelley scholarship over the last decade, in Curran's phrase, to an ever-increasing "emphasis on the skeptical basis of Shelley's worldview" ("Spenser and Shelley"). That discussion has recently been extended in a lively debate between Jerrold Hogle and Stuart Sperry. Where Hogle brilliantly analyzes what he calls Shelley's "mobile process" of open-ended vision (vi), Sperry qualifies the thrust of such skeptical readings with his emphasis on Shelley's "desire to project a vision embodying long-studied conclusions as to the nature of man, life, and destiny" (*Shelley's Major Verse* xi).

imagination that located the highest moments of cultural achievement in terms of their genius for revealing "the operations of the
human mind" (*PW* 205). Shelley vowed to replace his defensiveness
toward the past with an eagerness to absorb all that was stamped
with "the eternity of genius" in those moments (*SP* 290). He saw this
historical line as a series of great creative surges uniting classical
Greece, the Italian Renaissance of Dante and Petrarch, and the English Renaissance of Spenser, Shakespeare, and Milton. It was still too
early for him to say whether any principle of decline or progression
informed this historical pattern. For now, he was satisfied to delineate the high points of creative efflorescence, unite them loosely according to the force of their mental drama, and proclaim an ambition to reproduce that energy.

Such a plan moved Shelley to group some of the most tremendous
presences in Western poetic history into a special tradition with
which he sought to affiliate himself. He built a pantheon of the
world's greatest poets in the preface to *Prometheus Unbound,* for instance, giving the principal seats to the Greek dramatists, Dante, and
Milton. He similarly distinguished Sophocles and Shakespeare in the
preface to *The Cenci.* Shelley worked extensively to link himself with
the tradition of these mighty spirits by adopting the major poetic
forms of their epochs: the terza rima of *Prince Athanase,* the eclogue
format of *Rosalind and Helen,* the revenge-tragedy motif of *The Cenci,*
the Greek drama of mind in *Prometheus Unbound.* In the most revealing expression of his new commitment to these forebears, he declared in the preface to *Prometheus Unbound* the absolute necessity of
following their examples: "[I]t is the study of their works . . . to
which I am willing that my readers should impute this singularity [of
style in *Prometheus Unbound*]. . . . [O]ne great poet is a masterpiece of
another which another not only ought to study but must study" (*PW*
205–6).

By patterning himself so determinedly after giant figures like
Sophocles, Dante, Shakespeare, and Milton, however, Shelley intensified the distressing question that had become so familiar to him
and his contemporaries: *how* was one supposed to stand up against
such towering examples? He could approach the task zestfully at
times, feeling "incite[d]" by "great ancestors" to "do that for our own
age which they have done for theirs" (*PW* 278). His six volumes of
poetry published between 1818 and 1822, as Curran points out (*Poetic Form* 17), show that the weight of such an aspiration did not
paralyze him creatively. But it did make him pause at times to consider how much more pressure was now on him. Thus at times the

moderns seemed to him like "puny generations" in the shadow of those giants who walked before the flood (*LPBS* 2:59). And the "very fragments" of his ancestors' "faultless productions" could seem to enforce "the despair of modern art" (*PW* 447). If we examine his guarded comments on literary tradition, we may find that his concern with the dead, though far from a source of incapacitating anxiety, was at least becoming a major preoccupation and one with significant bearing on his response to Spenser. His very evasiveness about the subject may also be seen as a kind of repression, which suggests a response to the past arguably even more complicated than Keats's.

Repression of the dead, as Mileur citing Freud reminds us, never works (195). The signs of where it may have caused difficulties for Shelley lay in his many brief, often unexpected outbursts on the power and the choking domination of the past. They flare up and relapse suddenly in his later poems with a recurrence that implies something like a semi-repressed obsession struggling to break out. Thus he alternately conceives of those "dead Kings" and their strong "Melody" as "the tales / Of mighty poets," "wise poets in the waste of years," the "fautless productions" of a bolder "age of gold" in "the world's young prime" (*PW* 586, 367, 447, 421). These reflections on the strength of the past often come with an ominous sense of threat. "[D]read antiquity" haunts the moderns with "rattling bones" (*PW* 377, 570). Its "imperial spirits / Rule the present from the past" (*PW* 468), and their spectral authority can be brutal. The "great bards of elder time" leave the current age "infected" with the "contagion" of their mighty song, the powerful "words" of their "antique verse" overwhelming "the shattered present" (*PW* 514, 416). Faced with this onslaught, Shelley could acknowledge a desire to "Forget the dead, the past" (*PW* 553). But the sound of "rattling bones," he well knew, could not be shut out, and the "ghosts" of the past would continue to "take revenge" on those who try to dismiss them (*PW* 553).

None of these reflections occurs during any sustained analysis of literary influence, which is probably why they have never been examined very closely. Instead they surface like the psyche's subtle, repetitve ways of gesturing a considerable but unstated preoccupation. Nowhere is the consuming and semi-repressed nature of this concern more evident than in the preface to *Prometheus Unbound*. Shelley purports there to describe the conception of his work, its aims, and its relation to various literary models. But his explanations frequently digress into contradictory theories of poetic influence, in which he both defends his originality and confesses his lack of it. He begins with a defense of the "license" to innovate upon great predecessors and insists on his independence from Aeschylus and Milton. Yet he later acknowledges that the "singularity" of *Prometheus Unbound* is owed to "the study of their works." Then he turns to the question of how "contemporary writings may have tinged my composition," and he returns again near his conclusion to the writer's "subjection" to the spirit of the age, whose general shape he is "willing to confess . . . I have imitated" (*PW* 205–7). Such an equivocating fixation on poetic influence makes this preface less a conventional introduction to *Prometheus Unbound* than a veiled drama of Shelley's apprehensions about the space left by his great ancestors for innovation. If we read *Promethus Unbound* as a psychodrama subliminally about the "despair of modern art," a reading I intend to pursue, we can find such a preface serving as an appropriate entryway to the poem that follows and to Shelley's state of mind in 1818–19.

The preface also shows him sharing Keats's particular way of configuring England's literary tradition. Like Keats, Shelley imagines Shakespeare and Milton towering godlike above all the other mortal English poets. Only Shakespeare among the English can stand up to the great tragic poets of classical Athens, and Milton's superlative achievement in religious epic makes him appear the divine genius of a higher world, "the sacred Milton" (*PW* 206). Of these two giants, Shelley leagues himself more obviously with Milton, probably sharing Keats's sense of Milton's special appropriateness for the mythmaking and epic-building enterprise of Romantic literary culture. His view of Milton's "sacred" status in this capacity particularly concerns me, for it recalls the scenario in which Keats found Spenser a more accessible guide.

Shelley never said that his life hinged on Milton's death. As he demonstrated in his remarks about the "superstition" that *Paradise Lost* had engendered (*SP* 290), he was also not averse to noticing Milton's errors. But he generally approached Milton with the kind of awed reverence that made Keats feel so intimidated. The language of his references to Milton, like Keats's, teems with images of domineering authority. Milton appears in *Adonais* as an immortal "Sire" who "reigns o'er earth" (lines 29–36). His "spirit-sighted countenance" in the "Ode to Liberty" (line 48) sternly chastises the political retrenchments of England's Restoration. In the short fragment "Milton's Spirit," his ghost rises to thunder and shake "[a]ll human things built in contempt of man" (line 4). Milton similarly emerges in *A*

Defence of Poetry as a bold destroyer of false creeds (*SP* 285), and the "supremacy of [his] genius" excludes everyone but Homer and Dante from the title of epic poet (*SP* 290–91). One can almost hear Dryden's phrase echoing in Shelley's imagination: "This man cuts us all out." The degree to which that thought preoccupied Shelley may be measured in his late fragment, "The False Laurel and the True." It presents Milton as one of the "eternal few" who wear the "wreath to mighty poets only due" and force the "Presumptuous" modern writer to don the "false laurel" of sickening flowers and poisonous dews (lines 1–2, 8).

Contemplating the "infection" wrought by such a mighty poet, Shelley may not have found Keats's murderous thoughts about Milton utterly foreign. His uneasiness about Milton's inflexible and wounding divinity, like Keats's response, also seems to have heightened his interest in Spenser's gentler "Tydings," which grew in direct proportion to his developing sense of Milton's severity. He ranked Spenser, as *A Defence of Poetry* makes clear, among the "eternal few." Within the English epic tradition, he found Spenser's model second only to Milton's. But quite unlike Milton, Spenser came to Shelley with both limitations and affability. Spenser's "official morality," contrasted with Milton's "bold neglect of a direct moral purpose" (*SP* 290), made him less of an eternal poet. Yet such a diminishment of stature also highlighted his approachability. Of perhaps greater significance, Shelley found this openness enhanced by his traditional association with beneficence. That characterization was not new to Shelley, but now, with Milton's hard siring much in his mind, he developed a special interest in the gentle and playful dimensions of Spenser that were being featured in Romantic literary culture. In *Rosalind and Helen*, modeled partly on *The Shepheardes Calender*, he embraced the tender and melancholy pathos of Spenser's love poetry. Putting on a Shenstonian hat in *The Letter to Maria Gisborne*, he treated Spenser as a playmate and toyed with his archaisms: "I'll leave, as Spenser says, with many mo, / This secret in the pregnant womb of time" (lines 103–4). He also sported devilishly with Spenser's bizarre characters, presenting himself "like some weird Archimage" hatching inflammatory works (line 106). In *The Witch of Atlas*, a fairy allegory with obvious links to *The Faerie Queene*, Shelley created a whimsical heroine whose magical "pranks" reflect the childlike playfulness that the Romantics found pervasive in Spenser. This amiable Archimago of a Spenser, to whom Shelley conspiratorily responded with such "a playful and perverse" spirit (Curran, "Spenser and Shelley"), could relieve the pressure that

England's other eternal writer of epic was fomenting. How much that relief meant to Shelley may be gauged by a brief sequence on intellectual guidance in *Prince Athanase*, his first significant poem after *The Revolt of Islam*.

Like Laon, Athanase is a young revolutionary poet-prophet with many general resemblances to Shelley. Also like Laon, he receives poetic and spiritual instruction from an elderly sage, Zonoras. Shelley connected Laon's tutor, we recall, with Spenser's spiritual educator Heauenly Contemplation. Probably remembering that association, he also places Zonoras in a Spenserian context with his opening description of the old man as "a weary wight" (line 155). As the sequence evolves, Zonoras takes on the specific attributes that Shelley was assigning to Spenser. A noble and inspiring poet-figure from an antique past, the "majestical" Zonoras inflames Athanase with "soul-sustaining songs of ancient lore" (line 171). But his "wan visage" and "withered mien" mark him with the melancholy pathos of a man who, like Spenser, has suffered much and lived to tell of it. His speech, also like the voice that so many of the Romantics heard in Spenser's poetry, is "clear and mild, / And sweet" (lines 172–73). Not surprisingly, Zonoras thus approaches Athanase, much as Spenser came to Keats in the "Induction" to *Calidore*, with a "calm and gentle" look (160). Instead of feeling imposed upon, Athanase welcomes this friendly mentor "[i]n patient silence" (line 163). The outcome of their pleasant sessions together may be Shelley's most significant comment on Spenser's unique attractiveness as a malleable guide, for Athanase eventually outstrips his master. Drawing upon his own "native strength," the young disciple teaches "Strange truths and new to that experienced man" (lines 178–79). We should not, of course, read the Zonoras/Athanase relationship as simply and solely a transparent allegory of the Spenser/Shelley dynamic. But the two couplings have enough in common for us to see in the mirror of *Prince Athanase* the mixture of respect, intimacy, and self-confidence that Shelley was feeling toward Spenser. Such was the combination of attitudes carrying him into the depths of Spenser's universe, where he felt it possible to receive the inspiration of "soul-sustaining songs" while turning around to counterinstruct his mentor in "Strange truths and new." It was as if the bigoted writer of *A View of the State of Ireland* was being replaced in Shelley's imagination with the moving but pliant singer of the *Complaints*, or more specifically, of *The Shepheardes Calender*.

Shelley began reading *The Shepheardes Calender* in August 1818 with a special eye to its amatory themes, which inspired him soon after to compose his own "modern eclogue," *Rosalind and Helen*.[2] Of all Spenser's works, *The Shepheardes Calender* may be one of the easiest to divest of ideology and read as a straightforward record of love's sorrowing passion. E. K. announces its principal theme as "the common Labyrinth of Love" (19), and it was indeed the "sore heart roote" (*December*, line 93) of that "common Labyrinth," as Shelley made clear in the "mournful talk" (line 60) of *Rosalind and Helen*, that now seemed more important to him than everything else in Spenser's poetry. Spenser's dedication to love, Shelley even argued, finally drowns out the "dissonance" of his "superstition" (*SP* 289). Displacing Artegall with Colin Clout in this manner entailed a major revaluation of what Spenser represents and how he can speak to a modern age.

It was especially useful to emphasize Spenser's amatory themes because of their obvious associations with his pastoralism, which as a traditional apprentice genre was the form Shelley wished to practice in this first phase of his new poetic enterprise. Working in the context of Spenserian pastoral was a logical way to situate himself with his great ancestors, at the point where they had begun their classic ascents to the higher genres. But there was something more strategic about his decision to follow Spenserian instead of, say, Virgilian or even Miltonic pastoral. Spenser had taken pains to reduce the pressures of poetic influence on himself, as he began his official career with *The Shepheardes Calender,* and it was that disarming attitude toward literary competition that Shelley particularly wished to absorb. He makes a point, for instance, of echoing Spenser's disclaimer that not much should be expected of a jejune poet like himself. Inexperience had moved Spenser, E. K. explains, "rather in AEglogues, then other wise to write, doubting perhaps his habilitie." For such a young, insecure poet, the "base" matter, "homely" manner, and pathetic sorrows of the pastoral tradition are invitingly manageable (18). In the preface to *Rosalind and Helen*, Shelley similarly emphasizes the humbleness of the pastoral form and the limits of his own

2. Havens notes that the first version of *Rosalind and Helen* was completed by 18 February 1818. He argues that this early version comprised primarily the Helen segment, which was a kind of blueprint for *The Revolt of Islam,* and was completed before Shelley began working on the epic in April 1817. Citing similarities between Rosalind's tale and Mary Shelley's rupture with Isabel Baxter in March 1818, Havens assigns an 1818 date for the Rosalind section. Because the Rosalind section features the kind of Italian landscapes Shelley was absorbing after he left England in March 1818, coupled with Shelley's statement about revising the pastoral in August 1818 (*LPBS* 2:31), Havens finds it likely that he composed the Rosalind section that August (218–19).

creative aspirations: "The story of *Rosalind and Helen* is, undoubtedly, not an attempt in the highest style of poetry. It is in no degree
calculated to excite profound meditation" (*PW* 167). It was not easy,
however, for Shelley or any of those Romantics who were building a
second Renaissance to restrain their aspirations, especially while
working in traditional genres that invited comparison with great predecessors. The pressure of those natural comparisons, as Jeffrey had
explained, inevitably left them feeling in direct competition with
their strongest forebears. What helped Shelley evade that pressure,
here, was Spenser's own sustained argument against it.

   The Shepheardes Calender, if read with the kind of interest the
Romantics brought to it, is one of England's great treatises against
the anxiety of poetic influence. E. K. explains in the preface, for
instance, that young poets should feel free of enforced competition with threatening precursors. All the great poets of the past had
started humbly, assured of a hereditary right, in fact, to fledge their
wings slowly instead of leaping headlong, like Keats and Shelley, into
the storm of epic competition:

> . . . the best and most auncient Poetes . . . [had] devised this
> kind of wryting, being both so base for the matter, and
> homely for the manner, at the first to trye theyr habilities:
> and as young birdes, that be newly crept out of the nest, by
> little first to prove theyr tender wyngs, before they make a
> greater flyght. So flew Theocritus. . . . So flew Virgile, as not
> yet well feeling his winges. . . . So Petrarque. So Boccace. . . .
> So finally flyeth this our new Poete, as a bird, whose princi-
> pals be scarce growen out, but yet as that in time shall be
> hable to keepe wing with the best. (18–19)

Spenser presents himself as this kind of unthreatened, self-assured
novice throughout *The Shepheardes Calender.* He is also certain that all
those who flew before him would support his venture. Colin freely
admits in the *June* eclogue that "Of Muses . . . I conne no skill" (line
65). He also laments the seeming diminishment of creative possibilities after Chaucer's death. Chaucer's "skil" is "fledde," Colin declares, and "I am not, as I wish I were" (lines 91, 105). Yet he can
imagine "some little drops" from the spring of Chaucer's inspiration
seeping into his own spirit, and he envisions a time when he will sing
like his brilliant master (lines 93–100). This impression of humble
sustenance from the "drops" of the past recurs even more strongly
in *November.* Thenot compares great poets to lofty trees whose "kind-

lye dewe drops" wet and invigorate lesser aspirants to poetic fame, "the little plants that lowly dwell" (lines 31–32). This is an "infusion sweete," as Spenser would later say, whose full fruits would blossom in time. For now, as Cuddie explains in the *October* eclogue, it is enough to absorb that "infusion" slowly, taking up the "slender pipes" (line 118) of pastoral poetry with the confidence that his preparation would lead eventually to the "trumpets sterne" of a greater song like *The Faerie Queene* (1. Proem. 1).

By crafting his own new beginning as that of a Spenserian pastoralist and adopting Spenser's humbleness about the project, Shelley was positioning himself to absorb this entire argument. It sanctioned him to resist the compulsion to march out suicidally against the mature strength of his giant predecessors, to draw reassurance from the conviction of their encouragement, and to rest confidently in a gradual progression to those stern notes of higher poetry—all luxuries rarely available for the young Romantics. How deeply Shelley connected them with Spenser's message is suggested by his variation on Thenot's "dewe drop" metaphor. His Rosalind, feeling great "joy" upon the removal of her own burdensome past and its haunting memories, compares her rejuvenation to the quickening effect of "twinkling rain-drops [falling] from the eaves, / When warm spring showers are passing o'er" (lines 367–68). The recollection implied here of Spenser's "joy" about "kindlye" drops from the springs of literary tradition may very well function as a more specific metaphor for Shelley's reception of the pastoral Spenser as he crept out of his own modern nest with a fledgling ambition to "keepe wing with the best."

Once again, however, we should recall that it took more than generosity from Spenser to inspire the Romantics to follow him. In this case, Shelley's new sensitivity to his "Tydings from the Heart" also made him seem more important than ever as a guide through the psychic landscapes of modern poetics. Traveling into his "Labyrinth of Love" could have only sensitized Shelley to Spenser's exploration of the heart's divisions—to his knowledge, we might say, of that other labyrinth of many apartments that Keats found constituting modern experience. No longer the arbiter of an "official morality," Spenser was beginning to strike Shelley as a voyager moving uncertainly like Guyon through not necessarily a perilous sea but, as Keats would say, an interior "mystery." As such, Spenser was also encouraging Shelley's evolution away from his early didacticism and philosophical idealism toward that "mystery" in which "two opposed ideas [may live] in the mind at the same time" (Thorslev 31). Shelley's new interest in this Spenser of the heart's conflict is evident in the divided structure of *Rosalind and Helen*. Shelley wrote Helen's story in 1817, shortly before he began *The Revolt of Islam*. In her tale, he was shaping a prototype for the heavily moralistic portions of the epic. Helen and her lover, Lionel, wage a noble but unsuccessful campaign against social and religious institutions in a scenario virtually identical to the reforming enterprise of Laon and Cythna. The rhetoric of didactic zeal here, replete with denunciations of the era's "outworn creeds" (line 718), turns this section into a model for the social lectures that Laon and Cythna deliver. The Rosalind section, composed in August 1818 while Shelley was reorienting his literary values and focusing on *The Shepheardes Calender*, condemns political oppression but is more obviously concerned with the workings of the human heart. More specifically, its drama of love's passion follows the kind of inner conflicts that beset the characters in *The Shepheardes Calender*. Shelley's heroine, for instance, bears the name of Colin Clout's disdainful lover, Rosalind, and her behavior is patterned upon the conduct of Spenser's Rosalind. As Spenser's Rosalind proves unfaithful to Colin, Shelley's namesake betrays Helen. The agonies of unrequited love that compose the basis of Spenser's complaints also become the focus of the modern Rosalind's sorrowful tale.[3]

The particular anguish that Shelley takes over from the "sore heart roote" of Spenser's characters entails the kind of poignant mental divisions that Keats was absorbing from Spenser about the same time. To appropriate that dimension of *The Shepheardes Calender*, Shelley reproduces many of the specific dramatic situations in which Spenser's characters describe their conflicts. In *September*, Diggon encounters Hobbinoll after "Thrise three Moones bene fully spent and past" (line 20) and describes his "miserye" and loss in "forrein costes" (lines 28–29). Rosalind similarly meets Helen after a long separation and tells her of misfortunes suffered in foreign lands. Where Hobbinoll laments the wavering of Colin's friendship in *April*, Shelley's Rosalind regrets her past disloyalty to Helen. Her bitter indictments of her husband's emotional sterility also recall Colin's anguished complaints of unrequited love in *June*. The interiority that Shelley thus adapts from *The Shepheardes Calender* may generally embody those "pathetic" emotions of the sorrowing heart that so pleased Mary Shelley (*PW* 188). But there is something more spe-

---

3. Mary Shelley openly preferred this "pathetic" picture of "the human heart" to the "abstruse truth" of Helen's sequence (*PW* 188).

cific about the mental situations. They all center in conflicts between ideal hopes and bitter realities, whether Hobbinoll's regret about a broken friendship, Diggon's lament about the crushing of his hopes for profit in foreign lands, or Colin's central complaint about Rosalind's betrayal of their love. Spenser usually leaves that pattern of division unresolved in *The Shepheardes Calender*. It is a clash of opposites—not, as in *The Revolt of Islam*, their eventual resolution—that Shelley incorporates into his own tale of broken trusts and shattered dreams.

The depth of his interest in Spenser's way of handling this duality is suggested by his studied appropriation of the more technical features of the psychodrama in *The Shepheardes Calender*. Its pastoral landscapes often present allegories, tapestry pieces like the ones Keats admired in *The Faerie Queene*, of the mind's division between truth and beauty. In *December*, for instance, Colin imaginatively contrasts fertile and desolate natural landscape. The contrast figures his own emotional collapse after Rosalind's desertion and his interior division between former ideals and present realities: "Where I was wont to seeke the honey Bee, / Working her formall rowmes in Wexen frame: / The grieslie Todestoole growne there mought I se" (lines 67–69). Shelley takes over the same maneuver to depict Rosalind's vivid sense of the contrast between her youthful attachment to the love of her heart and the disaster of a cruel marriage that was forced upon her. Like Colin's agony, her sorrow darkens an attractive pastoral retreat, which changes from a "lucid flood . . . [under] yon dome's eternal blue" (lines 114–22) into a "Gloom" of "grey shadows" when she enters it (lines 130–38). Like the chiaroscuro of Colin's *December*, this checkered landscape is a projection of the viewer's division between the ideals of a dream and the facts of a grim reality.[4]

We should expect by now, however, that transplanting the root of sorrowful division from Spenser's song involves some important prun-

---

4. Shelley found Spenser's metrical virtuosity just as valuable for working out these polarities of mind. At first glance, the style of his "modern eclogue" may seem foreign to the poetry *The Shepheardes Calender*. But while he avoids all the eccentricities of style that stamp Spenser's hand so definitively on *The Shepheardes Calender*, he does follow closely Spenser's general strategy of shifting metrical structures to punctuate the mental divisions of his characters. While the elegiac stanzas of *November*, for instance, with their radical compressions of line length—"O hevie herse," "O carefull verse"— enact the agony of Colin's bereavement, his lyrical song of praise to "fayre *Elisa*" in *April* reveals in the dancelike motion of the following stanza his experience of joyous love:

ing. That old process takes on a new, constructive character, however, due to Shelley's greater receptiveness to Spenser and poetic
tradition generally. Instead of "ruthlessly subverting" Spenser's system, as Gleckner finds Blake recurrently doing (*Blake and Spenser*
187), Shelley now deepens the patterns of mental doubling in *The*

> Lo how finely the graces can it foote
>   to the Instrument:
> They dauncen deffly, and singen soote,
>   in their meriment.
> Wants not a fourth grace, to make the daunce even?
> Let that rowme to my Lady be yeven:
>   She shalbe a grace,
>   To fyll the fourth place,
> And reigne with the rest in heaven.
>   (lines 109–17)

Colin even glosses his shifting metrics by claiming that his irregular rhythms spring
from the turbulence of his divided thoughts:

> I wote my rymes bene rough, and rudely drest:
> The fytter they, my carefull case to frame:
> Enough is me to paint out my unrest,
> And poore my piteous plaints out in the same.
>   (*June,* lines 77–80)

Shelley makes a similar point about the metrical irregularity of *Rosalind and Helen* and
its relation to the upheaval of his characters' feelings: "I resigned myself, as I wrote,
to the impulse of the feelings which moulded the conception of the story; and this
impulse determined the pauses of a measure, which only pretends to be regular inas-
much as it corresponds with and expresses the irregularity of the imaginations which
inspired it" (*PW* 167). That principle gives rise to the same basic correlation of metrical and psychological doubling, though the exact forms differ, that helps energize
Spenser's psychodrama. Rosalind's tormenting sense of guilty elation over her cruel
husband's death, for instance, registers in the eerily abrupt repetitiveness of her te-
trameter triplet:

> They laughed for he was dead: but I
> Sate with a hard and tearless eye,
> And with a heart which would deny
>   (lines 240–43)

When she later recalls the genuine love of her youth, however, her sensation of transitory bliss becomes apparent in the musical anapests and feminine endings of these
very different rhythms:

> I'll tell thee truth: I loved another.
> His name in my ear was ever ringing,
> His form to my brain was ever clinging
>   (lines 276–78)

Shepheardes Calender, and in such a way as to improve himself. He does away with Spenser's more overtly didactic eclogues and the moral apothegms that punctuate them, just as he dispenses with the Mab-like lecturing of the Helen section. More significant, he intensifies the mental probing of Spenser's love conflicts so as to refine his own treatment of passion in Helen's story. His main correction of Spenser's study of the heart is to discard all of the Petrarchan conventions of *The Shepheardes Calender,* which in his view graft an enervating literary system and moral ideology onto the poem's mental action.[5] Hence he removes all those familiar accoutrements of Renaissance Petrarchism—poetry contests, shepherds' delights, conventional lovers' conceits and complaints, even the whole calendar motif—and cuts more directly or, we might say, carries Spenser more deeply into the inner labyrinths of the heart. In place of the rather conventional lovesickness of Spenser's shepherds, Shelley's characters go through a complex range of mental experiences. Rosalind's lover, for instance, does not die brokenheartedly of unrequited love, as Colin expects to do. Instead he goes mad and dies laughing wildly after learning that he and Rosalind are siblings. Rosalind's "hell" of experience thus takes her far from the pastoralism of Spenser's *Calender* into the tormented world of *Childe Harold's Pilgrimage.* Put another way, Shelley's treatment of her sorrow recovers and extends the core of anguish that Spenser veils over with the web of his Petrarchism.

In the Helen section of Shelley's poem, we may find a similar "heart roote" in need of recovery from another kind of systematizing. Helen speaks of the pain "gnawing the core / Of my bitter heart" (lines 776–77). But Shelley's journey into that core is impeded, like Spenser's, by his devotion to a system, certainly not Petrarchism, but a literary and ideological system nevertheless. The poetic style of his eighteenth-century didacticism and the ideology of *The Revolt of Islam* take over in long sections of the Helen story, beclouding Shelley's interiority just as Spenser's Petrarchism shadows his own drama of the mind. Cutting Spenser free of his systems to range through the life of the mind, then, could not have seemed for Shelley all that different from restraining his own more radical moralism to get at the "core" of a "bitter heart." The self-redemptive aspect of Shelley's revisionism, in fact, may explain why he chose to retain the Helen section even after he had changed the entire form

5. Gleckner finds Blake reacting in a similar way against Spenser's Petrarchisms (*Blake and Spenser* 27–70).

of his pastoral with Rosalind's story. His growth from one tale to the other is at once the main point of *Rosalind and Helen* and the key to his new Spenserian poetics.

Just how much was to be gained from revising Spenser's pathos became more apparent as Shelley began to recognize its close relation to his own visionary idealism. He was learning that Spenser not only explores the labyrinth of the heart in his amatory themes but can also rise as a love poet to the kind of prophetic millennialism that Shelley still aspired to in his own art. There may be much to blame with Spenser's Petrarchism. But his commitment to writing hymns of heavenly love places him, as Shelley was coming to see it, in a chivalric tradition whose worship of love had renovated European culture, planting "trophies in the human mind of that sublimest victory over sensuality and force" (*SP* 289). What is divine in those poets who sang a "perpetual hymn of everlasting love" is passed on to the moderns as the spirit of imaginative creativity, in which the outpouring of love seems synonymous with an enlargement of the imagination and a revelation of "the hidden beauty of the world" (*SP* 289, 282). The "perpetual hymn of everlasting love" in Spenser thus makes up the eternal portion of his art that can inspire Shelley's own prophetic vision. All this did not come clearly into focus for another few years. Yet by late 1817, Shelley was already associating the Spenserian "soul-sustaining songs" received by Prince Athanase with the visionary inspiration of the "wine" of "Love" (lines 279–80). In *Rosalind and Helen*, he was presenting the love of his own Spenserian psychodynamics as the "essence of our being," "a law of life," "an irrefragable truth" (*PW* 188). The Spenser who stood behind all this still needed to have his imagination liberated from the trammels of his ideology. But as a poet of "Heavenly Love" who could also sing of the "sore heart roote," he must have seemed all the more qualified for importation into a modern doubling poetics, and more specifically positioned to help Shelley work out the visionary strain of that dichotomous song.

The experience of writing *Rosalind and Helen* also suggested what form a new Spenserian poetics might take after the disappointment of the extended narrative format of *The Revolt of Islam*. In discovering the gentle Spenser of lyrical complaints, who defended short poetic flights (at least early in one's career), Shelley now had the authorization to keep his Spenserianism within a condensed form. That message did more than reduce the burdens of adaptation. It also moved Shelley, as he grew increasingly appreciative of Spenser's contrary vision, toward the same important conclusion Keats was

reaching about the appropriate poetic form for modern approximations of that vision. A revisionary Spenserianism grounded in the
dualities of the present, Shelley began to realize, would need to assume the form of a lyrical fragment in order to convey the indeterminacy of modern experience. Such a conviction made diffuse
Spenserian epic, or possibly epic in general as it was traditionally
understood, seem incompatible with a contemporary poetics. It
would not be until he wrote *A Defence of Poetry* that Shelley could feel
confident about this point. But he was already moving toward it in
1818 and thus preparing himself for the kind of terse antiallegorical
allegory that would place him, along with Keats, at the pinnacle of
Romantic Spenserianism.

Much as the breakthroughs of *Rosalind and Helen* were encouraging Shelley,[6] he still recognized the poem's limitations. Though he
was learning much about how to adapt Spenser's duality, he was yet
far from the sort of complex allegorical and prosodic revisionism
that distinguishes *The Eve of St. Agnes*. He even described *Rosalind
and Helen* as a tale of "idle melancholy," and after its publication he
tended to dismiss it as "a mere extempore thing . . . worth little . . .
possessing only what little merit . . . it aspired to" (*LPBS* 2:31, 199).
Granted, it was only supposed to be a first flight, and as such it
certainly inspired confidence about going further; but it still left all
that new terrain unexplored. Added to this was the nagging fact that
Shelley could not, despite his best efforts, yet accommodate Spenser's conservatism. Although he had found a way to make it into
something positive, it still vexed him and continued to inhibit his
responses to Spenser. Not long after *Rosalind and Helen* was completed, as we shall see, he was still fuming at Artegall. The pressure
that Spenser had been exerting on him, however reduced, was still
there and still troublesome. *Prometheus Unbound* became the psychic
battleground on which Shelley would try to put this conflict to rest,
or, better yet, transform it to his advantage.

II

Several weeks after completing *Rosalind and Helen,* Shelley began the
gigantic labor in *Prometheus Unbound* to build upon what he consid-

6. He gave it the prominent title position in his 1819 volume of lyrics, anxiously
watched over its publication from abroad, and asked for copies to be sent to his
friends and literary associates in England. On three separate occasions he requested
copies for himself to distribute in Italy (*LPBS* 2:106, 111, 113, 117, 198–99).

ered the highest triad of literary culture: the poetry of classical Greece, Dante's Italy, and Renaissance England. Naming Aeschylus, Dante, Shakespeare, and Milton as his principal guides (*PW* 205–6), he determined to construct a millennial drama of psychic rehabilitation. He also intended to make that drama pivot upon the Spenserian conflict of mutability and eternity that had preoccupied him for so long. To work out the paradigm of separation, reunion, and millennial joy that controls his story of Prometheus and Asia, Shelley extends the basic patterns of fractured realities and eternal ideals in the Redcrosse/Una narrative that he had already incorporated into *The Revolt of Islam*. More specifically, he now transforms the enspiriting influence of love in *The Faerie Queene* into the figure of Asia as the central vehicle of Prometheus's rehabilitation. He also associates the apocalyptic scene of world renovation that her agency induces both with Redcrosse's vision of the New Jerusalem and with the millennial overtones of the celestial love that is honored at Una's betrothal feast. But he still feels that Spenser's vision, just like Aeschylus's and Milton's, needs to be cleansed, its contradictions between eternity and the productions of time purged from the error of his day. That struggle, and its bearing on Shelley's effort to purify himself, makes up much of the psychic action of *Prometheus Unbound*.

If all this happens in *Prometheus Unbound*, then we must question why Shelley was silent about Spenser when he spoke so openly about the influence of his other precursors. The answer, I think, lies in the very way he discusses them. These highest figures in his pantheon of immortals are not only to be emulated, he makes clear in the preface to *Prometheus Unbound*, but are also to be surpassed. *Prometheus Unbound* is not, Shelley argues, "as the name would indicate, a mere imitation of the Greek drama, or indeed if I have been successful, is it an imitation of anything." Rather, it must be considered as "a drama, with characters & mechanism of a kind yet unattempted" (*LPBS* 2:219, 94). The enormity of this intention is staggering. Just a few weeks after his tentative first flight among "the best and most ancient Poets," Shelley now planned to soar with them to their loftiest heights, and, what is more, leave them trailing behind. Icarian forebodings, even when flying under the general encouragement of Spenser, were inescapable. Those concerns drove him toward a particular Spenserian model that he was not so eager to discuss, the Despair episode.[7]

---

7. Attention to the literary backgrounds of *Prometheus Unbound* has always focused

Shelley's preoccupation with the perilous nature of his attempt registers throughout the defensive remarks about imitation and originality that dominate his preface. Speaking with "candour" and "unaffected freedom" (repetitive claims which should arouse our suspicions about his protesting too much), he "confess[es]" that his poem must be "tinged" by the influence of contemporary writings. Even the loftiest of writers, he argues at great length, must adopt the literary forms of their day, which is an inevitable "subjection." But the "spirit" of their writing retains its individuality, and herein lies the essential originality of his own work (*PW* 205–7). Although Shelley does not make the connection overtly, his argument also seems directed to the "subjection" of powerful literary traditions, whose spirit if not form, he hopes, will be surpassed in the "collected lightening" of the present (*PW* 206). The defensive nature of these claims about being "tinged" by influence suggests that Shelley is neither wholly candid nor confident about his relation to the past. Moreover, one only needs to put together his statement about being "infected" by the "mighty dead" with his denial of Spenserian influence in the preface to *The Revolt of Islam* to suspect that his silence about Spenser here might also be a pregnant one.

What lay beneath the silence, and more generally behind his defensiveness about poetic "subjection," seems to have surfaced throughout the letters he was writing about the time he began *Prometheus Unbound*. Considering, for example, Satan's doomed cast against God's priority in *Paradise Lost,* he quoted a line disturbingly relevant to his own usurping confrontation with the past: "ominous conjecture on the whole success" (*LPBS* 2:35). Shakespeare's genius drove him to assert defensively, "There is nothing which the human mind can conceive it may not execute. Shakespeare was only a human being" (*LPBS* 2:40). But of course, as many of the Romantics were coming to understand, Shakespeare and his peers could seem

---

on the Greek context that Shelley calls attention to in his preface (Zillman [62], Wasserman [282–92], Flagg [33–34], and Curran [*Shelley's Annus Mirabilis* 38]). Curran looks beyond the Greeks to Eastern mythology (34–100) and treats Milton's background in close detail (54–60). Spenser, however, receives only peripheral treatment in Curran's and other discussions of Shelley's models. Even those few works devoted to the Shelley/Spenser dynamic give main emphasis to the Greek sources of *Prometheus Unbound.* Bloom does offer some highly provocative suggestions, however, about the way that "Spenser, not Aeschylus, becomes the prototype [of *Prometheus Unbound*], and Faery Land, the complete visionary projection with its ambiguous interleaving of the varying states of existence (earthly paradise, our life, earthly hell), becomes the local habitation out of which the poem's lyrical discourse arises" (*Shelley's Mythmaking* 95).

more than human beings and too large for mere mortals to compass. Shelley's apprehension of that possibility brought him near the edge of creative despair. His letters of autumn 1818 teem with references to despair and despondency, sometimes related to his unhappy domestic life but just as often left unexplained or connected openly with artistic despair: "I have depression enough of spirits"; "I have neither good health or spirits just now"; "O if I had . . . strength & equal spirits"; "I can conceive a great work . . . [but] Far from me is such an attempt" (*LPBS* 2:64, 68, 70–71). On one occasion, he even spoke sympathetically of Byron's despair about his own work (*LPBS* 2:58).

As Shelley struggled with his inclinations toward a similar despair, at a time when the opportunities and difficulties of Spenserian art were fresh in his mind, he began to consider the applicability of Spenser's Despair episode to his own state. Keats might have recommended that identification, knowing from firsthand experience that the Cave of Despair is where poets suffering from creative despondency belong. But Shelley needed little help, having already made the association early in his career between Despair's insinuations and his own questions about the validity of imaginative experience. In *The Revolt of Islam,* moreover, he had discovered the Despair episode's relevance to his struggle to overcome those questions. He must have also known that Spenser himself, by alluding to the Prometheus myth near the outset of the Despair sequence, had hinted at a connection between the two stories (1.5.35). This background might have been enough to make Spenser's allegory seem a useful model for the central drama of psychic recovery and integration in *Prometheus Unbound.* But in Shelley's mind a different, even more compelling juxtaposition was also begining to emerge among Redcrosse's battle with Despair, Prometheus's fight against greater gods, and his own apprehension of being subjected to domineering forebears.

Such a configuration suggested that making Prometheus's conflict a partial recasting of Redcrosse's struggle could also dramatize the tensions of trying to carry out the monumental revisionary labor of *Prometheus Unbound.* In this way, the poem would become a sustained act of revisionism with a subtext about the pressures of revising. It was a brilliant stroke, though not entirely new. At just about the same time, Keats was doing something quite similar in *Hyperion* by transforming Milton's angelic warfare into a drama about old orders giving way to new cycles—new poetic cycles, in particular, with the birth of Apollo. What made Shelley's maneuver more effective, however, was his focus on the center of conflict and rejuvenation in the model he was appropriating for his own creative experience. Redcrosse, of course, defeats his blocking foe in the fallen world and passes on to a redemptive vision of the New Jerusalem. That history could be transformed into the psychodrama of mutability and secular millennialism in *Prometheus Unbound*. Perhaps even more significant, it could also serve as an inspiration for Shelley's victory over the despair of being able to carry out such a revision of Spenser, or of any of the towering precursors he was now confronting. The very act of drawing this new personal application out of Spenser's story, in itself, constituted a kind of successful revisionism, a mark of that victory. Hence the Despair model, besides offering the source material for a revisionary poetics, could also provide a key to help Shelley understand and disarm the pressures of what he was doing. This is why Bloom is probably right to say that *Prometheus Unbound* is "analogous (and not, I think, by accident)" to Book 1 of *The Faerie Queene* (*Shelley's Mythmaking* 92).

Although Shelley never acknowledged these links with Spenser openly, he implied their significance throughout the ensuing months of composition. It became habitual during this span for him to associate *The Faerie Queene* with his work in progress. Shortly after beginning the poem, for instance, he linked its radical politics to his own demonic reading of the encounter between Artegall and the Giant. When he finished *Prometheus Unbound,* he considered posting the manuscript to England in a parcel containing his edition of *The Faerie Queene.* Still later, he spoke at once of stylistic details in *Prometheus Unbound* and the Spenserian stanzas of *Adonais* (*LPBS* 2:70–71, 120, 297). This pattern narrowed strikingly to the personal relevance of the Despair episode when Shelley paused from act 1 of *Prometheus Unbound* to write a short lyric, "Stanzas Written in Dejection, Near Naples." Its technical structure of five modified Spenserian stanzas borrows directly from *The Faerie Queene,* and its theme of dejection plainly echoes the Despair sequence. Its meditation on the tranquility of the grave resembles both Despair's seductive recommendation of suicide—"Sleepe after toyle, port after stormie seas, / Ease after warre, death after life does greatly please" (1.9.40)—and Prometheus's languid yearning for the comfort of death—"Peace is in the grave. / The grave hides all things beautiful and good" (I, 638–39):

> Yet now despair itself is mild,
> Even as the winds and waters are;

I could lie down like a tired child
And weep away the life of care
Which I have borne and yet must bear,
Till death like sleep might steal on me,
And I might feel in the warm air
My cheek grown cold, and hear the sea
Breathe o'er my dying brain its last monotony.
(lines 37–45)

Such a dramatic conflation of Spenser's Despair, Prometheus's anguish, and Shelley's own dejection suggests how trenchantly that pattern of relations was engaging him as he worked upon *Prometheus Unbound*. Moreover, the lyrical shortening of Spenser's pentameter line implies his specific wish to heighten and bring home to his own pulses the emotions at the center of Redcrosse's encounter with Despair.

Shelley suggested himself that the psychic action of *Prometheus Unbound* embodies, on one level, that experience of despair and its particular associations with his "subjection" to mighty precursors. He often conceptualized Prometheus's enslavement in terms of the subordination of modern poets to the undying voices of the past. Shortly after the completion of act 1, for instance, he connected Prometheus's craggy prison grounds with the habitation of those "imperial spirits" who haunt and oppress belated poets. Rome's great artistic ruins appeared to him as magnificent but dominating and oppressive structures, like the jagged rocks imprisoning Prometheus. It seemed as though the power of those "shattered [Roman] columns" could only "baffl[e] . . . succeeding generations," who, much as Laon faces the monuments of mightier times, must confront in the ruins of Rome "a city as it were of the dead, or rather of those who cannot die, and who survive the puny generations which inhabit and pass over the spot which they have made sacred to eternity" (*LPBS* 2:59). Elaborating on this association between Prometheus and those "puny generations" diminished by the eternal dead, Shelley thought about poets who were enslaved, like Prometheus, by despotic rulers and their own fears of inferiority. Tasso's literal imprisonment under aristocratic tyranny thus seemed related to his apprehension about rivaling poetic forebears. His was "an earnest mind" whose "adventurous" steps halted in confronting prior excellence (*LPBS* 2:47). Shelley connected this fate more obviously to Prometheus's with his grim description of Tasso's "low and dark" dungeon, whose details remarkably match the "Dongeon deepe" in which Redcrosse despairs (1.7.15) and the bleak Caucasian landscape in which Prometheus suffers.

In a related configuration of the same period, Shelley depicted Raphael's St. Cecelia and her followers as a group arranged like Prometheus, Ione, and Panthea. They are restricted by what we might take as the angelic version of Jupiter's plagues, the divine harmonies of a higher order of beings, which leave them rapt in silence as they stand amid broken musical instruments (*LPBS* 2:51–52). For Shelley, it must have seemed like an ambiguous icon of religious devotion and, in its relation to the personal context of *Prometheus Unbound*, artistic capitulation before a convoluting sound, like the din of Keats's planetary music, that drowns out all other song. In his most telling suggestion that *Prometheus Unbound* enacts just such a disturbing allegory of poetic relations, Shelley now described Byron's works as the mirror of their creator's "despair" (*LPBS* 2:58)— an observation, also implied in the recently finished *Julian and Maddalo*, that had its own subtle application to *Prometheus Unbound*. All together, these associations suggest that Prometheus's dire struggle against Jupiter's omnipotence may be glossed, on one level of the poem's action, as a drama of Shelley's own anxious conflict with domineering forebears. Shelley even raised the Oedipal implications of such a contest when he portrayed the Jupiter of *Prometheus Unbound* as a child destroyer (I, 178–79).[8]

My focus on the Spenserian basis of this struggle in *Prometheus Unbound* is not to deny the poem's other sources, or its many different psychological and philosophical contexts. Nor do I mean to imply that *Prometheus Unbound* is simply a testament of Shelley's despair of measuring up to the past. Quite the contrary, as we shall see, he acted on the redemptive aspects of the Despair episode to apply Redcrosse's eventual triumph over despair to his own situation. Making that application stick, however, was no easy matter, which is why Shelley ultimately remained ambivalent and silent about his overall engagement with Spenser in *Prometheus Unbound*. We may find, therefore, that much of the passion, joy, anguish, and uncertainty in *Prometheus Unbound* emanates from the coalescence of these confrontations between Redcrosse and Despair, Prometheus and Jupiter, Shelley and "the dead Kings of Melody." Comprehending this pattern of relations in *Prometheus Unbound* can help us better understand some of the work's most problematic features: its volatile

8. For a sustained discussion of Oedipal implications in Prometheus's conflict with Jupiter, see Waldoff ("The Father-Son Conflict").

mood swerves, its compositional lapses, its depth of conditionality, and its ambiguous stance toward poetic tradition.[9]

To discern how Shelley's adaptation of the Despair episode comments on itself, both executing and reflecting on the labors of poetic revisionism, we must examine the basic circumstances of Shelley's contention with Spenser in *Prometheus Unbound:* his complicated efforts to recast the Despair sequence as a drama of the mind's struggle for visionary enlightenment in the face of its own despair at the world's "wretched interchange of wrong for wrong." Such a redemption of one of the "eternal" truths of Spenser's drama controls much of the dramatic action in the opening of *Prometheus Unbound* and throughout its first act. Prometheus here undergoes a cycle of temptation, fall, and rebirth similar to Redcrosse's in its axis of despair. Much as Redcrosse is locked up to wither in the damp and darkness of Orgoglio's prison, Prometheus is chained and doomed to a tormenting decline amid the storms and solitude of the Caucasus. Misdirected pride enthralls both characters and saps their memories of humiliating defeat; where Redcrosse blocks out the encounter with Orgoglio (1.8.43), Prometheus forgets his curse of Jupiter. Their parallel conditions further merge when Prometheus, implacably though hopelessly braced against Jupiter, vows commitment to his own empire of "despair" (I, 15). Shelley depicts the perversity of this blind rage with the Spenserian device of landscaping mentality, which he had used so extensively in *The Revolt of Islam.* He thus makes the rock-strewn prison grounds of the Caucasus—"Black, wintry, dead, unmeasured; without herb, / Insect, or beast, or shape or sound of life" (I, 21–22)—an extended metaphor of Prometheus's inward sterility, in the way that Spenser presents a "craggie clift" and "Ragged rocky knees" to picture Redcrosse's decay (1.9.33–34). To intensify this scene of mental anguish, Shelley borrows even more specific patterns of imagery from the Despair episode. Prometheus's grief is figured as piercing "spears" (I, 31), which recall the "swords point" of Redcrosse's guilt (1.9.48). His "eyeless" gaze (I, 9) resembles the "hollow pits" of Redcrosse's "sad dull eyes" (1.8.41). The herbless blight surrounding him mirrors the "withered flowers" of Redcrosse's decaying flesh (1.8.41). Considering this pattern of

9. These questions have been taken up at length by, among many others, Wasserman (*Shelley* 283, 307–10), Curran (*Shelley's Annus Mirabilis* 12, 108), and Bloom (*Poetry and Repression* 95–96). Perhaps the most pressing debate concerns Shelley's measure of success at integrating his myriad sources, with Curran finding him brimming in "confidence" about the "reorganization of literary models" (*Shelley's Annus Mirabilis* 108) and Bloom seeing him nearly "overcome" by tradition (*Poetry and Repression* 96).

frequent correspondences, we may even link Jupiter's devouring
eagle, a standard feature of the Prometheus myth, with the "ghastly
Owle" that surmounts Despair's cave (1.9.33).

This opening reformulation of Spenser's mental portraiture also
conflates Despair and Jupiter as embodiments of the inner distortions that Redcrosse and Prometheus endure. Like Despair, Jupiter
is most renowned for his subtle malevolence. Shelley's description of
his soul, gaping "like a hell within" (I, 56), evokes Despair's apella-
tion, "man of hell" (1.9.28). The poisoning nature of Jupiter's tyranny resembles the literal poison that Despair offers Redcrosse. Jupiter's chief weapon, the thunderbolt, besides appearing as a
traditional attribute of his power, also recalls the club of Orgoglio,
prideful extension of Despair, whose thunderbolts subdue Redcrosse. This final link is tightened by Spenser's association of Orgoglio's tyranny with Jove's malicious torment of men and gods
(1.5.33; 1.8.9); Jove's cruelty is identical to that wrought by Shelley's
Jupiter, the "Foul Tyrant both of Gods and Human-kind" (I, 264).

These patterns of relation become even more complicated when
Shelley launches a psychic battle among unlike characters denoting
polar states of mind. Such a psychodrama relies on the very Spenserian method of allegorizing mental conflict that Godwin had probably told Shelley about during his disciple's first encounters with
Spenser. Shelley's debt here to the particular strategies of the Despair episode is pronounced. Prometheus curses Jupiter (I, 262–
301), for instance, revealing his own mental fixity in the manner of
Redcrosse's tirade against Despair: "Thou damned wight" (1.9.37).
Appropriately, Jupiter's minions next appear as embodiments of this
degenerate impulse, just as Despair issues from his cave to figure
Redcrosse's spiritual bankruptcy. Like Despair, they couple advice
for luxurious, deathlike submission with assertions of moral unfitness. Mercury, whose plumed feet resemble the "winged heels" of
the victimized Trevisan (1.9.21), spearheads the assault. He urges
capitulation to Jupiter's tyranny, offering the lassitude of eternal
"voluptuous joy" as reward for such moral suicide (I, 426). When
this attempt fails, the Furies heighten Prometheus's anguish with indictments of his moral depravity. They follow Despair's testimony,
likened by Spenser to a flight of "Infernall furies" (1.9.24), that noble
aims engender only increase of woe; such bitter knowledge, the
Furies insist, argues for but one option, which is twice named "despair" (I, 553–96). The Furies's "emblem" of such failures (I, 594),
like the painted "table" of sin that Despair shows Redcrosse (1.9.49),
brings their prey to the edge of collapse. Throughout this harangue,

Ione and Panthea drop words of sympathy recalling the encouragement Redcrosse receives from Una. Like Redcrosse, Prometheus
then avoids near disaster by mustering the will to resist his op-
pressors. This triumph, entailing generous pity for Jupiter and his
slaves, falls short of complete renewal, again like Redcrosse's. Prometheus, still debilitated at the end of act 1, requires fuller maturation, just as the enervated Redcrosse needs enlightenment after his
bout with Despair.

As this scenario develops, prosodic clashes act like Spenser's to
punctuate its shifts of mind. The mental fixedness of Prometheus's
rage, for example, issues in the same monosyllabic beats that witness
Redcrosse's dull inflexibility when calling Despair "Thou damned
wight" (1.9.37): "But thou, Jupiter, who art the God and Lord: O
thou . . . I curse thee" (I, 282–86). This boorish rhythm soon gives
way to Mercury's slippery rhetoric, a shift recalling the entry of Despair's "subtile tong," as the mood of resignation dominates both
psychodramas. Despair's languorous rhetoric thus anesthetizes Redcrosse spiritually and tempts him to the brink of suicide:

> He there does now enioy eternall rest
> And happie ease, which thou doest want and craue,
> And further from it daily wanderest:
> What if some litle paine the passage haue,
> That makes fraile flesh to feare the bitter waue?
> Is not short paine well borne, that brings long ease,
> And layes the soule to sleepe in quiet graue?
> Sleepe after toyle, port after stormie seas,
> Ease after warre, death after life does greatly please.
> (1.9.40)

Leading Prometheus to a similar crisis, Mercury displays a linguistic
dexterity that closely matches Despair's mellifluous sibilants, his soporific cadences, and his befuddling rhetorical questions:

> Yet pause and plunge
> Into Eternity, where recorded time,
> Even all that we imagine, age on age,
> Seems but a point, and the reluctant mind
> Flags wearily in its unending flight,
> Till it sink, dizzy, blind, lost, shelterless
> (I, 416–19)

In fashioning these Spenserian rhythms, Mercury even borrows particular words from Despair. His mind flagging "wearily" echoes Despair's "wearie wandring way" (1.9.39) and his list of woes—"dizzy, blind, lost, shelterless"—recalls Despair's like compilation of "Feare, sicknesse, age, losse, labour, sorrow, strife" (1.9.44). This developing pattern continues with the vigorous interruptions of Ione and Panthea, whose timing and cadence approximate Una's. Ione even mimics Una's iterations—"Come, come away" (1.9.53)—when she cries, "they come: they come / Blackening the birth of day with countless wings" (I, 440–41).

Shelley draws just as deeply upon the psychodynamics of the Despair episode to enact Prometheus's eventual rejuvenation and access to millennial vision. In dramatizing the "inscape" of Prometheus's triumph, he consistently appropriates the drama of Redcrosse's rehabilitation in the House of Holinesse and final victory over the blocking dragon of evil. Jupiter emerges in act 3, for instance, as a conflation of Despair and "that old Dragon" (1.11.motto). He is blind, like Despair, and he dispenses the venom of Hercules's shirt, just as the dragon burns Redcrosse with the inner pangs felt by Hercules (1.11.27). Both "old dragons" symbolize, among other things, everything that stands in the way of a second Eden—this "old earth," we might summarize, the "tickle" state of mutability—and both fall, giving way to a marriage and the regaining of paradise. Upon Jupiter's defeat, the citizens of the world emerge from their homes in disbelief, much as the denizens of Una's "Eden" hesitantly leave their fortifications when Redcrosse proves victorious. The great apocalyptic scene that follows draws much of its visionary resonance from Redcrosse's glimpse of the New Jerusalem and the millennial overtones of his betrothal feast in a restored Eden of love. Where Archimago's "clokt" evil is unmasked amid the sound of the "heauenly noise" at the betrothal feast (1.12.34, 39), the "painted veil" and "loathsome mask" of falsehood is "torn aside" at the apocalyptic conch blast of Shelley's Spirit of the Hour (III, iv, 190–93). Redcrosse's "exceeding merth" and melting heart in the "pleasures manifold" of Una's love (1.12.40) seem reembodied in Prometheus's self-dissolving love for Asia: "And we will search, with words and looks of love / For hidden thoughts, each lovelier than the last, / Our unexhausted spirits" (III, iii, 34–36). In the "full content" of Redcrosse and Una there is place for "Ne wicked enuie, ne vile gealosy" (1.12.41). "Nor jealousy, nor envy, nor ill shame" can spoil the harmony of the renovated world over which a reunited Prometheus and Asia preside (III, iv, 161). The song that ushers in this new millennium, celebrating a redeemed human community in which all men walk "One with the other" (III, iv, 132), reproduces Redcrosse's joyful vision of cosmic harmony in God's New Jerusalem, where the heavenly hosts pass "to and fro . . . in gladsome companee" (1.10.56). Shelley can sing the great apocalyptic hymn to love at the end of *Prometheus Unbound,* act 3, we may conclude, because he had traveled with Redcrosse through the fires of hell to the New Jerusalem of Una's "everlasting love."

If Shelley's adaptation of the Despair episode is also an allegory of creative despondency, this close adherence to Redcrosse's experience ultimately makes that subtext an allegory about the triumph over despair of creative freedom. To retrace Redcrosse's progress toward the New Jerusalem is to redeem Prometheus, which is also for Shelley to liberate himself from the despotism of his great precursors. Yet his journey with Redcrosse and Spenser is also an occasion itself for potential despair, the despair of ever gaining full independence from the past. Dramatizing one's progress toward liberation in the very terms of Spenser's allegory can actually reinforce one's enslavement to his paradigm. Thus Prometheus finds himself in Redcrosse's demoralizing situation throughout act 1 precisely because Shelley relies so heavily on Spenser during that sequence. In order for Shelley to free Prometheus and lift himself out of the Cave of Despair, it is necessary for him to transform as well as follow Spenser's model.

This revisionary process begins as early as act 1 and reaches a height of intensity during Prometheus's apocalyptic liberation in act 3. Much of the ecstasy of that millennial scene proceeds from Shelley's self-enfranchisement in purging Spenser's errors as the two of them stride forth together toward the New Jerusalem. What is so provocative about this revisionism in *Prometheus Unbound* is that it manifests both Shelley's new strategy for correcting himself and a lingering degree of his older antagonism toward Spenser. In both respects, it is stunningly detailed. That mixture of innovation and regression suggests that Prometheus's liberation and Shelley's own ascent out of the Cave of Despair are both realized and left incomplete in *Prometheus Unbound.*

The overall aim of Shelley's revisionism is to jettison the morality of the Despair sequence while heightening its interiority for applications to the complexity of imaginative experience in the nineteenth century. Thus he takes considerable pains to displace the ideological structures of the Despair episode with pointedly psychological ones. That shift in emphasis begins with the opening lines of *Prometheus Unbound,* where Shelley replaces the traditional Christian iconography of Despair's habitation—the shrieking owl, the wandering

spirits, the greedy grave—with a network of glacial images evocative
of the mental symbolism of frozen Alpine scenery in "Mont Blanc".
To reinforce this substitution, he also does away with the familiar
echoes and distortions of Christian theology in Despair's cozenage.
Jupiter's slaves, in contrast, wage secular combat by insisting on the
futility of mental reform. Shelley punctuates the altered psychological emphasis with Prometheus's overt gloss of these links among
character, landscape, and mind. He calls the Furies "thought-execut-
ing ministers" (I, 387) and finds them objectifying the warped dimensions of his own mind: "Methinks I grow like what I contemplate, / And laugh and stare in loathsome sympathy" (I, 450–51). On
a larger scale, Prometheus senses "types" of his "woe-illumined
mind" throughout the desolate landscape imprisoning him (I, 637,
645). His triumph over such torments of mind, furthermore, hinges
on his own mental reform, which occurs without the kind of preve-
nient grace that Spenser bestows through Una. Although Prometheus's eventual illumination may parallel Redcrosse's in terms of an
interior renovation of the psyche, his renewal proceeds from his re-
nunciation of everything that blocks visionary perception rather
than from the kind of ideological schooling Redcrosse goes through
in the House of Holinesse. In fact, as Keats would have known, the
training that prepares Redcrosse for a spiritual vision is precisely the
kind of erroneous moralism, based on penance, suffering, and hatred, that Prometheus must transcend in order to behold imaginative realities.[10]

Hence, as Shelley understands it, the dragon that Redcrosse must
slay is not only an embodiment of mutability but also a manifestation
of the very kind of antivisionary system that Redcrosse defends.
From the perspective of his redeemed alter-ego, Prometheus, Redcrosse would see that he is actually battling against Heauenly Contemplation when he goes up against "that old Dragon." In *Prometheus
Unbound,* the whole theological basis of Spenser's allegory is thus cast
off so that Shelley can redeem its psychological truths about the
mind's struggle toward visionary enlightenment in a world of time,
death, and error.

Shelley not only exorcises Spenser's system but attacks it with
amazing pertinacity. In replacing Spenser's owl with an eagle, for
instance, he does more than simply dismiss Spenser's Christian iconography of despair and supply a more appropriate Jupiterean im-

10. Gleckner finds Blake similarly disturbed by the ideological disciplining that goes
on in the House of Holinesse, a schooling whose principles represent everything
Blake fought to overcome in his wars of Eternity (*Blake and Spenser* 61).

age. Making Jupiter's eagle a symbol of sinister cruelty also exposes the moral oppressiveness of the House of Holinesse and its ideals of Christian salvation, which are associated with eagle imagery during Redcrosse's final redemption. Shelley clarifies this indictment of Spenser's piety with his epithet for the bird, "Heaven's winged hound" (I, 34). He extends this subversive assault on Spenser's heavenly ideology by transforming Despair's grim furnishings into the most obvious religious trappings—altars, shrines, priests, a crown of thorns—and placing the whole set of devotional accoutrements in Jupiter's foul den, which is generally named "Heaven." This reversal makes Spenser's Christianity the oppressor rather than the deliverer of mankind, a point that Shelley emphatically stresses by calling the tyrannical Jupiter "Heaven's fell King," "O Mighty God," "the God and Lord" (I, 140, 17, 282). He makes the same point throughout his revision of Redcrosse's final victory over the dragon. Jupiter is meant to appear like a cross between Despair and "that old Dragon" in this scene, but his blind violence issues from "heaven" and its "eldest Faith" (III, i, 1, 10), not from Spenser's conventional sources of evil. And where Spenser's townspeople behold vanquished evil in the dragon's carcass, Shelley's witness the fall of Jupiter in abandoned religious symbols: altars and shrines. The inhabitants of the House of Holinesse rather than the House of Pride, we might say, come together in Shelley's "old Dragon."

As if to drive home that point, Shelley goes as far as to honor Spenser's necromancers, who in their passion for beauty and their love of imagination seem the more fit companions for his own rejuvenated lovers. The cavern of the mind to which Prometheus and Asia finally retire is shaped by the spirit of none other than Acrasia, that arch-enchantress. Its "difference sweet" of whispering birds, fountains, and winds (III, iii, 39) replicates the "sweet diversitie" of "Birds, voyces, instruments, winds, waters" in her bower (2.12.70). Pendant fruit drips heavenly nectar in the manner of her "bounches hanging downe" toward "luscious wine" (2.12.54). "[L]inked ivey tangling wild" (III, iii, 136) proliferates like her profuse "trale of yvie" (2.12.61). But unlike her retreat, Shelley's cave is free of "discord" and filled only with "harmonies divine" (III, iii, 38). It is as if what Shelley sees as the "evil" of the Palmer, and the ideology that he so rigorously enforces, is displaced by Spenser's redeemed Acrasian imagination. Or so it seems, though we shall have to return to that point and qualify it, as Shelley does.

Shelley's subversion of Spenser's system is most dramatic during the millennial vision at the close of act 3, which also entails his heaviest borrowing from The Faerie Queene. This is the point where Spenser's idea of visionary illumination and his own finally lock horns. Shelley was adamant, like Blake in his Spenserian revisionism, about the possibilities of restoring Eden in the here and now, not in the distant future that Spenser forlornly yearns after at the end of the *Mutabilitie Cantos.* To emphasize that difference in *Prometheus Unbound,* Shelley inverts Spenser's pattern of relations between heaven and earth, bringing Redcrosse's New Jerusalem down off the mountain into the nineteenth century. He displaces Spenser's idea of a transcendent heaven, for instance, with a modern paradise in the rehabilitated mind and thus envisions the perfect worldly city instead of Redcrosse's heavenly one. Elaborating on that shift of emphasis, Shelley replaces Spenser's "gladsome companee" of angels with a visionary company of mortals, transforming those angels who "wend" like men into men who walk "One with the other even as spirits do" (III, iv, 132). He even reverses the direction and purpose of Spenser's millennial sounds. Eden's trumpets aspire toward heaven, which gives off its own "heauenly noise" to draw the gaze of mortals upward (1.12.39). But Prometheus's conch brings heaven to earth. It also unmasks not Archimagean evil but religious authority—mantled in the veil of shrines, altars, priests, and tomes—which is the true Covering Cherub that blocks man from paradise. The very illumination that Spenser honors becomes the infection of blindness that Prometheus must remedy. (Redcrosse, we should recall, and Shelley would surely have noticed, is actually blinded by his vision of the New Jerusalem.) Put another way, the truth of visionary imagination that Spenser only dimly perceives is released from the ideological veil of his own revelation.

By now, of course, Shelley knew that illuminating the truth within Spenser's darkness also means deepening the core of ambiguity in his vision. Although Shelley passionately aspires to an apocalypse of the imagination in *Prometheus Unbound,* especially in what Yeats called "the ecstatic lyricism of that famous fourth act" (*Autobiographies* 65), he ultimately leaves his paradise regained conditional. As many readers of *Prometheus Unbound* have noticed, the enthusiasm at the end of act 3 is qualified by the reminder that we are not exempt "[f]rom chance, and death, and mutability" (III, iv, 201). Indeed, Shelley's "old Dragon" of mutability is always threatening, like the "serpent" at the close of *Prometheus Unbound,* act 4, to rise up and clasp "Eternity" in its coils (IV, 565–67).[11] Spenser, as Shelley now

---

11. The movement of *Prometheus Unbound,* Curran argues, is not to "regain paradise, at least as that term is customarily employed in Christian commentary. Chance, mutability, death—qualities which God excludes from Eden and which Shelley at-

saw it, had that fact of prophetic illumination partially right. Redcrosse is told that he cannot enter the New Jerusalem, that he must go "Backe to the world" and renew his pilgrimage (1.10.63). Archimago, like Shelley's serpent, can always slip free of his bondage, and the Blatant Beast remains ever on the loose. Yet for all his acceptance of the eternal contradictions between "the world" and the New Jerusalem, Spenser finally trusts in and yearns, however hesitantly, for that distant time when "all shall changed bee, / And from thenceforth, none no more change shall see" (7.7.59). Redcrosse cannot wait to end his mission and "shortly backe returne unto this place" where chance, death, and mutability do not exist (1.10.64). The mature Shelley, who like Blake may finally be much more passionate than Spenser in his millennial idealism, still cannot "backe returne" in such a way. His empire of the spirit is ever at war with Jupiter's "disentangled doom" (IV, 569). Shelley's need to emphasize that difference, or to redeem the duality locked inside of Spenser's vision, may be why he brings Prometheus and Asia, in the end, to a reconstructed Bower of Bliss. The doubleness at the heart of Acrasia's bower, we recall, represents for many of the Romantics the deepest truth of Spenser's poem, or the one which says the most about modern experience. If we recognize how its "chiaroscuro" comes into the "far goal of Time" where Prometheus and Asia finally rest (III, iii, 174), we may understand the depth of Shelley's conditionality in *Prometheus Unbound* and the extent to which unlocking Spenser's vision helps him explore it. It is this self-redemptive recovery of Spenser's imaginative truth that ultimately carries Shelley out of his own cave of creative despair and enables him to celebrate his independence of vision in Prometheus's apocalyptic liberation. That Shelley should thus assume the position of a rehabilitated Redcrosse at the borders of a New Jerusalem of poetic tradition helps account for the great outpouring of joy in the Spirit of the Hour's proclamation of a renovated universe.

The patterns of adaptation I have just outlined demonstrate, in many ways, a constructive revisionism by which Shelley appropriates all that is eternal in Spenser while also purging his own "longing for an Absolute Center" (Hogle viii).[12] Casting off Spenser's "reasoned

tempts to deny in *Queen Mab* and *The Revolt of Islam*—retain their integrity in this regenerate world" (*Shelley's Annus Mirabilis* 65).

12. In the preface to *Prometheus Unbound*, he acknowledged his "passion for reforming the world" and claimed that he had restrained his didacticism: "[I]t is a mistake to suppose that I dedicate my poetical compositions solely to the direct enforcement of

system," as he puts it, is obviously a way to act on his "abhorrence" of his own earlier didactic poetry (*PW* 207). Yet as much as we should note the self-redemptive aspects of his Spenserian revisionism in *Prometheus Unbound,* it is difficult not to see fairly significant traces of his previous excesses. More than one of his critics, from the poem's first appearance, has observed or complained about the volatile character of its anti-Christianity. Its repetitive attacks on altars, priests, and heaven should remind us of similar patterns in *Queen Mab* and *The Revolt of Islam,* even though Shelley takes obvious measures to tone down his former lecturing style. Moreover, the extreme pertinaciousness with which he reverses details of Spenser's orthodox iconography suggests as much an angered impatience with his model as a studied determination to build on Spenser. We have seen how impatience of that sort, "mad obstinacy" to some Spenser loyalists, had arisen in the past from his uneasiness about following so conservative a guide and risking the subordination of his own independent vision. Although Shelley had learned by now to transform his quarrel with Spenser into something positive, there is evidence that he was still feeling some of the old concern about being put in "subjection" by the company of spiritual foes. In the middle of composing *Prometheus Unbound,* he remembered Artegall's encounter with the Giant and reiterated his antagonism to Spenser (*LPBS* 2:70–71). That recollection, coming in the midst of a poem deliberately conceived as a struggle with great forebears, must have seemed rather ominous to Shelley. He knew that Artegall wins the battle, that it is not even a contest.

How much Shelley may have still been troubled by his nearness to Spenser's orthodoxy is suggested in his correspondence by his frequent diatribes on Christianity, which intriguingly recall the power relations of *Prometheus Unbound* in their recurrent images of tyranny and restraint. Many of these images are particularly associated with Jupiter's oppression as "God and Lord" over psychological and, we might add, creative freedom. While denigrating the "monstrous form" of the Crucifixion, for instance, Shelley mentioned a painting by Guido in which Christ, St. John, and Mary Magdalene assume the exact postures of Ione, Panthea, and Prometheus as they are suffering under Jupiter's rule. The resemblance between the two groups may be taken to imply Shelley's apprehension of the way Christian

reform, or that I consider them in any degree as containing a reasoned system on the theory of human life. Didactic poetry is my abhorrence" (*PW* 207).

visions, like Guido's and Spenser's, could impose on his own. Whenever he thought about those visions, his imagination turned to religious images of constriction, such as hair shirts and sacrifice (*LPBS* 2:48, 52). His recollection of Spenser's Giant points to the personal application of those images. The Giant, like himself, is a democratic revolutionary friendly to man and implacably girded against omnipotent power. Also like Shelley, he specifically battles against the religious hierarchies at the center of Spenser's Christian vision. Shelley even described his current poetic ambitions in terms of the Giant's revolutionary struggle: "I shall be content . . . [to] cast what weight I can into the right scale of that balance which the Giant (of Artegall) holds" (*LPBS* 2:71). Where Keats brought the Giant back to strike down Artegall and Talus, however, Shelley made no mention of a similar rebirth. The implications are still more discomforting if we consider that the Giant reference comes in the midst of a letter to Peacock about the subordinate position of poetry in modern culture. The lyric on despair had just been written a few weeks earlier. It was also about this time that Shelley made those comparisons between Prometheus's enslavement and the plight of modern artists trapped in the prisonhouse of cultural tradition.

All this is not to claim that Shelley did despair about his creative freedom; he was far from giving up, as his self-redemptive Spenserian revisions confirm. Rather, it tells us how concerned he was about gaining that freedom, not only from Spenser but from all the "imperial spirits" who watched over *Prometheus Unbound.* If we suspect that, notwithstanding his many transformations of the past in *Prometheus Unbound,* Shelley's sense of constriction persisted right through his revisions of Spenser's millennialism, then we must find something incomplete about Prometheus's reenactment of Redcrosse's visionary triumph at what was supposed to be a concluding celebration of creative independence—as if Despair's shadow, the Covering Cherub of the "city of the dead," was still casting a dark cloud over the poem's consciousness. Shelley, at least, seems to have felt that way, and not simply because he went on, after a nine-month hiatus, to write another act. The deliberate suppression of any reference to Spenser in his original preface, which he wrote after he finished act 3, suggests the uneasiness he was feeling about their relationship. The scenario was not unlike what had happened after *The Revolt of Islam.* Whatever apprehensions he was indeed harboring about his own creative independence were much deepened six months later. In October 1819, a packet from England brought him a review of *The Revolt of Islam* condemning its derivative nature.[13] That criticism must have hit a sore spot, for he responded by expanding the preface of *Prometheus Unbound* to include his contentious arguments for originality. He still repressed Spenser's impact, even cancelling a draft reference to the Elizabethan age (Zillman 636). But the ruling spirits of the past, as Shelley said himself, "cannot die," and these defenses could not shut out his doubts about his own "subjection" to Spenser's authority. It is not surprising that he turned now, undoubtedly aware of the potential self-applications, to Spenser's allegory of flimsy imitation and artificial genius, the story of the False Florimel (*LPBS* 2:125). Clearly, some new way of absorbing Spenser and understanding the whole dynamics of cultural influence was necessary in order to give *Prometheus Unbound* a more satisfying conclusion.

It may be true that Shelley did not rejuvenate the Giant during the first three acts of *Prometheus Unbound*. But after that October review, he did begin to regird himself not solely to challenge what Artegall represents but also to subdue or refit that even more formidable figure, the Giant of poetic tradition. More precisely, he began to develop a theory of cultural transmission that would open up the literary past by reconceptualizing it as a fertile ground of inspiration containing the seeds of its own enrichment in a modern poetics. The aim here was to address the fundamental dilemma of Romantic influence theory: how to validate the second Renaissance by linking it with the first while affirming its capacity to supersede that magnificent origin. Shelley tried to solve the problem by proposing a theory of wavelike cultural regeneration specifically connected with sociopolitical reform.

Periodic surges of major social reform, Shelley argues, had triggered aesthetic renewal throughout the generations. "The mass of [creative] possibilities," he explains in the revised preface to *Prometheus Unbound*, "remains at every period materially the same" (*PW* 206). That "mass of possibilities" is brought to life, he continues, by great movements of social and political reform. Hence the democratic political innovations of classical Athens, republican Italy, and Commonwealth England—his triumverate of culturally superior epochs—were the chief inspiration for the creative outpourings of those great moments in Western cultural history. The writings of

13. This review was John Taylor Coleridge's "*Laon and Cythna. The Revolt of Islam*" (reprinted in Newman I. White 133–50).

these periods "are the productions of the vigour of the infancy of a new nation, as rivulets from the same spring" that feeds "the greatness of the [world's] republics" (*LPBS* 2:122). To this "cause" of political vigor, he elaborates in *A Philosophical View of Reform*, "if to anything, was due the undisputed superiority of Italy in literature and the arts over all its contemporary nations. . . . The most unfailing herald, or companion, or follower . . . of beneficial [political] change is poetry" (*SP* 231, 239).

This way of uniting history's great political republics with cultural highpoints is the first stage of a theory of perpetually self-renewing processes of literary transmission. Shelley establishes the basic principle of that theory by arguing for a cyclical link among these periods of great social innovation, with each breakthrough incorporating and building upon the achievements of its model. Hence Athens was the "predecessor" and "image" of Renaissance Italy, and through the Italians "[w]hat the Greeks were" became "the influence and inspiration" of what "we are" (*SP* 231, 219). Moreover, the "republics and municipal governments of Italy" had flowed into the emancipating movements of the English Reformation, which in turn had helped stimulate the outburst of European revolutions around the turn of the nineteenth century (*SP* 231, 239). What seems most significant to Shelley about this cyclical wave is its steady habit of improving upon itself. The brilliance of Greek institutions was imperfect, marred by inequalities among the sexes and practices of slavery that would be wiped out by future generations. The Reformation's "emancipation of mankind" was also "imperfect," its religious strife transcended by a later age. Every great social breakthrough had been "partial and imperfect," with its strengths incorporated and its errors corrected by the next wave of reform (*SP* 231).

If we keep Shelley's notion of political and artistic interconnection in mind, we can see what this idea of a steady "progress of philosophy and civilization" meant in terms of the current debate about literary transmission. Each *poetic* revolution, the argument follows, also integrates and refines the imperfections of *its* precursor movement. The "more complete development" of social institutions during the Elizabethan age, Shelley concludes in *A Philosophical View of Reform*, resulted in a "new spirit" of literary achievement (*SP* 231). That claim opens up a Mammon's cave of possibility for contemporary poets if one believes, as Shelley certainly did for a brief time late in 1819, that the democratic revolutions of modern Europe were surpassing all previous sociopolitical breakthroughs in human history. "If England were divided into forty republics," he suggests in the expanded preface to *Prometheus Unbound,* "each equal in population and extent to Athens, there is no reason to suppose but that, under institutions not more perfect than those of Athens, each would produce philosophers and poets equal to those who . . . have never been surpassed" (*PW* 206). If the institutions were to become yet "more perfect" than those of Athens, one could go on, there is no reason to suppose but that poets would be produced who would even outperform those giant sons of genius. "The fact is," Shelley indeed continues in his essay *On The Manners of the Ancient Greeks,* "modern Europeans" have made "the most decisive [improvements] in the regulation of human society" (*SP* 220). An "unimagined change in our social condition" is well under way, he elaborates in the preface to *Prometheus Unbound,* and its "companions," the "great writers of our own age," are thus destined to outsoar all of "the dead Kings of Melody" (*PW* 206). It is that conviction, and the theory of political/literary renewal behind it, that enables Shelley to conceive of England rising phoenixlike out of and above the glorious achievements of the political and the poetical past: "The literature of England, an energetic development of which has ever followed or preceded a great and free development of the national will, has arisen, as it were, from a new birth" (*SP* 239). The claim meant so much to him that he took it almost verbatim out of *A Philosophical View of Reform* and used it two years later for the rousing conclusion of *A Defence of Poetry.*

Though still incipient, this theory and the confidence it inspired were already developing by late 1819. Just before Shelley began the last act of *Prometheus Unbound,* he eagerly prophesied imminent social reforms and the creative regeneration they would inspire. "[W]e are on the eve of great actions," he told his friends the Gisbornes, and that promise left him "full of all kinds of literary plans" (*LPBS* 2:150). Armed with this enthusiasm, he began to receive his great poetic forebears joyfully as fraternal spirits engaged in a common enterprise. He dropped the provoking Oedipal imagery of devouring fathers, for instance, and spoke of poets as "mothers who prefer the children who have given them most trouble" (quoted in Zillman 34). Such an altered stance toward literary influence made the paternal generosity of Calderón's *Cabellos de Absalón* particularly attractive, "full of the deepest & the tenderest touches of nature. Nothing can be more pathetically conceived than the character of the old David, & the tender and impartial love, overcoming all insults & all crimes, with which he regards his conflicting & disobedient sons" (*LPBS* 2:154). With this confidence about lineal relations prevailing, Shelley

launched ebulliently into act 4 of *Prometheus Unbound,* whose millennial joy may be read as the genuine accomplishment of Prometheus's
liberation and, following the personal allegory, of Shelley's own triumphant reconciliation with the past. It now seemed possible to welcome all his illustrious predecessors as the muses to propel him forward, "as it were, from a new birth," instead of holding him back.
Spenser, in particular, could be received as one of the great products
of an "imperfect" revolution rather than being fought off as a bas-
tion of orthodoxy. The new feeling of collaboration with the spirit of
the past finally inspired Shelley to assimilate a host of "disparate
traditions and cultures," as Curran puts it (*Shelley's Annus Mirabilis*
112), in the "ecstatic lyricism" of his final act, which is an impassioned masque about freedom and harmony.

But the triumph was not yet complete. As the wave of conservative
reaction grew in the early 1820s, Shelley felt increasing doubts about
the political basis of his whole theory of cultural progression. Even
after the ecstasy of that last act, then, he was not completely free of
discomfort about the weight of tradition bearing down on *Prometheus
Unbound.* In the same breath with which he sighed about the "mediocrity" of poets locked in fruitless imitation, he called his own lyrical
drama "a very imperfect poem. I begin to learn," he spoke of the
burden, "'quid valeant humeri, quid ferre recusent' ['what your
shoulders refuse, and what they are able to bear']" (*LPBS* 2:290).
Upon the completion of *Prometheus Unbound,* what he designated his
"severest test," he lamented, "Mine is a life of failures" (quoted in
Zillman 35). With this diffidence in mind, we may find the epigraph
Shelley directed to Aeschylus—"Audisne haec, Amphirae, sub ter-
ram abdite?" ["Do you hear this, Amphiaraus, in your home beneath
the earth?"]—reflecting a measure of self-deprecation, not arro-
gance as it is traditionally read, especially if we gloss it with the Cic-
eronian context of a disciple's unworthiness before his master. Shelley himself suggested such an interpretation, when he spoke just as
he was finishing *Prometheus Unbound* about Rome's buried dead who,
in their mockery of the "puny generations" that pass over them (or,
we might add, shout down to them), refuse to die.

The force of these unresolved apprehensions may be why he
never directly acknowledged Spenser's influence on *Prometheus Unbound,* as if the outcome of his own Despair episode was still too
equivocal for him to discuss it openly. He even defended such reti-
cence, though obliquely, in the final lines of his revised preface. He
claims there a preference for the solitary refuge of private failure to
public recognition of aesthetic breakdown: "[I]f his [the poet's] at-

tempt be ineffectual, let the punishment of an unaccomplished purpose have been sufficient; let none trouble themselves to heap the
dust of oblivion upon his efforts; the pile they raise will betray his
grave which might otherwise have been unknown" (*PW* 207). Better,
one might paraphrase, to grapple silently with the past than to call
attention to "an unaccomplished purpose." Shelley had come a long
way toward accomplishing that purpose, but he still felt himself positioned in a vexing "purgatory," between the "Hell" and the "Paradise of poetry" (*LPBS* 2:258). Before he could fully integrate himself
with Spenser and consolidate his overall relationship with poetic tradition, he would have to refine those theories of cultural transmission that were gradually helping him create a "Paradise of poetry" in
his own imagination.

III

The great leap forward in Shelley's theorizing on cultural transmission came in 1821 with *A Defence of Poetry*. And a stunning refinement it was, emerging as Romanticism's most sophisticated declara-
tion of its right to inscribe itself in that scroll of mighty poets that
had seemed folded up to Keats and so many others going all the way
back to Dryden. The *Defence* is so eloquently complex in its theories
about the mental dynamics and the ontological implications of the
creative act itself that little attention has been given to its origin as a
response to the question of how well the moderns were performing
that act in relation to their predecessors.[14] The immediate provocation of the essay, Peacock's *The Four Ages of Poetry* (1820), confronted
Shelley with a retrograde view of literary history. Poetry, as Peacock
argued, necessarily declines in vigor and relevance as cultures move
from primitive to sophisticated conditions. Considering Shelley's recent efforts to formulate a progressive view of literary history, we
can understand why this argument "excited," as he explained, "my
polemical faculties so violently" (*LPBS* 2:258). He felt a "sacred
rage" against Peacock's "unhorsing" of poetry, and he resolved to
"break a lance" with Peacock in "the lists of a magazine" by con-

---

14. Wittreich reads both *Adonais* and *A Defence of Poetry*, in a pairing on which I
intend to elaborate, as works that honor the fruitful dynamics of cultural transmission
(*Visionary Poetics* 88–89).

structing an alternative, more optimistic view of cultural development (*LPBS* 2:261). Shelley wondered if he was prepared for such a
battle, caricaturing himself as "the knight of the shield of shadow
and the lance of gossamere" (*LPBS* 2:261), but it was only a few days
later when he entered the lists, once and for all, against Peacock and
all those who despaired of a second Renaissance.

It is difficult to overlook the parodic Spenserianism of his chivalric
metaphor, and the élan with which he presented it. One thinks of
Keats, in a different sort of bind, puffing himself up to cross the
"Draw Bridge of Credit," or coupling Moneta's austerity with Venus's coquettish laugh. If Keats was toying with Spenser and not
feeling too distressed on those occasions, then Shelley's little allegory
suggests at least two things: that the whole issue of cultural transmission, of such major consequence to him now, was inseparable from
his long, eventful relationship with Spenser; and that despite the
tensions and setbacks in that relationship, there was still something
reassuring, even relaxing, about shouting down to the mighty dead
with Spenser by his side. Both points, we shall see, figure prominently in *Adonais;* what makes this possible in *Adonais* is the intellectual drama of the *Defence,* through which Shelley expands his recent
theorizing on literary influence in such a way as to induce a final
rapprochement with Spenser while bringing himself to the brink of
the "Paradise of poetry."

Shelley continues to argue in the *Defence* for a reciprocal relationship between political and poetical innovation, but he insists now
that neither form of renewal necessarily takes precedence over the
other. It is an "idle inquiry," he explains, to "demand" which movement, political or artistic, precedes and inspires the other. They "ac-
compan[y]" and sustain each other, "co-existing" as the signs and the
instruments of the spirit of renewal that transforms all facets of cultural life (*SP* 283, 296). That emphasis on reciprocity gives the arts a
certain independence from the political sphere, which frees Shelley
from building a "defence" of poetic progress on the shifting sands of
current political action. It also enables him to contemplate how the
cycle of literary transmission works within itself, regardless of the
historical evolution of political improvement.

In concentrating on artistic developments, however, Shelley takes
over the basic principle of interconnected, self-refining cycles in his
political theory. The question is how to show that history's great poetic moments have their own inherent dynamics linking them together, with each breakthrough arising from and renovating the
creative achievements of its precursor movements. Answering that

question could rescue the second Renaissance from the charges of belatedness that all the Romantics, in one way or another, had been struggling against. With so much at stake, it is no wonder that Shelley is so passionate about declaring the existence of such a cycle that perpetually renews itself. "The sacred links of that chain," he exclaims, "have never been entirely disjoined, which descending through the minds of many men is attached to those great minds, whence as from a magnet the invisible effluence is sent forth, which at once connects, animates, and sustains the life of all." It is that connecting, ever animating "effluence" that obviously concerns him, as he goes on to explain that a "great poem is a fountain forever overflowing with the waters of wisdom and delight" to be quaffed as the stimulant for later generations. The "Past" may thus be conceived, or we should say reconceived, as "an inspired rhapsodist [who] fills the theatre of everlasting generations with [the] harmony" of such "great poems" (*SP* 286–87, 291). That sound is not the thronging "disturbance" that could intrude on Keats, but a harmony that ever inspires its own refinement in the theater of mind where succeeding generations outlive Hazlitt's last act and continue to perform their new poems. Shelley's favorite way of conceptualizing this perpetual evolution of poetry is to describe literary influence in terms of self-renewing cycles of germination. The "faculty" of transmitted effluence, he characteristically declares, "contains within itself the seeds . . . of its own . . . renovation" (*SP* 287).[15] The key point is to show *how* that process of germination operates through the ages in such a progressive fashion.

The explanation presented in the *Defence* may not seem new to Shelley scholars, but its implications for a theory of poetic influence have rarely been appreciated. Shelley's basic thesis is that all superior poets are linked together by their mutual apprehension of the "eternal proportions" of truth (*SP* 282), but the limitations of their times have also forced them to cloud those "proportions" in veils of error that must be continually torn aside by their successors.[16] The "eternal poets," as Shelley describes them, "imagine and express" the "indestructible order" of things, the "eternal, the infinite, and the one"

15. Continuing the metaphor, Shelley also writes: "All high poetry" is like "the first acorn, which contained all oaks potentially." The poet "beholds the future in the present, and his thoughts are the germs of the flower and the fruit of latest time" (*PW* 291, 279).

16. Wasserman explicates Shelley's concept as follows: "Although poetry as an integral thought containing the principle of its own integrity is eternally relevant, it must be continuously re-created in man's successive transient conditions" (*Shelley* 210).

(*SP* 279). Each poet's vision of that order constitutes the "effluence" that is transmitted as the inspiration to his successors. Hence the "immortal compositions" of poetic history, Shelley goes on, may be recognized "as episodes to that great poem which all poets, like the co-operating thoughts of one great mind, have built up since the beginning of the world" (*SP* 287). In building up the "great poem" that unites them, however, all of the "eternal poets" have been forced by the error of their time to grasp only a portion of that "indestructible order" and to cloak their vision in the false materials of their day. "Every epoch, under names more or less specious, has deified its peculiar errors," and the "vices" of the poet's contemporaries must become "the temporary dress" in which his "creations must be arrayed" (*SP* 282). Hence even though a "Poet therefore would do ill to embody his own conceptions of right and wrong, which are usually those of his place and time, in his poetical creations," none may fully escape this subjugation. Even Dante and Milton had to "walk through eternity enveloped and disguised" in "the mask and the mantle" of their "distorted" superstitions (*SP* 289–90). The ramifications here for a theory of progressive literary transmission are staggeringly provocative.

The natural extension of this argument, as Shelley goes on to say, is that while each new contributor to history's "great poem" absorbs his predecessor's vision of truth, he must also correct the errors that distort it. The "eternal proportions" of that cyclical poem thus go through a self-perpetuating process of increasing purification with each new creative "episode." Time forever "augments," Shelley explains, the "beauty" of its ongoing poem and "for ever develops new and wonderful applications of the eternal truths which it contains. . . . [A]fter one person and one age has exhausted all of its divine effluence which their particular relations enable them to share, another and yet another succeeds, and new relations are ever developed" (*SP* 281, 291). By way of example, Shelley cites the love poetry of Christian Europe, which had integrated and in its own "abstract purity" "renovated" the spirituality of pagan art. Seeing literary transmission in this way finally enables Shelley to conclude that every "great poet" must "inevitably" draw inspiration from and "innovate upon the example of his predecessor" (*SP* 288–89, 280). Such a reading of poetic history transforms the "Past" from a blocking agent into the outline of an incompleted prophecy, from which the "everlasting generations" can be inspired to draw ever new relations, another after another. "[P]aradise," a "Paradise of poetry" as Shelley puts it on another occasion, can thus be "created as out of the wrecks of Eden" (*SP* 289). That conviction, and what it says about the possibilities of building a second Renaissance out of the massive wrecks of the first, lies behind Shelley's famous paeans to the spirit of the modern age: "[T]he world as from a resurrection, balancing itself on the golden wings of knowledge and of hope, has reassumed its yet unwearied flight into the heaven of time. . . . [O]ur own will be a memorable age" (SP 288, 296–97).[17]

Besides helping to release the flood of creative energy that distinguishes the last year and a half of Shelley's life, this theory of poetic influence profoundly alters his stance toward Spenser. On the one hand, it allows him to drop his antagonism to Spenser's error. There is still no mistaking that error. In fact, Spenser has to be relegated to the second order of "supreme poets," along with Euripides, Lucan, and Tasso, for having so "frequently affected a moral aim" (SP 283). His error, however, now seems but the veil of his true genius, "the mask and the mantle" in which he "walked through eternity enveloped and disguised" by his time's decay (SP 290). Correcting Spenser's limitations is thus no longer a self-inhibiting attack but one more part of the overall process of purification by which Shelley adds his own episode to time's "great poem." He now sees the errors of all his predecessors being "washed in the blood of the mediator and redeemer, Time," and he can, at last, forgive Spenser for being the kind of conservative poet who would deign to become "a poet laureate" (SP 295). Shelley even goes so far as to see the eternal part of Spenser, like the revisionary Redcrosse who battles the very dragonish orthodoxy he mistakenly supports, struggling against his fallen self's investment in the wars of monarchy and religion. Much as Spenser clung to that error, Shelley now acknowledges, his imaginative faculties helped to "drown the dissonance of arms and superstition" in his own mind (SP 289). So the true genius in him made him ever strive to become like the witch of Atlas, that Spenserian enchantress who arranges her imaginative pranks against conventional values. That is why he can be counted as one of those opponents of tyranny who made England "an island of the blest" (Letter to Maria Gisborne, line 32). Part of Spenser thus had it right all along. But his resistance to orthodoxy was incomplete, his vision locked in the superstitions of his time, and the eternal portion of him needed completion in a new episode of the cyclical poem that he had helped to construct.

17. This theory of a perpetually self-refining process of poetic transmission shares much with the notion of prophetic lineage that Blake was building up as his own source of inspiration. Wittreich has extensively discussed the complicated strategies of the prophetic line in Visionary Poetics.

Recovering the lineaments of truth from the veil of his predecessors' errors is one way of characterizing the poetics of Shelley's
final months. "Poets, the best of them," he summarized during his
last year, "are a very camaeleonic race: they take the colour not only
of what they feed on, but of the very leaves under which they pass"
(*LPBS* 2:308). What he took from Spenser's leaves helped make up
the fabric of his own final poetic accomplishments. Purifying Spenser, no doubt, continued to help him in that ongoing effort to arrest
his own didactic impulses and sink himself in the mystery of life's
labyrinthine dualisms. And there seemed no question now that in his
capacity as a prophet of "everlasting love" Spenser could inspire the
visionary illuminations of "the great writers of our own age" (*SP*
289).[18] But the eternal part of Spenser's imagination was also addressing Shelley in a way that he had never understood before writing the *Defence*.

This fresh insight grew out of his recognition of the striking parallels between his new theory of cultural transmission and his developing notion of the duality of all experience. It now became apparent
to him that the interplay of a transient vision of the day with an
eternal episodic poem duplicates and participates in that dynamic of
eternity and the productions of time that he was finding basic to
modern poetic experience. The very process of struggling to build a
second Renaissance, then, by engaging in the wavelike rhythms and
contraries of literary influence—what Bloom calls the "dialectics of
literary tradition" (*Map of Misreading* 38)—could become in itself an
act of empowerment for a modern poetics of duality. That stunning
revelation, as Shelley would make clear in *Adonais*, had been dimly
perceived by Spenser. Shelley's own eagerness to extract and illuminate it from Spenser's error-laden universe may be why he characterized himself, in creating his own mature poetic vision, both as a
"weird Archimage" (*Letter to Maria Gisborne*, 106)—that old master of
duality—and as a Spenserian champion of doubt, transiency, and
equivocation: "the knight of the shield of shadow and the lance of
gossamere."

IV

What Shelley means by immersing himself in "the One" has always
been a central question in readings of *Adonais;* the various often con-

18. Bloom suggests that Spenser's visionary sensibility helped Shelley carry out
mythmaking exercises in a series of late poems, *The Sensitive Plant, The Witch of Atlas,*
even *The Triumph of Life* (*Shelley's Mythmaking* 162–65).

flicting answers that have been posited are legion.[19] Without trying
to settle that debate, I wish to suggest how much more fruitful it can
become if we move it into the context of Shelley's developing engagement with Spenser. Actually, Curran has already begun to do
that by reading *Adonais* as a response to Keats's later poetry, though
he is not so concerned as I with how *Adonais,* a poem in Spenserian
stanzas about mutability and eternity, elaborates Keats's Spenserianism in that other great lyrical drama of reality and idealism,
The Eve of St. Agnes. Curran finds *Adonais,* as a reply to Keats's 1820
Lamia volume, extending Keats's willing descent into the welter of
mortal experience, a "dying into life" that ultimately enriches poetic
creativity. In Curran's view, Shelley's self-sacrificial submission to the
"breath" of an apocalyptic force may be associated with his acceptance of the destructive and preservative "breath" of the West Wind,
which is "the creative principle itself." Hence "the One" can be identified with "the basic impulse of creation itself, which destroys worlds
to create them anew, which forces the breaking of hearts and the
destruction of perilously integrated psyches." To embrace this "creative urge" is both a "voiding of personality" and a "paradoxical discovery of the self as a universal force through a refining away of all
that is not imagination" ("*Adonais* in Context" 178–79). It is Curran's
contention that Shelley goes farther than Keats, who was always
prone to the seduction of enchanted isles, in this capitulation to the
"basic impulse of creation itself." We have seen, though, how Keats
traveled quite far himself into the contrarieties of the "Mansion of
Many Apartments," even giving up his preoccupation with that quest
in the end because it held him back from becoming one with the
experiences of the divided heart. Rather than debate about who
went the furthest, however, I would like to focus on the likeness of
the journey, especially in its Spenserian dimensions. Curran's notion
of a descent into disruptive processes that also participate in eternal
rhythms of creativity seems congruent with the main idea of Spenserian revisionism that both Keats and Shelley were developing: a
poetics designed to complicate Spenser's intersection of eternity and
this "tickle" state. Keats's way of opening up that dichotomy in a
condensed antiallegorical allegory, we may suspect, was a key inspiration for Shelley's recourse to the Spenserian format of *Adonais.*

Yet Shelley was also deeply concerned, as we have seen, with the
interplay between Spenserian duality and the flux of poetic history.
We only need recall the circumstances of Keats's death, as Shelley

19. Curran's recent essay, "*Adonais* in Context," provides a useful summary of the
critical background.

understood them, to recognize how centrally *Adonais* is engaged with that parallel question of literary transmission. Keats had died, Shelley believed, at the hands of malicious reviewers, whose "savage criticism" and "spoken daggers" were threatening to depress art and set up the hirelings of a diseased imagination, represented by the likes of "Mrs. Lefanu, and Mr. Barrett, and Mr. Howard Payne, and a long list of the illustrious obscure" (*PW* 431). In responding to the depredations of these "literary prostitutes," Shelley aimed to show how the "unextinguished Spirit" of Keats's poetry, and the creative excellence it manifests, surmounts the hostile errors of the day to live on in eternity. That intention makes *Adonais* a kind of poetic *Defence of Poetry*, or a passionate expression of the dynamic between rupture and continuity in Shelley's theory of cultural transmission. Keats, like Milton, Dante, Spenser, and all the "eternals" honored in the *Defence*, had to be liberated from the errors of his time and place in order to live on in history's "great poem." If we thus read *Adonais* as not only a "correction" of the errors surrounding Keats but also a paean to the ever-renewing flux of poetic history, we should not be surprised to find it filled with the rhetoric of the *Defence*'s influence theory. References to "the enduring dead," the "Eternal," their "transmitted effluence" abound in *Adonais*. Even "the One," a term used in the *Defence* to describe the eternal qualities of art (*SP* 279), may be associated with the rhetoric of poetic influence in *Adonais*. Just as the "One," in Curran's sense, subjects the poet to mutability in order to subsume him into the eternal rhythms of creativity, poetic history refines away the temporal forms of art to preserve its "eternal proportions."

What makes Spenser so important to *Adonais* is Shelley's recognition that he understood, albeit faintly, this connection between the duality of creative experience and the flux of poetic history. The subject of cultural transmission, as Shelley knew from current Spenser criticism and from his own interactions with *The Shepheardes Calender*, is one of the main preoccupations of Spenser's poetry. On numerous occasions Spenser celebrates the immortality of song, presenting the *Epithalamion* as an "endlesse moniment," *The Faerie Queene* as a "labovr" for "eternitie," and his *Complaints* as verse that "For ever . . . shall live." But he is even more specifically concerned about the continuity of poetic achievement amid the decay of time and—a point that would have surely captivated Shelley—before the onslaught of its detractors. *The Teares of the Muses* is a sustained complaint about the "open shame" into which poetry has fallen in an unsympathetic age (line 61). It has virtually been put out, laments the muse Euterpe—and this should make us think of the blind rabble's attack on Keats in *Adonais*—by "Ignorance", who "armd with blindnesse and with boldnes stout, / (For blind is bold) hath our fayre light defaced" (lines 265–66). In Book 4 of *The Faerie Queene*, Spenser laments that "wicked Time" doth "out weare" and quite deface the "famous moniment[s]" and "workes of heauenly wits" (4.2.33). That knowledge leaves him anxious to transcend "cursed Eld the cankerworme of writs" and particularly rescue Chaucer's essence through "infusion sweete / Of thine owne spirit, which doth in me surviue" (4.2.34). This is the same problem of "transmitting effluence" across the boundaries of time and cultural inhospitality that Shelley was trying to solve in the *Defence*.[20]

Among Spenser's many efforts to affirm the triumph of such "transmission," one passage from *The Ruines of Time* must have seemed acutely relevant to Shelley's plans for *Adonais*. It is the brief lament for Sidney that Hunt regarded as the prime embodiment of Spenserian duality, an observation he would have been eager to share with Shelley.[21] Sidney is shown here to transcend the "obscure obliuion" to which time, mutability, and ignorance would consign him, rising up to join a heaven of eternal poets:

> But now more happie thou, and wretched wee,
> Which want the wonted sweetnes of thy voice,
> Whiles thou now in *Elisian* fields so free,
> With *Orpheus*, and with *Linus*, and the choice
> Of all that euer did in rimes rejoyce,
> Conversest, and doost heare their heauenlie layes,
> And they heare thine, and thine doo better praise.
>
> (lines 330–36)

Shelley did not need Hunt to tell him that such a rescuing of Sidney's song in a poet's heaven is also a way of dissolving the mutability of this "tickle" world into God's heaven, that such a key passage collapses the duality of human experience with the flux of poetic transmission. Spenser may not have the details properly sorted out, as Shelley saw it. Yearning to escape mutability now seemed erroneous, especially if it meant trusting in a Christian heaven. Shelley would have also denied that the eternal poem sung by Sidney and

20. MacCaffrey finds Spenser committed to dramatizing "the battle against the enemies of poetry" (343).

21. Baker notes the parallel between the heaven of poets in both poems ("Spenser and Shelley" 256).

his immortal peers was unavailable to human ears. Yet Spenser's
drama of a poetic death leading to eternal song still provided a useful metaphorical paradigm for his own theory of how poets die or
are refined into the great episodic poem of history. The relationship
in *The Ruines of Time* between that dying into life and the larger
drama of Mutabilitie's contention with the gods also formed a kind
of blueprint for his own final juxtapositions of literary history and
poetic vision. Redeeming these "eternal proportions" of Spenser's
art from the errors of the past could thus help consummate Shelley's
ongoing effort to center himself in the literary and psychological
intersection of actuality and transcendence. It could also make
Keats's triumph "against Oblivion" in the poets' heaven of *Adonais*
not only the next episode in time's cyclical poem but a commentary
on how such episodes happen. To resurrect Spenser in this way,
Shelley turned to his more elaborate handling of Sidney's apotheosis
in *Astrophel.*

We know that Shelley synthesizes in *Adonais* a spectacular variety
of source material from the pastoral tradition. But, as several critics
have demonstrated, he may take the most from Spenser's elegy for
Sidney, *Astrophel.*[22] Shelley's choice of the *Faerie Queene* stanza alone
suggests a special link with Spenser, and his structural approximation of Spenser's elegy implies an even more specific tie to *Astrophel.*
The opening two-thirds of both elegies are lamentations, which are
followed in both poems by consolatory endings—a common pattern
in the tradition of English pastoral elegy. The fifty-five stanzas of
Adonais make a more direct connection with *Astrophel,* specifically approximating its fifty-four stanzas.[23] I do not need to restate the many
other structural, linguistic, and imagistic parallels between the two

22. Silverman has devoted the most attention to the background of *Astrophel.*
23. The difference is significant, and I shall discuss it shortly. *Astrophel* is in six-line
stanzas. The first two-thirds of the poem makes up a pastoral lament for Sidney,
which is followed by a consolation titled *The Doleful Lay of Clorinda.* The question of
whether Spenser actually composed *The Doleful Lay* has never been settled, but Spenser scholars now tend to agree that the style of *The Doleful Lay* suggests his authorship
of all or at least part of the poem. Its multiple stylistic affinities with *Astrophel* lead
most Spenser scholars to regard the two works as a single unit, "contrasting parts of a
complex whole" (Oram 565). Romantic editions of Spenser's poetry often group the
two poems together as a single composition by Spenser. Some editions, like the Bell
text probably used by Keats, present *The Doleful Lay* as a continuous part of *Astrophel*
without even separating it by title, page breaks, or line numbers. Judging from Shelley's response to these works, I would say that he read them as a single poem. To
ensure clarity of reference, my citations of passages from *The Doleful Lay* follow the
numbering of *The Yale Edition of the Shorter Poems of Edmund Spenser.*

poems that have already been noted by Curran and Silverman. As Curran observes, however, a convincing explanation of why Shelley follows the example of *Astrophel* and how he may transform it has yet to be made ("*Adonais* in Context" 169). We may come to that understanding by recognizing how Shelley recovers the eternal dualities of artistic vision and poetic transmission locked inside Spenser's elegy.

Probably on Keats's specific instigation, Shelley fashions *Adonais* as a "succession" of allegorical panels in the manner of *The Revolt of Islam*. Only now, like Keats in *The Eve of St. Agnes*, he is moved by the indeterminacy of his own mature thinking, the "dual force" of his psychology (Curran, "*Adonais* in Context" 174), to condense that paneling into a brief, highly complex series of ambiguous pictures. His particular focus on a single Spenserian text makes his revisionism even more compact. Where Keats generally recovers the duality of Spenser's castle motif, Shelley specifically intensifies the contraries of his mutability theme in *Astrophel*. The elegy for Sidney presents a classic Spenserian tension between mutability and the New Jerusalem. Spenser bewails Sidney's vulnerability to the "direfull stound[s]" of a fragile mortal existence (line 123), but he also finds consolation in the "blisfull Paradise" of "heavens joy" (*Doleful Lay*, lines 68, 93), to which Sidney ascends and rests, as the end of *The Faerie Queene* would have it, "eternally / With Him that is the God of Sabbaoth hight." That vision of transcendence, of course, seems fraught with error to Shelley, notwithstanding Wasserman's platonizing claim that *Adonais* ascends toward an "infinite spiritual life" (*Shelley* 305). But Shelley does find some traces of its "eternal proportions" in Spenser's devotion to Sidney's poetic immortality and in his passionate sensitivity to the division between "heavens joy" and "our owne selves that here in dole are drent" (*Doleful Lay*, line 94). Shelley's effort to free those eternal realities from the veil of Spenser's time and place makes up much of the antiallegorical allegory of *Adonais*.

To rectify Spenser's withdrawal from the dualities of *Astrophel* for instance, Shelley produces a tableau of allegorical contrasts that humanize Spenser's etherealness and consolidate his own duality of vision in *Adonais*. Where Spenser enshrines Sidney in a "blisfull Paradise" of immutability, Shelley describes Keats as a "ruined Paradise" (line 88), characterizes his burial place in Rome as both a "Paradise" and a "grave" strewn with "wrecks" (lines 443–45), and installs him, at last, in a "Heaven" filled with tempests, veils, and death (lines 490–95). In a similar correction of Spenser's transcendent impulse, Shelley replaces Sidney's Stella, whose spirit "did flit" out of her "corps" to join her lover in heaven (line 177), with Keats's Urania, who is "chained to Time, and cannot thence depart!" (line 234). To punctuate this earthward reversal, he also rewrites Sidney's metamorphosis from a flower to a star as Keats's "incarnation . . . of the stars" in the flowers that his "leprous corpse" exhales (lines 172–74). Sidney even reappears in *Adonais*, if we read the pun rightly, as "A rose," one who "fought" and "fell" and "lived" and "loved," instead of an immutable star (lines 400–404). Where eternal beds of flowers surround Sidney in Spenser's heaven, Shelley's Urania drops "eternal flowers" amid the rough "camps and cities . . . [a]nd human hearts" of the transient world (lines 209–16). Even when Keats/ Adonais finally rises to join "the Eternals" as a star, the "splendours" in the heaven to which he ascends "[m]ay be eclipsed," may be "veiled" though never completely "blotted" out (lines 388–92). Put together, this sequence of changes reverses Spenser's movement beyond the temporal world to recover his vision of the tenuous ground where mutability and eternity become one, the "One." It is such a strengthening or illumination of his buried insight that helps Shelley work out his own vision of that intersection in *Adonais*.

Nowhere is this process more richly evident than in Shelley's presentation of himself as a re-created Sidney. Putting his famous (to some, infamous) self-portrait in such a context can resolve some of the critical confusion surrounding a passage that to many has seemed egregiously self-pitying.[24] Shelley encapsulates the entire Spenserian revisionism of *Adonais* here by picturing himself as a poet wrought out of the "eternal portions" of Spenser's vision, as they lie embodied in the mixture of truth and error that is the Sidney of *Astrophel*. Both Sidney and Shelley are gentle shepherd-poets, Sidney derived from that "gentlest race that ever shepheard bore" (line 2) and Shelley one of "that gentle band" of shepherd-poets who mourn for Keats (line 299). Both devote themselves to the poetry of love, Sidney hymning "layes of love" (line 35) and Shelley appearing himself as "a Power . . . a Love" (line 281). Both gain insight and achievement in lands, perhaps landscapes of the imagination, beyond their conventional homes, Sidney pursuing his craft in "forreine soyle" (line 92) and Shelley singing "in the accents of an unknown land" (line 301). These parallels are most significant for the way that Shelley changes Sidney, or creates himself by freeing the eternal part of

24. Wasserman tries to defend the passage by emphasizing Shelley's desire for transcendence (*Shelley* 321). But that reading still fails to account for the qualifying oxymorons by which Shelley presents himself as both strong and weak, a "Power / Girt round with weakness" (lines 281–82).

Sidney (and Spenser, of course) from error. Spenser presents two Sidneys, the vulnerable shepherd-poet and the "immortall spirit" (*Doleful Lay*, line 61), clearly giving privilege to the latter. Shelley, however, restores the frail Sidney and merges him into the transcendent one, in effect bringing Spenser's vision down from heaven and folding it into the world of time, chance, and mutability. Such a maneuver is for Shelley not only a process of extracting "[a] portion of the Eternal" from Spenser in order to shape his own vision (line 340) but also the consummate step in correcting his own past visionary extremism by disciplining Spenser's.

This aim of recovering Sidney/Spenser's participation in the "tickle" world from his transcendentalism helps explain the tapestry of vulnerability that makes up Shelley's portrait of himself. Where the mortal Sidney reveals his weakness in his "palled face" (line 163), for instance, Shelley appears as a "frail Form, / A phantom among men" (lines 271–72). Sidney gasps out his pain in "wasting breath" (line 165), just as Shelley exhales his suffering in a "partial mone" (line 298). The "flowers and grylonds" (line 153) that have faded from Sidney's wounded body are like the "faded violets" and "pansies overblown" that crown Shelley's head (lines 289–90). (Notably, Shelley does *not* wear the eternal "daintie violets" that deck the heavenly Sidney [*Doleful Lay*, line 72].) Where Stella's "fairest face" smiles down on Sidney's rent flowers (line 155), moreover, the "killing sun smiles brightly" on Shelley's "withering flowers" (lines 286–87). The wounded Sidney is "Unpitied, unplaynd, of foe or frend" (line 136), just as Shelley is "companionless . . . neglected and apart" (lines 272, 296). Finally, where Sidney is "deformed" with "crudled blood and filthie gore" (line 152), Shelley's suffering is revealed in his "branded and ensanguined brow" (line 305). It is this very "dying into life" on Shelley's part, this deepening of Sidney/Spenser's frailty, that ultimately enables him to participate in the eternal dualities of the "One." Hence where Spenser would finally separate the two Sidneys, and favor "Sweet without sowre, and honny without gall" (line 26), Shelley integrates them in the various oxymorons of his self-portrait: "A pardlike Spirit . . . A Love in desolation masked . . . a Power / Girt round with weakness" (lines 280–82). The double-sided poet who emerges out of the veils of Spenser's error is "the knight of the shield of shadow and the lance of gossamer," whose "Power" comes from his "weakness," whose vision of eternity is grounded in that "direfull stound" from which Spenser yearns to escape. It seems a capping point of revisionary brilliance, if we follow out this pattern of re-creations, that Shelley's wound comes metaphorically from "the hunter's dart" (line 297). Sidney, of course, is the unparagoned hunter in the "brutish" wilderness of *Astrophel*, who is also Spenser voyaging through this wide world of change. For Sidney to be wounded by his own dart, when he reappears as Shelley in *Adonais*, is thus for Spenser to be wounded by his own humanity, or turned into a "Power" by Shelley's recovery of his "weakness."[25]

Rewriting the hunt motif of *Astrophel* also helps Shelley integrate his redemption of Spenser's dualism with his recovery of Spenser's ideas about the flux of poetic influence. Much as Spenser is preoccupied with the immortality of the soul in *Astrophel*, his own version of the traditional hunting accident in the Adonis legend reveals that he is also deeply concerned with the continuity of poetic transmission. That accident, as it is presented in *Astrophel*, has all the rudiments of an allegory about Ignorance's attack on culture. Sidney emerges in the beginning of *Astrophel* as the epitome of cultural refinement, consummately skilled in statesmanship, soldiery, and the fine arts: "For both in deeds and words he nourtred was, / Both wise and hardie" (lines 71–72). Shelley only needed to consider Spenser's own quarrels with those Blatant Beasts like Burleigh who would depress art to realize that Sidney's hunting foray against "the brutish nation" (line 98) could be read as the "contention" waged by the "kings of thought" in *Adonais* against their "time's decay" (lines 430–31), against the likes of Stephen Gosson in Sidney's case or the *Quarterly Review* in Shelley's own. Hence the mortal wound inflicted on Sidney by a "cruell beast" (line 116) is not simply an allusion to his battlefield experience in Flanders or to the precariousness of human existence; in this special allegory, it is also an emblem of those error-ridden disruptions in cultural progress that Shelley was trying to understand and redeem in the *Defence*. Sidney's enshrinement in a heaven ringing with sweet carols, where he inspires his shepherd followers to sing in his honor, also becomes a celebration of that endless flux of decomposition and refinement through which poetic "effluence" is transmitted across the ages. At least, that is the way Shelley sees it when he depicts the insidious reviewers who destroyed

---

25. This transformation of Spenserian conditionality must be counted as one of the supreme examples of Romantic antiallegorical allegory. Earl Schulze, recently discussing Shelley's efforts to "mount allegory against allegory," argues that "Shelley's strategy is to undermine traditional allegorical method, which presupposes a world of stable values, in order to free the mind . . . from the gross delusion through which it dooms itself" (34). This is the "strategy" that operates at the highest level of Romantic Spenserianism, and we would be hard-pressed to find a more complete embodiment of it than *Adonais*.

Keats as "the unpastured dragon in his den" and then proceeds to immortalize Keats in a heaven of poets from which he "Beacons" to his followers (lines 238, 495). Shelley knows, however, that Spenser did not clearly understand this eternal portion of his own allegory, having submerged it in his more conventional disquisition on the immortality of the soul. Recovering his buried truth about the intersection of mutability and eternity in the dynamics of poetic transmission thus becomes for Shelley one and the same with redeeming the duality of vision from his Christian allegory.

Such a recovery of Spenser's influence theory matters deeply to Shelley's sense of his own relationship with the mighty dead, supplying the basis for much of the passionate drama of sorrow and consolation at the heart of *Adonais*. How much is at stake may be judged by the focus and intensity of Shelley's opening revisions of *Astrophel*. At the beginning of *Astrophel*, Spenser hints at his concern with cultural transmission by contrasting Sidney's bright promise, outlined in a sustained record of his youthful accomplishments, with his rudely abbreviated career, lamented in the opening invocation to fellow shepherds. The issues here of poetic progress and discontinuity are only latent, however, as the first section of the elegy relapses into a fairly conventional history of Sidney's pastoral deeds. Shelley immediately draws out and intensifies the urgent question buried in this allegory of Sidney's thwarted development: is the creative power of the giants from the past, like Sidney's burgeoning talent, lost forever to succeeding generations, never to be recuperated? Agonizing over the death of Keats, and its seeming affirmation of that question, Shelley yearns to believe in the eternal self-renewal of poetic tradition. Keats's "fate and fame," he declares, "shall be / An echo and a light unto eternity," just as Milton's "clear Sprite / Yet reigns o'er earth." The unbroken light of such poets will beam "till the Future dares / Forget the past" (lines 7–9, 35–36). In that implication of what the future might dare, however, lies a great apprehension of creative discontinuity, which Shelley finds increasingly manifested in Keats's untimely death. With a few monumental exceptions, all that remains of the past is the inferior taper light of minor poets burning "through that night of time / In which suns perished." Most sublime poets "Have sunk, extinct in their refulgent prime" (lines 40–43), and Keats begins to appear as the most recent example of this hard fate. His music of love, which Shelley would like to commend as a sustaining power for all generations, no longer travels "from kindling brain to brain," for his "passion-winged Ministers of thought" have died into the eclipse of "cold night." The sword of his poetry, instead of melting the sheath of time and convention as the *Defence* would have it, has been "consumed before the sheath . . . quenched in a most cold repose" (lines 74, 107, 178–80). Such a doom does not simply suggest that Keats and the tradition he had come to represent have been forgotten; rather, it raises for Shelley the much more disturbing possibility of losing access to the "kindling" power of that tradition, being cut adrift as a belated poet in the dark night of time.

The irony here, as Shelley grieves over his precarious artistic inheritance, is that his very engagement with the issue of poetic transmission, by clarifying Spenser's focus in *Astrophel,* actually contributes to the disruption of poetic continuity. It exposes Spenser's blindness and thus lessens his light. Yet in that loss is also a gain, for Spenser's eternal spirit is being reilluminated from out of the darkness of his own error. That point is not yet obvious to the mourning poet of *Adonais.* But the image of Keats exhaling breath and dissolving in order to buy a "grave among the eternal" (line 58) suggests that Spenser's life-through-death passage into *Adonais* is beginning to enlighten Shelley's own mind about the dynamics of poetic history. That journey inspires a full revelation when Shelley unveils the truth about literary influence buried in Spenser's shepherd song. Clorinda's song about Christian dying into immortal life becomes in Shelley's procession of shepherds a hymn about the eternal flux of cultural transmission. The sequence begins when Urania, without fully comprehending her words, succinctly articulates the dialectic of poetic progress. As a "godlike mind soars forth" (line 258), she declares, its brilliance is dimmed by the ephemera of the day. Its sinking, however, augurs the removal of its transitory coverings and the enshrinement of its eternal spirit among "its kindred lamps," which glow throughout the "awful night" of time and change (line 261). This testament to poetic energy coming out of dissolution is then memorialized in the appearance of the shepherd-poets who mourn Keats. Byron, who had appeared two stanzas earlier asserting his strong identity, now comes to grieve in a self-effacing manner, "veiling all the lightenings of his song / In sorrow" (lines 267–68). Moore and Hunt similarly curtail their selfhood in pathetic gestures of mourning. Yet it is precisely such dissolutions of the self that make them into "enduring monuments" (line 266). This is the eternal truth about the dynamics of poetic history that a redeemed Spenser, one who is dying into the eternal life of *Adonais,* gives to Shelley.

It is in Shelley's controversial self-portrait that his meditation on that process and its relation to his engagement with Spenser reaches an access of understanding. While this passage emblematizes his idea of poetic vision, as we have seen, it also marks a peak of enlightenment about his own situation within the whole process of literary change. His most plangent quotation of *Astrophel* occurs at the climax of his self-portrait, and it expresses his new understanding of how his dialogue with Spenser manifests the deepest truths of poetic transmission. He specifically echoes a passage near the end of *Astrophel* about lamenting our own eventual decline in the deaths of others: "Thus do we weep and wail, and wear our eies, / Mourning in others, our own miseries" (lines 311–12). Emerging in *Adonais* to mourn Keats in precisely this way, Shelley appears as one "Who in another's fate now wept his own" (line 300). This is the only direct, or nearly direct, quotation of Spenser in all of Shelley's poetry. Its great significance lies in the way it epitomizes for him not only his particular conversation with Spenser but the essential relation among all eternal poets. That is a relation, or a "fate," based on endless decompositions in the very process of refinement that binds together all poets in their episodes within time's "great poem." To mourn Spenser's death is to correct him, which is also to make him eternal. The same may be said of Keats, who is also mourned and "corrected" in *Adonais*, as well as of all the other eternals whom Shelley counts as his forebears. The same, finally, may be said of Shelley, himself, in his relation to his own successors. Thus he can see his own future of eternal life through death in the fates of Keats and Spenser, which further explains why he presents himself as a "Power" in "weakness" and as a Christ-figure who dies to be reborn.[26]

This insight, like inspired readings of the eternal significance of Christ's death, is both sorrowful and redemptive. It ultimately carries Shelley to the brink of consolation for Keats's death and into his most significant modification of *Astrophel*, which is his insertion of one extra stanza in *Adonais* at the parallel position where Spenser concludes his lament for Sidney in stanza 36 of *Astrophel*. Stanza 37 of *Adonais*, instead of veering into a consolation, as Spenser's next stanza does, pinpoints and accepts the cause of Keats's death. That swerve from *Astrophel* actually consolidates everything Shelley was re-

26. I do not agree with John Archer's contention that Shelley increasingly turns away from the cultural past, but Archer's brilliant point about Shelley's proleptic vision of himself being refined and reconstituted in future poets makes an apt conclusion to my reading of his dialectical theory of poetic influence: "Shelley's poetic theory is characterized by a radical prolepsis rather than an awareness of the burden of the past. He would not have been surprised to find his poetry, or his sections of the great cyclic poem, living on in certain passages of Browning or Yeats" (271).

covering from Spenser about the dynamics of poetic transmission. He comes now to accept Keats's killers, the enemies of culture, as instruments, however unwitting, in the process of dissolution and cleansing that bestows everlasting fame. "But be thyself, and know thyself to be!" Shelley confronts them, "And ever at thy season be thou free / To spill the venom when thy fangs o'erflow" (lines 327–30). The implication is that such "o'erflowing" of criticism, as destructive as it may seem, ultimately helps pare away all that is mortal in Keats. Shelley furthers that process himself when he announces in the preface to *Adonais* his "known repugnance to the narrow principles of taste on which several of . . . [Keats's] earlier compositions were modelled" (*PW* 430). What killed Keats, therefore, has a "season," a necessary function in that cycle of poetic relations that ensures his immortality. It also takes a killing of Spenser, Shelley knows by now, to eternalize him as a harbinger of that truth, a truth that reconciles Shelley to the disruptions of poetic history and inspires him to proceed through the great sweep of consolation that closes *Adonais*.

If we follow this line of revisionism to the end of *Adonais*, we can see how its rapturous conclusion both re-creates Spenser's "hevenly quires" (*Doleful Lay*, line 63) as a pantheon of eternal poets and proclaims Shelley's own dedication to the perpetual rhythms of transmission that have built up their episodic poem. At the end of *Astrophel*, Sidney appears in an eternal heaven of saints that gleams through the "dole" and darkness of worldly change (*Doleful Lay*, line 94). Such Christian Neoplatonism, as Curran has argued, is transformed in Shelley's "One" into a vision of everlasting creative flux ("*Adonais* in Context" 169, 179). It is a flux, I would like to add, directly associated with Shelley's idea of poetic history's dialectical continuity. His descriptions of change and permanence in "the One" strongly recall his particular ways of characterizing the interplay of loss and gain in poetic transmission. The mutable shapes of temporal life fade like "shadows" and dying flames in the manner of Keats's poetic dissolution. Worldly achievement, like his, is "eclipsed" in a temporary veil. But also like the eternal portion of his endeavor, the unextinguished spirit of the One shines on through the night of time (lines 461, 389–92). The imagery used to depict the continuity of this spirit even more strikingly intersects with Shelley's method of conceptualizing poetic transmission. Keats "sleeps" to "wake" in the One with "the enduring dead" of poetic history. The part of them that endures is a "portion of the Eternal, which must glow / Through time and change." Their light "kindles the Universe," passing the "transmitted effluence" of their vision across the boundaries of time and chance. By "waging contention with their time's decay," casting off their mortal shrouds, they have become all "of the past . . . that cannot pass away." They are the "Eternal," the same name given in the *Defence* to the undying makers of history's cyclical poem (lines 336–40, 478, 407, 431–32, 495). These phrases are so deeply interwoven with the rhetoric of Shelley's influence theory that we must consider the flux of the One, whatever else it may represent for him, as the culminating symbol of his dialectical poetic history.

Such a reading seems confirmed by Shelley's specific way of populating the kingdom of the One. He fills it with poets who tragically died before consummating their promise, which may simply be a way of paying a last tribute to Keats's special fate. Yet there is something more calculated about his presentation of Chatterton, Sidney, and Lucan as the "inheritors of unfulfilled renown" (line 397). He imagines their "mortal thought" fading into oblivion, their renown incomplete, before their eternal spirits are redeemed (line 398). This is precisely the way he characterizes Keats's fate, as a model of poetic history, throughout *Adonais*. The culmination of that pattern in Shelley's eternity suggests that his vision of the One is a revelation of the workings of cultural transmission, as epitomized in the metaphor of a young poet's abbreviated career. Like Keats and his young compeers, the individual poet must die or give up the "mortal" part of his work before gaining eternal life. Thus his achievement, like Keats's, must inevitably be unfinished, to be completed only in the perpetual elaborations of the literary tradition that he absorbs, continues, and proleptically inspires. His works are to that tradition what Keats's short burst of creativity is to the overall achievement of all poets: one episode, from which "new relations are developed," in that ongoing poem "which all poets . . . have built up since the beginning of the world."

Shelley's final acceptance of this destiny at the end of *Adonais* helps explain the suicidal overtones and the complicated balance of ecstasy and apprehension with which the poem concludes. Giving himself over to the dialectical rhythms of poetic history means surmounting "the eclipsing Curse" of time and birth, becoming one with "the Eternal" (lines 480, 495). But that voyage beyond "cold mortality" (line 486) entails tremendous self-sacrifice, the death of Shelley's own temporal art and the submission of his eternal parts to a process of ongoing purgation in the future cycles of literary transmission. Hence the contradictions of being redeemed or "borne" away "darkly," of experiencing apocalyptic rapture along with a fearful sense of loss. "I am borne darkly, fearfully, afar," Shelley thus apprehends the death of his mortal part. But in that loss he can

also envision himself purified and made one with the "Eternal" poets
of "Heaven" (lines 492–95). It is an apotheosis, finally, that participates in the basic psychological dualism of *Adonais,* through which
the mutable intersects with the eternal in a rhythm, like the dance of
the earth and moon in *Prometheus Unbound,* of endless and harmonious contraries.

All this may seem a long way from *Astrophel.* But if Peacock had
been on the scene to caution once again, "That was not the lesson
which Spenser intended to convey," Shelley no doubt would have
repeated himself: "Perhaps not, it is the lesson which he conveys to
me." Spenser had been conveying this particular lesson to him at
least as far back as the *Defence.* It was a lesson to be extracted not just
from *Astrophel,* but also from *The Ruines of Time, The Shepheardes Calender, The Faerie Queene,* in short, from the preoccupation with poetic
influence and continuity that pervades the whole of Spenser's art.
Perhaps most significant, it was also a teaching that intersected with
Spenser's other lesson about the duality of poetic vision, which he
had been conveying more and more to Shelley over the last several
years. Shelley's way of receiving those lessons had also changed radically from his earlier championship of the Giant. Instead of just tear-
ing at Spenser's veils as before, he now uncovered the truths hidden
within, freeing himself from error in the process of absorbing them
as eternal lineaments for his own poetic vision. By drawing out and
uniting those interconnected truths about the duality of poetic vision
and the flux of cultural transmission, he finally created in *Adonais* a
poetics of experience that authorizes its own continuity with the
products and processes of tradition. It is for that reason arguably the
most successful contribution to Romanticism's second Renaissance,
and it comes out of the the the most sophisticated integration, ever, of
those two portions of Spenser's genius that had always seemed so
important to the Romantics' renewal of the past: his fluidity as a
transmitter of poetic "effluence" and his intellectual relevance as a
painter of the mind's chiaroscuro. With *Adonais,* more capaciously
than anywhere else, Spenser's song becomes the empowering voice
of the present.

If we are to conclude that Spenser's song reaches its Romantic
apotheosis in *Adonais,* it seems only fitting to end with a few salient
points about how the timbre of his music is transmitted into the
prosodic and linguistic rhythms of Shelley's poetry. Here Shelley
and Keats, notwithstanding all they shared in their evolving Spenserianism, finally part ways, with Keats moving toward an ever-
increasing directness of style and Shelley growing more and more self-
consciously stylized. The ever-deepening duality in their Spenserian

poetics should reveal to us how surprisingly like-minded they can be, despite their very different creative temperaments, in their responses to the most pressing cultural concerns of their time. But this last contrast in their Spenserian styles ultimately tells us how Shelley undertakes a more elaborate revisionary task of building up a theory of poetic influence and an articulate style for it.

Adonais can seem quite un-Spenserian because of Shelley's persisting resistance, probably strengthened now by Keats's example in The Eve of St. Agnes, to Spenserian archaisms and expletives. But these were only Spenser's mortal wrappings as Shelley now understood, the mask of his time and place, to be cast off in order to preserve the eternal portion of his style. Shelley had come by now to consider the highly formalized styles of the great poetic traditions—the choral language of Greek tragedy, for instance, and the ritualistic lamentations of the elegiac tradition—as the eternal language of time's cyclical poem, the rhetoric of poetic history that stands beyond the prejudices of time and place. He was assembling those rhetorical formalities into what he called a "highly wrought" style (LPBS 2:294) that would be appropriate for his own episode in history's "great poem." Adonais is one of the most "highly wrought" of English poems in this respect, especially in its duplications of the ritualistic mourning of Bion and Moschus. Much of the high formality that has impressed so many readers of the poem actually comes from Shelley's sophisticated integration of Spenserian patterns of assonance and alliteration—the formal, eternal portion of Spenser's musicality, as Shelley heard it. His own incorporation of that music into the pageantry of sound that complements the ritualistic processions of Adonais is as deft as it is "highly wrought":

"Wake, melancholy Mother, wake and weep!" (line 20)

"Most musical of mourners, weep anew!" (line 37)

"Nor to himself Narcissus, as to both" (line 141)

"Made bare his branded and ensanguined brow," (line 305)

"Which wields the world with never-wearied love"

(line 377)[27]

27. The lines above these verses trace the patterns of Shelley's assonance, and the lines below indicate his alliterative effects.

Leigh Hunt may very well have been thinking about these effects when he said that Spenser would have been pleased with *Adonais* (quoted in Silverman 26). Without making the poem seem obsolescent, they give it a quintessentially Spenserian character—the stylistic character of his ritualistic part, we should add, that is for all time.[28]

Perhaps the greatest technical achievement of *Adonais*, however, is its condensed, revisionary form of the same metrical dualities that Keats found in Spenser and adapted so effectively for *The Eve of St. Agnes*. Shelley had intensified Spenser's prosodic contraries before, to deepen his vision of duality, but never in such a compact form. That heightened tension is maintained throughout *Adonais*, always punctuating and elaborating the poem's continual recovery of Spenser's mental and cultural contraries. The opening threat to tradition in Milton's symbolic death, for instance, is registered in a jarring measure whose abrupt stops intensify Spenser's most turbulent rhythms and suggest an even greater threat to cultural continuity in the belated, divisive age of the nineteenth century:

> Most musical of mourners, weep again! //
> Lament anew, // Urania! // —He died, //
> Who was the Sire of an immortal strain, //
> Blind, // old, // and lonely, // when his country's pride, //
> The priest, // the slave, // and the liberticide, //
> Trampled and mocked with many a loathed rite
> Of lust and blood.
>
> (lines 28–34)

---

28. The same point applies to Shelley's integration of Spenserian language into a timeless speech of the tribe of all English eternal poets. He does import, as Keats had done in *The Eve of St. Agnes*, some venerable-sounding Spenserian words that would not have seemed utterly outdated in the nineteenth century: "sprite," "lorn," "brake," "brere," and "hoary." But he is more concerned with cultivating a formalized language of pageantry that comes in part from Spenser but could be equally at home in the loftier passages of Shakespeare, Milton, and Wordsworth. The result is a diction both traditional and modern, the timeless speech of generations of High English poets heard in stylized phrases like "obscure compeers," "refulgent prime," "ambrosial rest," "garlands sere," "magic mantles rent," "unprofitable strife," "Invulnerable nothings." The majestic flow of these phrases moves and sounds like the very kind of timeless, ritualistic processions that march through *Adonais:*

> And others came . . . Desires and Adorations,
> Winged Persuasions and veiled Destinies,
> Splendours, and Glooms, and glimmering Incarnations
> Of hopes and fears, and twilight Phantasies
> (lines 109–13)

As Shelley yearns to believe in a continuity that transcends these disruptions, the meter relaxes into the sort of even patterns that commonly balance Spenser's couplet endings. Hence Milton's immortal union with Homer and Dante is accompanied by the metrical regularity of the following lines:

> he went, unterrified,
> Into the gulph of death; but his clear Sprite
> Yet reigns o'er earth; the third among the sons of light.
> (lines 34–36)

But Shelley frequently disrupts even his couplets, the conventional center of harmony in Spenser's stanza, to reinforce the looming threat of cultural annihilation that dominates the opening segment of *Adonais*. Where his stanzas might be expected to strain most for metrical resolution, therefore, they often fall into these more extreme versions of Spenser's discord:

> Died on the promise of the fruit, is waste;
> The broken lily lies—the storm is overpast.
> (lines 53–54)

> Into a shadow of all sounds:—a drear
> Murmur, between their songs, is all the woodmen hear.
> (lines 134–35)

> Leave me not!' cried Urania: her distress
> Roused Death: Death rose and smiled, and met her vain caress.
> (lines 224–25)

Nowhere is this harmony of revisionary methods more evident than in Shelley's climactic reworking of Spenser's Christian cosmography. As Shelley's dualistic vision of poetic creativity and his dialectical notion of cultural transmission coalesce in his portrait of the "One" and the "many," his heightening of Spenser's metrical tension becomes particularly condensed. Many readers of *Adonais* have been enraptured with the ecstatic mellifluence of the concluding stanzas. Yet others, like Angela Leighton, hear unsettling discords in Shelley's final affirmations. The contradiction is essential to the revisionism of *Adonais*, whose most extreme metrical clashes now culminate Shelley's ongoing extension and enrichment of Spenser's dualities. Stanza 44, which celebrates the eternal life of great poets, is a model of unbroken euphony:

The splendours of the firmament of time
May be eclipsed, but are extinguished not;
Like stars to their appointed height they climb,
And death is a low mist which cannot blot
The brightness it may veil. When lofty thought
Lifts a young heart above its mortal lair,
And love and life contend in it, for what
Shall be its earthly doom, the dead live there
And move like winds of light on dark and stormy air.
(lines 388–97)

But jarring stops fill the very next stanza, itself a catalogue of human and cultural disruptions that are a basic part of eternal processes:

The inheritors of unfulfilled renown
Rose from their thrones, // built beyond mortal thought, //
Far in the Unapparent. // Chatterton
Rose pale,— // his solemn agony had not
Yet faded from him; // Sidney, // as he fought
And as he fell and as he lived and loved
Sublimely mild, // a spirit without a spot, //
Arose; // and Lucan, // by his death approved: //
(lines 397–405)

In an even more dramatic gathering of tensions, Shelley's famous vision of the One moves from intense metrical discord in its body to the relaxed closing hexameter—"The glory they transfuse with fitting truth to speak" (line 468)—and then to increased disruption in the following questions:

Life, // like a dome of many-coloured glass, //
Stains the white radiance of Eternity,
Until Death tramples it to fragments.— // Die, //
If thou wouldst be with that which thou dost seek! //
Follow where all is fled!— // Rome's azure sky, //
Flowers, // ruins, // statues, // music, // words, // are
    weak.
The glory they transfuse with fitting truth to speak.

Why linger, // why turn back, // why shrink, // my Heart?
(lines 462–69)

These ever-mounting rhythmical clashes help explain why *Adonais* can seem to end both apprehensively and ecstatically, disrupting poetic traditions and conventions that it also seems to honor, declaring a vision of unity that it simultaneously deconstructs. The very dualities of experience that it finally affirms are fundamentally embedded in its stylistic contraries and—one final turn of the screw—in the revisionary relation of those contraries to the Spenserian paradigm and its buried truths.

Because it watches itself so successfully making Spenser's accents into the voice of a new song, *Adonais* may be read as both the encapsulation and the completion of the Romantics' Spenserian project. It was a project, we may now conclude, central to the shaping of Romanticism's dialectical poetics and particularly important to its building of a second Renaissance. It could inspire stunning creative breakthroughs or become a cause of error, leading the Romantics down the errant pathways of abortive epics. But it was always close to the most compelling concerns of their art and, perhaps most significant, it helped them find themselves as poets who arrived late, but not necessarily too late, in a great tradition. It was particularly enabling for Keats and Shelley, helping them create a modern vision of experience and a sophisticated lyrical poetics responsible for what some have called the Romantics' most successful integrations of the past, "the most perfect" of their poems (Curran, "*Adonais* in Context" 181). Considering how much Spenser assisted in their renewal of the first Renaissance, it seems fitting to discover in *Adonais* their most succinct and poignant expression of how poetic influence works. From "kindling brain to brain," the past lives on in the art of the present that it inspires. But just as it is the death of Keats that "animates the creations" of Joseph Severn's pencil (*PW* 431), so it takes a lessening of the past to ensure and make room for its continuity in the refinements of the present. The Romantics' reception of Spenser, especially in the works of Keats and Shelley, is their best testament of how that process works. *Adonais* is its crowning song, a hymn that so many English poets had been building up since the beginning of Spenserianism.

Works Cited

Addison, Joseph. *Epistle to Sacheverell*. Chalmers, *Works* 9: 529–30.

Aikin, John, ed. *The Works of the British Poets*. Vol. 2. Philadelphia, 1819.

Allott, Miriam, ed. *Keats: The Complete Poems*. London: Longman, 1970.

Alpers, Paul J., ed. *Edmund Spenser*. Harmondsworth: Penguin, 1969.

———. *The Poetry of The Faerie Queene*. 1967. Columbia: University of Missouri Press, 1982.

Archer, John. "Authority in Shelley." *Studies in Romanticism* 26 (1987): 259–73.

Baker, Carlos. *Shelley's Major Poetry*. Princeton: Princeton University Press, 1948.

———. "Spenser and Shelley." Diss. Princeton University, 1939.

———. "Spenser, the Eighteenth Century and Queen Mab." *Modern Language Quarterly* 2 (1941): 79–92.

Bate, Walter Jackson. *The Burden of the Past*. New York: Norton, 1970.

———. *John Keats*. London: Chatto & Windus, 1979.

Beattie, James. *Dissertations*. London, 1778.

———. *The Life and Poetry of James Beattie*. Ed. Sir William Forbes. Vol. 1. London, 1824. 2 vols.

Bell, John, ed. *Bell's Classical Arrangement of Fugitive Poetry*. London, 1789–1810. 18 vols.

———, ed. *The Poetical Works of Edmund Spenser*. The Poets of Great Britain. Edinburgh, 1778. 8 vols.

Berger, Harry. *The Allegorical Temper*. New Haven: Yale University Press, 1957.

———. "The Spenserian Dynamics." *Studies in English Literature* 8 (1968): 1–18.

———. "Two Spenserian Retrospects: The Antique Temple of Venus and the Primitive Marriage of Rivers." *Texas Studies in Literature and Language* 19 (1968): 5–25.

Bhattachereje, M. M. *Keats and Spenser*. Calcutta: University of Calcutta Press, 1944.

Birch, Thomas, ed. *The Fairie Queene*. Vol. 1. London, 1751. 3 vols.

Bloom, Harold. *The Anxiety of Influence*. London: Oxford University Press, 1973.

———. *A Map of Misreading*. London: Oxford University Press, 1975.

———. *Poetry and Repression*. New Haven: Yale University Press, 1976.

————. *Shelley's Mythmaking*. Ithaca: Cornell University Press, 1959.

Bohme, Traugott. *Spenser's literarisches Nachleben bis zu Shelley*. Berlin: Mayer & Muller, 1911.

Bond, R. P. *English Burlesque Poetry 1700–1750*. Cambridge, Mass.: Harvard University Press, 1932.

Boyse, Samuel. *The Vision of Patience*. 1741. Bell, *Bell's Classical Arrangement of Fugitive Poetry* 11: 49–60.

Boyd, Henry Hugh. *The Woodman's Tale, after the Manner of Spenser*. London, 1805.

Bradley, Laurel. "Eighteenth-Century Paintings and Illustrations of Spenser's *Faerie Queene:* A Study in Taste." *Marsyas* 20 (1979–80): 31–51.

Brewe, Claude C. *Shelley and Mary in 1817*. London: Keats-Shelley Memorial Foundation, 1971.

Brogan, Howard O. "The Cap and Bells, or . . . The Jealousies." *Bulletin of the New York Public Library* 77 (1974): 298–313.

Byron, George Gordon, Lord. *Byron's Letters and Journals*. Ed. Leslie A. Marchand. Vol. 4. Cambridge, Mass: Belknap Press, 1973–82. 12 vols.

————. *Childe Harold's Pilgrimage*. *Lord Byron: The Complete Poetical Works*. Ed. Jerome McGann. Vol. 2. Oxford: Oxford University Press, 1980–86.

————. *The Critical Heritage: Byron*. Ed. Andrew Rutherford. New York: Barnes & Noble, 1970.

————. *The Works of Lord Byron*. Ed. Rowland E. Prothers. Vol. 9. London: John Murray, 1904. 13 vols.

Cameron, Kenneth Neill, ed. *The Esdaile Notebook: A Volume of Early Poems by Percy Bysshe Shelley*. New York: Knopf, 1964.

Campbell, Thomas. *Gertrude of Wyoming*. London, 1809.

————, ed. *Specimens of the British Poets*. Vol. 1. London, 1819. 7 vols.

Chalmers, Alexander. "Life of Spenser." Chalmers, *Works* 3: 3–11.

————, ed. *The Works of the English Poets*. London, 1810. 21 vols.

"Chalmers's English Poets." *Quarterly Review* 12 (1814): 60–75.

Cheney, Donald. *Spenser's Image of Nature*. New Haven: Yale University Press, 1966.

Church, Ralph, ed. *The Faerie Queene*. 4 vols. London, 1758.

Cibber, Theophilus. *The Lives of the Poets*. Vol. 1. London, 1753. 4 vols.

Clairmont, Claire. *The Journals of Claire Clairmont*. Ed. Marion Kingston Stocking. Cambridge: Harvard University Press, 1968.

Clarke, Charles Cowden. *Recollections of Charles and Mary Cowden Clarke*. London, 1878.

Coleridge, John Taylor. "Laon and Cythna. The Revolt of Islam." *Quarterly Review* (1819): 460–71.

Coleridge, Samuel Taylor. *Coleridge's Literary Criticism*. Ed. J. W. Mackhail. London: Henry Frowde, 1908.

————. *The Collected Works of Samuel Taylor Coleridge*. Gen. Ed. Kathleen Coburn. Princeton: Princeton University Press, 1969– . 13 vols. to date.

————. *Conversations at Trinity*. Ed. C. Wilmott. London, 1836.

————. *The Literary Remains of Samuel Taylor Coleridge*. Ed. Henry Nelson Coleridge. London, 1836.

————. *Coleridge's Miscellaneous Criticism.* Ed. Thomas Raysor. Cambridge: Harvard University Press, 1936.

————. *The Notebooks of Samuel Taylor Coleridge.* Vol 3. Ed. Kathleen Coburn. Princeton: Princeton University Press, 1957– . 4 vols. to date.

————. *Seven Lectures on Shakespeare and Milton by the late S. T. Coleridge.* Ed. John Payne Collier. London, 1856.

————. *The Unpublished Letters of Samuel Taylor Coleridge.* Ed. Leslie Griggs. New Haven: Yale University Press, 1932.

Collins, William. *Ode on the Poetical Character. The Poems of Gray, Collins, and Goldsmith.* Ed Roger Lonsdale. New York: Longman, 1969. 427–35.

Cory, Herbert E. *The Critics of Edmund Spenser.* 1911. New York: Haskell House, 1964.

————. "Spenser, Thomson, and Romanticism." *PMLA* 26 (1911): 51–91.

Crabbe, George. *The Poetical Works of George Crabbe.* Ed. A. J. Carlyle and R. M. Carlyle. London: Henry Frowde, 1908.

Craik, George, ed. *Spenser and His Poetry.* 3 vols. London, 1845.

"Critical Observations on the Writings of the most celebrated Original Geniuses in Poetry. By W. Duff." *Monthly Review* 43 (1770): 305–7.

Crompton, Georgia. *The Conditions of Creatures.* New Haven: Yale University Press, 1974.

Croxall, Samuel. *An Ode Humbly Inscrib'd to the King.* London, 1714.

————. *Another Original Canto of Spencer's Fairy Queen.* London, 1714.

Cullen, Patrick. *Infernal Triad: The Flesh, the World, and the Devil in Spenser and Milton.* Princeton: Princeton University Press, 1974.

Cummings, R. M., ed. *The Critical Heritage: Spenser.* New York: Barnes & Noble, 1971.

Curran, Stuart. "*Adonais* in Context." *Shelley Revalued: Essays from the Gregynog Conference.* Ed. Kelvin Everst. Totowa, N.J.: Barnes & Noble, 1983. 165–82.

————. *Poetic Form and British Romanticism.* Oxford: Oxford University Press, 1986.

————. *Shelley's Annus Mirabilis.* San Marino: Huntington Library, 1975.

————. "Spenser and Shelley." *The Spenser Encyclopedia.* Ed. A. C. Hamilton. Toronto: University of Toronto Press (forthcoming).

Davies, Phillips C. "A Check List of Poems, 1595 to 1833, Entirely or Partly Written in the Spenserian Stanza." *Bulletin of the New York Public Library* 77 (1974): 314–28.

De Maar, Harko Gerrit. *Elizabethan Romance in the Eighteenth Century.* Zalt: N. V. Van De Garde, 1924.

DeNeef, A. Leigh. *Spenser and the Motives of Metaphor.* Durham: Duke University Press, 1982.

Denton, Thomas. *The House of Superstition.* 1762. *A Collection of the Most Esteemed Pieces of Poetry . . . By the Late Moses Mendez and Other Contributors to Dodsley's Collection.* London, 1770. 225–30.

Dermody, Thomas. *The Harp of Erin, Containing the Poetical Works of the Late Thomas Dermody.* London, 1807.

Dickstein, Morris. *Keats and His Poetry.* Chicago: University of Chicago Press, 1971.

Downman, Hugh. *The Land of the Muses.* Edinburgh, 1768.

"The Dramatic Works of John Ford." *Edinburgh Review* 36 (1811): 275–86.

Duff, William. *Critical Observations*. London, 1770.

Dundas, Judith. *The Spider and the Bee: The Artistry of Spenser's Fairy Queene*. Urbana: University of Illinois Press, 1985.

Elliott, John R., ed. *The Prince of Poets: Essays on Edmund Spenser*. New York: New York University Press, 1968.

The Examiner Examin'd. London, 1713.

Finney, Claude. *The Evolution of Keats's Poetry*. Vol. 1. New York: Russell & Russell, 1936. 2 vols.

Flagg, John Sewell. *Prometheus Unbound and Hellas*. Salzburg: Institut für Englische Sprache und Literatur, 1972.

Fletcher, Angus. *Allegory: The Theory of a Symbolic Mode*. Ithaca: Cornell University Press, 1964.

Frushell, Richard C. "Spenser and the Eighteenth-Century Schools." *Spenser Studies* 7 (1986): 175–98.

———. "Spenser Imitations and Adaptations: 1660–1800." *The Spenser Encyclopedia*. Ed. A. C. Hamilton. Toronto: University of Toronto Press (forthcoming).

"Gertrude of Wyoming." *Quarterly Review* 1 (1809): 242–58.

Giamatti, A. Bartlett. *Play of Double Senses: Spenser's Faerie Queene*. Englewood Cliffs, N.J.: Prentice-Hall, 1975.

Gittings, Robert. *John Keats*. London: Heinemann, 1968.

———. *The Mask of Keats*. London: Heinemann, 1956.

Gleckner, Robert. *Blake and Spenser*. Baltimore: Johns Hopkins University Press, 1985.

———. *Blake's Prelude: Poetical Sketches*. Baltimore: Johns Hopkins University Press, 1982.

———. *Byron and the Ruins of Paradise*. Baltimore: Johns Hopkins University Press, 1967.

———. "Keats's 'How Many Bards' and Poetic Tradition." *Keats-Shelley Journal* 22 (1978): 14–22.

Godshalk, W. L. "Prior's Copy of Spenser's *Works*, 1679." *Papers of the Bibliographical Society of America* 61 (1967): 52–55.

Godwin, William. "Inkle and Yariko." *Four Early Pamphlets*. Ed. Burton R. Pollin. Gainesville, Fla.: Scholars' Facsimiles & Reprints, 1968.

———. *Life of Chaucer*. London, 1804.

———. *Uncollected Writings*. Gainesville, Fla.: Scholars' Facsimiles & Reprints, 1968.

Goldberg, Jonathan. *Endlesse Worke: Spenser and the Structures of Discourse*. Baltimore: Johns Hopkins University Press, 1981.

Goldsmith, Oliver. *The Miscellaneous Works of Oliver Goldsmith*. Ed. James Prior. Vol. 4. New York, 1855. 4 vols.

Gray, Thomas. *The Poems of Thomas Gray, William Collins, Oliver Goldsmith*. Ed. Roger Lonsdale. London: Longman, 1969.

Greenlaw, Edwin, et al., eds. *The Works of Edmund Spenser*. Baltimore: Johns Hopkins University Press, 1932–57. 11 vols.

Griffin, Dustin. *Regaining Paradise: Milton and the Eighteenth Century*. Cambridge: Cambridge University Press, 1986.

Grundy, Joan. "Keats and the Elizabethans." *John Keats: A Reassessment*. Ed. Kenneth Muir. Liverpool: Liverpool University Press, 1969. 1–19.

————. *The Spenserian Poets.* New York: St. Martin's Press, 1969.

Haller, William. *The Early Life of Robert Southey.* New York: Octagon Books, 1966.

Halpern, Martin. "Keats and the Spirit that Laughest." *Keats-Shelley Journal* 15 (1966): 69–86.

Hamilton, A. C. *The Structure of Allegory in The Faerie Queene.* Oxford: Clarendon Press, 1961.

Hard, Frederick. "Lamb on Spenser." *Royston Memorial Studies.* Chapel Hill: University of North Carolina Press, 1931. 124–38.

Haswell, Richard. "Shelley's *The Revolt of Islam:* The Connexion of Its Parts." *Keats-Shelley Journal* 25 (1976): 81–102.

Havens, R. D. *The Influence of Milton on English Poetry.* Cambridge: Harvard University Press, 1922.

————. "Rosalind and Helen." *JEGP* 30 (1931): 217–25.

Hazlitt, William. *The Complete Works of William Hazlitt.* Ed. P. P. Howe. London: Dent, 1930–34. 21 vols.

————. *Lectures on the English Poets; The Spirit of the Age.* Ed. Catherine Macdonald Maclean. London: Everyman, 1967.

Headley, Henry. *Select Beauties of Ancient English Poetry.* London, 1787.

Hildebrand, W. H. "Shelley's Early Vision Poems." *Studies in Romanticism* 8 (1969): 198–215.

Hirst, Wolf. "Lord Byron Cuts A Figure." *Byron Journal* 13 (1985): 36–51.

Hogg, James. *The Poetical Works of the Ettrick Shepherd.* Vol. 5. London, 1839. 5 vols.

Hogle, Jerrold E. *Shelley's Process: Radical Transference and the Development of his Major Works.* New York: Oxford University Press, 1988.

Horton, Ronald Arthur. *The Unity of The Faerie Queene.* Athens: University of Georgia Press, 1978.

Huggins, William. *The Observer Observ'd.* London, 1756.

Hughes, John, ed. *The Works of Mr. Edmund Spenser.* Vol. 1. London, 1715. 6 vols.

Hume, David. *The History of England.* Vol. 4. New York, 1851. 6 vols.

Hunt, James Henry Leigh. "Annotations of Craik's Spenser." University of Iowa Libraries. Iowa City, Iowa.

————. "Annotations of Todd's Spenser." Victoria & Albert Museum Library. London.

————. *The Autobiography of Leigh Hunt.* Ed. J. E. Morpurgo. London: Cresset Press, 1949.

————. *The Correspondence of Leigh Hunt.* Ed. Thornton Hunt. London, 1862. 2 vols.

————. "English Poetry Versus Cardinal Wiseman." *Fraser's Magazine* 60 (1859): 747–66.

————. *The Feast of the Poets.* London, 1815.

————. *Imagination and Fancy.* New York, 1845.

————. *Leigh Hunt's Literary Criticism.* Ed. Lawrence Huston Houtchens and Carolyn Washburn Houtchens. New York: Columbia University Press, 1956.

————. *The Poetical Works of Leigh Hunt.* Ed. H. S. Milford. London: Oxford University Press, 1923.

Hurd, Richard. *Letters on Chivalry and Romance.* London, 1762.

Hyde, Michael W. "Notes on Shelley's Reading of Godwin's *Enquirer.*" *Keats-Shelley Journal* 31 (1982): 15–24.
Jack, Ian. *Keats and The Mirror of Art.* Princeton: Princeton University Press, 1968.
Jeffrey, Francis. *Contributions to The Edinburgh Review.* Boston, 1854.
———. "Keats's Poems." *Edinburgh Review* 34 (1820): 203–11.
Johnson, Samuel. "Life of Prior." Chalmers, *Works* 10: 105–18.
———. "Life of West." Chalmers, *Works* 13: 135–37.
———. *Samuel Johnson.* Ed. Donald Greene. Oxford: Oxford University Press, 1984.
Jones, Frederick L. "Shelley and Spenser." *Studies in Philology* 39 (1942): 662–69.
Jones, Leonidas M. *The Life of John Hamilton Reynolds.* Hanover, Vt.: University Press of New England, 1984.
Jones, William. *The Palace of Fortune.* Chalmers, *Works* 18: 491–95.
Jortin, John. *Remarks on Spenser's Poems.* London, 1734.
Keats, John. *The Keats Circle.* Ed. Hyder Edward Rollins. Cambridge: Harvard University Press, 1965. 2 vols.
———. *Keats: The Complete Poems.* Ed. Miriam Allott. London: Longman, 1970.
———. *The Letters of John Keats.* Ed. Hyder Edward Rollins. Cambridge: Harvard University Press, 1958. 2 vols.
———. *Poems.* London, 1817.
———. *The Poems of John Keats.* Ed. Jack Stillinger. London: Heinemann, 1978.
King, Everard. *James Beattie.* Boston: Twayne, 1977.
———. "Beattie and Byron: A Study in Augustan Satire and Romantc Vision." *Aberdeen University Review* 48 (1980): 404–18.
Knox, Vicesimus, ed. *Elegant Extracts.* London, 1809. 2 vols.
Krier, Theresa. *Gazing on Secret Sights: Spenser, Classical Imitation, and the Decorums of Vision.* Ithaca: Cornell University Press, 1990.
Kucich, Greg. "Leigh Hunt and Romantic Spenserianism." *Keats-Shelley Journal* 37 (1988): 110–35.
———. "'A Lamentable Lay': Keats and the Marking of Charles Brown's Spenser Volumes." *Keats-Shelley Review* 3 (1988): 1–22.
———. "The Spenserian Versification of Keats's *The Eve of St. Agnes.*" *Michigan Acadamician* 16 (1983): 101–8.
Lamb, Charles. *Lamb as Critic.* Ed. Roy Park. Lincoln: University of Nebraska Press, 1980.
———. *The Letters of Charles Lamb.* Ed. E. V. Lucas. Vol. 1. London: J. M. Dent, 1935. 3 vols.
———. *The Works of Charles and Mary Lamb.* Vol. 4. Ed. E. V. Lucas. London: Methuen, 1903. 6 vols.
Landor, Walter Savage. *The Complete Works of Walter Savage Landor.* Ed. Stephen Wheeler. Vol. 15, part 3. London: Chapman and Hall, 1936. 16 vols.
Lau, Beth. "Further Corrections to Amy Lowell's Transcriptions of Keats's Marginalia." *Keats-Shelley Journal* 35 (1986): 30–38.
———. "Keats and Byron." *Critical Essays on John Keats.* Ed. Hermione de Almeida. Boston: G. K. Hall, 1990. 206–22.

Leigh, Chandos. "America." *Poems Now First Collected*. London, 1839.

Leighton, Angela. "Deconstructive Criticism and Shelley's *Adonais*." *Shelley Revalued: Essays from the Gregynog Conference*. Ed. Kelvin Everst. Totowa, N.J.: Barnes & Noble, 1983. 147–64.

Levinson, Marjorie. *The Romantic Fragment Poem*. Chapel Hill: University of North Carolina Press, 1986.

Lewis, C. S. *The Allegory of Love: A Study in Medieval Tradition*. 1936. New York: Oxford University Press, 1958.

Lloyd, Robert. *The Progress of Envy*. London, 1756.

Lockerd, Benjamin J., Jr. *The Sacred Marriage: Psychic Integration in The Faerie Queene*. Lewisburg: Bucknell University Press, 1987.

Lowell, Amy. *John Keats*. Vol. 2. Boston: Houghton Mifflin, 1925. 2 vols.

MacCaffrey, Isobel. *Spenser's Allegory: The Anatomy of Imagination*. Princeton: Princeton University Press, 1976.

Martin, Philip. *Byron: A Poet Before His Public*. Cambridge: Cambridge University Press, 1982.

McCracken, David. "Godwin's Literary Theory: The Alliance Between Fiction and Political Philosophy." *Philological Quarterly* 49 (1970): 113–33.

McFarland, Thomas. *Originality and Imagination*. Baltimore: Johns Hopkins University Press, 1985.

———. *Romanticism and the Forms of Ruin*. Princeton: Princeton University Press, 1981.

McGann, Jerome J. *Fiery Dust: Byron's Poetic Development*. Chicago: University of Chicago Press, 1968.

Mellor, Anne K. *English Romantic Irony*. Cambridge: Harvard University Press, 1980.

Memoirs of Fairyland. London, 1716.

Mendez, Moses. *The Blatant Beast*. 1758. *European Magazine* 22 (1792): 331–36, 417–22.

Mickle, William. *Syr Martin*. Chalmers, *Works* 17: 541–53.

Mileur, Jean-Pierre. *Literary Revisionism and the Burden of Modernity*. Berkeley: University of California Press, 1985.

Moorman, Mary. *William Wordsworth: A Biography*. Vol. 1. Oxford: Clarendon Press, 1957. 2 vols.

Morton, E. P. "The Spenserian Stanza in the Eighteenth Century." *Modern Philology* 3 (1913): 365–91.

Mounts, Charles. "Coleridge's Self-Identification with Spenserian Characters." *Studies in Philology* 47 (1950): 522–33.

———. "Wordsworth's Transparent Sobriquet." *Huntington Library Quarterly* 15 (1951): 201–8.

"Mrs. Tighe's Psyche." *Quarterly Review* 5 (1811): 471–85.

Mueller, William R., ed. *Spenser's Critics: Changing Currents in Literary Taste*. Syracuse: Syracuse University Press, 1959.

Murrin, Michael. *The Veil of Allegory*. Chicago: University of Chicago Press, 1969.

Neve, Philip. *Cursory Remarks on Some of the Ancient English Poets*. London, 1779.

Newlyn, Lucy. "Wordsworth, Coleridge, and The Castle of Indolence Stanzas." *Wordsworth Circle* 12 (1981): 106–13.

Nohrnberg, James. *The Analogy of The Faerie Queene*. Princeton: Princeton University Press, 1976.

Oram, William A., ed. *The Yale Edition of the Shorter Poems of Edmund Spenser.* New Haven: Yale University Press, 1989.

Parker, Patricia. "The Progress of Phaedria's Bower: Spenser to Coleridge." *English Literary History* 40 (1973): 372–97.

Patrides, C. A. "The Achievement of Edmund Spenser." *Yale Review* 69 (1980): 427–43.

Paul, C. Kegan. *William Godwin: His Friends and Contemporaries*. Vol. 1. London, 1876. 2 vols.

Peacock, Thomas Love. *The Works of Thomas Love Peacock*. Ed. H. F. B. Brett-Smith and C. E. Jones. Vol. 6. London: Constable & Co., 1924–34. 10 vols.

Pettit, E. C. *On the Poetry of Keats*. Cambridge: Cambridge University Press, 1957.

Pitts, George Richard. "Romantic Spenserianism: 'The Faerie Queene' and the English Romantics." Diss. University of Pennsylvania, 1977.

Polwhele, Richard. *The Influence of Local Attachment with Respect to Home*. 1791. London, 1798. 2 vols.

Pope, Alexander. *The Poems of Alexander Pope*. Ed. John Butt. London: Methuen, 1963.

Potter, Robert. *A Farewell Hymne to the Country*. 1749. Poetical Calendar. 5: 51–64. London, 1763. 12 vols.

Prior, Matthew. *Colin's Mistakes. The Poetical Works of Matthew Prior*. Ed. Reginald Brimley Johnson. London: George Bell, 1907.

———. *An Ode Humbly Inscribed to the Queen*. Chalmers, *Works* 10: 178–81.

"Psyche, with Other Poems." *Monthly Review* 66 (1811): 138–52.

Quilligan, Maureen. *Milton's Spenser: The Politics of Reading*. Ithaca: Cornell University Press, 1983.

Rajan, Tilottama. *Dark Interpreter: The Discourse of Romanticism*. Ithaca: Cornell University Press, 1980.

Ragussis, Michael. "Narrative Structure and the Divided Reader in *The Eve of St. Agnes*." *English Literary History* 42 (1975): 378–94.

Read, William Alexander. *Keats and Spenser*. Heidelberg, 1897.

Reiman, Donald, ed. *The Romantics Reviewed, 1793–1830: Contemporary Reviews of British Romantic Writers*. New York: Garland, 1972. 9 vols.

Reynolds, John Hamilton. *The Letters of John Hamilton Reynolds*. Ed. Leonides Jones. Lincoln: University of Nebraska Press, 1973.

———. "Milton and Spenser." *John Hamilton Reynolds. Poetry and Prose*. Ed. George L. Marsh. London: Humphrey Milford, 1928.

———. *The Romance of Youth*. 1817. *The Garden of Florence and Other Poems*. London, 1821.

Richards, Michael Reynard. "The Romantic Critics' Opinions of Elizabethan Non-Dramatic Literature." Diss. University of Tennessee, 1972.

Richardson, Samuel. *Selected Letters of Samuel Richardson*. Ed. John Caroll. Oxford: Oxford University Press, 1964.

Ridley, Gloucester. *Melampus, A Poem in Four Books*. London, 1781.

Ridley, Maurice Roy. *Keats' Craftsmanship: A Study in Poetic Development*. Oxford: Clarendon Press, 1933.

Rogers, Neville, ed. *The Poetical Works of Percy Bysshe Shelley*. Clarendon Press, 1975. 4 vols.

Ruff, James. *The Revolt of Islam.* Salzburg: Salzburg Institut für Englische Sprache und Literatur, 1965.

Rutherford, Andrew. *Byron: A Critical Study.* Palo Alto: Stanford University Press, 1961.

Sale, Roger. *Literary Inheritance.* Amherst: University of Massachusetts Press, 1984.

Schulman, Samuel. "The Spenserian Enchantments of Wordsworth's 'Resolution and Independence.'" *Modern Philology* 79 (1981): 24–44.

Schulze, Earl. "Allegory Against Allegory: 'The Triumph of Life.'" *Studies in Romanticism* 27 (1988): 31–62.

Schwartz, Lewis M. *Keats Reviewed by His Contemporaries.* Metuchen, N.J.: Scarecrow Press, 1973.

Scott, John. *Critical Essays on Some of the Poems of Several English Poets.* London, 1785.

Scott, Sir Walter. *The Letters of Sir Walter Scott 1787–1807.* Ed. H. J. C. Grierson. London: Constable & Co., 1932–37. 12 vols.

———. "Todd's Edition of Spenser." *Edinburgh Review* 7 (1806): 203–17.

———. *The Poetical Works of Sir Walter Scott.* Ed. J. Logie Robertson. London: Oxford University Press, 1931.

Shawcross, John T., ed. *The Critical Heritage: Milton 1732–1801.* London: Routledge, 1972.

Shelley, Mary. *The Journals of Mary Shelley.* Ed. Paula R. Feldman and Diana Scott-Kilvert. Vol. 2. Oxford: Clarendon Press, 1987. 2 vols.

Shelley, Percy Bysshe. *The Esdaile Notebook.* New York: Knopf, 1964.

———. *Letters of Percy Bysshe Shelley.* Ed. Frederick L. Jones. Oxford: Clarendon Press, 1964. 2 vols.

———. *Shelley: Poetical Works.* Ed. Thomas Hutchinson; rev. by G. M. Matthews. London: Oxford University Press, 1970.

———. *Shelley's Prose.* Ed. David Lee Clarke. Albuquerque: University of New Mexico Press, 1954.

Shenstone, William. *The Letters of William Shenstone.* Ed. Marjorie Williams. Oxford: Basil Blackwell, 1939.

———. *The Schoolmistress.* Chalmers, *Works* 13: 326–29.

Shilstone, Frederick W. *Byron and the Myth of Tradition.* Lincoln: University of Nebraska Press, 1988.

Silverman, Edwin. *Poetic Synthesis in Shelley's Adonais.* The Hague: Mouton, 1972.

Simpson, David. *Irony and Authority in Romantic Poetry.* Totowa, N.J.: Rowman and Littlefield, 1979.

Southey, Robert. "Todd's Works of Edmund Spenser." *Annual Review* 4 (1805): 544–55.

Spence, Joseph. *Observations.* Ed. James M. Osborn. Vol. 1. Oxford: Clarendon Press, 1966. 2 vols.

———. *Polymetis.* London, 1747.

Spencer Redivivus. London, 1687.

Spenser, Edmund. *The Faerie Queene.* Ed. Thomas Birch. London, 1751. 3 vols.

———. *The Faerie Queene.* Ed. Ralph Church. London, 1758. 4 vols.

———. *The Fairy Queen: Written by Edmund Spenser.* Ed. Jacob Tonson. London, 1758. 2 vols.

———. *The Faerie Queene.* Ed. Thomas P. Roche. New Haven: Yale University Press, 1978.

——. *The Poetical Works of Edmund Spenser. The Poets of Great Britain.* Ed. John Bell. Edinburgh, 1778. 8 vols.
——. *Spenser's Faerie Queene.* Ed. John Upton. London, 1758. 2 vols.
——. *Spenser's Works.* Ed. John Henry Todd. London, 1805. 8 vols.
——. *The Works of Edmund Spenser.* Ed. Edwin Greenlaw et al. Baltimore: Johns Hopkins University Press, 1932–57. 11 vols.
——. *The Works of Mr. Edmund Spenser.* Ed. John Hughes. London, 1715. 6 vols.
——. *The Works of that Famous English Poet, Mr. Edmond Spenser.* London, 1679.
——. *The Yale Edition of the Shorter Poems of Edmund Spenser.* Ed. William A. Oram et al. New Haven: Yale University Press, 1989.
The Spenser Encyclopedia. Gen. Ed. A. C. Hamilton. Toronto: University of Toronto Press (forthcoming).
Sperry, Stuart. *Keats the Poet.* Princeton: Princeton University Press, 1971.
——. "Richard Woodhouse's Interleaved and Annotated Copy of Keats's *Poems* (1817)." *Literary Monographs* 1 (1967): 101–64.
——. *Shelley's Major Verse.* Cambridge: Harvard University Press, 1988.
St. Clair, William. *The Godwins and the Shelleys: The Biography of a Family.* New York: Norton, 1989.
Stepanik, Karel. "The Problem of Spenserian Inspiration in Keats's Poetry." *Brno Studies in English* 2 (1960): 5–74.
Stillinger, Jack. *The Hoodwinking of Madeline and Other Essays on Keats's Poems.* Urbana: University of Illinois Press, 1971.
——, ed. *The Poems of John Keats.* London: Heinemann, 1978.
Stockdale, Percival. *Lectures on the Truly Eminent English Poets.* 2 vols. London, 1807.
Storey, Mark. *Byron and the Eye of Appetite.* New York: St. Martin's Press, 1986.
Taylor, Irene. *Blake's Illustrations to the Poems of Gray.* Princeton: Princeton University Press, 1971.
Thompson, William. *An Hymn to May.* Chalmers, *Works* 15: 32–37.
——. *Sickness.* Chalmers, *Works* 15: 38–56.
Thomson, James. *The Castle of Indolence.* Chalmers, *Works* 12: 455–67.
——. *The Seasons.* Chalmers, *Works* 12: 413–53.
Thorpe, James, ed. *Milton Criticism.* London: Routledge, 1951.
Thorslev, Peter L., Jr. *Romantic Contraries: Freedom Versus Destiny.* New Haven: Yale University Press, 1984.
Tighe, Mary. *Psyche, with Other Poems.* 1795. London, 1811.
Todd, Henry John, ed. *Spenser's Works.* Vol. 1. London, 1805. 8 vols.
"Todd's Edition of *Spenser's Works.*" *Critical Review* 7 (1806): 411–16.
Tonson, Jacob, ed. *The Faery Queen: Written by Edmund Spenser.* Vol. 1. London, 1758. 2 vols.
Trueblood, Paul G. *Lord Byron.* New York: Twayne, 1969.
Tucker, Herbert F., Jr. "Spenser's Eighteenth-Century Readers and the Question of Unity in *The Faerie Queene.*" *University of Toronto Quarterly* 46 (1977): 322–41.
Tuve, Rosemond. *Allegorical Imagery.* Princeton: Princeton University Press, 1966.
Una and Arthur. Cambridge, 1779.

Upton, John. *A Letter Concerning a New Edition of Spenser's Faerie Queene to Gilbert West*. London, 1751.

———, ed. *Spenser's Faerie Queene*. London, 1758. 2 vols.

Vendler, Helen. *The Odes of John Keats*. Cambridge, Mass.: Belknap Press, 1983.

Vicario, Michael. "The Implications of Form in *Childe Harold's Pilgrimage*." *Keats-Shelley Journal* 33 (1985): 103–29.

"The Vision of Don Roderick. A Poem." *Quarterly Review* 6 (1811): 221–35.

Waldoff, Leon. "The Father-Son Conflict in *Prometheus Unbound:* The Psychology of Vision." *Psychoanalytic Review* 62 (1975): 79–96.

———. *Keats and the Silent Work of Imagination*. Urbana: University of Illinois Press, 1985.

Warton, Joseph. *An Essay on the Genius and Writings of Pope*. Vol. 2. London, 1782. 2 vols.

Warton, Thomas. *Observations on the Fairy Queen of Spenser*. 1754. London, 1807. 2 vols.

———. *The Poetical Works of the Late Thomas Warton*. London, 1802. 2 vols.

Wasserman, Earl. *Elizabethan Poetry in the Eighteenth Century*. Urbana: University of Illinois Press, 1947.

———. *Shelley: A Critical Reading*. Baltimore: Johns Hopkins University Press, 1971.

Weller, Earle Vonard. *Keats and Mary Tighe*. New York: Century Co., 1928.

Wells, William, ed. *Spenser Allusions in the Sixteenth and Seventeenth Centuries*. Chapel Hill: University of North Carolina Press, 1972.

Wesley, Samuel. *The Battle of the Sexes*. 1723. London, 1724.

West, Gilbert. *Abuse of Travelling, a New Canto of Spenser's Fairy Queen* (given in Chalmers, *Works* as *On the Abuse of Travelling. A Canto, in Imitation of Spenser*). Chalmers, *Works* 13: 175–80.

———. *Education, a Poem: in Two Cantos, Written in Imitation of the Style and Manner of Spenser's Fairy Queen* (given in Chalmers, *Works* as *Education: A Poem, Written in Imitation of the Style and Manner of Spenser's Fairy Queen*). Chalmers, *Works* 13: 180–87.

White, Newman I., ed. *The Unextinguished Hearth*. Durham: Duke University Press, 1938.

White, R. S. *Keats as a Reader of Shakespeare*. Norman: University of Oklahoma Press, 1987.

Wilkie, Brian. *Romantic Poets and Epic Tradition*. Madison: University of Wisconsin Press, 1965.

Wilkie, William. *A Dream. In the Manner of Spenser*. Chalmers, *Works* 16: 177–78.

Williams, Kathleen. *Spenser's World of Glass*. Berkeley: University of California Press, 1966.

Wittreich, Joseph Anthony, Jr. *Angel of Apocalypse: Blake's Idea of Milton*. Madison: University of Wisconsin Press, 1975.

———, ed. *The Romantics on Milton*. Cleveland: Case Western Reserve University Press, 1970.

———. *Visionary Poetics: Milton's Tradition and His Legacy*. San Marino, Calif.: Huntington Library, 1979.

Wolfson, Susan J. "Composition and 'Unrest': The Dynamics of Form in Keats's Last Lyrics." *Keats-Shelley Journal* 34 (1985): 53–82.

————. *The Questioning Presence: Wordsworth, Keats, and the Interrogative Mode in Romantic Poetry*. Ithaca: Cornell University Press, 1986.

Wordsworth, William. *The Critical Opinions of William Wordsworth*. Ed. Markham L. Peacock, Jr. Baltimore: Johns Hopkins University Press, 1950.

————. *The Female Vagrant*. *Lyrical Ballads*. Bristol, 1798.

————. *The Letters of William and Dorothy Wordsworth*. *The Later Years (1821–28)*. Ed. Ernest de Selincourt; rev. by Alan G. Hill. Vol. 4. Oxford: Clarendon Press, 1978. 5 vols.

————. *The Prelude: 1799, 1805, 1850*. Ed. Jonathan Wordsworth, M. H. Abrams, and Stephen Gill. New York: Norton, 1979. Textual citations follow the 1850 version.

————. *The Prose Works of William Wordsworth*. Ed. W. J. B. Owen and Jane Worthington Smyser. Oxford: Clarendon Press, 1974. 3 vols.

————. *The White Doe of Rylstone*. *William Wordsworth: The Poems*. Vol. 1. Ed. John O. Hayden. New Haven: Yale University Press, 1981. 2 vols. 741–97.

"The Works of Edmund Spenser." *Edinburgh Review* 7 (1806): 203–17.

Wurtsbaugh, Jewel. *Two Centuries of Spenserian Scholarship*. Baltimore: Johns Hopkins University Press, 1936.

Yeats, William Butler. *Autobiographies*. London: Macmillan, 1955.

————. *Essays and Introductions*. New York: Macmillan, 1968.

Zillman, Lawrence John, ed. *Shelley's Prometheus Unbound: A Variorum Edition*. Seattle: University of Washington Press, 1959.

Zimmerman, Dorothy Wayne. "Romantic Criticism of Edmund Spenser." Diss. University of Illinois, 1957.

Index